Macon **Black** *and* White

Andrew Manis's book *Macon Black and White* reminds us all how flawed communities can be even when they occupy a place in our memories as nearly perfect. This is a rare book, which fairly traces the trajectory of race relations in a southern city throughout the twentieth century. Unlike many polemical studies of race, this work is wonderfully nuanced, neither shying away from egregious violence nor unwilling to depict some white people as enlightened beyond their time. Beautifully written and cogently argued, every community should receive the gift of such a healing narrative about the tortured course of race relations.

—Wayne Flynt, Distinguished University Professor,
Auburn University

African American freedom movements in the 20th century South, like the Jim Crow social order they eventually toppled, were diverse and local, and drew on a deep sense of place. In *Macon Black And White*, Andrew Manis reveals root, branch and blossom of this struggle in one extraordinarily telling town. Like no other scholar before him, Manis marches us from black Union soldiers to Black Power militants in the streets of Macon. While he never downplays the venomous power of white supremacy, he reveals that neither black nor white in Macon was ever as simple as color and caste. As if this breathtaking epic of a century in black and white were not enough, Manis also offers some sane and useful advice for bridging the racial chasm in our communities. This is a consummate work of the historian's craft, and a first-rate act of citizenship, too.

—Timothy B. Tyson
Associate Professor of Afro-American Studies at the
University of Wisconsin-Madison

It is often through the study of individual communities that the subtle and not so subtle dynamics of Southern race relations are most effectively conveyed. Andrew Manis demonstrates that this is certainly the case in his remarkably thorough and poignant chronicle of Macon's turbulent racial history. From the depths of Jim Crow to the mixed achievements of the Civil Rights Movement and the often troubling legacies of both, Manis uses the past to provide a timely appraisal of the present. His book is a landmark contribution to the modern history of Georgia and the South.

—John C. Inscoe, editor
The New Georgia Encyclopedia

With his customary clarity and sensitivity to detail and nuance, Professor Manis has made a very significant contribution with this historical examination of black and white relations in Macon, Georgia during the 20th century. His work is well researched, insightful, and superbly written, meeting the highest scholarly standards yet easily understandable to the average reader. For those interested in 20th-century African American and white relations, not just in Georgia but in the U.S. generally, this book is a must read.

—Sandy Dwayne Martin
professor of Religion, University of Georgia
author, *Black Baptists And African Missions*
and *For God And Race: The Religious And Political
Leadership of AMEZ Bishop James Walker Hood*

Macon Black and White is more than the history of one small Georgia town. What happened in Macon over time is a reflection of attitudes, social norms, and the clash of cultures that separation and inequality were bound to bring about. Manis's vivid descriptions of well-researched cold facts will haunt some readers and enlighten others.

—Charles E. Richardson
columnist, *The Macon Telegraph*

Macon
Black *and* White

An Unutterable Separation

in the American Century

Andrew M. Manis

Andrew Manis (signature)

Mercer University Press
and
The Tubman African American Museum
Macon, Georgia

Cloth: ISBN 0-86554-761-0   MUP/ H573
Paper: ISBN 0-86554-958-3   MUP/P306

© 2004 Mercer University Press
1400 Coleman Avenue
Macon, Georgia 31207

First Edition.

Library of Congress Cataloging-in-Publication Data

Manis, Andrew Michael.
 Macon Black and White : an unutterable separation in the American century / Andrew M. Manis.-- 1st ed.
   v. cm.
 Includes bibliographical references and index.
 Contents: "The White man's Georgia" : Macon and Black disfranchisement—Unsafe for democracy : lynching and the Great War—The governors and the Klan—The beginnings of interracialism—Tiptoeing toward freedom : challenging Jim Crow in war and postwar Macon—Macon and "massive resistance"—Bloc votes, boycotts, and Baptists : disintegrating Jim Crow in 1960s Macon—A new nadir : Macon's race relations in the era of Black power—Macon, race, and the culture wars—Still unutterable, still separate : Blacks and Whites in the Ellis years—Epilogue : prescriptions for racial healing.
 ISBN 0-86554-761-0 (hardcover : alk. paper)—ISBN 0-86554-958-3 (pbk. : alk. paper)
 1. Macon (Ga.)—Race relations. 2. African Americans—Georgia—Macon—Social conditions—20th century. 3. African Americans—Civil rights—Georgia—Macon—History—20th century. 4. Civil rights movements—Georgia—Macon—History—20th century. 5. United States—Race relations—Case studies. I. Tubman African-American Museum. II. Title.
 F294.M2M323 2004
 305.896'0730758513'0904

                                                                    2004014602

This book is dedicated to

Joseph M. ("Papa Joe") Hendricks

and the memory of

William P. ("Daddy Bill") Randall,

who represent the best of Macon, both white and black,

and whose lives inspire the rest of us

to keep on struggling for justice and reconciliation.

Contents

Preface

In late 1999, the city of Macon, Georgia, found itself in a maelstrom of national media attention over the public statements of John Rocker, then a pitcher for the Atlanta Braves and a proud son of Macon. In an interview published in *Sports Illustrated*, Rocker had launched a tirade of disparaging and racially insensitive remarks about New York City, giving rise to spirited conversations across America. The spotlight grew brighter and hotter when news outlets discovered that just days before Rocker's statements his hometown had inaugurated C. Jack Ellis as its first African-American mayor. The news media sought interviews with the new mayor and a meeting between Ellis and Rocker gained nationwide attention. For several weeks after of the incident, the national and local press intensely scrutinized Rocker and Macon regarding their respective attitudes toward racial and other sorts of diversity.

Ironically, the election campaign that landed Ellis in the mayor's office had generated surprisingly little public discussion of race. No doubt it did stimulate considerable *private* discussion, but Ellis' fairly easy victory, with 53 percent of the vote over an elderly former mayor, did not generate any great hue and cry. Although it did spark celebration among black Maconites, the election seemed to signal a city experiencing a racial coming of age.

The Rocker incident, however, destroyed that mythology and temporarily broke the silence that looms over Macon and much of the nation on matters of race. Having recently survived the mayor's somewhat more controversial re-election effort, Macon now finds itself in the middle of the Ellis years with race as the unspoken subtext beneath virtually every issue faced by the city and county governments.

Like the Rocker controversy, the publication of this book will no doubt generate similar, surely less sensational, but hopefully more constructive, conversations about a subject many would prefer to ignore. The contract for this book was signed just days after the Rocker incident put the subjects of Macon and race relations in the same news stories. Again ironically, just as the book was being conceived, John Rocker's comments gave this project an added urgency. In many ways the heat generated by that controversy put considerable steam in the author's engine over the next four years of research.

In spring 1999, I received a call from Joseph M. Hendricks, a professor and former dean of students at Mercer University who had done more than anyone to integrate black students into Macon's most influential institution of higher learning. "Papa Joe," as students of both races call him, was well known as one of the "good white people" who had quietly and without fanfare aided the civil rights movement in the city. I had met Hendricks prior to his call, but because of my scholarly and personal interest in race and religion, I wanted to get better acquainted. So I was delighted when he asked to visit me to talk about a project he had in mind. A day or two later Hendricks arrived in my office with Carey O. Pickard, director of the Tubman African American Museum, and retired businessman Gus B. Kaufman.

A few years earlier Hendricks had been a central resource for Southern writer Will Campbell's efforts to produce *The Stem of Jesse,* a book on the integration of Mercer University. Hendricks and Kaufman had both been members of the Macon Council on Human Relations and had carefully watched racial developments in the city over several decades. Having read and discussed Campbell's book with appreciation, they nevertheless thought the Mercer story needed to be put into wider context by looking at racial developments in Macon as a whole. They conceived the idea of another book, a prequel that would focus on an earlier period and go beyond Mercer to tell the larger story of civil rights in Macon. They had already enlisted support from Carey Pickard and the Tubman Museum—along with an anonymous donor—and a commitment from Mercer president Kirby Godsey to see the final product published by Mercer University Press. All they needed was an author.

It was clear, however, that they had come not to enlist me, but for recommendations on someone who might be interested in undertaking the project. After half an hour or so of learning what Hendricks and company had in mind, in an act of shameless self-promotion, I told them I had written in the field of civil rights history and that I myself was interested in becoming their author. After reading my earlier books, they decided that had stumbled onto the right person for the job.

x

I am glad they did. While a book about Macon, the city where I live, probably would not have been the next item on my "To Do" list, I have probably learned more from this research and writing than any of my previous efforts. For starters, I decided early on to give the book a focus much wider than even Hendricks, Kaufman, and Pickard had in mind. Until this work, most of my research had looked at the civil rights era. Since I was being asked to investigate the period before the 1950s, I eventually chose to go back to the Age of Segregation and look developmentally at the lives of black and white Maconites over the course of the entire twentieth century. Mostly I chose to get such a long running start on the stories Hendricks and Kaufman hope to hear because I simply wanted to learn something new. Later, I realized it would also be wise to expand the chronological boundaries of my expertise. In so doing I may have "accidentally" written a rare study of black-white relations in America. Searching the Library of Congress catalogue in every way I could think of turned up only one or two other investigations focusing on black-white relations in a single city over an entire century. There is no question, however, that no other treatment takes such a thorough look at race relations in Macon.

What I bring to this study is the perspective of both an outsider and an insider. Having lived in Macon for less than ten years, I have not done enough time here for natives to consider me a true Maconite. Indeed, as is the case in many antebellum Southern cities, "newcomers" can spend half a lifetime in Macon and still have natives say, "Well, you're not from here, are you?" This outsider status allows a certain distance and a willingness to tell the unvarnished truth. I suspect the Macon Chamber of Commerce will never include a copy of this book in its newcomer packets, but I do hope its members will engage me and one another about its contents.

On the other hand, I have grown to love the city I now call home, and as an honorary Maconite, I am fairly certain the book will prove to native-born Maconites that the author knows the "feel" of their city. He has done more than make a few research trips to Macon. He has lived here, has enjoyed living here, and expects to live the rest of his life here. I can promise that he at least knows how properly to pronounce *Pio Nono* Avenue. (Don't worry, native Maconites, this secret is between us.)

There are two promises, however, I cannot make. I cannot say that this book discusses every important development in black-white relations over the course of the entire twentieth century. Every particular episode chosen for inclusion in any narrative reflects the historian's selectivity, and this is particularly the case when the historian is ranging over more than a hundred years. There were perhaps other events or developments that were as determinative as those I have chosen to spotlight. There will no doubt be some long-time Maconites who will remember some events I have left out, or who will remember differently those events I have put in. Such is the case whenever one writes history that remains a part of a city's living memory. Nevertheless, I stand by the choices I have made, while recognizing that other historians, professional or amateurs, may have made different ones. Specifically, I was deeply into the writing when I realized what I must now confess to be the most gaping hole in this work: the story of Macon's Catholic community and its efforts in black education. That story, with particular attention to the St. Peter Claver parish, will have to await a future telling.

The other thing I cannot promise is complete objectivity. Such is a noble, but ultimately unattainable aspiration. No one writes or reads a book without a point of view and no author could eliminate it even if he or she wished to do so. Rather than pretend that this is a purely objective, unbiased history of black-white relations in Macon, I feel it is better and more honest to acknowledge my point of view, or at least the frame of reference from which I write. That has very much to do with the city that *is* my hometown, Birmingham, Alabama, and the period during which I grew up there. Born in 1954, the year of *Brown v. Board of Education*, my childhood was spent in the most cataclysmic years of that city's history. In those civil rights years, the city developed an irony I am still trying to understand. Besides the nicknames generated by its chamber of commerce—"The Pittsburgh of the South" and "The Magic City"—Birmingham had also earned two others. Its white citizens called it "The City of Churches," while its African American community called it "Bombingham."

I am certain I never realized any of this until much later, but trying to get to the bottom of the brutal irony of those two nicknames has driven my efforts as a historian to understand the interaction of religion and race in America and the South. Growing up in Birmingham during the Civil Rights years, being warned not to play outside because of recurring "nigger trouble," hearing an announcement one Sunday morning about the deaths of four black girls a few miles away and a few years my senior, noticing my baseball coach's celebration over Martin Luther King's assassination—all these events had a profound effect on me. More than anything else, these events have shaped my views on race, religion, politics, culture, values, and almost everything else. Thus, between the lines of almost everything I have ever written for publication has been a deep desire to contribute to the demise of the sort of racism I saw close up as a boy—and other kinds as well.

One of the other personal roads that brought me to this point was religious faith. While still in high school I felt a sense of vocation into the ministry. Significantly even this calling crosses paths with the racial events of my youth. Just as I was thinking of becoming a minister, Birmingham's First Baptist Church experienced a much-publicized schism over whether to allow a black woman and her daughter into its membership. Having grown up in the Greek Orthodox Church, I could not quite fathom what these Baptists, who always seemed a little weird to my parents, were thinking. Nor could I understand why the prospective membership of two harmless black females was even a matter of controversy. Despite some initial disillusionment, I attended a Baptist college in Birmingham, where my professors helped clear away some (though by no means all) of the weirdness from the Baptists. Thus I eventually went into the Baptist ministry. Later, personal and professional developments made it necessary to lay aside my ministerial vocation, but the impulse is still very much a part of me. Thus, I wear two hats—ordained (though currently "laid off") minister and professional historian of religion and race in America.

Most of what readers will encounter in this book is written by the historian. But my professional colleagues who review the work may be startled by the epilogue. In that section I offer the conclusions and generalizations obligatory for the historians. For my fellow Maconites, however, I also suggest some practical prescriptions for racial healing. I do this not only because of my other, ministerial hat, but mostly because I believe that history matters most when it helps shape and even change the present. And in our fifth century on this continent, there is no change America and Macon could experience that is more crucial—and more overdue—than a radical change in matters of race. If this book creates some opportunity for frank conversation on that tangled subject and helps bring about some healthy change in my adopted city, it will have been worth the effort.

As always, it is altogether fitting and proper to say "Thank You" to the many persons who helped me along the way. Financial support for this project was made possible by Carey O. Pickard, director of Macon's Tubman Museum, and one of his anonymous donors. I have appreciated Carey's eagerness to see this book finished and look forward to working with him and the museum staff to promote discussions of the book for the greater good of our community. I thank Carey, along with Gus B. Kaufman, for their conscientious reading of the manuscript and their helpful suggestions for improving it.

Many persons at my home institution, Macon State College, have helped ease the burden of this work. Al McCormick, former chair of the division of Social Sciences, advocated for me and this project with former Dean of the College Thomas Isherwood (now president at Reinhardt College) for extra funds to provide a research assistant. Their mutual decision to help fund this research sped the process along, largely due to the aid provided me by my eventual assistant, Chadwick Dent. For two full years Chad found articles for me, read them, typed them up, filed them, and otherwise did everything he could to help me. He graciously performed what was often very tedious work without complaint and with great competence. I would also like to thank many, many students in my classes over the past three years whose never-ending quest for extra credit led them to "volunteer" to dig up and write up other articles for my perusal.

I must also thank Tracey Toole who helped me wade through a massive amount of material by typing summaries of almost a hundred years worth of news articles.

I hope director Pat Borck of the Macon State College Library will also accept my gratitude, along with Mary Morris, and Richard Sager who ably lent a hand every time I called upon them. Colleagues and friends on the faculty are also due my thanks, especially Myra Jackson, who read the manuscript, encouraged me and my ideas, and served as a primary source by allowing me to interview her about her experiences of racism in Macon. As always, my friend and colleague Harriet Jardine cheered me on and made it possible to use her faith community, the High Street Unitarian-Universalist Church, as a focus group on whom I tried out some of this material in lectures over two consecutive Black History Months. I am grateful for the support of the High Street congregation, which is always an eager, challenging, and gracious audience. I also thank the Reverend Lonzy Edwards and the members of the Mt. Moriah Baptist Church for their invitation to talk about this research in their hospitable company.

Other Macon State colleagues whose friendship and encouragement always lighten the load are Stephen Taylor, Joe Lamb, Bob Durand, and Ben Tate. Finally, nobody in the Social Science division at Macon State College could get *anything* done without the superb assistance and good-natured humor of Debra Slagle.

In addition I thank Anthony Dixon, a native of Fort Valley, Georgia, and a graduate student in history at the University of Indiana. As part of his Ph.D. studies, he contacted me about serving a summer as a research intern. For a historian, having a free assistant for two months is almost like winning the lottery, and Anthony spent several days with me in Atlanta doing archival research. Without him I would have had to linger there much longer than I ultimately did.

Not that lingering would have been so very painful, as working at the Robert W. Woodruff Library of the Atlanta University Center was the most pleasant research experience of my career. The staff of the department of archives was unfailingly helpful and friendly in every request I made of them. Thus I wish to thank the director of the archives, Karen Jefferson, reference archivist Cathy Lynn Mundale, archivist Alexandra Bernet, and library technical assistant Antoine James.

Surely no one deserves the statement "without which I could not have done this" more than Muriel McDowell-Jackson, at the genealogy and archives department of the Washington Memorial Library in Macon. In addition to help dig up occasional details, she permitted the use of all the photographs in this book. In addition I am grateful to Christopher Stokes and Willard Rocker for their occasional errands in my behalf.

At Mercer University there are also many people to thank, beginning with president R. Kirby Godsey, whose eagerness to see this book come into being and whose encouragement convinced me to undertake it. At the Jack Tarver Library, I thank assistant director Theresa Preuit, as well as Judy Ellis, Russell Palmer, and Valerie Edmonds for their help. I particularly appreciate the help provided me in the department of special collections by Susan Broome, Arlette Copeland, and Robert G. Gardner. In the department of English, I am grateful to Andrew Silver, who made available to me transcripts of some of his interviews with principal figures in the integration of Mercer

University. Finally, I am grateful to Marc A. Jolley, publisher at Mercer University Press for his interest in this project and the almost effortless way he helped move this book to completion. I also thank other staff members at the press, Marsha Luttrell, Jenny Toole, and Barbara Keene.

One of the great pleasures of doing recent local history is the opportunity to meet and interview Maconites whose perspectives have been invaluable for developing a contemporary sense of the city. Forty-six of my neighbors in Macon agreed to sit with me and answer my questions. Even when their points of view did not match my own, I found them all gracious, kind people who genuinely care about their city and wish to see it progress in every possible manner. I deeply appreciate their community involvement and their willingness to give me some of their time. Macon is indeed fortunate to have citizens like these and I am fortunate to be able now to call most of them my friends.

Of course, I am also most fortunate in having the support of my wife, Linda, whose love and good cheer are always "a shelter in a time of storm." We have weathered another research project with our sanity and our love intact, and I hope by the time she sees this book in print we will have had time to take golfing lessons.

Finally, I extend my deepest, most heartfelt appreciation to Joseph M. Hendricks. This book is mostly his brainchild. Without him I would not have been asked to write it, and without his help the task would have been an onerous one. He brought the project to me and sat for a formal interview and countless informal ones by telephone. He helped me figure out what to look for and whom to talk to next. He and his wife, Betty, hosted me in their home more times than they or I can count, and have been my most ardent cheerleaders. Mostly, I thank Joe for his lifetime of putting money where his mouth is and putting his life on the side of the angels on matters of race in Macon. If, before I leave this world, my name were mentioned in the same sentence with his, I could die a contented man. His interracial activities in the 1960s, when it was dangerous to do so, earned him a cross-burning in his front yard and the admiration of African Americans and other progressive-minded Maconites. His leadership, and that of black Maconites like the late William P. Randall, left Macon better than they found it. For this reason, this book is dedicated to them.

While I was working on this project, I celebrated my fiftieth birthday. As is the case for many, this milestone became the occasion for a good deal of introspection. Having that experience while trying to produce a book that impinges on real life in a real city has created different hopes for this book than anything I have written before. At this point in my life and career, and in my current way of thinking, whether this project has come to a successful conclusion depends less on the judgment of professional historians than on what my fellow Maconites say and do in response. Another century has come and gone and still we ask how long this disease of race will continue to afflict us as a people and nation. This project ends with the author's hope that this book will hasten at least one American city toward that good day when at least this particular affliction will have become an unpleasant memory.

Introduction

In 1895, shortly before the arrival of a new century, Afro-America passed its torch of leadership to a new generation—and to a new leader. In February of that year, Frederick Douglass, firebrand orator and leader of the nineteenth century abolitionists, closed his eyes in death. But on 18 September, Booker T. Washington, president of Tuskegee Institute in Alabama, stepped to the dais to address the Cotton States and International Exposition in Atlanta. When he concluded his speech, white women in the audience tossed flowers on the stage at his feet and Georgia governor William Atkinson bolted up from his seat to shake the Wizard of Tuskegee's hand and congratulate him for the advice he had given both his people and the white South.

A new, accommodationist style of black leader had been recruited for the New South and soon a new century. What made this transition of black leadership so significant was the comforting—to white Southerners, at least—advice Washington had given. The "Atlanta Compromise," as his speech soon came to be called, advocated that African Americans temporarily accept political and social inequality without protest. In exchange, Southern whites would aid and encourage "their colored people" to uplift their race economically through faithful stewardship in agriculture and industrial education. In fairly short order, prominent white newspapers like the *Atlanta Constitution* had concurred with the governor and proclaimed Washington the new and improved leader of Southern blacks—at least when compared to the more inflammatory likes of Douglass. The Atlanta paper viewed the speech as "the beginning of a moral revolution in America" and consecrated Washington as "a wise counselor and safe leader." Here was a pragmatic, sensible black leader the white South could live with.[1]

Unlike its counterpart in the capital city, however, the *Macon Telegraph*, did not mention Washington's celebrated speech. Instead, much of its space covered a speech, also delivered on the opening day of the exposition, by a prominent Maconite, Judge Emory Speer. In a fulsome paean to the glories of America and the South, Speer also expressed the common racial ideology of turn-of-the-century Macon. "The young and strong civilization of the West," he exulted, "assimilated all the healthy blood that came. But the old Anglo-Saxon stock has ever predominated." Momentarily diverging from the reigning myth of the era that bemoaned Reconstruction's "negro rule," Judge Speer confidently asserted, "There was never the slightest danger of continued negro control in the local affairs of a Southern state. Those who had apprehended it had done well to consider that of all the American Union the Southern people present the largest percentage of the Anglo-Saxon stock.... Even now there is but 1 $^{1/4}$ per cent of foreign blood in the population of this state."

Judge Emory Speer, 1905, Maconite who spoke at the Cotton States Exposition on the same day that Booker T. Washington gave the famous "Atlanta Compromise" speech. (Courtesy of the Washington Memorial Library.)

Moving toward his rhetorical conclusion, Speer looked to the future, calling on his fellow Georgians to "see to it that the American stock which made the country shall dominate its institutions and direct its policy and work out its destiny on the lines our fathers marked." As for the appropriate role for Georgians descended from Africa, without consultation his remarks sounded as if ghostwritten by the sage of Tuskegee: "The opportunity for technical education is the greatest benefaction his friends can bestow on the negro. The skill of the graduate of an industrial college is his capital. He has been taught to appreciate the dignity of labor. He is not striving for the unattainable.... How incomparably superior is his condition to...one who has merely acquired a fatal facility of speech."[2]

Some five days later, Charles R. Pendleton, editor of the *Telegraph,* weighed into the discussion of Washington's speech. Quoting the *Philadelphia Bulletin,* the editor suggested that "with a few more leaders of the robust sense of Booker T. Washington of Alabama, the negroes in the South would not be in danger of losing the ballot...." Washington had won over the South's opinion-makers with his most famous utterance signaling blacks' acceptance of Jim Crow: "In all things that are purely social we can be as separate as the fingers, yet one as the hand in all things essential to mutual progress."[3] Unuttered in this salute to Washington was white Macon's assumption that social separation was the only viable solution to the South's "negro problem." This assumption was dangerously called into question the next time Washington's name appeared prominently in the *Telegraph.* Ten months into the new century, the first droplet of what became a storm appeared with an 16 October 1901 dateline and one line of text: "Booker T. Washington of Tuskegee, Ala., dined with the president this evening." Subsequent references to the incident would not be so matter of fact.[4]

The following day's paper carried an exclamatory editorial titled, "Mr. Roosevelt!!," taking the new president to task for trespassing on sacred territory. "God set up the barrier between the races," argued editor Pendleton. He continued: "No president of this or any other country can break it down. A dinner given by one man to another in the home and privacy of his family means that the guest or his son may woo and win the host's daughter. When the one man is a white man and the other black, it means that there is but one more step to miscegenation—a sinful and willful breaking of God's plain law.... We shall hear more of this."[5] Indeed, four days hence another Pendleton piece disagreed with the *Atlanta Constitution*'s view that Roosevelt's political appointments of African Americans posed a greater problem. Such a perspective, the Maconite argued, "amounts to an abandonment of the purest instincts of the Caucasian blood—a grave, thoughtless blunder." Southerners cared not about Washington's erudition or personal cleanliness. What concerned the white South was preserving the "pure white blood which

God gave." For the president of the United States, "the fountain head of our social life," to break the barrier of social separation was "an affront to the white race." Returning to the theme of intermarriage he had expressed in his first editorial on the matter, Pendleton feared that result in "a composite American...with brown skin and kinky hair." Such a possibility was "as forceful as it is revolting to the Caucasian who loves and wishes to perpetuate his race."[6]

Reaction in Macon mirrored that in Atlanta and elsewhere throughout the South. Officials at the Capitol denounced Roosevelt's act as an outrage. Governor Allen D. Candler warned hysterically that it would "bring on rape and lynching and bloodshed and riot." Meeting in Columbus at the end of the month, the Georgia Daughters of the Confederacy adopted a report by state historian Mildred Rutherford calling on Georgians not to blame blacks for the affront.[7] In a barrage of editorials, Pendleton continued explicitly to utter the assumption of Southern race relations of the era. "A race that cannot intermarry with the ruling race of a country must remain forever a class apart.... The negroes must either go forth and establish a commonwealth of their own or remain in a white man's country and suffer the consequences." The average Southern white man, he averred, was fond of blacks "'in his place' of a subordinate who shows no desire for social equality." At this point, Washington jeopardized his status as a wise leader. Worse still, his daughter Portia told a northern reporter of having eaten with a young Southerner while in school in Framingham, Massachusetts. Thus, despite claiming disinterested in social equality, Pendleton concluded that "it is now clear enough that he and his family want it and are seeking it for themselves."[8]

The incident also sparked an effort in the state legislature to separate the races on streetcars. At the beginning of the twentieth century, the Georgia General Assembly had passed surprisingly few Jim Crow restrictions. Convicts leased by the state were segregated, as were railroad coaches, by laws passed in 1891. Sleeping cars were segregated in 1899. In reaction to both the White House incident and the local situation in Macon, state senator Thomas S. Felder renewed his efforts to pass a bill he had introduced during the previous session. The bill, proposed in response to a Bibb County grand jury presentment, would have required all transit companies in the state to segregate the races either by separate cars or compartments. "I introduced the bill because the people of Macon urged me to do so," Felder told reporters. The language of the grand jury's statement was unmistakable, expressing deep concern about the mixing of whites and blacks, which the jurors viewed as "a never ending and ever increasing source of friction and crime." Eventually, despite being reported out favorably by a Georgia House committee, the bill was tabled by the senate, and ultimately defeated.[9]

Such was the state of black-white relations in Macon and Georgia at the beginning of the twentieth century. Ninety-three years have revealed a vastly different Macon. In January 1994, thirty years on the other side of the civil rights revolution, the city's largest institution of higher learning, Mercer University, commemorated the arrival of its first students of color. At a Founder's Day convocation, the Mercer community both repented of the racial sins of a formerly segregated South and gloried in its status as the first Georgia university to lower its racial bars voluntarily and without a court order. In his introductory remarks, Mercer president R. Kirby Godsey lauded his predecessor, Rufus C. Harris, who "challenged the prevailing order [and] placed moral conviction above cultural expectation" by admitting these students. Godsey continued: "No passing of time, no future episodes can ever eclipse the significance of their coming to this place.... they enabled this University to build a new tradition.... Sam Oni, Bennie Stephens and Cecil Dewberry made Mercer University a different and a better University for every student, black or white, Hispanic, or Asian, or American who will ever attend one class here.... They are founders of Mercer University."[10]
      Observing the proceedings, however, were the students of ethics professor Joseph M. Hendricks, one of the figures most influential in the integration of the university. Hendricks had required his charges to attend the ceremony and record their reactions. One of those freshman students commented on the segregated fraternities, sororities, and cafeterias still prevalent on the campus. Another student observed similarly segregated seating arrangements at the convocation itself and could not help noticing the irony: "I saw how the black people were more dressed up than the white people. And as if by some unutterable

separation by dress code the black people filled the pews by themselves."[11]

These two sets of events serve as powerful bookends of the twentieth century. Viewed together they capture the change and continuity of black-white relations in Macon, Georgia. Between the two events lie a multitude of changes. This book, a survey of black-white relations during the twentieth century, offers rebuttal to the impassioned argument of racial pessimists that little has changed in Macon or in America. When separation, and the badge of inferiority implied in it, had the force of law as well as social custom, the "white over black" social arrangements were buttressed by an unquestionable sense of sacredness. The reality in this new century is that both federal *and* state laws protect against racial discrimination. This protection in turn has made it possible for contemporary college students to approach race relations with what now seems a genuinely self-evident truth that all men and women really *are* created equal. Neither these young people nor the society around them always or perfectly "live out the true meaning" of this creed, but in ways that were unimaginable in the time of Booker T. Washington the creed itself is a given. So much for the change.

Yet throughout the "American Century," when the United States rose to international prominence as the "beacon of liberty," an ironic continuity remained. As the Mercer freshman observed, an "unutterable separation" has characterized black-white relations in Macon throughout the twentieth century and persists in different forms into this new millennium. In different ways and with different meanings, this unspoken division is the constant that holds this story together. Significantly, the key adjective vacillates in meaning between "unutterable" and "unuttered." Early in the twentieth century this separation meant African-American Maconites were expected to follow Booker Washington's advice and accept segregation and second-class status without complaint. Only to themselves and only in the language of future hope were they able to "speak now against the day." Or if they ventured to speak a dissenting word to the hardening Jim Crow system around them, they were obliged to do so in the coded language of the slave spirituals, like the ancient Hebrew prophets who used cryptic signs or parables, for which most of their white audience had neither eyes to see nor ears to hear. Their separation was thus unutterable for fear of the retribution earned by stepping out of their place in the racial pecking order.

For whites this separation was unuttered because of its taken-for-granted status and its sacred inviolability. As good and typical Americans, most white Maconites agreed with their editor that to ignore this racial separation was "a sinful and willful breaking of God's plain law." Comment on this reality was unnecessary, for like the antebellum planters' paternalistic social pyramid, the era's New Southerners entertained no debate and tolerated no doubt that Jim Crow arrangements were just as God intended. The separation was unuttered—except on occasions when comment from the North or when some unruly Southerner said or did something to challenge the moral legitimacy of Jim Crow. At those points, defenders of the racial faith spoke up forcefully.

By the 1920s and 1930s certain Maconites, both black and white, began to make more interracial efforts to cushion the harder edges of "separate but equal." Again, these efforts had a covert, publicly unutterable quality about them. The Commission on Interracial Cooperation, founded by Atlanta Methodist layman Will Alexander, and Jessie Daniel Ames's Association of Southern Women for the Prevention of Lynching, began to spread their interrelated influence across Georgia and the South. Sometimes together and sometimes separately, a small number of black and white citizens of Macon worked cautiously to address the inequality of the Jim Crow system, almost always without directly challenging its separateness. Even this conservative approach, however, posed danger for these race workers, making it necessary to keep their progress publicly unuttered and separate from the conservative white mainstream.

After defeating Germany in World War II, the United States saw its own racist practices undermined by the logic of its struggle with Nazi ideology. After American soldiers spilled oceans of blood to halt Hitler's racially-driven policies, the notion of returning to a region that segregated its own "inferior" race seemed senseless. The irony, pointed out during the war years by the black press's "Double-V" campaign to vanquish racism not only abroad but also at home, was not lost on racial progressives North and South, and least of all on African-American veterans returning home ready to press for change. Consequently, from the 1940s through the cataclysmic 1960s, like other Southern cities, Macon began to see dramatic shifts in the willingness of both blacks and a significant minority of whites to work both separately and cooperatively to reverse the separation of the racial status quo and its longstanding unutterability. The eventual result was a comparatively calm process of desegregation. Of course, a "promised land" was never fully reached, and African Americans were forced by prejudice and hysteria to sing "stony the road we trod" all along the way. But for this Middle Georgia city the changes of the civil rights era avoided the extremes of violence so evident in other parts of the South and other parts of Georgia. In the contemporary era, has tempered, but not completely ended, its separateness. White moderates and black activists spoke that change into being, while racial conservatives in Macon continued the tradition of non-utterance by submitting, often with clenched teeth, to federal court orders.

More recently, as the gains of the national and local civil rights movements have gradually taken hold in America, and the most egregious and dehumanizing elements of legal racial separation have disappeared, another sort of unspoken separateness continues to shape events, attitudes, and human relationships in Macon. The dawn of the twentieth-first century found a black political class strong enough to elect C. Jack Ellis as the city's first African-American mayor in 1999. By that time, blacks had gained majority status within the city limits and taken over many of the reins of power. Since 1970 large numbers of whites forsook the central city for the northern and western suburbs in Bibb County. Thus in a new century, race and a persisting inability or unwillingness to talk about it remain a central strong factor in the social and political life of Macon, particularly in public education and tensions between city and county governments.

There is, of course, a final, inescapable, moral in the unutterable separation that continues to hamper human relations in Macon and the nation. Going down the list of *unutterable*'s definitions inevitably brings one to "unspeakably evil or tragic." How else to characterize so longstanding a flaw in the American character. For the 385 years since a Dutch man-o-war delivered a cargo of twenty "negars" to the first American colony, for the 180 years since white Europeans began a settlement on the Ocmulgee River and named it after Nathaniel Macon, race has defied the human ability or will to fashion imaginative, charitable solutions to bigotry. Despite undeniable progress during the twentieth century, black and white Americans *still* cannot coexist in ways that grant equal life chances to any newborn child thrown by fate into this geographical space. That irreducible reality can hardly be anything but unspeakably tragic. Call it the "racism problem" as I do, or call it the "negro problem" as did our white Southern forebears, it remains at times a scar and at others an open wound that has continually debilitated the health of our national and local bodies politic.

Part of the unutterable tragedy is because Macon is largely a humane city in which to live and one that prides itself on both its patriotism and its religious piety. Given the nation's founding documents, citizens must attend to any community's inability fully to embody such foundational American values. The Declaration of Independence, of course, begins by articulating the value of equality, and although Macon and the nation have taken giant steps in that direction, the goal of genuine equality remains unrealized. Even earlier, when Puritan refugees inaugurated their settlement of the Massachusetts Bay Colony, their leader John Winthrop called their communal experiment a "city on a hill." Inherent in that conception was a note of exceptionalism. Massachusetts, and by extension America itself, was to be different and exemplary. Since that 1630 "inaugural address," Puritan and non-Puritan Americans alike have accepted these ideas, particularly in the South. Yet through the generations Winthrop's words have called upon his listeners to contract with themselves to embody a long list of human values. Among the imperatives were these: "For this end, we must be knit together, in this work, as one man. We must entertain each other in brotherly affection. We must be willing to abridge ourselves of our superfluities, for the supply of others' necessities."[12]

To be certain, it did not take long for Puritans and other Americans to neglect such values or even to assume them inapplicable to the descendents of Africa. Nonetheless, equality, mutual concern, and exceptionalism have laid claim on Americans, who in turn have claimed to have created such a community as an example to the world. Having heralded such values for so long without embodying them more completely, especially in matters of race, makes our continued separation all the more unutterable.[13]

One can, however, choose to call the glass half full, and while this narrative admittedly emphasizes the persistence of racial separation in Macon over the course of the twentieth century, the narrative does not only reveal apartness or inequality. It is also a story of courage, by both blacks and whites, sometimes separately and sometimes together, working to push Macon to realize the ideals of our founding documents. To be sure, like the larger civil rights story in America, Macon's story properly highlights black agency. Most of the heroes are African Americans whose mostly independent efforts eventually made them the most important agents of change in a conservative Southern city. But as one of my students recently taught me, since African Americans have been the numerical minority in the United States, they could have accomplished no real change in their status without white support. Without some whites on board, the "freedom train" could never have even left the station, much less gotten as close to its destination as it has.

In American race relations, most whites have typically discounted most of what African Americans have said in their pursuit of freedom, equality, and racial justice. This dismissiveness made it necessary for blacks to convince progressive whites, who in turn could help convert the more conservative white majority. Although not necessarily any more successful in evoking change, white supporters of equality had the advantage of at least appearing to be disinterested parties in the social struggle. For example, present-day whites *expect* African Americans to advocate affirmative action, since African Americans directly benefit from such a policy. When advanced by other whites, however, the argument will often be considered more seriously by racially conservative whites. Without winning a certain percentage of whites to their points of view, African Americans would still be much further away from the goal of racial justice in Macon and America. Since relationships between persons and groups are by definition two-way affairs, improvement in those relationships require effort on both sides. Hence, some of Macon's heroic advocates of racial equality have been whites. This narrative tells their stories as well as those of black protagonists. To do so takes nothing away from black agency or accomplishment, but it does acknowledge both the logical reality and the historical record that strategically the freedom struggle had to be a matter of "black and white together."

In some ways, however, one must disconnect harmonious race relations from black achievement of equality. These two values have not typically occurred together. Any honest historian must admit that to the extent that equality for blacks has been achieved, it has often been won at the expense of harmonious relations with whites. Thus in Macon, as in America more generally, success in desegregation is more visible than successful integration. Desegregation speaks more to the legal end of the Jim Crow system and setting African Americans on the same level as whites relative to the law. Integration speaks of mutually satisfying voluntary relations between the races. Macon's unutterable separation persists in part because blacks and whites have not established enough harmonious voluntary relationships with one another. This rift exists largely because of white backlash against the gains of the civil rights movement, both nationally and locally.

Still, the change in black status in America is a success story. In Booker T. Washington's day few could have predicted that a hundred years later another Republican president would not only have African Americans in the White House dining room, but also in his Cabinet—or that Macon would have a black mayor. So the success in this story is that legal desegregation happened in certain sectors of life in Macon. Moreover, it did so with little of the violence, bloodshed, or social upheaval of some other civil rights venues such as Birmingham, Selma, Augusta, and others. Human effects rarely have singular causes, and thus no one factor can account for the mostly peaceful change in black status during the twentieth century, at least not in Macon, Georgia. What then were the key elements making this change possible in Macon?

First, the editorial stance of the *Macon Telegraph* provided an important and growing progressive tradition among opinion-makers in the city. When in 1914 Charles R. Pendleton died and William Thomas Anderson took full ownership of the paper, Macon began to benefit from the *Telegraph's* more progressive approach to race. For the next thirty-one years, until his death in 1945, Anderson's voice, and that of his managing editor and chief editorial writer, Mark Ethridge, rang out clearly against lynching and the Klan. Other race-baiting groups also drew Anderson's fire. After the Great War journalists wrote of Anderson's influence: "Soon the American Facist [sic] Association and Order of the Black Shirts arose in Atlanta to assure Nordics that it would make the south safe for white supremacy.... The black Shirts were making headway in Atlanta and had enrolled twenty-one thousand members, thanks largely to the craven conduct of Atlanta newspapers in permitting the organization to grow unmolested, when the *Macon Telegraph* launched an editorial campaign which soon put them out of business." Key to this successful campaign was a front page Anderson editorial titled, "Crack the Head of This Newest Nasty Thing."[14]

A second pillar on which peaceful racial change stood was the activism of the Macon branch of the National Association for the Advancement of Colored People. The NAACP was not the conservative or passive organization some historians have claimed when comparing it to civil rights era organizations like the Southern Christian Leadership Conference (SCLC) or the Student Nonviolent Coordinating Committee (SNCC). Historian Stephen Tuck, in a revisionist view, has convincingly shown that the NAACP was clearly the most influential organization in the struggle for equal rights in Georgia.[15] The work of the Macon branch bears out Tuck's view. Responding to discrimination in the military during World War II, a group of black Maconites re-organized a branch of the NAACP in 1942. (The membership of an earlier NAACP effort before World War I had dipped in membership and lost its charter.) While eventually William P. Randall, an NAACP member, would stand out as its most important black spokesperson, the civil rights movement in Macon would enjoy a fairly decentralized leadership focused on the ranks of the Macon branch.

Third, beginning in the 1930s a number of organizations emphasizing Christian interracial activities began to establish a foothold in Macon. Chief among these were the Commission on Interracial Cooperation (after 1944 renamed the Southern Regional Council), the Association of Southern Women for the Prevention of Lynching, the Georgia Council on Human Relations, and its Macon branch. These organizations increased the level of interracial contact between African Americans and racially progressive whites throughout the South. While most institutional churches did not support these efforts in any formal way, individual members met periodically to discuss racial matters, hoping to equalize separate but unequal resources for blacks in Macon and the state. Slowly, the goal of such groups would evolve beyond their tacit acceptance of a more just version of segregation to that of ending Jim Crow altogether.

The final progressive factor in Macon was the leavening influence of Mercer University, and to a lesser degree, Wesleyan College. The record of Mercer, like any white-controlled institution in Georgia during the period of segregation, is mixed, particularly because of the school's historic relation to the Georgia Baptist Convention. As Baptist ministers and laypersons served on Mercer's board of trustees, and annual Baptist conventions saw frequent democratic wrangling over liberal theological teaching, the state convention exercised a conservative influence on the ways the school dealt with race issues. But while presidents of Mercer usually (but not always) proceeded cautiously, farther down the flow chart, in the classrooms, individual professors made important contributions, challenging conservative ideas and practices, influencing succeeding generations of students toward more humane views on race. Sometimes, most formidably in the post-World War II prophetic teaching of G. McLeod Bryan, Kelly Barnett, and Joseph M. Hendricks, they inspired a cadre of radical Christian activists to challenge the racial mores of segregated Macon. The same is true of professors like Carl Bennett and Thomas Gossett at Wesleyan.

This panoramic view of black-white relations in twentieth-century Macon will illustrate these perspectives through an episodic approach. Each of the ten chapters presents a historian's-eye-view of a cluster of events roughly representative of Macon's racial situation for each decade of the twentieth century. Efforts to survey an entire century must necessarily have some limits. Any scheme for organizing or periodizing a hundred years of development will inevitably have an arbitrary quality. This is certainly true of the tendency to divide history into ten-year periods with characters unique to themselves. Major shifts do not naturally arrange themselves into neat ten-year intervals. Nevertheless, I do believe that by looking carefully at these ten year "snapshots," the important representative events can reveal the development of black-white relations in Macon through the years. Since a book of this kind cannot present a hundred such snapshots, ten chapters can be a manageable way to depict both the continuities and the changes that gradually developed as blacks and whites interacted in Macon over a century's time.

Each chapter focuses on an "event" (or cluster of related events) that represents the most significant vantage point for viewing and evaluating the ways African-American and white Maconites interacted in each decade. In some cases the purpose is to see how these interactions developed in response to local events. Other chapters investigate events in the larger state or national contexts. In each chapter, I choose to focus on the local, state, or national event that I judge to be of greatest moment in shaping race relations in Macon during the particular decade under consideration.

Chapter 1, "'The White Man's Georgia': Macon and Black Disfranchisement," looks at Macon's responses, both white and black, to the 1907 gubernatorial contest between Hoke Smith and Clark Howell. In one of the South's most racially charged elections of the era, the Smith-Howell race centered on the effort to reduce the role of the Negro in Georgia politics by disfranchising black voters by constitutional amendment. Central to this story is the role of former populist leader Tom Watson who agreed to endorse Smith when the candidate committed himself to disfranchisement. The chapter thus investigates Maconites' reactions to both the campaign and its central issue, with particular focus on black Georgians' efforts to protest disfranchisement at an "Equal Rights Convention" held in Macon in February 1907.

The next two chapters examine the racial aftermath of the World War I era and the 1920s. Chapter 2, "Unsafe for Democracy: Macon, Lynching, and the Great War," looks at the rise in racial violence in Macon in the period after World War I. The 1920s marked an important resurgence of Ku Klux Klan activity in many parts of the country and marked the organization's heyday in Macon. Chapter 3 investigates the prominence of the Klan in Macon and the strong criticism of it voiced in the *Macon Telegraph* by W. T. Anderson and Mark Ethridge.

Chapters 4 and 5 look at the immediate prelude to the civil rights era in Macon. Focusing on the 1930s, chapter 4 discusses the beginnings of interracial work in the city, led by the black and white Maconites who became involved with the activities of the Commission on Interracial Cooperation and the Association of Southern Women for the Prevention of Lynching. In the context of these South-wide organizations, the chapter also places the establishment of the Booker T. Washington Community Center, which became Macon's most visible agency working to improve black conditions within "separate but unequal" Jim Crow arrangements. The fifth chapter looks at the ways segregation in Macon was increasingly subverted in the wake of America's war against Hitler's racist Nazi ideology. Crucial to this story are the roles of the Macon branch of the National Association for the Advancement of Colored People (NAACP) and racially progressive professors at Mercer University.

The following three chapters describe Macon's entry into the era of the black freedom struggle during the 1960s and '70s. Chapter 6 investigates the reaction of Macon to the Supreme Court's historic *Brown v. Board of Education* ruling under the title, "Macon and 'Massive Resistance.'" Chapter 7, "Bloc Votes, Boycotts, and Baptists: Disintegrating Jim Crow in 1960s Macon," narrates the end of racial segregation in the city's businesses and schools during the 1960s and early 1970s. Focusing on the mid- to late 1970s, chapter 8 highlights the rise of Macon's black political class and the nadir of twentieth-century black-white relations.

The ninth chapters lumps together the political milieu of 1980s and '90s to survey the ways white and black Macon reflected trends in the what were known nationally as the "culture wars." Although less overtly than in previous eras of Southern history, through an appeal to certain code words, race remained central to battles in both Macon and the United States at large. Chapter 10 investigates black white relations during the tenure of C. Jack Ellis as Macon's first black mayor. It discusses how Ellis' election both affected and was affected by black-white relations in the city and county. The epilogue follows up this survey of 100 years of black-white relations with a few general observations and ends with some prescriptions for racial healing.

1

"The White Man's Georgia": Macon and Black Disfranchisement

By the time Booker T. Washington and Judge Emory Speer gave their speeches at Atlanta's Cotton States Exposition, black Maconites, like African Americans across the South, had suffered a considerable reversal of fortune since their 1865 Jubilee. Celebrating Emancipation circumspectly, lest they give offense to their white neighbors, blacks in Middle Georgia in reality had little in which to rejoice. Emerging from slavery with virtually "nothing but freedom" to their names, most left the plantations and migrated into Macon.[1] In less than a year after Appomattox, black Maconites doubled their numbers to more than 6,000. Many scavenged among garbage dumps and eventually built shantytowns on the outskirts of the city. These concentrations of poverty soon bred cholera and smallpox, and by the end of 1865 black carpenters could not build coffins fast enough for the 500 blacks who had succumbed to disease.[2] Still, despite the fears of survival in their post-slavery world, black Maconites did celebrate their chainlessness and, thanks largely to the Union army and the Republican party, matters would get better before they would get worse.

As elsewhere in the South, an almost tangible fear descended also upon whites in Macon. Worried mostly about the unknown, they were most immediately concerned about their war-torn economy and the presence of Yankee troops. In addition, they were all but doubled over with a fear and loathing of their former slaves, "drunk with the feeling of power which their sudden liberation had given them," as the city's official history later described them. "When," asked the editor of the *Macon Telegraph* in January 1866, "shall our eyes be taken off of ebony in uniform in our city."[3] Having feared the rise of the "black Republicans" since before the War, now white Southerners feared the presence of African Americans in public life during the years of Reconstruction and Redemption.

This fear of blackness took aim at both freedpersons whose efforts at advancement marked them as "trying to be white" and at whites who showed too much concern for them. "Black success," noted historian Glenda Gilmore, "threatened what southerners called 'place.'"[4] Emancipation signaled blacks' first tentative steps out of slavery. Any strides further along the road to economic and political success rattled white sensibilities and social arrangements. Thus, by the beginning of the new century the arrival of Jim Crow and black disfranchisement had done much to reverse black progress and return African Americans as nearly as possible to their former, inferior place in the Southern pecking order.

BLACK POLITICAL ACTIVITY AND
WHITE INTIMIDATION

In Macon, as elsewhere in the state, violence would be whites' first instrument in the effort to return blacks to their accustomed place. Moving into the city after the War, many blacks found encouragement from Yankee troops to taunt devastated white Maconites. As 1866 wore on, the federal provost marshall was swamped with clashes between whites and former slaves.[5] The following year blacks chose Macon as the site of a Georgia Equal Rights Association meeting, called to urge blacks to register to vote in a referendum regarding a new state constitution. In August 1867 six armed whites attacked an African-American church, killing three blacks and wounding eighteen, apparently to intimidate them from gathering in their churches for political activity.[6]

Blacks voted for the first time in Georgia in April 1867, when they chose thirty-seven of their own as delegates to a constitutional convention that also included 120 white members. Under the new constitution adopted in 1868, blacks were enfranchised and elected two black members of the state senate and twenty-five to the House. By September, however, white members of the legislature voted to expel all its black members, including Henry McNeal Turner, the African

Methodist Episcopal minister who represented Macon in the House.[7] Before exiting the chamber, however, the angry legislator delivered a blistering denunciation of the House's action. Intending to "hurl thunderbolts" at those who questioned his manhood, he asked the legislators, "Because God saw fit to make some red, and some white, and some black, and some brown, are we to sit here in judgment upon what God has seen fit to do?" Taking aim at the piety of white Georgians, he marveled: "It is extraordinary that a race such as yours…living in a land where ringing chimes call child and sire to the church of God—a land where Bibles are read and Gospel truths are spoken, and where courts of justice are presumed to exist; it is extraordinary that, with all these advantages on your side, you can make war upon the poor defenseless black man. You know we have no money, no railroads, no telegraphs, no advantages of any sort, and yet all manner of injustice is placed upon us."

Barely able to contain his growing bitterness, he advised black Georgians: "Never lift a finger nor raise a hand in defense of Georgia, until Georgia acknowledges that you are men and invests you with the rights pertaining to manhood." In his closing, Turner issued a final warning: "You may expel us, gentlemen, by your votes, today, but while you do it, remember that there is a just God in Heaven whose All-Seeing Eye beholds alike the acts of the oppressor and the oppressed, and who, despite the machinations of the wicked, never fails to vindicate the cause of Justice, and the sanctity of His own handiwork." Then, as he led his fellow black delegates out of the House chamber, Turner turned, faced the white legislators, and as Jesus had once counseled his disciples, scraped the dirt off his shoes. [8]

The speech availed nothing except to draw the ire of whites. The editor of the *Columbus Weekly* immediately opined that if Turner were to be lynched, "we should neither be seized with astonishment or regret." A Macon Klansman also sent Turner a letter that warned: "Radical H. M. Turner: Your course of conduct is being closely watched by the owls of the night; do not be surprised if you should be aroused from slumber err long by a boo hoo, boo hoo."[9] The Klan also managed to scare almost all African Americans away from the polls in the 1868 presidential election. In the face of terrorist activity and widespread voting fraud, in 1870 Macon blacks once again elected Turner to the Georgia House—only to see whites once again resort to intimidation. Threatened with death unless he immediately left town, Turner holed up in his home, protected by 150 armed supporters, who told city authorities they would torch the city if one black were harmed. He and other blacks were charged with inciting to riot. Although their convictions were overturned on appeal, the minister was again denied his seat in the legislature.[10]

The election of 1872 spawned outbreaks of violence in Atlanta, Savannah, and Wilkinson County, but Macon saw the worst of them when black Maconites marched to the polls in military formation. Encountering a group of angry whites, shots rang out and according to one report, one white and three black Maconites were killed, along with a handful of wounded on both sides. The *Americus Sumter Republican* later commented that the black Maconites had been taught a lesson in being "good, peaceful, law-abiding citizens." Similar incidents of violence continued throughout the 1870s and '80s as local Ku Klux Klan leader Horace Maynard actively combatted black property ownership or political activity in Macon and environs.[11]

Disfranchisement and the 1906 Governor's Race

While such intimidation lasted into the Redemption era, most of the black voting did not. When white, conservative Democrats regained unrivaled control of state politics, Georgia found itself in the vanguard of the South-wide movement to remove African Americans as a political issue by removing them from the voter rolls. The first step in this process was the provision of a cumulative poll tax in a new state constitution adopted in 1877. This means of limiting black voting was quite successful, reducing the percentage of blacks who voted from 53 percent in 1876 to 8 percent in 1900.[12] The decline was reinforced by the establishment of the white primary. This ploy allowed only whites to vote in primary elections on the theory that the Democratic Party could restrict its voting members to those who were white. As a private organization, a political party did not fall under the rule of the Fifteenth Amendment, which only prohibited *states* from abridging the right of blacks to vote. The white primary was adopted in Atlanta in 1892, Augusta in 1900, and Macon in 1901.[13] Thus by the elections of 1904 only 250 blacks (6.25 percent) voted in Bibb County out of a total black registration of 4,000.[14] These tactics had all but eliminated black voting in Georgia. In the 1880s and early nineties, however, another phase of disfranchisement efforts was prompted by a new threat of interracial politics posed by the rise of Tom Watson and Georgia populism.

As the most important leader of the Southern agrarian movement, Thomas E. Watson led efforts to break the power of conservative Democrats whom members of the Farmers Alliances believed to be controlled by Northern industrialists. Championing the cause of Southern farmers against big business interests, Watson and the Populists began to appeal across racial lines to black voters. A native of Thomson, Georgia, who studied at but never graduated from Mercer University, Watson had always opposed social equality between the races. Despite this view, however, he advocated interracial political alliances based on their strict economic interests as farmers. Still, longterm racial animosities always remained just below the surface of this coalition, and once Populism gathered enough influence actually to challenge the Democrats, the agrarian movement was vulnerable to any race-baiting opposition. Conservative Democrats anxious to retain their power eagerly played the race card, denouncing the Populists as radicals. By voting with African Americans, they would return Georgia to the mythical horrors of Reconstruction and "negro rule."[15]

Stymied by the Democrats through much of the 1890s, Watson reversed his views, concluding that only by eliminating the black vote could the white vote ever be successfully divided between reform candidates and the pro-business Democrats. Any division of the white vote gave blacks the important swing vote, and conservatives could always exploit white voters' reluctance to give blacks this much "control." Thus, as long as conservative Democrats could fend off all reformist challenges with warnings of the "Negro domination" of Georgia politics, agrarian reform remained an impossibility. So in September 1904 Watson pledged to back any reform candidate for governor who would support the disfranchisement of blacks by constitutional amendment.[16]

In 1899 and 1901, Thomas W. Hardwick, who like Watson was a Mercer man from Sandersville, sponsored bills to disfranchise African Americans through both a literacy test and a grandfather clause. Most "machine Democrats," however, opposed the bills for different reasons. Macon's Augustus O. Bacon, a member of the US Senate, had declared in 1904 that "Negro rule" was tantamount to "mongrel rule," and that white supremacy was necessary for the salvation of the South. He nonetheless opposed Smith's disfranchisement plans, arguing that the white primary was sufficient to disfranchise black voters. Others feared the measure would disfranchise too many illiterate whites. In the end, both efforts failed, but Hardwick continued to drum up support for finding ways to further exclude blacks from the voter's rolls.[17] Finding a political soulmate, Hardwick wrote a letter to Watson just three days before Hoke Smith launched his campaign for governor in a speech in Madison. Hoping to nail down his support of Smith, he assured Watson of Smith's plan to advocate disfranchisement. "Until the South is finally rid of the negro even as a political potentiality," he wrote, "she will never again have either freedom of thought or independence of action." Reminding him of his pledge to support any disfranchising Democrat, Hardwick appealed, "the man is here. I call on you to help!"[18]

In his Madison speech, just as Hardwick had promised, Smith forcefully called on the state to disfranchise black Georgians by constitutional amendment. Launching one of the most racially-charged campaigns in the history of the South, Smith warned that political equality was tantamount to social equality. He announced his opposition to both, as they would lead to miscegenation. Through the summer and fall, his platform appeared repeatedly in the *Atlanta Journal.* In November he told a Bainbridge audience that "an educated nigger is a curse to his race and a menace to the progress and prosperity of American institutions." By year's end, he had made disfranchisement the most important issue of the campaign, publishing his views in a pamphlet titled "White Supremacy in Georgia and How to Protect the Rights of the People." Throughout the entire year leading up to the election, Smith's typical stump speeches warned of the almost apocalyptic danger of inaction: "This is a white man's country, and we are all agreed that not only in the state at large, BUT IN EVERY COUNTY AND IN EVERY COMMUNITY the white man must control by some means, or life could not be worth living." His plans called for a constitutional amendment combining an education test to disfranchise illiterate blacks with a grandfather clause to keep uneducated whites on the voting rolls. Along the way, by September 1905, Smith had convinced Watson to come onboard.[19]

A former secretary of the interior under President Grover Cleveland, Hoke Smith was opposed by *Atlanta Constitution* editor Clark Howell, a staunch machine Democrat and opponent of Watson and the Populists. He opposed disfranchisement as unnecessary and reminded his audiences that Smith had opposed Hardwick's earlier bills as "unfair, unjust, and undemocratic." In a debate with Smith in Columbus, he argued further that by adding an educational qualification for voting, Smith's plan would enfranchise some 93,000 educated blacks, while eliminating "the votes of many an old democratic hero who was too busy shedding his blood in defense of Georgia to learn 'readin,' 'ritin,' and 'rithmetic.'" Fearful that black agricultural workers would abandon their duties, he warned, "Make the ballot the prize of education and every negro child in Georgia will trot right straight from the cabin to the college."[20]

Commenting on the campaign, *Macon Telegraph* editor Charles R. Pendleton showed his leanings by carrying a full text of only Howell's speech. He denounced Smith's alliance with Populism, charging that "a miserable plot to overthrow democracy...for selfish ends was being hatched and Watson is on the nest." He also dismissed disfranchisement as a serious issue, noting that "as a political menace, the negro is subsiding." Rather, he saw African Americans as "a more disquieting factor" as an element in "our social fabric," and called for "wise statesmanship" in dealing with the problem.[21] Such statesmanship, it went without saying, ought to be present in any candidate for governor. Southern blacks, of course, were expected to exhibit similar restraint. Pendleton therefor advised black Maconites to heed the advice of the Reverend Silas Floyd of Augusta. In a recent Emancipation Day speech, Floyd had called on blacks to improve their condition in the South by seeking "the friendship, aid and co-operation of our white neighbors in the South" rather than seeking refuge in the North. In a naively optimistic column, Pendleton informed his readers that blacks had more opportunity in the South than in other regions of the country: "White bankers, white physicians, white merchants, white lawyers and so on show him the same consideration they do their white clients. He is aided on every hand provided he shows himself worthy of aid and confidence."[22]

MACON AND THE EQUAL RIGHTS CONVENTION

For their part, black Maconites doubted that their situation was as rosy as most whites believed. As the year began, City Clerk T. L. Massenburg reported that Macon's white citizens endured a death rate of 8.47 per thousand, compared to 14.68 for the city's African Americans.[23] Such *quantity* of life issues made white efforts to eliminate black political power all the more questionable. So to protest the general of tenor of the developing governor's race, as well as their general *quality* of life, blacks from across the state gathered on 14 February for an Equal Rights Convention in Macon.

Led by the Reverend William J. White of Savannah, editor of the *Georgia Baptist*, and inspired by the Niagara Movement, some 500 delegates met in Macon to address virtually every aspect of black life in Georgia. A string of speakers launched a barrage of criticism against peonage, the convict lease system, exclusion from juries, unequal school funds, and especially Hoke Smith's disfranchisement plan. While some white observers commented on White's generally conservative leadership of the group, the minister nonetheless sounded anything but Washingtonian, as he admonished his audience that "we must agitate, complain, protest, and keep protesting against the invasion of our manhood rights...and above all organize these million brothers of ours into one great fist which shall never cease to pound at the gates of opportunity until they shall fly open."[24] Scholar W. E. B. Du Bois also addressed the gathering, disavowing any wish to associate with "any who do not wish our company, but we do expect in a Christian, civilized land, to live under a system of law and order." Most blacks, he asserted, were "fit for the ballot," calling on the delegates to "insist on full civil rights" for their people.[25]

As a group the convention issued a "declaration of principles" that defended the reputation of black Georgians as law-abiding and upright. The document criticized the state's efforts in the public education of black students and called on officials to apportion funding more equitably. They also commended those Georgia counties willing to summon African-American men to serve on juries and recommended that the practice be used across the state. On the central issue of the gubernatorial campaign, the convention lauded fair voting practices as "the bedrock principle of American citizenship" and advised black Georgians "to pay their taxes and qualify themselves as voters by registering," particularly because the poll tax funded the state's public school system. Denouncing the state's developing Jim Crow system, the principles rejected segregated seating on public conveyances as "harsh, degrading and unjust.... The present system is so operated that our people may be and are frequently subjected to many indignities, such as smoking, drinking whiskey, etc., in the presence of our wives, mothers, and daughters."[26]

By far the convention's most controversial comments, however, belonged to the aging Henry McNeal Turner. By 1900 Turner had been consecrated a bishop in the AME Church and was one of the era's most outspoken Southern black leaders. Having been ousted from both the Georgia House of Representatives and from his job as Macon's Republican-appointed postmaster, he had grown pessimistic regarding the prospect of racial justice in the United States. As a result, he became a fervent advocate of emigration to Africa. In 1899, under Turner's influence, some 100 black Maconites petitioned Congress for funding to emigrate to Liberia. By 1906 Turner viewed black conditions in Georgia as worse than slavery, dismissing other blacks' concerns about the perils of emigration. "Talk about dying in Africa!" he exclaimed, "My God! Can we die any faster than we are being murdered here?... To remain here in the face of discrimination, disfranchisement and all that is cruel and low, makes us monumental fools...." In his Macon speech, he said, "To the Negro in the country the American flag is a dirty and contemptible rag.... [H]ell is an improvement upon the United States when the Negro is involved."[27] Not surprisingly, Turner was, according to historian, Donald Grant, "almost universally disliked by white Georgians."[28]

Among those who disliked Turner's views was Macon's editor Pendleton. Scoring the Atlanta newspapers, he complained that "an undue amount of notice is being taken of the foolish remarks made...by the old negro Bishop Turner." Pendleton dismissed the bishop's "usual quantum of denunciation of the nation and its treatment of the negro," commenting that "it matters very little what this old and disappointed negro says." He took Turner's denunciation of the flag as a "dirty rag" as a mere "outburst" expressing Turner's disappointment in the Republican

Party which had "deceived him." He gave Turner his due, however, in commending his admonitions to emigration: "Bishop Turner is so far in advance of his race in the recognition…that this is a white man's country and that the negroes ought to migrate to Africa where they could try their practice hand at statesmanship and empire building and enjoy all the social equality in sight in their heart's content."[29]

The Equal Rights Convention elicited enough comment from Pendleton to suggest the general range of white public opinion on race relations in Macon. First, Pendleton addressed the issue of voting rights and the proper place of blacks in southern society. The white race had earned the franchise through "thousands of years of endeavor in that direction." Thus, to give that privilege to a race that had not made such an endeavor and only recently emerged from slavery would be "anything but equal rights." He also feared that education would mean "unfitting him for manual labor." To educate and lift them above common labor would be for African Americans "peculiarly disastrous," adding, "There is for him no field in the learned professions. Conditions have confined him to the physical and hardier channels of toil."[30]

In a later editorial, Pendleton acknowledged "an inborn racial antagonism" that God did not intend, and commented more generally on the race problem in the United States. First, he placed blame on Northern Republicans for the "penalties that are consequent upon the negroes' freedom." He explained that "at emancipation, he [the Negro] was untutored and unguarded and allowed to roam the fields and the country at large. Later under Reconstruction, he turned his liberty into license, in crimes that entailed wholesale slaughter and violence. It is not his fault that he was left to the promptings and instincts of his wild and destructive nature without hindrance and without restraint."[31]

Typical of most white Southerners, the editor further argued that the South had no race problem before the end of the Civil War. He lauded both the loyalty of the former slaves and the affection of the former slave owners. After the war, however, "untutored and unguarded and unrestrained" former slaves gained citizenship and voting rights, a radical change that strained race relationships and hindered black opportunity. Citing the comments of John E. White, pastor of Macon's white First Baptist Church, Pendleton praised the Jim Crow laws legislated after 1866 as "the strong hand of kindness and guidance" to "a confused race." More recent educational philosophies such as that of W. E. B. Du Bois had "lifted him entirely out of his place among the people who would be more than glad to use him...if he were only willing to serve." Servility thus marked the condition for harmonious race relations, as Pendleton noted: "We are quite willing to care for them as freedmen if they had remained dependent upon our direction."[32] As elsewhere in the South, blacks in Macon were only willing to adopt such dependence when pragmatics demanded.

MACON AND THE GOVERNOR'S RACE

In mid-February Hoke Smith made a campaign visit to Macon, delivering his stump speech to a large audience at the city auditorium. During his remarks, ten members of the Mercer University Hoke Smith Club enthusiastically cheered their hero, shouting, "Rah! Rah! Hoke Smith! Hoke Smith! Hoke Smith!" The candidate defended his support for "Jeffersonian Democracy," sound money, and disfranchisement. Blacks should be completely eliminated from voting and whites should control the education of the Negro. Skeptical of black potential, he asserted, "A mule, no matter how much you might try to drive him cannot be converted into a thoroughbred race horse."[33]

In the same issue carrying the story of Smith's Macon appearance, the Pendleton claimed not to care who was elected governor, citing loyalty to principles rather than particular candidates. He argued that the Democratic Party should be controlled by its own members, and not be steered by Tom Watson, who made "no pretense of being a Democrat."[34] Within a month, however, Pendleton printed a letter to the editor denouncing Smith's efforts to allay fears that disfranchisement might also eliminate some white voters. When Smith suggested this problem could be avoided by having registrars ask difficult questions of blacks and easier questions of whites, Pendleton was livid:

> Here is a man standing before the people of Georgia asking for their suffrage for the highest position within the gift of her people, who if elected will have to take the solemn oath that he will uphold and support the constitution of the state and United States, openly and above board proposing a scheme of

lawlessness and riot and pointing to her citizens to the paths of perjury.... If Mr. Smith fairly proposes a law that cannot honestly be executed the great state of Georgia, ten thousands times over would be better off without any law upon her statutes.

Disfranchisement to Pendleton was merely a "hobby horse" on which Smith hoped to ride into office. The poll tax and the white primary had already effectively disfranchised blacks. So few black Georgians were still registered to vote in the 1906 election that the fear of "Negro rule" was groundless. Pendleton himself wished to eliminate blacks from the political process, and believed that Republican enfranchisement of blacks had been "born of hate and madness." But the Smith-Watson disfranchisement scheme was also a grievous wrong, and "one crime committed offers no justification of the second." The correspondent then finished with a flourish: "Away with that sentiment that stirs up the passions and widens the breach, already too much strain between the races, who Hoke Smith and every other man knows must dwell together either in peace or in war. Perish the ambitions of that man who is willing to sacrifice the peace of his country upon the altar of personal interest."[35]

Macon's contrary opinion was advanced by Judge A. L. Miller, president of the Georgia Bar Association and a Smith supporter. In a 2 August letter to the *Telegraph,* Miller argued that education merely rendered African Americans more discontented. "Disfranchisement and deportation," he wrote, were the only solutions to the "Negro problem." He thus advocated that the United States sell the Philippines to Japan and use the proceeds to send blacks back to Africa.[36]

As the campaign developed, Pendleton and the *Macon Telegraph* seemed to oppose Smith more vigorously than Howell. Smith consistently defended himself against arguments put forth by Pendleton, and launched a number of counterattacks. On 10 August, just twelve days before the primary election, Smith made another visit to Macon to refute arguments raised by the *Telegraph*, which Pendleton claimed "more than any other has gotten right at the core of this campaign, and has exposed the worm gnawing there." Smith told his Macon audience that their newspaper "does not speak your views and it is not fighting for your rights." On disfranchisement, Smith argued that the Fifteenth Amendment, which guaranteed blacks the right to vote, should be circumvented, "even if by fraudulent administration." He added, "We can frame a bill to disfranchise the negro and not mention 'niggers' or 'color.'" Since, Smith argued, "the negro was better as a slave than now," all blacks "within the borders of the state should be deported and should not be allowed to return." Pendleton responded to Smith's speech with a lengthy editorial that concluded, "Mr. Smith's exhibition of himself, and his venomous attack on the *Telegraph* and its editor, shows that the heat of the dog days…has upset his spleen and unbalanced his brain. We trust that a case of rabies will not ensue."[37]

The following day he ran a half page article summarizing a speech by Statesboro Congressman W. G. Brantley. Labeling the article, "Disfranchisement Ably Discussed," Pendleton allowed Brantley's words to make his own case that white supremacy could be defended without unnecessarily disfranchising black voters. Arguing that white Georgians were in agreement regarding white supremacy, Brantley wrote, "There is not a white man in Georgia worthy of the name who does not believe in supremacy of the white race." Brantley pointed out that there were too few black voters in Georgia to pose a realistic threat. He cited figures from the Comptroller General's office that because of the poll tax only some 68,000 blacks had voted in 1904. "I do not believe," he concluded, "there are exceeding 75,000 negroes in Georgia who could vote if they desired to do so."[38] Brantley's (and Pendleton's) argument was based on the assumption that white voters supported white supremacy, but might differ on how best to maintain it. They rightly argued that Smith was unnecessarily stirring up prejudice and fears of "negro rule," not because of any serious threat to white supremacy, but merely for political gain. In the context of race relations, however, the morality of white supremacy was never in question; the issue was how to protect and maintain it.

Still, in spite of his determination to see Smith defeated—partly because of his disfranchisement plans, but mostly because he saw Smith as giving Watson and the Populists too much power in the Democratic party, Pendleton showed a measure of journalistic fairness by allowing opposing voices to be heard in the *Telegraph*. He ran another letter by Judge Miller, in which he deemed the coming balloting the most important election since 1870, when the Democrats regained control of the Reconstruction legislature. He predicted a Smith victory as a "final decree in favor of white supremacy." Miller concluded, however, with a dire warning: "If not, God save old Georgia! For what man of all of us can tell when the negro will hold the balance of power between a divided people?"[39]

Yet the *Telegraph's* opposition was more than obvious as election day arrived. Pendleton continued to editorialize against the Smith campaign, and on election eve gave little space to advertise a Smith rally at the Grand Opera House. In contrast, he prominently advertised a "monster rally" for Howell at the city auditorium, where "All the shame of hypocrisies of Hoke Smith will be shown up in their true light." That same issue carried an anti-disfranchisement article by perhaps the most prominent Maconite of all, Augustus O. Bacon, who served Georgia in the United States Senate. Once again, the senator assured readers of the "absolute necessity of making white supremacy the controlling issue," but argued that such a goal was being accomplished by the white primary. White voters, he warned, would be unnecessarily divided by the disfranchisement proposition. Moreover, he feared that a disfranchisement amendment would be overturned by the Supreme Court as a violation of the Fifteenth Amendment.[40]

On election day, the appeals to race continued as Howell supporters distributed circulars bearing Bishop Turner's picture, reminding voters that he had written a letter to President-elect Grover Cleveland in support of Smith for secretary of the interior. The brochures also told of Smith's black appointments during his service in the Cleveland administration.[41] These last-minute efforts were of no avail. A year and a half of race-baiting campaigning by both candidates had taken effect. As one historian put it, "the long and bitter gubernatorial campaign had degenerated into a contest in denunciation of the Negro." Another called it "the most demagogic, race-baiting politicking Georgia had ever seen."[42] Once the candidates decided to appeal to the voters' powerful fear of "Negro rule," the more Negrophobic candidate was almost destined to prevail. Fearful enough to base his campaign on Negro disfranchisement, Hoke Smith was clearly that candidate, and the wave of racial passion he created swept him into office. Statewide, he amassed 104,796 votes to 70,477 for his four opponents. He won 110 of Georgia's 145 counties, compared to 6 by Howell.

In Bibb County, Smith won handily, garnering 50.16 percent of the votes to Howell's 35.75 percent.[43] Macon's support for Smith was thus some 10 percent weaker than his statewide total of some 60 percent of the total vote. Pendleton's editorial stance, which marshaled opposition by other prominent Maconites like Senator Bacon, likely explains Smith's somewhat weaker showing in Macon. After the election, Pendleton bowed to the will of the people, pledging to support the new governor. He had little choice, for despite his vigorous opposition, fully half of Macon's voters disagreed with the *Telegraph* in support of both Smith and disfranchisement.

Twelve days after the primary election, Maconites took prominent roles when state Democrats met in Macon for their nominating convention. The outcome of the general election was a foregone conclusion. Smith faced only token opposition from a Populist candidate named J. B. Osburn who would draw only 148 votes in November. The convention was thus a coronation of Smith as Georgia's defender against railroad interests and "Negro rule." Elected chairman of the convention, Macon's Judge A. L. Miller told delegates that the primary had above all settled the issue of white supremacy. "We said by that primary," he exulted, "that we intend to govern the black man as we deem fit and that he shall never govern us." For his part, Smith called on the state to solve the "Negro problem" through a constitutional amendment passed by the legislature and ratified by the people in a general election. Such a measure would protect Georgia elections "against ignorant and purchasable negro votes."[44] After the convention, the *Augusta Herald* correctly noted that nothing in Smith's platform was more popular or "contributed more to his splendid victory" than his disfranchisement plank. Though somewhat less fervently than the state as a whole, Macon could join Augusta in being proud of and rejoicing in a victory "for the cause of white supremacy and of the determination of the Democratic party to make this for all time a white man's state."[45]

Once Hoke Smith was safely in office, his floor leaders introduced his disfranchisement plan into the General Assembly in July 1907. George W. Williams of Laurens county and Thomas Hardwick brought the bill to the House, while Macon's Thomas S. Felder shepherded the bill through the state senate. The amendment provided that any male citizen would be eligible to vote if he had paid all taxes required of him since the adoption of the 1877 constitution. All who had served in the military in any American war or their descendants were eligible. The amendment's educational clause required ability to read or write and understand any paragraph of the constitution.[46]

In the House, the bill's most vocal opponent was Bibb County Representative Joe Hill Hall. As a member of the committee on constitutional amendments, he presented a substitute bill. When an opposing representative implied that Hall had not sufficiently supported disfranchisement, Hall replied in his own defense: "I have never opposed negro disfranchisement in any speech I ever made. I am on record as favoring any bill that would disfranchise the negro because he was a negro, but never a bill that would disfranchise any white man and enfranchise a negro." In reality, Hall's was the more stringent disfranchisement bill. Hall opposed the Williams bill because it included an education qualification that Hall feared would eliminate too many uneducated white voters. He also opposed it because he believed it gave voting registrars too much power. His bill relied on the cumulative poll tax to eliminate only black voters, who would be ineligible to register unless they could produce tax receipts back to the time they came of age, or back to the 1877 constitutional convention.[47]

On 2 August, when the committee recommended the Williams bill to the House rather than Hall's, the Macon legislator objected bitterly: "You are fixing it so you may disfranchise my children and yours in the future. You had better go slow. You are aiming at the negro, but you may strike a white man.... What? Me discuss my bill before *this* committee? I guess not." At that, he walked out of the committee meeting vowing to fight for his measure before the full House.[48]

When the Williams bill reached the House on 12 August, Hall opposed it vigorously. "I have no patience," he argued, "with a white man going about saying, 'a white man is superior to a negro.' When he does, it makes us doubt whether he really believes it." He called emancipation "the greatest crime ever enacted," objecting that under the Williams bill registrars could ask any questions they wished:

> You say it's easy to ask a nigger a hard question and disqualify him. I stand here and tell you that it will be just as easy to ask a white man who is not going to vote right a hard

question and thus disqualify him, and also to ask a nigger who is going to vote right an easy question and qualify him.... Do you know that under this clause the descendants of Jefferson Davis...who served the confederacy, are not enfranchised. Of course, they are protected by other clauses; but even then you put the son of a negro soldier in the federal army above the descendants of these great southerners.

He finished his speech noting that the people of Georgia had voted for Smith "because you promised them that it would disfranchise 90 percent of the negroes and none of the whites, and I'm showing you where it disfranchises no negroes but lots of white men."[49] Hall managed to convince only a handful of his colleagues, and two days later the House adopted the Williams bill by a vote of 159–16.[50]

Debate in the Senate ran along the same lines as that in the House, but with the roles of prominent Maconites reversed. Unlike Hall in the House, Thomas Felder sponsored the amendment bill in the senate. When an opposing senator registered concern that whites might also be disfranchised by the education clause, Felder assured the senator that the grandfather clause and the character requirement would protect whites while eliminating black voters. When that argument was unpersuasive, Felder resorted to the Populist argument that the issue had been discussed all over the state and 111 counties had expressed themselves fully in favor of the measure. His rhetorical ace in the hole, however, was an overt appeal to race. He argued that even if the amendment disfranchised an occasional white Georgian, it would at the same time exclude 490 blacks. "Would not that community be better?" he asked. He concluded with a clarion call: "This is a white man's country and they should control it. Our ancestors fought for it and died in the efforts to gain it." The amendment eventually passed the senate by a 37–6 vote. Once differences between the House and senate bills were ironed out, the full senate adopted the disfranchisement amendment on 18 August 1907.[51]

In passing the amendment, however, both houses ignored the protests of a contingent of prominent black leaders from around the state, including some from Macon. Led by H. H. Proctor of Atlanta, the group presented a memorial to the General Assembly and attended the debate in the senate. Their statement listed five objections to the amendment. First, they viewed it as unnecessary and likely to provoke political agitation and racial strife. Second, it would disturb labor conditions and retard cooperative efforts toward law and order. Next, they argued that the bill was undemocratic and subverted the principles of popular government. Fourth, it was unconstitutional. Fifth, they believed the bill would have a morally degrading effect. In elaborating these arguments, they feared the bill gave too much power to voter registrars. They objected that the bill was a "stab at the negro race" that would reduce them to "complete political serfdom." Promising to fight the measure all the way to the US Supreme Court, they appealed to the members' sense of fairness:

> We have contributed in our way no little to the prosperity of this state. We have cleared your forests and tilled your fields; we have constructed your railways and spanned your streams with bridges; we have built your houses and tended your cattle; we have cooked your food and cared for your little ones; we have served you by night and by day, in the time of peace and on the field of battle; we have done for you the best we could. And in this hour when our liberties are in the balance, and while all the world looks on, we ask you to do us as you would have us do to you. For forty years your people have contended that they ought to be left alone to regulate the affairs between the races, and you have from a thousand platforms pledged to the negroes, to the nation and to the whole world that if this was allowed, you will deal with absolute fairness between your white and black citizens. The nation has granted your request and some of our ablest leaders have advised their people to trust you and withdraw themselves from politics. Many of our people have acted on this advice. Will you disregard your solemn vows and trample your honor in the dust by passing this bill?[52]

A week later another contingent of black citizens of Bibb County went to the state capital with another concern, petitioning the state legislature to kill a bill proposing that all Negro societies be placed under a bond of between $5000 to $20,000. The group was led by W. O. Emory and C. N. Robinson, but their concerns were again ignored by the lawmakers, and the bill was adopted.[53]

Thus adopted by the General Assembly, the disfranchisement amendment then went before the state's voters a year later on 7 October 1908, when it passed by a vote of 79,968 to 40,260. In Bibb County 1,053 out of 5,234 qualified voters in Bibb County voted for the disfranchisement, and 903 opposed it.[54] In a series of editorials over the next few days, the *Atlanta Journal* celebrated the victory, declaring that Georgia "takes her place among the enlightened and progressive states which have announced that the white man is to rule. She has declared in clear and specific terms for Anglo-Saxon supremacy...." The *Journal* also celebrated that the November elections would be the last time that the "ignorant and corrupt negro will participate in Georgia."[55] To have defeated the amendment, asserted the *Journal*, would have "set the clock back in Georgia for generations to come, but instead, the generations unborn will rise up to call us blessed for the work we have accomplished.... This is the white man's Georgia from now on."[56] Once it became Georgia law, the disfranchisement measure efficiently accomplished its purpose. Black voter registration in Georgia fell precipitously, from some 68,000 in 1904 to only 11,285 in 1910, when white registered voters numbered 261,145.[57]

Thus, in this context, whites viewed any political participation at all by blacks as too much. The appeals to racial prejudice, led by the two seekers of the state's highest political office, legitimized racist extremism. If the gubernatorial candidates could so thoroughly denounce black Georgians, their rhetoric also served to enable the more common element to use harsher methods of defending white supremacy. The campaign of 1906 and its efforts to disfranchise African Americans both contributed to and was the result of a larger "cultural Negrophobia" sweeping Georgia and the South. To that fear Macon was as susceptible as any other city.

CULTURAL NEGROPHOBIA

This need to protect white supremacy was as hysterical as it was groundless. "Negro rule" had never approached reality in any Southern state, and in Georgia, where conservative Democrats took back control of the legislature by 1870, the "horrors of Reconstruction" were mild and very short-lived. Yet the racist rhetoric of the 1906 governor's campaign was both a cause and a product of the white imagination run wild. Throughout the South during the 1890s and the early years of the twentieth century, ideas of "Negro retrogression" dominated white opinion of their African-American neighbors. Depending on the version of the ideology one accepted, most white Southerners held that, apart from white control, blacks would either revert to a childlike state or to their "beastly natures." Rather than making progress as a race, the argument ran, the former slaves were certain to descend into a natural barbarism, leading inexorably to crime and the rape of white women. As a result, this era became the heyday of lynching and race riots, a period that historian Rayford Logan called the "nadir" of African American history in the United States.[58]

Fueling these negative images of African Americans at the turn of the twentieth century were a series of influential books that ostensibly gave "scientific" support to the ideas of black inferiority and retrogression. In 1896 Frederick Hoffman published *Race Traits and Tendencies of the American Negro*, in which he portrayed sexual obsession as a peculiarly black characteristic and argued that the problem had worsened since the end of slavery. Four years later, Charles Carroll sounded the same themes and minced no words in his title, *The Negro a Beast*. The book argued that blacks had subhuman status, having been created on the sixth day, with the animals rather than with humankind.[59]

At roughly the same time that Hoke Smith began his campaign to eliminate the black vote, there appeared a literary development destined to influence white opinion as much as the governor's race. North Carolina-born minister Thomas Dixon published his novel, *The Clansman,* and sold over a million copies within a few months. In 1915 it would be made into America's first blockbuster film, *The Birth of a Nation.* A stage version of the novel attracted large crowds in Atlanta during fall 1905 and added to growing racial tensions in the city. *The Clansman* popularized common Southern views of Reconstruction as an era when corrupt Northern Republicans colluded with newly-freed and enfranchised blacks to control the vanquished and victimized Southland. The novel also depicted black men as educationally illiterate, politically incompetent, and sexually obsessed with white women. In addition,

Dixon's writings portrayed the Ku Klux Klan as a heroic force that rescued the South from the control of the beastly Negro.[60] All these views were quite prominent among whites in Macon.

Dixon's play (and the film version) drew audiences in the North as well as the South. In early January 1906, the *Telegraph* carried a news report of *The Clansman*'s large, enthusiastic crowd at the Liberty Theater in New York City. Touring with the theater company, Dixon told the audience that critics had warned him that his play would not be well received in the North. "Your reception tonight," he informed them, "has convinced me that there is no North and no South, but we are one people." Later that month, in an address at New York's Baptist Church of the Epiphany, he told his audience that colonization was the only long-term solution to the Negro problem. On black inferiority he asserted, "Today the negro is 4,000 years behind the white race and he will always be so. For that piece of time he occupied one of the richest and most fertile countries in the world, and he never improved it in any way; never dug up any of the minerals; never built a ship or a house or even constructed a cart until the white man showed him how." In a startling admission, he warned that the Negro would not "continue to submit to the injustice with which we treat him in the North and the South." He thus concluded, "We must remove the negro or we will have to fight him." Dixon's appearance was once again covered in the *Macon Telegraph*.[61]

By September 1906, however, after the gubernatorial campaign had roiled the racial waters of the state, several papers grew uneasy about *The Clansman*'s potential for making trouble. The *Augusta Herald* opined that the production had contributed to "race conditions in this State," and called on theater managers to bar blacks from attending the play. Reprinting part of the *Herald*'s editorial, Pendleton concurred, arguing that the production tended to "excite the baser passions of both races…. There may be sleeping passions and hatreds there that no white man can measure or understand." Thus, as a matter of prudence, so as not to "play with fire so near to the gunpowder," he recommended that Southern theaters refuse to book the production. Macon's proprietors ignored Pendleton's advice, however, and scheduled a performance for 25 September.[62]

Despite these misgivings about Dixon's work, four years later another of Dixon's plays—*The Sins of the Father*—was performed in Macon. The *Telegraph* enthusiastically publicized the production, carrying two articles about it just before the play date. One article recounted a standing room only audience of 2,000 in Richmond, Virginia, riveted by the play's message against the evils of interracial marriage and miscegenation. After the performance, Dixon told his audience that his play was written to combat the intermixing of the two races. Such practices, he warned, "would destroy the character of American manhood." The other article carried a review of the play by Dorothy Dix, the most prominent female journalist in America at the time. She wrote that racial intermarriage "endangers the health or life of every pure white woman and...threatens the very sanctity of the race.... 'The Sins of the Father' is more than a play. It is a sermon, a tract, a clarion call to maintain the purity of the white race that must thrill the heart of every man."[63] During the company's visit to Macon, Dixon invited members of the Mercer University Kappa Alpha fraternity, of which the playwright was a member, to attend the performance as his guests. The Mercer brothers responded by giving a banquet at the Lanier Hotel in Dixon's honor.[64]

At the same time that Maconites lapped up the publicity generated by *The Clansman* and Dixon's other racist diatribes, they were also being fed a steady diet of articles touching on the theme of black criminality and sexual obsession. Newspapers throughout the South commonly referred to African American males as "beasts," "brutes," or "fiends," often in lurid headlines. The "unmentionable" crime (the black rape of a white woman) was mentioned with great frequency, even though by far the majority of lynchings of the period were based on accusations of crimes *other* than rape.[65] In Macon, the *Telegraph* often informed readers of Mississippi Governor James K. Vardaman's harsh rhetoric regarding blacks. In January 1906, during the Georgia governor's race, Maconites read excerpts of Vardaman's annual message to the Mississippi legislature. Urging lawmakers not to waste state money for black education, he argued, "As a race the negro is deteriorating morally every day. Time has demonstrated that he is more criminal as a free man than as a slave, that he is increasing in criminality with fearful rapidity, being one-third more criminal in 1890 than he was in 1880.... You can scarcely pick up a newspaper whose pages are not blackened with an account of an unmentionable crime committed by a negro brute...."[66] Although Pendleton later lodged his disagreement with Vardaman on black education, he continued to run stories about him, as well as about South Carolina Senator "Pitchfork" Ben Tillman, whose racial rhetoric was similar to Vardaman's.[67]

Similarly, just days before the 22 August primary election, the *Telegraph* carried a story of Joe Morris, a twenty-year-old black man who languished in the Bibb County jail, protesting his innocence of the crime of shooting a family in Baldwin County. Fearing he might be lynched, he was incarcerated in Macon until his trial. Nonetheless, accounts described Morris as "skulking in the thickets in the darkness, and living more in the manner of beast than man."[68]

When the press did not depict blacks as brutes or fiends, it often poked fun at them in light-hearted, derisive stories. One such story half-seriously warned of the "hoodoo" practices being used against Andrew Bryant, a black resident of East Macon. With the headline, "White Powder 'Hoodoo' Terrorizes Neighbors," the account made great sport of Bryant's concerns and added to the unflattering picture of blacks in Macon.[69]

Thus, by August 1906 Macon had already passed a Jim Crow law to segregate blacks and whites on streetcars, which in Pendleton's view was "far preferable to indiscriminate mixing." In addition, white fearfulness about "negro criminality" led the Macon City Council to instruct the police to "strictly enforce" the city's vagrancy laws. Aldermen unanimously supported the motion designed to address the "evil" of "hundreds of negroes in the city, who congregated about the saloons, blocked the sidewalks, and had no visible means of support," as "crowds around the negro dives were being augmented day by day."[70]

Of course, Macon was hardly the only part of Georgia where such conditions had fueled tensions and turned the state's cities, with their large black populations, into a racial tinderboxes. Mixing Smith and Howell's racist political speeches with the push for disfranchisement, the furor over Thomas Dixon's plays, and the generally demeaning manner in which blacks were depicted in the Southern press made an explosion seem almost inevitable. Exactly one month after the primary election put Hoke Smith on the way to the governor's mansion, the capital city endured one of the greatest eruptions of racial violence in American history.

MACON AND THE ATLANTA RACE RIOT

The early years of the twentieth century saw a number of race riots break out in both the North as well as the South. Along with Atlanta, riots developed in 1900 in both New Orleans and New York. Springfield, Ohio (1904), Greenburg, Indiana (1906), and Springfield, Illinois (1908), all felt the travail of racial tension. In loss of life and property, however, the Atlanta riot was the worst of these racial earthquakes.[71] On the afternoon of 21 September the *Atlanta Evening News* carried two dramatic headlines on the front page: "Sheriff in Automobile Saves Negro from a Mob" and "Girl Jumps into Closet to Escape Negro Brute." The next day, Saturday, 22 September, the riots began in earnest. Crowds gathered in the central Five Points section of the city, and by that afternoon had been agitated by another series of lurid headlines, all on page 1 of the *Evening News*:[72]

COPS TEAR OBSCENE PICTURES FROM
DECATUR STREET DIVE

NEGRO RESTAURANTS INCUBATORS OF VICE; 60
LICENSES REFUSED

NEGRO INSULTER HEAVILY FINED

INSULTING NEGRO BADLY BEATEN
AT TERMINAL STATION

BOLD NEGRO KISSES WHITE GIRL'S HAND

HUNDRED LASHES AND '23' FOR SQUEEZING
LADY'S ARM

Not to be outdone, the *Atlanta Journal* rushed into print with two of its own extra afternoon editions. The first announced, "Negro Attempts to Assault Mrs. Mary Chafin Near Sugar Creek Bridge." A while later the second headline screamed: "ANGRY CITIZENS IN PURSUIT OF BLACK BRUTE WHO ATTEMPTED ASSAULT ON MRS. CHAPIN—RESCUED FROM FIEND BY PASSING NEIGHBOR."[73]

By 9:00 P.M. that night some 2,000 white Atlantans milled around Decatur Street swapping exaggerated stories of new assaults, dialing up their fury with every comment. The city's law enforcement agencies were denounced for allowing such travesties and tub-thumping fire-eaters called the crowd to take matters into their own hands. "Kill the niggers!" became the war cry. For the next four days, the city descended into chaos, as white mobs attacked blacks virtually at will.[74]

One report told of mobs attacking a streetcar, looking for blacks. The trolley was pulled away from its wires and in semi-darkness three victims were beaten to death. Snipers shot at other streetcars, leading their conductors to refuse to continue their runs. Governor Joseph Terrell mobilized eight local infantry companies to help restore order. By Monday morning the *Macon Telegraph* reported that sixteen companies of infantry, one battery of light artillery, and one squadron of cavalry patrolled the city under the command of Colonel Clifford Anderson of the Georgia State Militia. Six blacks were shot down in an attack on a streetcar, and by Monday morning the *Telegraph* reported sixteen dead and many others wounded.[75]

In addition, the governor called out companies of militia from Griffin, Barnesville, Jackson, Rome, Cedartown, and Macon, which sent two companies known as the Floyd Rifles and the Volunteers. Another company, the Hussars, remained in Macon in case violence flared there. The Floyd Rifles patrolled two black districts known as "Hell's Half Acre" and "Devil's Dip." Scattered gunshots were heard all through the night, and one officer from a Macon company reported that every man on the streets was armed and women sat on their verandas with shotguns across their laps.[76]

Back in Macon, Pendleton laid the blame for the "Atlanta Situation" on a combination of black brutishness and white exploitation, both political and commercial. At base, he found the roots of the upheaval in the nature of the black race. The surprise, he suggested, lay in that such a paroxysm had not happened earlier, particularly given the existence of "hundreds of low negro dives where congregate thousands of this naturally barbaric race for the practice of vice in all its beastly forms." Marveling that blacks seemed to "court death in its most cruel forms at the hands of the mob," he argued that "the passion of the brute one aroused is stronger than any fear."

Pendleton then echoed reports and rumors about Decatur street dives that tempt their black clientele with lewd posters hawking various liquors with pictures of suggestively (un)dressed white women posing in the embrace of black men. Such advertisements, Pendleton reminded his readers, were produced by white entrepreneurs. More seriously, however, the editor noted that similar billboards in Macon, Atlanta, and other Georgia cities were being used to beckon audiences, black as well as white, to the same theaters to see *The Clansman*. He argued that "the suggestive juxtapositions of white women and black men put on the stage before promiscuous crowds is just about as sensible as removing danger from a powder magazine by sticking a lighted match to it."

The brunt of Pendleton's criticisms fell on the liquor and theater interests exploiting both sexuality and race for commercial gain. But his displeasure at similar exploitation by Smith and Howell for political gain seeped out. While calling on officials to suppress lurid advertisements, the unsavory dives, and "idle, loafing negroes," he aimed a quick parting shot at Georgia's leaders: "our politicians must quit playing the negro up in politics when he is trying to keep out of politics. For a year and more he has been made too conspicuous in Georgia."[77]

The *Telegraph's* advice was quickly followed by Macon's leaders, as both Mayor Bridges Smith and the City Council barred the showing of Dixon's play in the wake of the disturbances in Atlanta. The capital city, Savannah, and Montgomery, Alabama, soon followed suit. For Pendleton and many others, however, the problem lay merely in the unwise decision to perform the play before "promiscuous" audiences including blacks and whites seated in separate sections. Critics faulted the decision to hold its performances in the South at such a volatile time, rather than the ideology presented in Dixon's scripts. In a separate opinion piece on *The Clansman,* Pendleton rejected the *Washington Post*'s denunciation of the play's historical outlook. "There are thousands of men still living in the South," he noted, "who can recall conditions fully as bad and wonderfully like those depicted by Mr. Dixon."[78] Nine years later, when the film version was released in D. W. Griffith's *Birth of a Nation,*

prominent Maconite and president of the Georgia Division of the United
Daughters of the Confederacy, Dorothy Blount Lamar, offered a
somewhat different evaluation of Dixon's work:

> ...the truth about the days of reconstruction has arisen and
> has put on the greatest production of the day in "The Birth of a
> Nation." It is a truthful portrayal of the sorrows of those times, it
> has done a magnificent work for us in setting the justice toward
> our troubles at that period before an uninformed north. I have no
> patience with those time-servers, who petition their city councils
> to prevent its presentation in the towns of our south. Our people
> know too little of what gave birth to the Ku Klux Klan.[79]

In addition to canceling performances of *The Clansman* scheduled
for Tuesday, 25 September, Macon authorities took other preventative
measures. Police kept close tabs on the purchase of guns by black
Maconites and the chief of police planted paid informants within the
African-American community.[80] Some of these concerns were sparked
by the frayed feelings created by events in Atlanta. But they also were a
response to a smaller outbreak in Macon two weeks before the Atlanta
riots. On 6 September a young black man named Henry Fews assaulted
two young whites, Will Solomon and Charles Adams, at the fairgrounds.
Whites in the crowd immediately subdued the perpetrator, wounding him
and taking him to jail. Two days later, when a mob broke into the jail to
take custody of him, the father and brother of the victims appealed to the
angry crowd to disperse and leave the suspect in official hands. When the
mob leaders eventually agreed, Macon law enforcement officials took
Fews to Atlanta for his protection.[81]

By Wednesday, 26 September, Atlanta had begun to settle back to
normal and Pendleton's editorial indicated that a relative calm prevailed
over Macon. Some days later, looking back over recent events, the
Telegraph took what at the time seemed a sensible moderate position
between two "hysterical" extremes. He denounced a *New York Evening
Post* editorial as "unfair, unjust, and outrageous." Accusing the *Post* of
gross ignorance of Southern conditions, he judged the Atlanta upheaval
as an exception to the general rule of good race relations in the South. He
asserted, "The wholesale denunciation of the white people of the South

by the *Post* and its attempt to make superior the black people, is the result of a 'hysteria' the equal of which we have not seen anywhere."

Bridges Smith, 1916. An Early twentieth century mayor who regularly wrote derisive columns about blacks for the *Macon Telegraph* (Courtesy of the Washington Memorial Library.)

In the same issue, he also rejected an article in a black newspaper called the *Topeka Plaindealer,* which carried the headline "The Negro Must Fight, Kill and Burn When Outraged As in Atlanta." Pendleton opined that "this fellow is even more hysterical than some of our white editors." In contrast, he had condemned the lawless mobs, the unjustifiable bloodshed, and the sensationalist journalism that had detonated the explosion. He also gently criticized Georgia's recent politics of race.[82] But not as sharply as Augusta attorney William H. Fleming, whose lengthy comments on the race problem the *Telegraph* ran in full. Fleming blamed Hoke Smith's campaign as a direct cause of the Atlanta riot. His rhetoric had contributed to a general lawlessness and a deepening hatred for African Americans. "In essence," he noted, "the chief difference between Mr. Smith and the mob was the difference between fraud and force—both knowingly defied the law of the land. The mob sought blood; Mr. Smith sought votes."[83]

For their part, black Maconites remained quietly apprehensive, and made efforts to avoid any trouble. "Some of the best Negroes" had informed the *Telegraph* that many of their number had temporarily fled into the country, "fearing that the disgraceful rioting in Atlanta might be communicated to Macon."[84] Another group visited the mayor and the city council to assure them and the white community that they supported the suppression of "negro dives" in Macon. They presented a resolution expressing their sympathy with city and county efforts to enforce the laws and offered their assistance in helping close down dives in the black sections of town. Pledging to help prevent any inflammatory meetings of blacks, the black leaders put pledged to be at the disposal of authorities in helping to reduce tensions in the city.[85]

Four months later, doubtless with the recent racial tensions still in mind, another group of blacks met to organize the "Good Government Club of South Macon." As they were described in the *Telegraph,* the "better class of colored men" gathered in the chapel of the Georgia Colored Industrial and Orphans' Home "with the object of bettering their moral condition." At the meeting the Reverend J. B. Bridges, president of the orphans' home, told the group it was time to "raise the moral standard of the race" by seeing to it that "members of our race who commit crime shall find no place among the race to seclude themselves from the law." Calling on his fellow black leaders to work with whites to eliminate the criminal element, he told them the fact that "white have all the law in their hands" was no excuse to "allow our criminals to go unpunished." This policy would prove to whites that the leaders of the black community favored law and order. Finally the group elected a slate of officers, with W. A. Kemp as president, L. W. Jenkins as vice president, Ira Kemp as secretary, and T. Billingslea as chaplain.[86]

Georgia lawmakers, however, seemed less than convinced that the state's African Americans would be able to overcome their animalistic nature to live as law-abiding citizens. In August 1907, in what the *Atlanta Constitution* called "an echo of the Atlanta-Macon riots of last year," the state house of representatives voted to appropriate a $5,000 military fund "for extraordinary occasions."[87]

Thus was life for African Americans in Macon and most of the South in this most dismal of eras in American race relations. Jim Crow had come to Macon and disfranchisement had reduced the black voice in Georgia politics to barely a whisper. At the same time, the voices of race-baiting politicians in the state became amplified manyfold. Their sound and fury would be audible for decades to come.

2

Unsafe for Democracy:
Lynching and the Great War

In the mid-twentieth century, theologian Reinhold Niebuhr became a part-time historian with the publication of his influential book, *The Irony of American History.* That same year, full-time historian C. Vann Woodward borrowed Niebuhr's category in a presidential address to the Southern Historical Association that he called "The Irony of Southern History." Both of these celebrated scholars added significantly to the longstanding efforts of historians to point out discrepancies between the ideal and the actual in the American experience. To call such inconsistencies "irony" is, of course, to put a positive face on them. They might just as accurately be called the "hypocrisy" of American history. Or like Niebuhr we could call them the "comic absurdities" that Americans have confronted "because so many dreams of our nation have been so cruelly refuted by history."[1] Either way, there is little doubt the treatment of blacks in a nation "conceived in liberty and dedicated to the proposition that 'all men are created equal'" is the most hypocritical or absurd of American ironies.

By the time Georgia-born Woodrow Wilson had become the first Southerner elected to the presidency since the Civil War, America's foreign policy had given new poignancy to the nation's primeval irony. On the eve of the twentieth century, a self-image of righteousness and growing economic and military power had dragged the United States grudgingly onto a world scene. The "splendid little" Spanish-American war, mostly an effort to protect international economic markets for American business interests, was pitched to the American people as a crusade to bring independence and democracy to Cuba and the

Philippines. Seventeen years into the "American century" and early in his second term, President Wilson responded to attacks on American ships and asked Congress to declare war on Germany. Having been re-elected with the help of the slogan, "He Kept Us Out of War," he now reversed his position and advocated American entry into the Great War. While the reasons for entering the conflict had more to do with freedom of the seas and commerce, again war became for an American president a righteous crusade. "The world must be made safe for democracy," argued the Presbyterian president with a "missionary diplomacy." Ironically, the era in which the United States took its place in the modern world as the defender of democracy, and used black soldiers in the process, was also the era of the widespread lynching of African Americans. One of the more virulent strains of this disease was to be found in Georgia. Macon was similarly infected and, at least for its black citizens, was rendered unsafe for democracy.

MACON AND THE GREAT WAR

Maconites enthusiastically celebrated the re-election of Woodrow Wilson in 1916. A crowd of partisans whooped and threw their hats into the air. Curran Ellis, president of the Woodrow Wilson Club, arranged for cannon fire to announce the great victory. The following Saturday night saw several hundred Maconites and other Georgians continuing their rejoicing at the state fair.[2] Just four weeks after his second inauguration, Wilson called on Congress to declare war on Germany and the nation quickly began to mobilize. Maconites, both white and black, registered their support for the effort to defeat the Huns. W. T. (William Thomas) Anderson, a newspaper man who had gained control of the *Macon Telegraph* when Charles R. Pendleton died in 1914, placed the Macon paper squarely in support of the war. On the day Congress adopted the war declaration, Anderson opined, "We are fighting for right and justice, the principles democracies have set up and which the last surviving autocracy is bent on tearing down as to further bulwark its own institutions." The following day his prose was even more grandiose: "America has voiced more ideals, has claimed unction for higher conceptions of right and wrong than any nation in the world, has stood as a great beacon burning across the Western horizon to all the liberty-loving downtrodden peoples of earth.... For this the common people the world over have come to love what we have for them stood for. We have taken that unction to ourselves, we have accepted the trusteeship of conserving and elaborating the new liberty on earth for all the earth...."[3]

Immediately after Wilson's address to Congress, Judge William H. Felton led a mass meeting at the city auditorium, where a large audience adopted a resolution supporting the president and American entry into the war. On 5 June Maconites answered Uncle Sam's call, as 5,964 males between ages 21 and 30 registered for the draft. Later that month, Macon was chosen as the state's mobilization center, necessitating the building of a camp to accommodate some 60,000 soldiers. The Bibb County Commission and the membership committee of the chamber of commerce set up a nine-man committee to raise the money for the project. In August, Camp Wheeler, as it came to be called, opened and would cost the city $215,000.[4] On Armistice Day, 11 November 1918, Macon's celebrations began by 2:00 A.M. Before the day ended, the city would celebrate victory with cannon fire, bonfires, seven brass bands, and a massive parade. Mayor Glen Toole issued a proclamation that touched on the themes of the war: "Our boys are victorious. Our enemies have been vanquished. Liberty is safe, and peace...will come to the people of the world, and democracy will rule."[5]

Black Maconites particularly distinguished themselves in their Americanism during the war effort. Initially, throughout the nation many blacks did raise questions regarding loyalty to a country defending democracy abroad while denying it to millions at home. It was a possibility realistic enough to lead W. E. B. Du Bois, editor of the National Association for the Advancement of Colored People (NAACP) organ, *The Crisis,* to write a column called, "Close Ranks," which argued that for the duration of the war blacks should "forget our special grievances" and fight for democracy with the allied nations. Indeed, African Americans did close ranks as over the course of the war more than 2 million registered for the draft and some 360,000 were accepted for service.[6]

In Macon, as the nation began mobilizing for war, editor W. T. Anderson commented on a raft of rumors that African Americans might conspire with German agents and refuse military service. Anderson suggested that blacks discovered in such plots "should be dealt with

severely and conspicuously…to properly impress others of their race."
Five days later the *Telegraph* carried the story of Coleman Akins, a black
man from McDonough, Georgia, whom federal agents arrested for
making "treasonous statements against the white people of the United
States." Reports suggested that Akins was part of an "organized
operation" advising blacks that they would be fools to enlist in the
military because "this is a white man's country and no place for the
negro." Nevertheless, Anderson dismissed this as an unlikely threat.
Blacks knew better than that, he assured his readers, and the great
majority of them were paying no attention to such efforts.[7] The wartime
activities of Macon's black citizens bore out Anderson's assessment.

Soon after the war declaration, a black organization called the
Macon Business and Civic League held a mass meeting to express their
desire for a black regiment in the city. Their resolution assured their
white neighbors of their loyalty, reminding them that black Americans
had always rallied to defend America "even when themselves were held
by the bonds of chattel slavery." They further resolved that "despite the
grievances that we may have against our government, both state and
national, we shall and do forget them in the hour of the nation's peril and
offer unreservedly our services." Asking to be allowed to serve "under
the same conditions under which other citizens are serving," the group
petitioned Georgia governor and Maconite Nathaniel E. Harris to
authorize a black National Guard unit.[8]

A month later, the state council for defense endorsed a plan for a
statewide patriotic meeting to be held in Macon on 25 May 1917 under
the auspices of R. R. Wright, president of the Georgia State Industrial
College. At the meeting black Georgians discussed various ways they
could support the war effort. Nearly 600 blacks from across the state
gathered in the Macon City Auditorium to focus their attentions on
supporting the war through enlistment and food production. B. S.
Ingram, principal of the Ward Street Negro School presided and the
Reverend J. T. Hall, pastor of the Stewart African Methodist Episcopal
(AME) Church, delivered the invocation. A combined children's choir
from three black schools then sang "It's Time for Every Boy to Be a
Soldier." Henry Lincoln Johnson recounted African-American efforts in
the nation's wars, asserting that "the black man forgets all the injustices
and wraps himself in the flag." While enunciating such pledges of

allegiance, they nonetheless reminded white Georgia of a certain "unrest among our people" that was resulting in black migration. While deploring such departures, they nonetheless pointed out the reasons for them. Among these were the white tendency to "judge the race by the sins of a few," rather respecting blacks' moral, intellectual, and religious feelings or their "desires for a square deal as a citizen." Such unrest also arose from inequalities in black education, in which teachers were poorly paid while teaching double sessions. They further pointed to the unfair administration of justice for blacks and unequal wages as causes of this unrest. Suggested remedies for these problems included more adequate schools, equitable distribution of public funds for recreational facilities, impartiality before the courts, a living wage, and a general effort to cultivate "good-will between the races."[9]

White leaders of Macon also addressed the group during a morning session. Mayor Bridges Smith welcomed the convention to the city and congratulated the delegates on their constructive efforts to shoulder the load. W. T. Anderson also commended the group and urged them to pay more attention to food production. He also advised them to ignore the migration impulse. Then General Walter A. Harris of the Georgia National Guard addressed them on enlistment needs and procedures. Black citizens answered their calls with promises to bear the sword in defense of democracy. The verbal sword they wielded, however, was double-edged, cutting to the heart of the matter:

> We are willing to fight in the trenches or to work in the field, or to do both. We simply ask that our brethren of the Republic shall recognize the fact that the days of slavery have passed: that all men are now free and equal and that the demands of the country come to kindly suggest that the battle for democracy and human rights include the negro as well as the white man and that human right can only be made safe in Georgia when lynching is absolutely wiped out: when every negro home, however humble as it may be, shall be as safe as any white man's home in our grand old state. We further suggest that democracy can only be safe when political inequality shall be wiped out, when every man under the same

laws shall have the right to go to the ballot box and cast one ballot and have the ballot counted.[10]

A month later 200 members of Macon's black community began a "Colored Red Cross Drive." R. S. Ingram, principal of the Monroe Street High and Industrial School, and Susie L. Morris led sixteen teams of fund raisers, while appeals were issued by most church pastors in the city.[11] Similar efforts were launched the following year in connection with the Liberty Bond campaign. The black chamber of commerce brought together ten community leaders, including the Reverends J. T. Hall, C. W. Burton, and W. M. Gaines, along with Ingram and the city's wealthiest African American, Charles H. Douglass. They rallied black Maconites to meet on 9 April 1918 at the City Auditorium to collect money for the bond drive. At the mass meeting, William E. Holmes, president of Macon's Central City College, promised that the black citizens of Bibb County would subscribe to $10,000 in Liberty Loan Bonds. Dr. J. T. Bell, chairman of the Colored Liberty Loan Committee, responded to blacks who argued that the United States did not deserve their loyalty, asking, "If this is not your country, where do you like and enjoy your liberty?" When several black soldiers entered the meeting, the audience gave them a standing ovation and seated them on the platform.[12]

Charles H. Douglass, ca. 1920s, was Macon's most prominent African American business leader in the first half of the twentieth century. (Courtesy of the Washington Memorial Library.)

In June 1918 some 3,000 blacks participated in a War Saving Stamp parade. White employers granted a half-day holiday to their black workers to allow them to join the celebration. A company of black soldiers and a white military band from Camp Wheeler led the procession, followed by a large contingent of women in Red Cross uniforms. Gathering at the city auditorium for a rally, a large crowd heard William Gaines, chairman of the Bibb County Negro Committee, pluck patriotic heart strings, as did pastors J. T. Hall, of Steward Chapel AME Church, and B. F. Percy, of First Baptist Church (black). Moved to quick action, the audience pledged $5,000 in a few moments time.[13] Commenting on the occasion, W. T. Anderson editorialized: "It meant not a little for the negroes to take so much money all at once. It meant sacrifice and putting up money until it hurt, for the colored portion of the population has known very little of the pleasant walks of that material prosperity on to which the white man has naturally and quite easily latched as it came along." He concluded his commentary, however, with foreboding hints about "what the war is bringing to the negro." As to how white-black relations might stand after the war, he noted, "conjecture is ready, [and] it is not entirely undisturbing."[14]

In addition to civilian work in support of the war, young black men from Macon entered the draft and served with distinction both at home and abroad. One of the first Georgians to see action in Europe was a Maconite named Eugene Jacques Bullard, who eventually joined the French Foreign Legion, becoming the first black combat pilot in the Lafayette Escadrille. Later, when white Americans received transfers to the US Air Corps, Bullard's application was denied.[15] For most of the war, the number of black soldiers stationed at Camp Wheeler stood at around 3,000, most of whom worked on labors battalions constructing the camp's drainage system and repairing the camp roads. In preparation for what would be the last few months of the war, in July 1918, 4,350 additional Georgians were drafted, a large number of whom trained for in infantry and artillery.[16]

When the war came to an end, the African-American soldier returned from the experience a disturbing "New Negro." Coalescing in black communities in the northeast, the New Negro Movement and the Harlem Renaissance produced in the 1920s a racially-proud and politically-militant literature, art, and social criticism. The war had created this aggressive new attitude that overflowed Northern boundaries to influence Southern blacks. Some 17,000 black Georgians, having contributed to a postwar world now safe for democracy, resented the absence of liberty back home. They had also encountered in France a white population relatively free of racial prejudice. Thus they returned with a taste for more of the democracy for which they had helped to make the world safe. Thus, as W. T. Anderson had anticipated, Georgia was unprepared for what the war had brought blacks. Their new assertiveness, and even their uniforms, as one historian described it, "provoked the feeling that white supremacy was somehow in danger." As a result the immediate postwar era saw white Georgians lynch several black veterans, some even in uniform.[17]

WARTIME RACIAL INCIDENTS

With little sense of the ironic, the same white Americans who defended democracy "over there," redoubled their efforts to deny it to blacks over here. Many Americans who view the South as the heartland of American racism, remain unaware that similar racial ideas were also popular in other regions. Two years before the Great War, the film *The Birth of a Nation* became the first *nationwide* box office smash. The year of the Armistice was also the year a Northerner named Madison Grant published *The Passing of the Great Race,* a book that warned against racial intermarriage lest the great Anglo-Saxon race be destroyed. The year after that, 1919, saw some forty race riots break out across the nation in what has been called the "Red Summer." The hateful reactions of white Southerners to the black soldier are thus a part of a larger American picture.

Even before the war, the *Telegraph* was disturbed by the increasing tendency of African Americans to neglect the "outward signs of deference" toward whites.[18] One such failure of racial etiquette was later recalled by William P. Randall, who in the 1960s would become Macon's most influential civil rights leader. On one occasion a white customer shouted "Auntie, Auntie," in an effort to hail Randall's elderly aunt, who operated a vegetables wagon along Walnut Street. Instead of stopping, she deliberately goaded her horse to continue. After several attempts, the customer finally got her to stop by calling out, "Vegetable

Woman!" She asked, "Didn't you hear me calling you?" She replied, "I heard you calling your auntie, but I don't have any white nieces."[19] During the war whites complained that blacks seemed indifferent to a deepening labor shortage. A *Telegraph* reporter wrote, "There are some to say that it is all brought about by the appearance of the soldiers here, but others say that the coming of the soldiers has nothing to do with it, and that as one man opinionates, 'The negro is getting more and more trifling every day he lives.'"[20]

That this negative evaluation of blacks was inaccurate was borne out by press reports that a good number of local blacks had gained enough financial resources to purchase automobiles. Those able to acquire such status symbols quickly became the targets of nightriders. In October 1917, several beatings were perpetrated by white Maconites Minus Hardison and H. Lewis Harrison against Dock Anderson, Henry Cliett, William Brown, and Jack Thomas, black residents of Bibb, Houston, and Crawford counties respectively. Eventually Hardison and Harrison were brought to trial before Judge H. A. Matthews, who charged the jury diligently to protect the rights of all citizens regardless of color.[21] Troubled by such intimidation, a group of some thirty whites in Houston and Crawford counties organized to protect black tenants and farmhands. In addition, they convinced Governor Hugh Dorsey to offer rewards for information leading to the arrests of nightriders.[22]

Despite occasional efforts at racial understanding, many whites were concerned about the labor shortage and the increase of black migrations to the North. Across Georgia many towns also passed "work or fight" ordinances to force blacks to work for whites or join the military. One black Maconite convicted for this offense was fined twenty-five dollars when she refused a job as a domestic. When she objected that she had children at home and her husband could support the family without her working, the judge informed that marriage did not exempt her from the law.[23] When blacks chafed at such attempts to curb migration, Police Chief Charles Rowden persuaded the Macon City Council to purchase forty magazine rifles as a means of social control.[24] Rowden also instructed detectives to investigate black poolrooms to discourage loitering. On 23 November 1917, Rowden's men arrested thirty men who were eventually called to explain in Recorder's Court why they did not work. Black business leader Charles H. Douglass pleaded for the release of the men, vouching for their characters and that they worked for some of the black establishments along Broadway Street. One of those arrested, he claimed, was a guest at Douglass's hotel. On Douglass's appeal, all but three of the men were released. The next day below a headline of "30 NEGROES BAGGED IN RAID BY POLICE," the *Telegraph* read: "Darkies Who Refuse to Work Are Taken in by Police and They Must Explain." Another sub-headline announced: "There Is Plenty of Work for the Negroes—One Wouldn't Work Unless Given a Motorcycle."[25]

White leaders in Macon also sought to reaffirm segregation laws and remind blacks that serving their country would effect no changes in the dominant racial arrangements. When a black soldier was brought to trial, the prosecutor's opening argument warned not just the defendant, but all African Americans in uniform: "I am going to show a nigger soldier that he is the same as any other nigger."[26] Whites in Macon had found the sight of African American in uniform distasteful. During Reconstruction, they had yearned for the day when they would no longer see "ebony in uniform." More recently, during the Spanish-American War, a black regiment at Camp Haskell, near Macon, had learned of a particular "hanging tree" from which a recent victim had been lynched. Afterward, the dead man was castrated and his testicles were displayed at a local pub. In response, the black regiment chopped down the tree and reduced it to firewood. They then tore down a sign in a park that read: "No Dogs and Niggers Allowed." When some of them demanded service in white restaurants, their superior officers disarmed the entire regiment and incarcerated them for twenty days.[27]

As a young twentieth century unfolded, clearly many white Americans in all regions of the nation reacted to black soldiers with alarm. The tensions were exacerbated by the US Army's practice of stationing blacks in the South. The famous Brownsville, Texas, riot of 1906 and the Houston riot of 1917, though taking place in Southern venues, were only harbingers of the more regionally diverse riots of the Red Summer of 1919. Thus, in April 1918, when Atlanta whites, including the governor and mayor, applauded a parade of some 10,000 black soldiers, the *Macon Telegraph* reported that white Georgians nevertheless had misgivings about the spectacle of blacks in uniform.[28]

That same year Macon saw two clashes between white and black soldiers. In March, an argument between a black private and a white clerk in a soda fountain, led some 300 members of his regiment to attack the store. This incident mirrored the Houston riot the previous year, when after weeks of harassment by whites, 100 members of the black 24th Infantry marched into the city and began firing at the police station.[29] Now, in Macon the 48th Infantry was called into the fray, and the blacks ran away as the guards approached. After two halt commands were ignored, the guards opened fire, wounding two and killing one of the escapees. Later that year, another small riot broke out on Broadway Street when a police officer arrested a black woman named Lillian Roberts for loitering. When she called to several black soldiers to come to her aid, the men surrounded the officer and threatened to kill him if he did not release the woman. When two police lieutenants and six provost guards dispersed the crowd and took Roberts into custody, she shouted, "Don't let this damned white man take me. You negro soldiers go git your guns and clean out these white folks. This ain't their country no how. It belongs to us."[30]

Of course, the country did not belong to blacks, and most Southern whites were determined to prove it, especially to "new Negroes" in uniform. These wartime racial incidents were only part of the lessons to be learned. For particularly slow learners, the era's racial pedagogy included lynching.

LYNCHING AND "MACON'S ORGY"

In the late 1880s, the number of lynchings rose precipitously until 1892 marked the high (or low) point when some 71 whites and 155 African Americans were lynched. Between 1880 and 1930 there were 3,343 lynchings in the United States, 80 percent of which occurred in the South. Georgia ranked second behind Mississippi among Southern states, with 460 lynchings in this period.[31] The prevalence of lynching and the helplessness of African Americans to oppose it are what made this era the "nadir" of the African American experience in the United States. A Mississippi black man captured the black predicament of the times: "They had to have a license to kill anything but a nigger. We was always in season." One of the greatest ironies of Southern history is that this region was simultaneously becoming known as both the lynching center of the United States and as the "Bible Belt," as evidenced by a 1889 lynching in North Carolina that was preceded by prayers. The sad irony elicited the comment by Ida B. Wells-Barnett that "American Christians are too busy saving the souls of white Christians from burning in hell-fire to save the lives of black ones from present burning in fires kindled by white Christians."[32]

Given the rhetoric of many leading white Georgians, the prevalence of lynching in the state is hardly surprising. Rebecca Latimer Felton, wife of state representative Dr. W. H. Felton, was one of the best known political wives of the era. Also known for playing a leading role in the Holiness movement of Georgia Methodism, Mrs. Felton told the *Atlanta Journal* in 1898: "[W]hen there is not religion in the pulpit to organize against this sin nor manhood enough in the nation to put a sheltering arm about innocence and virtue, it requires lynching to protect woman's dearest possession from...drunken human beasts, then I say lynch a thousand a week if necessary." Tom Watson, who died in 1920 serving as a US Senator, had earlier in his career spoken of the need "to lynch him [the Negro] occasionally, and flog him, now and then, to keep him from blaspheming the Almighty, by his conduct, on account of his smell and his color." In Watson's view lynching proved that "a sense of justice yet lives among the people," and was thus "a good sign." Similar ideas resided within more common elements of the Georgia population. A Sandersville man wrote, "I say *hang*, if need be *Roast* a thousand [Negroes] a week, until they are convinced that at least that one hellish phase of their nature must be restrained."[33] Whether the rape of white women by blacks or the lynching of black men by whites revealed more of human nature's hellishness is a question most white Georgians of the era did not appear to ask.

Macon was also the venue of a number of lynchings, three of which came on the heels of the Great War. Historian Fitzhugh Brundage lists six such incidents in Bibb County between 1880 and 1930—one each in the 1880s and '90s, one in 1912, and three during or after the war, between 1918 and 1922.[34] This comparative flurry of vigilante justice suggests that Macon, like the nation as a whole and the South in particular, was caught up in racial concern over rising African-American aspirations. The rash of lynchings, and spectacle of one of them in particular, seems also to have moved the *Macon Telegraph* to stiffen its opposition to the practice.

After a respite of more than a decade, lynching returned to Macon with the 3 February 1912 lynching of Charley Powell, who had assaulted a young white woman. As two deputies attempted to spirit Powell out of town for his safety, a railroad worker tipped off a mob of some 100 men who were searching for the prisoner. Finding the trio in a boxcar along the Central of Georgia Railroad line about a mile south of the city, the vigilantes overpowered the deputies and dragged the handcuffed Powell away. They quickly hanged Powell from the nearest telephone pole and riddled his body with bullets. The next day newspaper headlines blared out the story: "NEGRO FIEND LYNCHED HERE." Nine hours after Powell was killed, another mob of some 200 whites advanced on the funeral home and demanded that the body be turned over to them. Over the objections of mortician C. S. Pursley, the mob decided to burn the body as an object lesson to the black inhabitants of the Tybee section of town. Pressing a wagon into service, the mob called out to black Maconites in Tybee to come see the spectacle. Those who did so watched in silence and fear.[35]

That night the Reverend T. W. Callaway entered his pulpit at the Tabernacle Baptist Church for his regular Sunday evening sermon. But taking an irregular topic, he indignantly denounced the incidents that had desecrated the Lord's Day earlier that morning. Comparing lynching to the crucifixion of Christ, Callaway told his congregation that "any man, whether white or black, who is put to death…without a fair and impartial trial of the law, is only short of murder and anarchy." He said that it was "a disgrace upon our state that during the last year she far exceeded all other states…in the number of lynchings." Further, he noted that the burning of the body was "a blight upon the fair name of Macon and Bibb County. He concluded that both pulpit and press, "and every patriotic Georgian," should denounce lynching and that officials and jurors should stop playing politics "with those they know to be guilty of such mob violence." The coroner's jury, however, did not heed the minister's advice, as it concluded that Powell's death had been caused by "unknown parties."[36] The following day C. R. Pendleton editorialized, "No punishment was too severe for the inhuman brute, but that punishment…could have, and should have, been speedily administered by the law."[37]

Four years later, Edwin C. Dargan, pastor of the white First Baptist Church, preaching on the Sunday that would later be designated Race Relations Day in many churches, touched on the same theme in his sermon. He told his congregation that sixty-nine persons had been lynched in 1915, an increase of 33 percent over the previous year. Moreover, more than a quarter of these incidents took place in Georgia, where lynchers "are seldom interfered with, much less punished. They have their own way, and being immune from penalties, the work of lynching by wholesale goes on." Dargan's remedy, however, was for Georgians to be swept up in a true religious revival.[38] A month later the new editor of the *Macon Telegraph*, W. T. Anderson told of a visit by a prominent Maconite to see a pageant called "The March of the States," at the New York Hippodrome. The man "turned half sick," reported Anderson, when the persons representing Georgia were depicted as men hanging from trees, as if to make the state synonymous with "lynch law." Anderson then said he expected some "demagogue and stump perching patriot" to make political hay out of such an insult and come to the defense of Georgia. He then called on his readers to face up the facts: "There is something wrong with us and we've got to do some surgery…. [I]t is high time for the sober, responsible people of every community to sit down quietly and look into affairs in their home counties, to devise ways and means to prevent another lynching ever being held in this State. The word LYNCH can never be allowed to stand as a synonym for the name GEORGIA."[39]

Under Anderson's leadership, the *Telegraph* thus began to stiffen its spine on racial matters and lynching in particular. The local lynchings in the Great War era pushed Anderson in that direction. This trend was further strengthened after 1925 when Mark Ethridge became associate editor and chief editorial writer.

The first of these incidents took place just two months before the Armistice, on 3 September 1918, when a black man named John Gilham was lynched for attempted rape. Gilham had escaped from a chaingang in neighboring Jones County two weeks earlier. While a fugitive, he attempted to assault two white women, a black woman, and two black girls. Pursued by a posse of farmers from the area around the town of

Gray, some 15 miles north of Macon, he was eventually caught by two African-American men from Macon, Charlie Jackson and Charlie Pitts. After being incarcerated in Macon for several hours, Gilham was released to Jones County Sheriff T. C. Middlebrooks. While being transported to Gray by Middlebrooks and two Macon police officers, an armed crowd surrounded the car and took Gilham from his escorts. The next morning Gilham's bullet-ridden body was discovered in a ditch not far from where he had been taken. Sheriff Middlebrooks, however, told reporters that he was certain that the lynching party had included several blacks. After a brief investigation, a coroner's jury closed the case with the verdict, "Death at the hands of persons unknown."[40]

Some six months after the end of the war to "make the world safe for democracy," news reports began telling of a rash of attacks on blacks, particularly black veterans, during the Red Summer of 1919. The *Macon Telegraph* carried the story of Willie Laney, a black veteran who, conscious of the lack of democracy for fellow African Americans, wrote threatening letters to the governors of Mississippi and Georgia. To Georgia's Governor Hugh Dorsey, he wrote:

> Dear Sir: You are the Governor of the State of Georgia, and I want you to consider that the negro was drafted during the world war to fight for this country as the white man, and I want you to understand that this thing of lynching in the state of Georgia must be cut out.... We went and killed Germans for your rights, and we can also kill Americans for our rights, and if I hear any more of lynching in the state of Georgia, I will come quickly and the people will weep after I leave, because I sweep from the cradle up. I will remember you this time.[41]

In a letter to the editor, a white Maconite later offered his advice regarding black-white tensions in the country. For him the attacks on blacks proved that the North was, as most Southerners expected, coming around to view race matters as did the South. All that was necessary for this, he suggested, was for blacks to migrate to the North in great enough numbers. He further argued that whites of all regions inevitably reject black "encroachment" because of the depreciation of their property values. Arguing finally that segregation was the only means of preventing repetitions of the East St. Louis, Missouri, lynching, one of the bloodiest postwar racial incidents. Referring to the opinion of the *Chicago Tribune,* the writer asserted that without Jim Crow "there can be no amity, no peacefulness, no mutual understanding and getalongability between the two races. The *Tribune* admits what the South has known always."[42]

Within a few months, "Red Summer" had come to Macon. In early November 1919, a Bibb County mob lynched a black man named Paul Booker for rape. On Sunday night, 2 November, a fifty-year-old white woman was attacked while walking home from church in an empty field a short distance from her home. A black man named Paul Booker reportedly grabbed, choked, and hit her on the forehead. Bleeding from the wound, the woman deliberately marked his shirt with blood for easier identification. Soon after the attack, two deputy sheriffs found "a suspicious looking negro" in a railroad boxcar near the crime scene. Noticing blood stains on his clothing, the deputies backed Booker into a corner and waited for assistance. By the time the sheriff arrived on the scene around midnight, word of the incident had spread and a large crowd had gathered around the boxcar where deputies continued to hold the suspect in custody. The sheriff convinced the mob to allow him to take Booker to his victim, who was hysterical and bruised around her neck and one of her eyes. Identifying Booker by the bloodstains on his shirt, she told the sheriff how she had deliberately wiped her bloody hands on his shirt.

At that, hoping to avoid a lynching, the sheriff told the armed mob, which had followed him to the victim's home, that the evidence was incomplete and that he had to return with the prisoner to the crime scene. The crowd then verified that the victim had positively identified Booker as the perpetrator. Why the sheriff did not escort this prisoner back to the safer confines of the jail was never fully investigated, but by 2:00 A.M. the mob found the deputies and the prisoner holed up in a shack near the railroad yard. The mob broke the windows and eventually tore down the shack, seizing Booker. The mob had grown to more than a thousand, as according to news reports, "there was not an automobile left in the down town district." The vigilantes riddled Booker's body with some fifty bullets, then dragged him by a rope around the neck for nearly 150 yards down the railroad track. Reportedly the mob, which found him still clinging to life after this ordeal, then poured gasoline on him and set him on fire. Finally, when the charred body lay lifeless, the crowd repeated the fiery process until only a "charred mass" remained.[43]

The following day a coroner's jury declared that Booker had come to his death "by violence at the hands of unknown parties." At the same time Bibb County Superior Court Judge Henry A. Mathews ordered the Bibb County Grand Jury to investigate the lynching. Directly connecting the incident with the Great War that in 1914 began "a great struggle between the forces of law and those of lawlessness. He judged lynchings to be "absolutely lawless," and said such actions proclaim "the untruth that the courts are not sufficient in the execution of justice." He added, "They say there is no protection by law from the flaming passions of the lawless; they saw the law is weak and contemptible."[44] The grand jury, however, failed to issue any presentments regarding the incident.

Anderson's 4 November editorial similarly scored the lynching, opining that "the spectacle of mob violence is all the sadder for being at our own doorstep." He speculated that white Maconites bore "no animosity against any other negro, no additional resentment against them as a race." Most of Macon's African Americans, he surmised, would approve that "a bad man met a quick and deserved death." He concluded by advising readers to leave the matter in the hands of the grand jury "and until it acts all the rest of us [should] forget all about it."[45] African Methodists, however, did not forget the racial difficulties of their times. Ten days after the Booker lynching, AME Bishop J. S. Flipper addressed their troubles at a conference in Macon on 12 November. Calling on African Methodists to work for peace and harmony, he nonetheless echoed the disappointment of many: "Many of us thought that our unstinted efforts in helping to win the war would cause a better feeling between the races, but instead we are facing the greatest crisis we have faced since Emancipation."[46]

Several weeks after the Booker lynching, Anderson commented on the traditional end of the year lynching report from across the South. He put a positive face on the volatile situation in Georgia. Contributing to the volatility was a combination of 3 million whites and blacks living in close proximity, of agitation among blacks regarding "this or that 'right' by secret and active professional agents," and of the presence of "riff raff" that generally hated blacks. Given all this, that there had been only twenty-one acts of fatal violence "makes a most remarkable demonstration…that there is no race problem in the Southeast."[47] Two years later, the lynching of John "Cocky" Glover would cause Anderson to re-evaluate that assessment.

On 29 July 1922, the Bibb County Sheriff's office received a call regarding a disturbance at Hatfield's poolroom at the corner of Broadway and the Wall Street alley. A young black man named John "Cocky" Glover, apparently inebriated, had angrily burst into the establishment and waved a pistol at patrons. Deputy Sheriffs Walter C. Byrd, Romas Raley, and Will Jakes, a black deputy, were sent to look into the matter. As they reached the entrance, Glover opened fire with a .25 caliber automatic. Byrd immediately fell to the ground and deputy Raley chased Glover through the poolroom. Glover shot wildly as he sped from the scene and severely wounded two patrons, Sam Brooks and George Marshall. The assailant ran out of the rear of the poolroom, crossed Mulberry Street, and proceeded down an alley toward the Ocmulgee River. Raley quickly called Chief Deputy Sheriff Lane Mullally, who led a search party through the East Macon, Tybee, and Pleasant Hill sections of the city. By morning the sheriff's department had set up roadblocks and were searching all entering or exiting trucks and held four black men in custody as suspects.[48] Deputy Byrd had been instantly killed, while Brooks and Marshall lingered for several days before succumbing to their mortal wounds.

Within an hour of the shooting, police had closed all black establishments in the downtown area. They drove all blacks out into the streets, including guests at the Douglass Hotel. Two or three of them resisted the officers and were arrested. Virtually the entire block from Mulberry Street to Broadway Street was cleared out. A black postman collecting the mail at night was harassed three times by whites and ordered "to git for home." Black delivery boys were beaten. Seven random African-American men were arrested as suspects All the while, the streets were filling up with curious whites who had learned about the shootings, many volunteering to join in the search for Glover. House-to-house searches were conducted, rousting citizens out of their homes in the black sections of Pleasantville, Unionville, Stinsonville, and South Macon. Groups of whites took pot shots at blacks they saw on the streets. They also made threats on Douglass's life, and twenty police officers guarded his home through the night. As police escorted him from his business to his home, a number of whites followed the party, spewing additional threats against Douglass and accusing him of harboring Glover in his hotel. One person in the crowd, who apparently had pent up disgust for successful blacks, even began circulating a rumor that in his last words Glover had implicated Douglass as "responsible for all of this." Two days later the rumors had grown serious enough to necessitate a denial from Chief Deputy Mullally, who told officials "Nobody on earth was responsible for that affair except a drunken menace.... Douglass could not be connected with it any more than I could."[49]

While the state Ku Klux Klan offered a $100 bounty on his head, Glover managed to elude the authorities for two full days, finally boarding a train to Atlanta in the early morning hours on Tuesday, 1 August. When the train reached Griffin, Georgia, around dawn, police boarded the train to take custody of the fugitive. Another patrolman was wounded as Glover was apprehended and turned over to Bibb County officers, who continued the trip back to Macon. On the way, Glover begged the officers to shoot him, pleading, "Please don't take me back to Macon." Just north of the city, they were stopped by a mob of an estimated 400 angry white men, who grabbed up Glover from the back floor board of the car. They took him across the Monroe County line, emptied shotguns into his body, and left him lying face up in a small, swampy ditch near the town of Forsyth.

The mob then decided to dump the body in the back of a truck and take it into Macon. As they entered the downtown area, the party waved their arms and shouted to pedestrians to come see their work. The mock funeral procession coming to a stop on Broadway between Cherry and Mulberry streets, the mob jerked Glover's remains out of the truck and dumped it in the street, where his clothing was cut to shreds and sold as souvenirs. Later, the nearly nude body was dumped in the foyer of the Douglass Theater. Someone shouted, "Get the gasoline," but the police arrived just before the body could be incinerated inside the theater. By that time hundreds of whites had had converged on the area and overwhelmed the police. Pushing and shoving, many shouted, "Burn him!" or "Hang him up." Others merely yelled, "Let's get a look at him." Many of the revelers did, however, manage to kick and beat the corpse. Even a number of women were present, clamoring as eagerly as their male counterparts to see the battered corpse.[50] In time, police officers intervened to claim Glover's body, which was eventually taken to Forsyth and buried in an obscure graveyard for African Americans.

In the immediate aftermath of the incident, the Macon City Council revoked the license of Hatfield's poolroom and discussed the similar closings of other black establishments. The Douglass Theater also remained closed. Governor Thomas W. Hardwick offered to send state troops to keep order in Macon, but Bibb Superior Court Judge Malcolm D. Jones declined, saying that the people of Macon were "law abiding citizens. They want to obey the law and keep order. At times, a few of them might get off the track, but not often. I do not anticipate any trouble. I expect the people now to resume their peaceful pursuits."

Meanwhile, the people of Forsyth registered their indignation that the mob had done their deed in Monroe County, which had not seen a lynching in some thirty years. A large delegation of citizens, including city and county officials visited the governor to lodge their complaints against the Bibb County lynch mob. They asked the governor also to sponsor his own investigation in order to clear Monroe County from any responsibility in the matter. In connection with these complaints, Flint Circuit Judge W. E. H. Searcy in Thomaston, Georgia, announced that he would direct the Monroe County Grand Jury to investigate the case. "I have no respect for people who engage in mob violence," he told reporters, "and it is my conviction that they ought to be punished."[51]

Segments of the white community in Macon also raised their voices in disgust. The Macon Rotary Club adopted a resolution condemning the sordid incidents. The *Telegraph* also printed a strong editorial denouncing the events of the preceding weekend, particularly scoring "the chasing and beating of innocent negroes" as "an offense against society" even worse than the lynching. Editor W. T. Anderson charged that Bibb County officers knew the identity of those in the mob, "who did not take the trouble to disguise themselves" and who parleyed with Deputy Mullally for the prisoner. Worst of all, Anderson wrote, was "Macon's Orgy" at the Douglass Theater, where in the light of day the mob showed itself to be "devoid of all sense of decency." He noted that the *Telegraph* had strenuously argued against passage of the Dyer anti-lynching bill in Congress on states' rights grounds. He added, however, that "there are far too many instances of flagrant flaunting of the law in this State to make it possible for us to defend the practice and permit the criminals to go unpunished.... If we in Georgia are spineless and permit taxpayers and innocent people who are entitled to the protection of the laws, stand aside and see those laws disregarded, what defense have we against the plan to have the National Government take charge of our home affairs?"[52]

The next day Anderson produced a second piece criticizing not only the mob at the Douglass Theater, but also the sheriff's office. The mob had engaged in a "death dance that would have done credit to the most adept and hardened head hunters of the savage countries." In so doing they made a spectacle of Macon and generated revulsion and resentment in the community. He rejected Deputy Mullally's statement that his office was "through with the affair." Reiterating his accusation that Mullally knew the identities of the lynch party, Anderson called on Bibb County to make its own investigation of the incident and not leave the investigation to the lesser prepared officials of Monroe County. A delegation of prominent white Maconites took this same perspective to Judge Mathews, urging him to call a special session of the grand jury to make a full investigation the Glover matter.[53]

For his part, Mullally denied that he had done less than his utmost to protect the prisoner and wrote a letter to Judge Mathews seconding the call for a grand jury investigation, which he hoped would exonerate him and put the blame squarely on those responsible for the lynching. Two days later, on 8 August, Judge Mathews followed these suggestions, ordering the grand jury to investigate the matter as violations of state laws covering unlawful assemblies and rioting, both of which were misdemeanors. In his charge, he warned that their deliberations would help determine whether the law or the mob would hold sway in Macon. "Unless some action is taken," he noted, "the lawless element will feel greatly encouraged and even justified in defying all constituted authority." He also reminded jurors that since the events at the Douglass Theater took place in the plain view of officers and other private citizens, there should be sufficient information to identify and indict the guilty parties.[54]

Clearly white Maconites were stirred up by "Macon's Orgy." Reverend W. H. Quillian, pastor of the Mulberry Street Methodist church and president of Wesleyan College, condemned the lynching in a sermon that also called on Macon officials to "make a clean sweep" and close all the city's poolrooms. The men's Bible class of the Vineville Methodist Church issued a statement in support of the grand jury investigation, as did a men's class at First Presbyterian Church. Beyond this, however, the Vineville Methodist Church memorial scathingly denounced the lawlessness of the events, the terrorizing of innocent blacks by the mob, and the failure of law enforcement officers to make any arrests. The statement excoriated those who were not caught up in a momentary frenzy, but who after nearly three days since the crime, "moved deliberately, in cold blood to lynch a culprit." In so doing, they had "so flagrantly flaunted the decencies of our community, and so openly raped our laws." Putting the onus on the deputies' who made no arrests, the memorial asked pointedly: "What would have happened if these officials having in custody this prisoner had said to the gathering mob, 'You may take him but you will do it at the cost of our lives and possibly yours?'...[W]e do not believe that any man would have sacrificed the lives of these officials for the sake of wreaking vengeance upon the prisoner." The Vineville men concluded: "Too often when such investigations are ordered, it results in a mere flurry, perhaps some indictments may be returned, and then the whole matter is dropped and forgotten. For once let this city and county demonstrate that we do not need Federal force nor Federal supervision for the defense of law and the safety of our people."[55]

On the opposite end of the spectrum, one white correspondent to the *Telegraph* commented in an open letter: "I do not belong to the Ku Klux Klan, but I had rather trust them to administer justice than any set of lawyers or jurymen or judges who will allow a proven criminal to keep his case in court from two to five years."[56]

On Monday, 29 August, the Monroe County Grand Jury met in Forsyth to begin its investigation into the Glover affair. Because the lynching had occurred in Forsyth, any forthcoming indictments for murder would be issued in Monroe rather than Bibb County. Two days into its investigation, the Monroe Grand Jury indicted five Macon men for murder in connection with Glover's lynching. Troy Raines, a grocer, Nathan Unice, a soft drink dealer, Gordon Herndon, a mechanic, H. L. McSwain, president of the Southern Cooperative Fire Insurance Company, and D. L. Wood, a hotel clerk, appeared before Judge W. E.

H. Searcy in Forsyth on 10 September. While in the Bibb County jail for several days since their indictment, the defendants received scores of visitors from Macon friends. Bibb County Solicitor General Charles H. Garrett, in charge of the Bibb investigation, attended but did not participate in the trial of the five, although evidence collected in the Bibb investigation was shared with Monroe.[57]

On the second day of the trial, Garrett and lead prosecutor Emmett Owen saw their case weakened when three of their witnesses contradicted testimony they themselves had given in the Bibb investigation. Reporters commented that "there was some indication" that these witnesses had been intimidated. One of the witnesses had told the Bibb grand jury he had seen Troy Raines participate in the Glover shooting; now at trial in Monroe, the witnesses testified that he did not recognize Raines. The prosecution managed only to elicit considerable conflicting testimony regarding the defendants. One witness, for example, had McSwain helping the officers protect Glover, while another testified to seeing him place a rope around Glover's neck. One witness identified Raines as a member of the firing squad that shot Glover, while another claimed Raines was unarmed.[58]

The next day, 12 September, Owen called one additional witness, whose testimony was inconclusive. For its part, the defense presented no witnesses, but did put the defendants on the stand to testify that they had gone to the lynch scene in order to help the Bibb County officers. They also testified that they had been eager to help end the killing of law officers by the "death gang...composed of negroes." They finally appealed to the jury that they were family men incarcerated for more than twelve days and were anxious to return to their homes. In closing arguments, the defense reminded the jury of the conflicting testimony of the state's witnesses, while Owen said the witnesses had presented "the most changed evidence" he had ever seen. Once given the case, the jury wrestled with the contradictory testimony, but only for half an hour. Their verdict was an acquittal—all the defendants, on all counts.[59]

As for the Bibb County investigation, on 11 September, within a week of beginning its work, the grand jury indicted five men in connection with the Glover incident, for rioting, assembling for the purpose of lynching, carrying concealed weapons without a license. These were H. L. McSwain and Nathan Unice, two of the defendants exonerated in the Monroe County murder trial, along with Herbert Block, manager of the Hotel Dempsey, city firefighter Guy Jones, and a fifth man whose name was not released.[60] For several weeks after these initial indictments, the grand jury kept its own counsel regarding the Glover lynching, until it issued its final presentment to Judge Mathews on 23 September. Additional indictments for rioting were issued to John C. Vann, Fred Whidden, Billy Smith, and Alva Hightower. Eventually, however, all indictments against all persons involved with "Macon's Orgy" were dropped. The grand jury did level stiff criticism at Bibb County deputy sheriffs and Macon police for their handling of the prisoner, particularly their feeble attempts to keep the prisoner from the mob, which the jury learned had had only eight or ten active members. The jury also denounced the officers for failing to identify members of the mob. Four city police officers were some 50 feet away from where Glover's body was hurled; none made any effort to interfere and none of those threatening to burn the body was arrested. The jury also opined that it had been within the officers' power to disperse the mob had they attempted to do so.[61]

After the grand jury report the white Macon Ministerial Union issued a statement commending the investigation. The ministers denounced the "mob spirit and its accompanying cowardice, cruelty, and perjury." They concurred with the Grand Jury, laying the blame for the incidents on county and city law enforcement officials. Their statement spoke of the community's disgrace, and called on officers to be good trustees of the good name of Macon by giving absolute fidelity to their responsibilities.[62]

Given its strong condemnation of "Macon's Orgy," the *Macon Telegraph* made surprisingly tepid responses to the Monroe County murder trial and the Bibb grand jury report. Anderson did raise mild questions regarding the discrepancies between evidence elicited by the grand jury and that gathered in the trial. But the editor made no accusations nor leveled any charges, leaving the matter to the Bibb grand jury's "manhood and courage."[63]

The Bibb grand jury's fortitude, however, was canceled out by its legal limits—it could only indict for misdemeanor offenses. Still, Anderson considered the report a small-scale victory. "Those actively connected with the lynching," he suggested, "have had to pay at least something that should stand as a deterrent to others as well as to themselves." He praised the jury for doing so well "under the circumstances," then launched into a paternalistic and patronizing lecture to black Maconites. The jury's report, he wrote:

> should make a powerful appeal to the colored people to co-operate in a way that will make what has been done truly effective. If our colored people were to yield to false counsel and represent a not of complaint and resentment rather than of gratitude, they would make it much harder for society to give the aid and protection to them that is deserved and that the great majority of whites desire to give.... [I]t would spell tragedy for our colored people to think in terms of privileges rather than of duties. The colored race has a future and a worthy place here in the South if they go in the way of Christian humility and service, but the assertion of the elements of false pride and misguided resistance on their part would mean ruin to them. The best colored people instinctively know this, but unfortunately there is a temptation to be false leaders and to be misled.[64]

Beyond these public statements of concern, however, the grand jury's presentment marked the end of the matter. None of those indicted sustained any legal penalties nor did the officers who had been judged derelict in their duties receive any disciplinary action for their part in the death of John "Cocky" Glover.

BLACK MACON AND THE "NADIR"

As for the black citizens of Macon, efforts were focused on convincing whites not to judge the entire race by the example of "Cocky" Glover and the "better class" of Negroes supported all lawful measures to clean up the city. L. J. May, a black leader in Macon, penned a letter to the *Telegraph* advocating that all of the city's poolrooms be closed down as "breeding places of crime." He asserted that closing Hatfield's poolroom would meet "the approval of every law-abiding and respectable negro." What was necessary was rather to close down all such dens, which "furnish a meeting place for the lowest element of humanity—crooks, bootleggers and criminals of every class."[65]

Two black religious organizations also went on record as supporting the elimination of crime and lawlessness and against "gun toting" in Macon. The Evangelical Ministerial Union criticized Glover as a part of "that lawless element of our race whom we find impossible to touch with that religious influence so essential to the salvation of the race, because they prefer to frequent the dives instead of the church." Their statement expressed regret for the incident that resulted in four untimely deaths, but also saw hope in Anderson's "righteous stand for the protection of the innocent law abiding defenseless hard working negroes." Another statement was issued by the trustees of Steward Chapel AME Church, which commended Anderson for coming "to the rescue and defense of the better class of colored citizens of Macon." All groups of people, the trustees noted, had "their black sheep," but the actions of one wayward soul is no reason for "some of the most industrious and law-abiding negroes should be beaten up, shot at and run off the streets." Such persons were worthy of both the protection of the laws and of white persons' respect.[66]

Along with these responses from Macon's black churches, and despite Anderson's advice that blacks avoid "complaint and resentment," some sounded muted notes of grievance. Just days after the Glover affair, there came a poignant commentary from J. L. Corwin, a black physician who had migrated from Macon to St. Louis. Having read "streaming headlines" about the lynching and the attacks on Charles H. Douglass, Corwin reminded Maconites that such acts "are driving the property-owning class of Negroes out of the State and leaving with you the class that you don't want." For his part, Corwin wrote, "I have lived in Georgia all of my life and I love her hills…. But I hate her mobs and her lawlessness as much as all of her good citizens do." He argued that the good black citizens who never frequented the pool hall district deserved to be protected. Corwin's own brother, Sam, was among the seven blacks taken into custody as a suspect in the Byrd shooting, "even though he had "served eighteen months in France and who has never carried a gun in his life, except to defend his country." Corwin closed his letter with pathos: "For the sake of Georgia's good name, for the honor of Georgia citizens, stop the lawlessness in the State…. I write these lines as one who loves his State and with the view and a hope that hate and prejudice will someday be suppressed."[67]

Near the end of August, "Inquirer" wrote a letter to the editor raising a number of questions regarding the affair. With the clear knowledge of gathering mobs, why did city officials decline the governor's offer to send troops to keep order? Why did Anderson smooth over the lawlessness of the city by commenting, "at time of few of them [Maconites] might get off the track, but not often." Since officers knew the identities of some of the lynchers, why were there no arrest? "Is it the duty of officials…to arrest men they knew to be murderers?" Finally, the anonymous writer asked, "Isn't it our duty to our State to speed up the anti-lynching bill now before Congress?" No answers to these queries were forthcoming.[68]

The Great War era was a period when the United States took its self-image as the beacon of liberty and the bastion of democracy to the international stage. The failure of democracy to include African Americans, even after they helped defeat the Kaiser, once again pointed up what blacks understood as the most obvious irony of American and Southern history. The upsurge of lynchings in the same era symbolized the failure of democracy. In Macon, those lynchings brought to a head issues that had been on the minds of blacks throughout the era.

For example, the Macon Business and Civic League, which would lead black patriotic efforts in Macon during the war, in the year before American entered the war, lodged protests with the Bibb County Board of Education concerning black schools. In April 1916, a committee of eight members of the league presented a petition to the school board asking that they relieve congestion in the schools. They also asked that the board provide industrial education to black children. After a mass meeting passed a resolution authorizing the committee to represent them before the school board, the petition asked for four additional grades to be added to the black public schools, raising their number to ten. It also asked that an industrial school be established in some central location of the city. Petitioners asked the board to discontinue double sessions in the black schools, in which the average class size was between seventy-five to ninety students. In East Macon, where average class size was ninety pupils, citizens made a similar request of the board. Chairing the board Judge A. L. Miller told the committee the board had considered their request, but that lack of funds and hindered any definite action. He further suggested that the committee elect a sub-committee of three members to confer with the school board. In 1922 "A Colored Patron" wrote to the *Telegraph* complaining that the board allowed teachers without degrees to teach in the black schools. "There is not another city in the State," wrote "Patron," "that allows undergraduates to teach in their schools." Unequal conditions such as these in Macon's black schools would remain until the civil rights era.[69]

Another area of complaint among black Maconites was a 1920 problem concerning water resources for residents of the Pleasant Hill section. City health officials had forced them to fill up their wells, but provided no water to take the place of that which had previously been drawn. Residents in eight homes on one block in Pleasant Hill signed a letter to the board of water commissioners. The letter bemoaned a "water famine" that left the residents without water for washing or drinking. Belatedly, the Commissioner made arrangements to run a water main to the complainants who wrote that they were "in a sufferin' condishun."[70]

Still another black Maconite called for higher wages and other general improvements in their plight. "We have made the white man what he is today, and are still making him stronger and stronger in wealth.... And I must say to our white citizens of Georgia. What we need is higher wages for our work and better treatment.... It has been proven that the negro is the best laborer on the globe and for that reason the negro deserves better pay. We are punished with unwritten laws very constantly which ought to be prevented."[71]

In the face of difficulties such as these, so rampant in the South, black Maconites joined with others in the "Great Migration" to the large cities of the northeast and Midwest. The resulting labor shortage greatly concerned many whites, including W. T. Anderson, who commented on it with some regularity. African Americans sometime pointedly explained the situation to Anderson and his white readers. Explaining the "exodus" from the South, one correspondent in 1916 cited as causes "the great disadvantages at which he [the Negro] is placed and the constant dangers that surround him. Low wages and high costs of living, severe pressure when in debt, and inadequate school facilities, to say nothing of other things adverse to his peace and prosperity place him at such disadvantages that contentment is next to the impossible. Then, because of what appears to be an unguarded anti-negro agitation, growing out of the crimes of a few, the negro is made to feel that popular sentiment is against him; that he is without proper protection of the law, and, therefore, surrounded at all times with imminent dangers." He advised whites that to give fair wages, humane treatment, better housing and schools, and "full protection of the law" would stop the black exodus.[72]

Less than a month later, on 30 October, Macon saw an abortive attempt at a major black exodus. A white "labor agent" scammed black Maconites into purchasing tickets to Michigan, where he promised them good paying jobs. The con artist coaxed two blacks, Dave Williams and Jim Anderson, to recruit as many as 500 to leave Macon for the North. Almost 300 would-be migrants actually bought tickets on the Southern Railway, and a crowd of 1,000 gathered to see them off. City and county officers dispersed the crowd and arrested Williams and Anderson for working as sub-agents, while they also arrested five others for loitering. In the process, the white agent, tipped off about the investigation by city and federal officials, failed to appear at the station.[73]

"A Colored Subscriber" angrily castigated white Macon for this "disgraceful occurrence," as well as for the lynching problem:

> And still you ask the question why the negroes are leaving. There was a time when the negro was lynched only when he committed rape on one of your women, but now, if he disputes his employer's word, or fails to give all of the road, or steals a pig, he is strung up and riddled by bullets. And nothing is ever done about it. It is always the same old story (unknown parties) and it seems to me that these emigrating agents are unknown parties, too.... the negro is carrying his children with him where they can inhale something else beside air pregnant with prejudice, hatred and strife.... God is not dead. The blood of my people from the swamps and secluded spots all over this Southland cries to you from the ground in tones you can never hear now. But always bear in mind, whatever you sow, that shall you reap.

Some days after this, the *Telegraph* printed an apology for accidentally allowing the letter to see the light of day. "A Colored

Subscriber," Anderson lamented, "had done his own race a grave injustice."[74] Seven months later, as the tide of migrating black Georgians increased to some 50,000, Anderson editorialized that wiser blacks should think again about leaving the South:

> There is every reason why the negro should be left in the South, why he should come to look on it as a permanent and continuing habitat…There is no appreciable race trouble in the South, and never will be again because both white and black understand each other on a tolerable and usefully workable basis to an extent far exceeding whatever has existed in this respect in the past. The climate and general attributes of the country are almost indigenous to the negro. Here in this semi-tropical country he works best and most healthy, lives more naturally and happily and is more useful to himself, his community and the country at large. Also he is the most efficient, if not the only efficient, labor the South can ever hope to get.[75]

Others, like William Russell Owen, pastor of the First Baptist Church, sought to convince white Maconites that "the Negro problem had moved north. "The North is in for a bad spell with the negro problem," Owen said in a 1920 speech. He continued, "The North is losing its feeling of protection over the negro and has come to regard him with a growing hatred. I found on this trip more growing hatred between the races in the North than one ever discovers here in the South…. There is a growing intermarriage between the whites and blacks and a flaming race hatred.[76]

Black Georgians and black Maconites appeared to believe, despite Anderson's optimistic assurances, that there *was* "appreciable race trouble" and would continue to leave the South in considerable numbers. In 1919 a young black man migrated to Macon from the South Georgia town of Cordele, where white violence against blacks had flared up once too often to suit him. After picking up a series of odd jobs in Macon, he was hired as a gang laborer at the Southern Railway Company. On 1 August 1922, the young man and one of his brothers had business in downtown Macon. As they approached the outskirts of the city, departing blacks warned them of trouble. Unable to turn back, they arrived at their destination to discover themselves in the middle of another lynch party. As they walked past mobs of whites in their frenzy, the young man left the macabre scene carrying with him the image of the mangled body of "Cocky" Glover. At their first opportunity, he and his wife and two children left Macon and Georgia never to return. From his new home in Detroit he would later write that he had seen "enough of the white man's brutality in Georgia to last me for 26,000 years."[77]

The young man's name was Elijah Poole, later to be changed to Elijah Muhammad, future leader of the Black Muslims, now known as the Nation of Islam. In the 1960s, during the height of the civil rights movement, many African Americans were torn between the Christian, nonviolent philosophy of Martin Luther King, Jr., and Elijah Muhammad's Black Nationalism. When mainstream American journalists heard Muhammad speak of "white devils," those at CBS produced a television documentary called *The Hate that Hate Produced*. Some of that "hate" had been produced in Macon.

3

The Governors and the Klan

Despite lynching, black migration, and continued racial separation, Macon in the 1920s enjoyed a period of moderate economic growth and the beginnings of progress in black-white relations. The flurry of lynchings before and immediately after World War I increasingly became an embarrassment to the state, while a resurgent Ku Klux Klan gained influence over Georgia politics and Macon's social setting. For the state as a whole, as well as for Macon, the main stories of the decade centered on two governors and the influence of the Klan. One chief executive, Hugh M. Dorsey, made a controversial exit from the governor's mansion with a strong denunciation of lynching and the state's general treatment of its black citizens. Another governor, Clifford M. Walker, was revealed to be a member of the Klan. This chapter analyzes Macon's reactions to both these governors and to the Klan, which was responsible for a number of flogging incidents during the decade.

BLACK MACONITES IN 1920S

By 1920 Macon's population had reached 52,995, and would grow by only 1.6 percent, to 53,829 over the next decade, with blacks numbering some 23,093 or 43 percent of the total.[1] Ninety-eight percent of white Maconites were native-born Americans, although a centennial history of the city published in 1929 remarked that "Macon's gates are open and a cordial welcome awaits worthy immigrants."[2] Leading Macon's industrial development in the 1920s were eleven textile mills, the largest of which was the Bibb Manufacturing Company. Five railroads and five paved highways moving outward to the rest of Georgia served the city. In 1925 a bond issue had paved an additional 31 miles of Macon's streets, and by 1926 automobile traffic increased enough to justify the installation of the city's first electric traffic lights on Cherry Street. Despite this increase in paved roads, Macon's black citizens endured mostly dirt streets and inadequate water and sanitation facilities.[3] The majority of Macon's African-American population was, of course, unable to migrate to the "Promised Land" of the North, despite the mob violence and lynching that threatened them. In addition to such major terrors, however, were the more mundane, minor inconveniences of life in the Jim Crow South.

The realities of segregation created a separate sphere for black economic development in Macon. Many blacks began with the mercantile business, catering to customers of their own race. By mid-decade black Maconites ran more than twenty retail establishments, two real estate companies, three mortuaries, two furniture stores, a coal company, and a printing company. Eight physicians worked through the black-owned Lundy Hospital. Exclusively serving Macon's black population, the Lundy Hospital included an operating room and an ambulance service. The predominantly white Macon Hospital also treated blacks on a segregated basis. Three dentists and two lawyers also served the black community.[4] In 1919 blacks established the Liberty Loan and Investment Company, which increased its deposits from $25,000 to $740,000 in its first three years. In 1921 the Middle Georgia Saving and Investment Company was organized to serve the black community in real estate as well as banking. Within two years the company had deposits of some $28,000, and over the previous year had transacted almost $228,000 in banking and $60,000 in real estate. Charles H. Douglass, Macon's most prominent black business leader, served as company president, while the Reverend W. R. Forbes was chairman of the board of directors.[5] Some 84 percent of black women in Macon worked as domestics. After the stock market crash and bank failures of 1928, blacks made up 60 percent of the unemployed in Macon. Unemployed blacks constituted 3.9 percent of the overall population to a full 7 percent of those employed, compared to unemployed whites who made up 2 percent and 4.9 percent, respectively.[6]

In 1920 black illiteracy rates remained high. Of Georgia's 328,838 illiterates over ten years old, 261,115 (79.4 percent) were African

Americans. Only 5.4 percent of white Georgians could not read, compared to almost six times that percentage (29.1 percent) of blacks in the state. Blacks comprised 1,451 (81.5 percent) of the 1,780 illiterates in Bibb County. Yet when reporting its findings to Governor Clifford M. Walker, the Georgia Illiteracy Commission only mentioned the approximately 70,000 whites who labored under this disability. Nevertheless, Rufus W. Weaver, president of Mercer University and an original member of the commission, organized Mercer students to identify illiterates in Bibb County and teach them to read in Mercer classrooms. Their work revealed that the commission's 1920 figures were dramatically low, as they discovered some 8,400 illiterates, most of them black. Between 1919 and 1925, more than 7,000 were taught to read, 5,000 of them by Mercer students.[7] This effort to eradicate illiteracy constituted one of the first examples of interracial work in the state. In early 1922, prominent Georgia educators and church workers, both black and white, met at the Mulberry Street Methodist Church in Macon to develop the program of the new Georgia Committee on Race Relations. Black attendees were heartened by the efforts, while they assured whites that they "do not want to meet the Southerners socially," but rather needed advice and aid for their churches, schools, and home conditions.[8]

In the 1920s Macon boasted but ten public schools for blacks. Only one of these, Hudson Industrial, was a secondary school. Salaries for school administrators were grossly unequal, with white male high school principals earning $125 a month and white female principal earning $75 a month. At the elementary level white male principals earned $60 a month, in contrast to the highest black principal who was paid $40 month. By the end of the decade African-American students in Macon constituted 39 percent of the total, while only 9 percent of expenditures went to black education. One study reported that statewide blacks received only about one-twenty-fifth of the total amount spent for public education, while figures compiled by the New Deal era Works Progress Administration showed that the state of Georgia spent $35.42 per capita on the education of its white students compared to $6.32 for black students.[9]

Black private education was centered in several schools in Macon. Ballard Normal School, operated by the American Missionary

Association and Macon's First Congregationalist Church since just after the Civil War. Central City College, which began elementary and secondary instruction in 1889, began its college department in 1920. The next year, a public school teacher named Minnie L. Smith founded Beda-Etta Business College, which gave instruction in typing, shorthand, bookkeeping, and banking. The St. Peter Claver Catholic School also educated black Maconites.[10] In 1923, black Macon made fundraising efforts to help rebuild Central City College after its buildings were destroyed by fire in 1921.[11]

Black educator R. S. Ingram wrote to the *Macon Telegraph* appealing for help in developing the new Negro High and Industrial School. Adopting a Bookerist perspective, he sought to assure whites that instruction at the school would be safely vocational. Styling the new school as a Tuskegee in the making, Ingram emphasized the "service" character of vocational training—"not merely the giving of information, theoretically, but actually doing the work with the hands, well and intelligently." Highlighting courses in shop work and carpentry for boys and sewing and domestic science for girls, he rejected a Du Boisian liberal education as "inflated and superficial." Disparaging mere "book learning," Ingram argued that when "taught to be more industrious, prosperous, more dependable and self-reliant through better methods of industrial education," blacks would improve their conditions and become more content with life in the South. He concluded his letter by underscoring that instruction at the new school would not challenge southern traditions of race relations:

> This city is fortunate because its Board of education and its Superintendent of Schools are wholly sympathetic toward a progressive industrial education program. The teachers of the several vocations here received their training at the best industrial institutions—Hampton, Tuskegee and Cheyney.... They are all Southern-born and reared and fully understand and respect the fixed sentiments and customs established for our goings that are conducive to peace and prosperity for us all.

Commenting on the letter, editor W. T. Anderson complimented Ingram's philosophy as sound and sane. "Many well-intentioned people who have no fundamental understanding of the colored race and its needs," he asserted, "have been championing the higher education for the Negro in the South." Such an error, he argued, betrayed an "unpardonable stupidity."[12]

Anderson also saw problems in the more activist perspective reflected in the recently-organized National Association for the Advancement of Colored People (NAACP), which had begun membership drives in most Georgia cities, including Macon. In a 1921 column, he lamented that "radical and shallow" leaders like W. E. B. Du Bois were replacing "the deeper, saner and more practical men of their race like Moton of Tuskegee." Noting the NAACP's meetings throughout Georgia, he warned that criticisms of the South and other efforts to estrange blacks from whites would retard rather than advance the status of blacks. If, on the contrary, blacks would "take the advice of his Best Friend and aspire to become a good servant in the large and best sense as well as the menial sense, there is nothing the better element of the white race in the South will not do for him."[13]

One cannot help marveling at the self-deception of Southern whites who believed that they were African Americans' best friends or could not understand when their black neighbors did not seem to think so. Such appeared to be the case with "A Colored Citizen," who addressed white Macon in a 1923 letter. He wrote, "It is not social equality, we want, but it is justice in the courts." It would take "more Christianity" for whites to see the racial realities of the era. "Here, our churches, schools and dwellings are burned," he reminded white Maconites, adding:

> and if we show any steps toward protecting our property we are lynched, our females as well as the males. The younger set of your boys between the ages of 16 and 25 years old, are very dangerous to my people, when they are in bunches, while our boys are not allowed to stand around at any place on the street. Your boys will see one of my race coming on the sidewalk, they will start advancing towards them five or six deep, taking all space on the walk, then when the man reaches them, he has to walk in the street. Some Christianity, is it not?... We can't say anything, if we do we are arrested and booked on disorderly conduct.... If a man of your race mistreats a man of

mine, the man of my race can't say a word, for if he does he is slain by a mob before twelve hours passes.... Although the Negro is understood better in the South than in the North, for government he desires the North.[14]

Thus, in spring 1921, by the time Governor Hugh M. Dorsey drew to the close of his two two-year terms, conditions of oppression and lynch violence against Georgia blacks had become serious enough for the governor, officials of the US Justice Department, and leaders of the fledgling Georgia Committee on Interracial Cooperation to discuss immediate action.[15] The eventual action of a lame duck governor would generate a torrent of denunciation from white Georgians.

"... AS TO THE NEGRO IN GEORGIA"

On 22 April 1921, three months before leaving office, Georgia's chief executive delivered a stinging condemnation of the state's dismal record on lynching in a pamphlet entitled, "A Statement from Governor Hugh M. Dorsey as to the Negro in Georgia." The statement reported on 135 cases of lynching and other violent attacks on blacks and called for reform. For his efforts, however, Dorsey was scathingly denounced across Georgia for embarrassing the state and violating its sense of honor. In 1920 he had lost a US senatorial campaign to Tom Watson, but his decision to weigh into the lynching issue effectively ended any further aspirations to elective office in the state.[16]

Ironically, it was Dorsey's indirect role in Georgia's most famous lynching that helped elect him to the governorship in 1916. Appointed solicitor general of the Atlanta Judicial Circuit in 1910, Dorsey led the prosecution of the infamous Leo Frank murder case in 1915. The manager of an Atlanta pencil factory, Frank was convicted for the rape and murder of thirteen-year-old Mary Phagan. Amid sensational news accounts and editorials from Tom Watson calling for the "Jew Pervert" to be executed, Dorsey convinced the trial judge to sentence Frank to death. The evidence was questionable enough to lead Georgia's outgoing governor, John Slaton, to review the case himself. Finding enough disputed testimony to doubt the verdict, Slaton infuriated the majority of Georgians by commuting Frank's sentence to life imprisonment. The angry throngs hissed, threatened, and hanged Slaton in effigy as he turned the governor's seal over to Maconite Nathaniel E. Harris. On 16 August 1915, they broke into Frank's cell in the state penitentiary in Milledgeville, took him to Marietta, and hanged him from a tree as Mary Phagan's relatives looked on. The following year, supported by Tom Watson as the prosecutor of Leo Frank and the protector of Georgia womanhood, Dorsey was elected governor.[17]

Macon was, of course, hardly a center of Dorsey strength in the 1916 gubernatorial election, as favorite son Nat Harris drew three votes to every one for the young lawyer. Outside of Bibb County, however, Dorsey won handily, taking majorities in 107 counties to Harris's 38. Besides this support for Harris, the *Macon Telegraph* viewed the Dorsey campaign, based as it was on the Frank case, as an obvious appeal to prejudice. Denouncing Dorsey's tactics as "the most nauseating politics ever known in Georgia." W. T. Anderson further argued, "The passions and animal instincts of a half-civilized people have never been so preyed upon, nor has anything of this kind ever been used before to pander to the blood thirst of insanity." Further, Anderson accused Dorsey of being the puppet of Tom Watson. He complained, "[W]e're not a lot of simple-minded but well-intentioned children to be sent into emotional paroxysms every time Tom Watson sounds a tocsin." After predicting a Dorsey defeat, election day force-fed Anderson what his editorial called "Our Dish of Crow."[18]

Once Dorsey was in office, NAACP Director Walter White's investigation of Southern lynching, and in particular those in Brooks and Lowndes counties in Georgia, brought pressure on the new governor to take some action against lynching in the state. In 1919 he proposed that the General Assembly pass legislation requiring juries in lynching trials to be composed of persons residing outside the counties where the lynching occurred. By reducing possible intimidation of juries and keeping mob members out of the jury pools, such a law promised to discourage verdicts that the deaths had "come at the hands of unknown persons." The bill's opponents in the legislature defeated the proposal.[19]

The following year, the governor received a petition from a new organization called the Commission on Interracial Cooperation calling on him to take action. Atlanta religious leaders C. B. Wilmer and Ashby Jones, headed the state's affiliate of the commission, the Georgia

Committee on Race Relations, met with Dorsey in a conference that studied economic, civic, and moral dangers posed by lynching. While denouncing lynching, the committee maintained a moderate segregationist stance by disavowing any influence from the NAACP, which was suspect throughout the white South. The committee publicized its opposition to social equality between the races, political race baiting, lynch law, mob violence, peonage, intimidation, and "propaganda to inflame the minds of whites and blacks with reference to race relations."[20]

Increasingly influenced by the committee, and now safely in the lame duck phase of his term as governor, Dorsey authorized members of the committee to ghost write a major statement on Georgia's treatment of its African-American citizens. Speaking at a meeting with the committee at the Piedmont Hotel on 22 April, Dorsey presented his audience a pamphlet that historian John Dittmer called, "probably the most candid and courageous attack on racial injustice issued by an American governor."[21]

Dorsey cited 135 unsolicited examples of mistreatment of blacks that Georgians had brought to his attention during the preceding two years. Only two of those instances, he noted, involved the "usual crime" against white women. On the basis of such a record, he argued, "we stand indicted as a people before the world…. the staggering sum total of such cases, which, while seemingly confined to a small minority of our counties, yet bring disgrace and obloquy upon the State as a whole, and upon the entire Southern people." He concluded by asserting that rather than Georgians, rather than outsiders, should further investigate the problem and suggest a remedy. He concluded his address with several proposals. First, he called upon churches throughout Georgia to teach to both races "justice, mercy, and mutual forbearance." Second, he called for compulsory education for students of both races. Third, he advocated two committees, one black and one white, to conduct conferences on race relations. Fourth, he called for the repeal of the wage labor contract law, which he said disregarded black rights. Fifth, he recommended the establishment of a state constabulary. Sixth, he proposed a fine to be assessed to every county where a lynching took place. Seventh, he proposed legislation giving the governor authority to remove any county officer whose negligence permitted a lynching. Finally, he proposed legislation authorizing the governor to appoint a commission to investigate lynchings.[22]

Reaction from across the state was initially mixed. While most press reaction was moderately supportive of Dorsey's good intentions, if not his methods, many Georgia politicos and other private citizens were indignant. The *Savannah Press* called the statement a "terrible arraignment" that put "Georgia before the world in a terrible light." Taking a more positive view, Clark Howell, editor of the *Atlanta Constitution* wrote, "Undoubtedly, the public sentiment has been aroused; and once aroused, the decent sentiment of the state can always be relied upon to assert itself and in the right direction. One thing is absolutely certain: An end must be put to conditions that have existed in Georgia." For Georgia itself to apply the remedy, he noted, was the easiest way to avoid federal intervention on the issue. While agreeing with the governor's hope of cleaning up the situation in Georgia, the *Telegraph* lamented that hostile Northerners had been presented "an official indictment by the highest official in the State," adding, "We won't get through denying this pamphlet for a long time to come." Most problematic to the *Telegraph* was the governor's "wholesale assaults and accusations against Georgia."[23]

Outgoing president of the state senate, Samuel L. Olive of Augusta denounced the governor, as did state Senator L. C. Brown of Athens. Brown introduced a resolution calling for a joint committee of the legislature to investigate the governor's allegations. The Reverend Caleb Ridley, pastor of Atlanta's Central Baptist Church, used his pulpit to excoriate both the governor and the ministers of the Georgia Committee on Race Relations. He also accused one particular church in Atlanta of mixing the races and encouraging the social equality of the races.[24] He organized a mass meeting in Atlanta for Saturday night, 21 May, where he circulated his own pamphlet rebutting Dorsey's statement and helped form the Dixie Defense Committee, Ridley accused the governor of "one of the vilest slanders ever heaped upon the people of Georgia." He called the governor "a political sore-head" who was licking his wounds after his defeat by Watson and was now "bidding for the colored vote." Warning that Dorsey might violate the principles of states' rights, he argued that "if the State laws do not force the white people to be more just to the negro the Governor is going to ask the United States government to come down here and force the white folks to behave themselves." He bitterly accused the governor of basing his pamphlet on lynching statistics provided by the Tuskegee Institute, condemning "any Southern white man who would condemn this alleged lynching record taken from a negro publicist without denouncing the brutal crime that excites our people to uncontrollable passions."[25]

White Macon also reacted to Dorsey's actions with fury. Three weeks after the original story broke, the Reverend Lincoln McConnell and more than fifty other Maconites commended Flint Circuit Court Judge W. E. H. Searcy for his criticisms of the governor. Their letter to the judge complained that Dorsey was damaging Georgia's reputation by his "unproved charges" against the state's judiciary. On Sunday, 22 May, the day following Ridley's meeting in Atlanta, Macon dentist C. A. Yarbrough, chairman of an organization called the Guardians of Liberty, led a mass meeting to consider ways of impeaching Dorsey. The Guardians were joined in the project by the Patriotic Societies of Macon, which included the Bibb County Civic League, the Protestant Federation, and other organizations. [26]

Even before the Macon meeting took place, however, W. T. Anderson judged impeachment a bad idea. To do so would give the appearance of a cover-up of wrongdoing. "The chronic and severest critics of the South," he asserted, "would say that the very way Georgia is stirred up proves the case against her." On the other hand, he later argued, any failure of the state legislature to impeach the governor would likely be interpreted as an endorsement of the governor's pamphlet. Rather than risking the perception that the legislature had given its "official approval" to Dorsey's statement, Anderson believed it would be wiser for the mass meeting to content itself with passing indignant resolutions concerning the governor.[27]

Between 1,500 and 2,000 white Maconites crowded into the city hall auditorium and adopted resolutions that called Dorsey "a traitor to his State and a libeler of every citizen of Georgia." The assembly called on the legislature to appoint a court of inquiry to conduct a thorough investigation of the governor's charges. They also called on the legislature to impeach Dorsey unless he produced satisfactory evidence. Miss Altel Benton, secretary of the Patriotic Societies, denounced Dorsey, telling the crowd: "We feel that the man in the Governor's chair has transgressed and trampled underfoot, walked up to and stabbed, our mother—Georgia. Let him perish who would blacken our mother. We ask God to help us vindicate Georgia."

Judge C. L. Bartlett, a former congressman, likened the governor to Benedict Arnold, and defended the honor of white Georgians. "The Caucasian shall be supreme," he declaimed, "and Dorsey cannot destroy that. What he has done has done more to ruin standards than any copper-backed Yankee from Massachusetts to the Potomac could do." W. G. McRae, a Mercer student who joined Yarbrough and C. E. Kennon on the committee that composed their resolution, accused the governor of violating "all law and precedent" by turning the investigation over to a committee of private citizens without the consent of the legislature. A brave Dorsey defender named Nelson Shipp dared to offer a substitute resolution affirming the governor's motives while rejecting his method. When he said he could not allow the governor to be slandered, he was booed and heckled by the crowd, which taunted Shipp with shouts of "throw him out." Carl F. Hutchison, representing the Dixie Defense League, condemned the ministers on the Georgia Committee for their role in producing the pamphlet. Ridiculing them as "city preachers," he advised them to "come down and mingle with the masses, take off their stiff collars, and get the point of view of the people."[28]

Afterward, a good deal of commentary critical of the mass meeting began to surface. Anderson reiterated his caution that Georgia's already sullied reputation would be further weakened if the state impeached its governor "for his efforts to stop lawlessness, alleged or otherwise." But then his resolve stiffened into a rather spirited defense of the governor. There was "no doubt in the world," her argued, that Dorsey's intentions were good and that in the matter of lynching Georgia's reputation was bad. He then added: "The great duty of Georgia is to clean house. And we are not going to get anywhere by spreading out skirts so as to conceal the fifth, and denounce those who say it is there. The trouble can be cured, and the Governor's pamphlet may be the means of arousing us to a determination to cure it. If so, it's a good job, whether exactly according to our notion or not." Some days later came a letter to the *Telegraph* from a Maconite who took issue with the mass meeting conveners. "I am a citizen of this great commonwealth," he reminded them, declaring "that the Governor has not libeled me." He found especially distasteful the group's denunciations of the ministers and their presuming to provide them their own code of ethics, noting "I have never allowed and never shall allow a lot of moral lepers to outline a code of ethics for me." In addition to these critiques, the *Savannah Press*, which had initially complained of the governor's actions, now refused to endorse the intemperate reactions of the mass meeting.[29]

White Maconites appeared to be of mixed opinion about the governor. The Reverend Bascom Anthony, pastor of the Vineville Methodist Church, who claimed he had never voted for Dorsey, told his congregation that he admired Dorsey as "a man who finds out the truth and is man enough to stand up and tell it regardless of personal popularity." Of the conveners of the mass meeting, he quipped, "I do not want such a crowd guarding my liberty." Lamenting Georgia's abysmal record in lynching, Anthony said, "Every citizen of Georgia who has ears long enough to fold about him as a mantle of innocency to ward off criticism may do so, but I, for one, think it wiser to mend our ways." Another Maconite wrote the *Telegraph* to defend Dorsey, noting that only 2 of his 135 cases had even been questioned. Trying to calm white fears, he wrote: "The negro does not and cannot threaten white supremacy. He neither desires nor expects social equality. The negro is not so stupid. He asks only for justice. Therefore we ask our fellow citizens to unite with us in upholding white supremacy by maintaining the principles of righteousness and justice upon which white supremacy depends." Disavowing any influence from the NAACP, the writer advocated segregated "but decent, sanitary, and adequate accommodations for both races, but opposed lynch law, race-baiting, and intimidation. At the other end of the spectrum of opinion, one anonymous correspondent pointedly raised questions about Dorsey's failure, while Atlanta's solicitor general, to investigate the mob that threatened then-governor John Slaton. To have done so would have killed his chances of being elected governor, implied "A Citizen," who added: "We are convinced that the document recently published by Governor Dorsey is more productive of mischief than of good to either race."[30]

For his part, Dorsey vigorously stood by his statement, both in responses to state officials who had differed with him on the issue, among these First Circuit Judge William E. H. Searcy, Judge E. T.

Shurley of the Toombs County Circuit Court, and Toombs Solicitor General M. L. Felts. The governor replied that he had no intention of personally trying all of the 135 cases he had cited, which was why he deliberately refused to name the specific counties or persons involved. Rather, he had hoped to awaken Georgians to "the staggering sum total of charges made against us as a people in connection with our treatment of the negro." By failing to appreciate the magnitude of the problem, he asserted, Georgians were subjecting themselves to "a peril overshadowing all others threatening our State."[31]

Less than a week later, Dorsey issued a more general defense in a communication "To the People of Georgia." He reminded his critics of the 415 lynchings that had occurred in the state since 1885 and only 15 percent of them had involved "the unspeakable crime." He further reminded them that no member of a lynch mob had ever been punished. To allow such a record to continue, he warned, was dangerously close to anarchy. "Every Southern man who will face facts," he challenged his readers, "knows that the negro is not treated with that justice which should characterize our dealings with this race of people who are in a great measure, the wards of the Caucasian." He concluded with a confession of faith in the people of Georgia: "I am convinced that, even in the counties where these outrages are said to have occurred, the better element regrets them, and…will condemn such conditions and take the steps necessary to correct them."[32]

In official actions, the governor recommended that the General Assembly consider the proposals listed in his pamphlet, particularly that the legislature increase a governor's authority to deal with racial disturbances and establish a state constabulary. In his farewell speech to state lawmakers, he reiterated the sentiments that had clouded in controversy his last three months in office. He ceremoniously called the names of fifty-eight blacks killed by mob violence in Georgia during his term as governor. Over against these victims, he noted, "we have hundreds who participated in these murders who have never been brought to justice, and in many cases no effort whatsoever made to apprehend or punish them." He advocated that peace officers be evaluated by some high-ranking official in any county where any mob crime had occurred and to execute immediate removal if the officers were judged derelict in their duties. He also recommended the formation of a state grand jury composed of citizens from all sections of the state and fully authorized to investigate and bring indictments against anyone participating in mob violence. Those indicted were to be tried before juries drawn from the entire state. His most drastic proposal was that governors be authorized to remove any sheriff found derelict in his duties. In his final appeal, he told the legislators: "Responsibility for the crime of lynching rests not only upon actors, but upon the community which shuts its eyes to the crime and permits and tolerates it, and upon legislators who refuse to enact laws to suppress it. It can and will be stopped when the better element who deprecate mob law, aggressively condemn it and determine to suppress the practice."[33]

Dorsey's efforts proved quixotic, however, as his proposals were immediately ignored by the General Assembly and the new governor. In his inaugural address, Thomas Hardwick defended the honor of the state against his predecessor's anti-lynching rhetoric and program. In the face of Dorsey's lynching statistics, Hardwick nonetheless asserted "that there is no State in this Union, and no country in this world, having within its limits anything like an even division of its population between white and black races, in which the relations between the two races are more harmonious than right here in the State of Georgia." Noting the small percentage of white crimes against blacks, he accused Dorsey of impairing "the friendly relations between the races in our State." Taking one last dismissive swipe at the outgoing governor, he promised to enforce the law, to impartially protect all citizens, white and black alike, "and not to write any pamphlets."[34]

Despite the failure of the Hardwick administration to follow up on his predecessor's concerns, both the rise of post-World War I racial incidents and Dorsey's principled stand for reform set the stage for an important debate over mob violence in Macon. In the mid-1920s, Maconites discovered that Dorsey's main antagonist in their city, C. A. Yarbrough, leader of the Guardians of Liberty, was also the head of the Klan in Macon.

MACON'S KLAN

The racial milieu of postwar Georgia eventually transformed the editorial stance of the *Macon Telegraph*. The spate of lynchings, especially that of

"Cocky" Glover, Dorsey's pamphlet, and the rise of the second Ku Klux Klan in Georgia and in Macon combined to stiffen W. T. Anderson's opposition to mob violence, lynching, and the Klan. Shortly after a group of Georgians led by W. J. Simmons met at Stone Mountain in 1915 to reconstitute the Klan, Anderson perceived a difference between the Invisible Empire's two incarnations. According to Southern orthodoxy, the first Klan had heroically restored order from the chaos of Reconstruction and "negro rule." Carpetbaggers had supposedly prodded blacks toward their natural criminality; the Klan put a stop to it. The happy result, Anderson averred, "was racial vindication, performed with expedition, justice, vision and sureness." He found the first Klan's record unimpeachable and the object of justifiable Southern pride.[35] However questionable his historical interpretation, Anderson recognized that this resurgent Klan, arising in a period of unrivaled white supremacy, was at best unnecessary. At worst, the Klan was criminal, as events in Macon would shortly reveal.

In 1919, fifteen white Maconites were initiated into the Dixie Klan No. 33 in ceremonies held in the Bibb County Superior Court room. One of the charter members told reporters that they had begun their local organizing effort to express their concern over black soldiers returning from the war. On New Year's Eve 1921, a black physician named F. P. Leaney was attacked for speaking rudely to a white drugstore clerk and army officer.[36] Having reorganized in Macon after the war, the "modern Ku Klux," as the *Macon Telegraph* dubbed it, was emboldened by the Dorsey controversy to increase its activities significantly by 1922.[37]

In July, the Macon branch of the Klan invited the city council to participate in one of their ceremonies and give permission to appear in full Klan regalia, including their hoods. The council entertained two other petitions, one from the Klan and another from a group of downtown business leaders, that the Klan to be allowed to hold its meeting in Macon City Auditorium. J. P. Durkee, "Kleagle" or leader of the Macon Klan, asked the council to designate one of its members to introduce the main speaker of the evening. The council allowed the Klan to use the auditorium, but denied the other requests, with a strong warning that police would enforce the council's anti-mask dictates. Some 300 Maconites gathered on 6 July to hear Caleb Ridley, who by this time had become the chaplain of the Georgia Klan, speak on the requisites for joining the Empire. To be a Klansman, he informed the audience, one must be white, American-born, a Gentile, a Protestant, and a gentleman.[38] These activities led Anderson to launch a strong campaign against the Klan focusing on its secrecy and its tactics of spying on local citizens looking for signs of vice and moral indiscretion.[39]

Macon's Knights of the Klan did not have to look for very long. A white Macon chiropodist named Robert F. Mills came under the Empire's scrutiny on suspicion of committing adultery. In January 1922 Mills had been kidnapped and taken to a cemetery along Columbus Road, where Klansmen flogged him with a whip. On the night of 4 November he was again victimized, as a car carrying five Klansmen forced Mills to pull over while driving home along College Street. When Mills's pistol failed to fire, the gang took his weapon, pulled him into their car, and drove off through Vineville, a Macon suburb. Backing down on threats to hang him, the gang settled for merely pistol-whipping Mills with his own gun. Returning home, Mills contacted the sheriff's office, complaining that he could not get adequate police protection because of the department's Klan contacts. Claiming to having recognized his attackers, he told sheriff's detectives, "I have seen them come and go from the Ku Klux lodge rooms, together with half of the police force and sheriff's force." The following day, W. T. Anderson called for a thorough investigation of city and county law enforcement agencies and a policy that all officers reveal all of their secret affiliations.[40]

The following day, as a number of local ministers mentioned the attack in their sermons, Kleagle J. P. Durkee denied that the attack on Mills was an "official" act of the Klan and announced that any members involved in any such lawless act would be banished from the organization and delivered to the authorities.[41] At the same time, the Macon Ministerial Union adopted a resolution criticizing the lawlessness that allowed such an attack. Judge Malcolm D. Jones charged the Bibb County grand jury to investigate the incident. The grand jury also took up the investigation another mob beating of sixty-nine-year-old D. S. Pinkston, a former lamp lighter for the Southern Railroad. Along with an elderly black woman named Eliza, who lived in the back room of his East Macon house, Pinkston was awakened in the middle of the night by a gang pretending to be from the sheriff's office. Placing Pinkston and

Eliza in their car, the gang drove to a wooded area and placed ropes around their necks. Then after voting not to hang them, the gang used leather straps to flog their victims. Attacking Pinkston not only for his "scandalous" relationship with Eliza, but apparently for his failure to pay alimony to his estranged wife, the gang departed with a warning to pay his wife ten dollars a week or else.[42]

Mills's wife soon issued public statements in support of her husband and denouncing the Klan. She told reporters: "If the Ku Klux Klan is '100 percent American,' why do they sneak around at night behind masks, and prey upon one helpless individual, in direct contrast to the laws of America which gives every citizen a right to a trial in open court?... I am in continual fear that they will take my children or do anything in the world that they can to my family or me. They are mean enough to do anything, I think, after seeing what they have done." Five days after the attack, Mills received a telephone message warning him to leave town on penalty of death. He and his older son quickly packed up their things and left town, leaving his wife and baby son behind.[43] Mills's departure effectively ended the inquiries into mob beatings until the problem flared up again in the late summer of 1923.

In the meantime, Klan issues in Macon swirled around the organization's influence in local and state politics and conflict over their rights to public activities in the city. Controversy arose in March 1923 when a national magazine claimed that Georgia Senator Walter F. George was a member of the Klan. George denied membership, but the incident gave a high profile to concerns about state politicians who may have quietly sought the support of the Klan. In the *Telegraph* reporter John W. Hammond argued that where once Georgia politicians trouped to the Hickory Hill home of Tom Watson, now in the 1920s they were seeking Klan counsel. By May, Anderson was editorializing that the Invisible Empire had successfully taken over state politics through its "hunger to control" and that the state Democratic Party had become "a gathering of rubber stamps" for the Klan.[44]

Controversy also erupted when Durkee presented a petition signed by a number of Macon business leaders, some of whom were Klan members. The document urged that "in the spirit of fairness" the city council grant the parade permit. Despite the protests of Mayor Luther Williams, the council granted the Klan's petition to parade through the

downtown area in full regalia, including masks. Durkee and Macon's
Dixie Klan No. 33 promised a political retaliation, vowing their support
to any candidate who would contest Williams in his fall re-election
campaign. In the weeks immediately after the controversy, Mayor
Williams found support for his anti-Klan stand in the pastor of the
prominent downtown Mulberry Street Methodist Church, the Reverend
Dr. Walter F. Anthony. Before a large congregation Anthony
commended Williams's opposition to the Empire, saying he had hoped
the city council might have unanimously supported his position.
"America today is cursed," said Anthony, "with the quackery of the
hooded minions, who, under shelter of night, and without process of law,
pretend to correct a nation's social and governmental ills. The Ku Klux
Klan is to the ills of the country what the cancer-cure quack is to the
physically afflicted. Both only hasten and aggravate the evils they
pretend to cure."[45] Williams was re-elected in the fall campaign.

On 18 June 1922, the Klan held its first public ceremony in Central
City Park. During the evening several hundred hooded Klansmen
marched through downtown Macon, watched by what the *Telegraph*
reported to be thousands of spectators gathered along Cherry Street.
Leading the parade were four mounted police officers, following by a
Klansman with a sign reading, "We were here yesterday, 1866."
Sprinkled among the parading Knights were placards. One read, "Duty
Without Fear and Without Reproach." Another claimed, "Vindicated by
Congress." Still another announced, "We are soldiers of the Cross, the
militia of Christ." Near the end of the parade a final sign promised, "We
will be here forever." Bringing up the rear marched a number of children
dressed in Klan robes. After the procession into Central City Park, the
"naturalization" ceremony, which lasted more than two hours, initiated
more than 400 candidates into the organization. Older members and the
inductees celebrated afterward with an early morning barbecue. A
network of robed picketers served as human cordons blocking
unauthorized persons from approaching the 100-foot square area where
the oaths were administered.[46]

The high-profile arrival of the Klan turned out to be a precursor to
the return of mob violence in the Bibb County area before the end of the
summer. Another series of floggings, along with the lynchings of two
blacks in Houston and Bleckly counties, led Governor Clifford M.

Walker to send Adjutant General Charles H. Cox to investigate the situation in Macon.[47] Meanwhile, the *Telegraph* again inveighed against the mob violence and the weak law enforcement officials who tolerated it:

> [W]hen there are no Negroes to be chased or hung, then the mob, become bold by its success, takes up the trail after white people. If the State of Georgia were really in earnest about wanting to stop mob activities and outrages, a law to the effect that if a Sheriff or his deputies lost a prisoner, that Sheriff should be automatically removed from office and made ineligible for other office. If that were the law there would be no lost prisoners. If the officers' lives or welfare were endangered like the prisoner's, they would dodge the mob or stand it off.[48]

That same day Macon attorney Charles H. Hall addressed a meeting of the Kiwanis Club, charging that the current lawlessness in Macon was an organized effort of the Ku Klux Klan and, without naming names, called for an investigation of a "prominent dentist" rumored to be the Klan's "whipping boss." Hall presented his ideas as resolutions, which were adopted by the Kiwanians and presented to all of Macon's civic clubs. The resolutions called on both city and county law enforcement agencies to bring the floggers to trial.[49]

As if to strengthen its resolve in response to press criticism, that very night the Bibb County Sheriff's office arrested a trio of East Macon brothers in connection with another flogging incident. S. R. Hudson, C. F. Hudson, and J. C. Hudson were involved in whipping a young black man on Clinton Road, in the northern section of the city near the Jones County line. As another black Maconite, Emory Roberts drove past the gang, one of the masked attackers climbed on the running board of Roberts' car. Fighting with the Klansman as he continued down Clinton Road, Roberts ran his car into an embankment. The Hudson's Ford crashed into the rear of Roberts' car as it came to a stop. Neighbors in the vicinity heard the commotion and quickly notified deputy sheriffs. When they arrived at the scene, they found one of the Hudsons watching as his brothers grappled with Roberts. After taking the Hudsons into custody, officers found their car near the Jones County line. Inside the car they discovered four other masks similar to those worn by the Hudsons, a small sledge hammer, and a piece of wet felt that had apparently been used to gag the earlier victim. They were charged with public drunkenness, rioting, and assault and battery. Officers also arrested Emory Roberts, holding him as a material witness.[50]

While the Hudsons awaited trial for the Emory Roberts incident, Sheriff James R. Hicks's investigation turned up witnesses who identified two of the Hudson brothers as part of a gang that had severely beaten Macon cab driver Ollie M. Perry earlier that month.[51] Later, Hicks arrested another suspect, as Perry himself identified Macon grocer J. F. Alexander as a member of the gang that had beaten him.[52] In an odd turn of events, in hopes of diverting attention from their Invisible Empire, the Georgia Klan in Atlanta sent three of their own detectives to Macon to help in the flogging investigations. M. O. Dunning, chief of staff of the Realm of Georgia, Ku Klux Klan, announced that headquarters in Atlanta had authorized their detectives to aid Sheriff Hicks' investigation as well as a $1,500 financial contribution to a reward for information leading to any arrests and convictions in the case. In addition, Nathan Bedford Forrest, Grand Dragon of the Georgia Klan, told reporters that even if the perpetrators were Klansmen, they had acted without Klan authorization or knowledge. The big news regarding the flogging cases, however, was the arrest of three more suspects, including C. A. Yarbrough—dentist, Guardian of Liberty, and Klan "whipping boss"—in connection with 1922 beatings of Robert F. Mills.[53]

Once Yarbrough was implicated in the floggings, Bibb County Solicitor General Roy W. Moore concentrated on prosecuting the "whipping boss," whose trial would dominate the city court through the fall months of 1923. In September lawyers for the Hudson brothers demanded to come to trial during the December court term, but a clogged court docket would postpone final disposition of the case against the Hudson brothers for several weeks. Along with the Hudsons, the group of defendants included J. P. Durkee, J. D. Patrick, a former deputy in the municipal court, and W. F. DeLamar, a Macon merchant. On 17 February 1924, City Court Judge Will Gunn closed the December 1923 court term before the clogged docket could allow the flogging cases to come to trial. The end of the court term effectively quashed the cases against the Hudsons and the others. Commenting on the Hudsons' case, prosecutor Moore had concluded that the incident was the result of drunkenness rather than an actual Klan flogging.[54]

As Yarbrough went to trial, Walter Anthony once more took to his Mulberry Street pulpit to denounce the Klan. He told the congregation, "The men who compose mobs are not patriots. They are generally the scum and criminal element of a community," adding, "Nobody but the dirtiest type of coward chooses the night, and numbers, and a mask to 'mete out justice' to wrongdoers." Near the end of his arraignment, he asked rhetorically, "Who but God shall ever be able to compute how much the South, Georgia, yes, and Macon, has suffered and is suffering from lawlessness." When he finished his sermon, Bishop W. N. Ainsworth, who was visiting the congregation, endorsed Anthony's sentiments. He then called on all present to stand if they supported the end of such lawless acts. Not surprisingly, everyone in the congregation rose to their feet.[55]

At trial one of the Klan detectives testified that Yarbrough had encouraged him to leave Macon in hopes that authorities would drop their investigation of him. Afterward, the state called Robert F. Mills, who described his January 1922 beating in detail and identified Yarbrough as the first to pistol-whip him. Though his attackers had been robed and hooded, Mills testified that he saw the men disrobing before they left the scene. On the second day of the trial another witness, W. O. Barnett, told the jury that he had been the victim of another Yarbrough-led flogging party in February of that year. On that occasion Yarbrough had Barnett beaten for abusing his wife and children, and for fathering a child by one of his employees. In other testimony, William C. Quarterbaum, student at Mercer University, revealed that Yarbrough and the Reverend E. Hewlette Connell, pastor of the Bellevue Baptist Church, had recruited him to inform them of anyone abusing liquor in the area. Also, two women testified that they had written local Klan leaders requesting that they discipline their husband and father for similar bad behavior.[56]

On 13 September, Yarbrough was greeted with an anti-Klan editorial in the *Telegraph* calling for Klan leaders in Atlanta to be punished along with any local members that might be convicted of mob violence. Anderson complained that in such cases "the local men suffer; the higher-ups slip through the net." National Klan leaders, he argued, "should not be allowed to escape simply because the actual whippings were executed by local men." In court that day he admitted membership in the Klan, though he denied being the local "whipping boss" or condoning the floggings. Conspicuously absent from his testimony, however, was any alibi explaining his whereabouts at the times of the floggings. The defense called a series of character witnesses, all Baptist ministers, who vouched for Yarbrough as a man of high morality. The Reverends Martin A. Wood, pastor of the Vineville Baptist Church, and J. C. Mays, former pastor of the South Macon Baptist Church, testified that they were not Klan members, while E. Hewlette Connell refused to answer any questions about the Klan.[57] In closing arguments, prosecutor Roy W. Moore waxed eloquent, charging the Klan with undermining the government of the community and asserting that Yarbrough had set himself up as God in the city and had become a law unto himself. After a five-day trial and just over three hours of deliberation, however, the jury acquitted the dentist of the charge of rioting. Two-thirds of the spectators in the courtroom rushed to congratulate Yarbrough for the outcome.[58]

Yarbrough's legal troubles did not end there, however. Nine days later he went on trial again in connection with the flogging of W. O. Barnett. The trial elicited little new evidence against Yarbrough, although his minister friend Hewlette Connell did contradict his own testimony in the first trial, admitting that had applied for membership in the Klan and had attended one meeting. This time around another five-day trial ended in a mistrial, after seventy hours of deliberation could not lead to a verdict. Nine jurors had, however, voted to convict.[59] In a third trial, this one in the Macon City Court in October, an expert testified that threatening letters sent to Barnett had been composed on the typewriter in Yarbrough's office. Once again, this time after fifty hours of jury deliberation, the trial ended in a hung jury. A fourth trial in December ended in a second acquittal.[60]

A separate trial of J. Frank Alexander for assault and battery in connection with the Barnett beating ended in the only conviction in any of the flogging trials. His conviction resulted in a sentence of six months on a chain gang. Before he had even begun his sentence, however, a petition was circulated to convince Governor Clifford M. Walker to commute Alexander's sentence. The newly elected US Representative Samuel Rutherford later approached *Telegraph* editor W. T. Anderson

asking him to write a letter to the governor on Alexander's behalf.
Anderson declined to write the letter, though he did correspond with
Judge T. E. Patterson of the state prison commission. He told Patterson
that the floggings had so harmed Macon's reputation that it would be a
shame "to pardon the only man who had been convicted of the crimes."[61]
In mid-November, after serving only two months of his sentence, without
the approval of the prison commission, Governor Walker commuted
Alexander's sentence and had him released. Alexander had been the
beneficiary of a letter from Yarbrough to the governor asking for
Alexander's release. Remembering Yarbrough's past contributions to his
political campaigns, the governor granted the request.[62]

THE POLITICAL KLAN

Alongside the controversy over the flogging trials, the year beginning in
the fall of 1923 became the year of the Klan in Macon, Georgia, and
national politics. Nationally, the race for the presidency created a
controversy over an anti-Klan plank in the Democratic platform. With
the exception of supporters of Alabama Senator Oscar W. Underwood's
candidacy, most Southern Democrats, fearing the loss of Klan support at
home, sought to block the platform committee from including an explicit
condemnation of the Klan in the platform. Before the Democratic
National Convention met in late June, the *Telegraph* called on the party
to take a hard, anti-Klan line: "The Democratic Party never had a better
chance in its life-time to make fine history.... If it has the courage to
insert in its platform a vigorous, unmistakable, condemnatory plank of
the selfish, narrow, destructive things the Klan has stood for, then it will
truly be a beacon light of American freedom in a fog of growing
oppression, molestation, depression, and injustice—the real and true
party of democracy." At the convention, however, Georgia's delegation
to the strongly opposed the anti-Klan plank, and many in the delegation
were put in a position of having to deny charges that 85 percent of their
number were Klan members. In an acrimonious ten-hour debate, the
evenly split delegates decided by one vote not to single out the Klan by
name. The Georgia delegation, however, had unanimously voted for the
minority plank. Once the results were in, the *Telegraph* accused the

Democrats of timidity, arguing that the Klan "should be bluntly and fearlessly designated in the fight against it...."[63]

Closer to home, however, Maconites saw the Klan become a political issue nine months earlier, as the trials of C. A. Yarbrough were ending. On 1 October, just days after the dentist's second trial ended with a hung jury, Bibb County Sheriff Jim Hicks fired two of his deputies, Romas Raley and Homer Hardison, from his staff. Claiming that the deputies had been uncooperative with him in the department's flogging investigations, Hicks also asked the county commission to fire motorcycle officer Charles L. Bowden. Another officer, Lucius G. Holmes, resigned his position rather than being fired. A fourth officer, Wilse Birdsong, was relieved of duty some days earlier, because of an outburst during the Yarbrough trial. Hicks did not indicate whether the dismissed officers had any Klan connections. Bowden, however, did tell reporters that he had once been a member, but had withdrawn.[64]

Reviewing the cases of Bowden and Birdsong, the county commission voted three to one to support the sheriff's decisions by suspending the officers. Hicks told the commissioners that he had dismissed the men not because they were Klansmen, but because they caused friction in the office. He backed up this claim by indicating that two other deputies who had been Klansmen were being retained. Hicks also complained that the officers' refusal to tend to the investigation necessitated that the department utilize the aid of M. O. Dunning and two other Klan investigators. Without them, Hicks admitted, "I could not have made progress in the flogging cases." For his part, Dunning verified Hicks's version of the events, telling the commissioners that he had revealed to the sheriff the identities of Klan members on his staff. This decision, he told them, was part of the Georgia Klan's efforts to clean up its own house. The commission suspended the men until an investigative committee recommended their reinstatement. Contradicting Hicks's authority, the county commission rehired the deputies.[65]

Hicks, however, was up for reelection with the primary scheduled for 14 February 1924, and faced strong opposition from Julian Peacock, who had the backing of the Klan. W. T. Anderson and the *Telegraph* endorsed Hicks, calling his department "one agency of the law not subsidized by the Invisible Government."[66] During the heated campaign, Hicks and Peacock made an emotional appearance before the League of

Women Voters in the election since women had gained the right to vote. Speaking to more than 200 in attendance, Hicks concluded his speech with a spirited defense of his record. Referring the crowd to endorsements by the Reverends Walter Anthony and William Russell Owen, the most prominent Methodist and Baptist pastors in the city, "Ask any one of them," Hicks challenged the audience, "and they'll tell you that Jim Hicks is doing his duty."

When one woman, an obvious opponent, called out, "Why don't you get some references from Rum Runner's Row?" Hicks recognized her as the wife of one of those he had arrested in a flogging case, and switched to the subject of the floggings. He happily acknowledged prosecuting Yarbrough, denouncing the jury's decision to convict Frank Alexander, while acquitting the leader. "It's a shame to convict that man," he asserted, "and let Dr. Yarbrough ride through the streets of Macon in a fine automobile, knowing as much about him as I do." He then implied that he had evidence of Yarbrough's sordid efforts to seduce a girl. "Yes, and I fired some deputies. Every one of them was a member of the Klan," he then announced, contradicting his earlier remarks to the county commission. Claiming he no longer employed any Klansmen in his department and never would again, he denounced the Invisible Empire: "They are a dirty set of cowards, those men who would attempt to take the law in their own hands…. I don't want the Ku Klux or the Ku Klux women to vote for me."

Responding to the league's questionnaire, Hicks categorically asserted he was not and never had been a member of the Klan, adding, "Everybody knows that the leaders of the Klan in Bibb County, including all members of the whipping gang, are now and have been for weeks actively at work to defeat me for sheriff." He said he expected not to receive any support from the Klan, saying, "As a matter of fact, everybody tells me that the Klan is fighting me. If Mr. Peacock wins, Dr. Yarbrough will have absolute control of the sheriff's office."

For his part, Peacock denied he was presently a member of the Klan, but admitted he had been a charter member of the Macon Klan when it was established in 1919. He later decided the Empire's program went beyond the mere preservation of the Southern heritage and white supremacy and never attended another meeting. He also acknowledged that some Klan members had publicly announced intentions to vote for Peacock.[67]

As Maconites went to the polls on 14 February, the Klan continued its campaigning for Peacock, registering its objections to the Democratic executive committee's decision to count all county votes at city hall. Their efforts were of no avail, as Hicks defeated Peacock by 680 votes. After the election, in which Roy W. Moore was re-elected as solicitor, Anderson editorialized that while Peacock was "an admirable fellow," many Maconites were nervous about his backing by the Klan. Moreover, he wrote, "officers who fly in the face of an organized minority…in doing their duty fearlessly and rightly, deserved to be rewarded, and not punished, and it certainly would have been construed as punishment if either Hicks the Sheriff or Moore the Solicitor had been defeated."[68]

Later that year, during statewide and national election campaigns the League of Women Voters submitted another questionnaire, which included queries about the Klan, to all candidates. Some of them, like A. W. Graves, a candidate for the state legislature objected to the questionnaire in general, while others objected specifically to the question on the Klan. W. T. Anderson editorially advised all the candidates to answer the questionnaire as fully as possible, so as to eliminate the Klan as an issue. Nevertheless, the issue remained significant in the 1924 elections.[69]

Klan influence became a central issue for most candidates throughout the state, and because of the flogging cases of the previous year, especially important in Macon. That issue intruded most notably into the race for US representative of the Sixth Congressional District between Ben J. Fowler and Samuel Rutherford. In September the Klan issue dominated a Fowler rally, as J. Ellsworth Hall roundly criticized Fowler's opponent Samuel Rutherford for refusing to give his opinion of the Klan. From such refusal Hall inferred that Rutherford was either a Klansman or a candidate backed by the Klan. He told the audience, "The Klan tried to beat Jim Hicks and Roy Moore but failed. Now they want to elect a county commissioner, an executive committee, and a congressman. It is just as dangerous now as it was then. The people of Bibb County next Wednesday will determine whether we will deliver the last blow to this political organization." Also denouncing Rutherford's silence was prominent Methodist church worker Louise C. Harrold, who judged Rutherford as "either ashamed, afraid, or ignorant." In another Fowler rally a few days later, Macon attorney Harry S. Strozier called Rutherford a "pussyfoot candidate" for having evaded questions regarding the Klan, saying "his answer has been to the effect that he didn't think he was under obligation to answer. He is the Klan candidate for Congress and does not dare come out and say that he isn't."[70]

Just before election day, the Rutherford campaign bought a half-page advertisement in the *Macon Telegraph* charging that Fowler had sought the support of C. A. Yarbrough. Citing an exchange of telegrams between L. S. Fowler, the candidate's brother, and Yarbrough. The ad explained that "the conversation referred to…was an effort on the part of Mr. L. S. Fowler to secure the support of the Klan." The notice concluded with a challenge: "Mr. Fowler be sincere and fair with the voters of your District!" Fowler labeled the charge "an infamous and malicious lie." In its own advertisement the Fowler campaign replied that "if Mr. Rutherford's Committee has the telegrams in hand, they have had opportunity since 15 August, to submit these telegrams to the voters.… [T]his cowardly attack was withheld until this last hour in the hope that I…would not have opportunity to make reply." In a final statement before the election, Rutherford specifically denied that he was a member of the Klan.[71] Fowler, the candidate from Bibb County, had made the Klan the central issue of the campaign and pressed it vigorously. The tactic failed to connect with the voters, however, as Rutherford, a resident of Forsyth in Monroe County, won easily. In spite of being viewed as the Klan candidate, or perhaps because of it, Rutherford carried every county in the district, including Fowler's home county of Bibb, where he polled 1,914 votes to Fowler's 1,686.[72]

Another race in which the Klan became a factor was the US Senate campaign between Thomas Hardwick and the incumbent Senator William J. Harris. Although a former senator and governor, Hardwick was overwhelmingly defeated by his Klan-backed opponent. In Bibb County, Harris took 2,685 votes to Hardwick's 930. Hardwick had cozied up to the Klan in his victorious 1920 gubernatorial race, but reversed his field while in office. Calling on the Klan to give up both its masks and its violence, Hardwick was defeated in his 1922 re-election efforts, trailing the Klan-supported Clifford M. Walker by more than 37,000 votes. Now in his run for the Senate, Hardwick became a crusader against the Klan and its stooge, William J. Harris. In the last days of the race he circulated materials claiming Harris to be not only supported by the Invisible Empire, but also a member. Harris denied ever having been a member or affiliated with it in any way. The crucial issue, however, was not Harris' support of the Klan, but its undeniable support of him and its desire to retaliate against Hardwick. Thus in analyzing the outcome of the race, journalist John W. Hammond claimed that from start to finish the Klan had actively campaigned for Harris. His sweeping victory, Hammond argued, "is an equally sweeping Klan victory in Georgia."[73]

One other race in Georgia revealed the power of the political Klan in 1924—the re-election campaign of Governor Clifford M. Walker. A Baptist lawyer from Monroe, Walker served as a trustee of both of the state's Baptist colleges, Mercer University and Shorter College in Rome. After being mayor of his hometown and solicitor general of the Western Circuit from 1909 to 1913, he was elected state attorney general in 1915. Five years later Walker lost a run for governor, although he outpolled his opponent Thomas Hardwick in Bibb County.[74] In 1922, with strong Klan support he defeated Hardwick, foiling the incumbent's re-election hopes. During the campaign Klan leaders like the Reverend Caleb Ridley made a number of speeches indicating Walker was acceptable and strongly denounced Hardwick as a turncoat. This time, however, he trailed Hardwick in Bibb County by a vote of 2,078 to 1,845.[75]

Once in the governor's office, he openly appealed to those who had put him the governor's office, speaking at a meeting of the Klan in Macon's Piedmont Hotel in November 1923. In the midst of Macon's prosecution of Yarbrough in the flogging cases, Walker called on the Knights to help him put his tax reform plan through the legislature.[76] Then in 1924, the preeminent "Year of the Klan" in national and state politics, the *Columbus Enquirer-Sun* reported that Walker secretly gone to Kansas City to speak to a national meeting of Klan officials, where he reportedly made derogatory remarks about Catholics and Jews. At first, Walker denied the allegations, saying he had been on vacation in Philadelphia at the time. Eventually, he was forced to admit that he had indeed spoken at the Kansas City affair, but he continued to deny his alleged anti-Catholic and anti-Semitic statements. He said he had nothing for which to apologize and would gladly give the same speech before any other group, including Catholics and Jews. He also said he was no longer sure of his membership standing.[77]

Responding to the revelations, the *Macon Telegraph* came to the defense of Walker, noting that despite his reputed Klan affiliation, he had in public speeches pled "with remarkable earnestness and manifest sincerity for the removing of prejudice and for good relationships among all classes of society." Anderson explained that he had alternately endorsed Hardwick and Walker at different times. He wrote: "So long as the Klan was responsible for the whipping of people and placed itself in the attitude of substituting itself for the Government, *The Telegraph* saw in it a dangerous menace and boldly opposed it and all of its masked methods. Since the Klan has been behaving itself and gives evidences of an improved point of view and attitude, there is not…the same danger in it…."[78] In another editorial, he focused more directly on Walker, writing:

> While Governor Walker might never have been Governor if it had been known that he was a Klansman and that he would appear before a klonvocation in Kansas City while we thought he was taking a vacation in Philadelphia, the Klan has so improved under somebody's influence, both in the things it says and in the things it has stopped doing, that Governor Walker may have rendered a great service to the Klan directly and to society generally by his counsel and influence. Anyway, the people of Georgia should get behind his program for a better day in Georgia just as heartily as if he had never been inside Klan ranks.[79]

In stark contrast to the *Telegraph's* editorial position on the issue, the *Athens Banner-Herald* withdrew support from Walker as result of the revelations of his Klan membership, pointedly commenting that "no honest man can served an invisible empire and the State of Georgia at the same time…. The American people are not in favor of any secretly controlled government, whether by the corporations, or oil interests, or the Ku Klux Klan."[80]

The revelation of Klan membership, however, hardly weakened Walker's chances of returning to the governor's office for a second term, as he ran unopposed in both the Democratic primary and the general election. There was little opposition even in Macon, which had voted for his opponent in his previous run. Walker received virtually all of Macon's votes for governor in 1924. How many of these voters were Klan members or sympathizers is unclear, of course, but four years later E. Y. Clarke, leader of the Georgia Klan, claimed to have over a thousand fellow members in Bibb County alone.[81]

Thus, Macon's record during 1924, the Year of the Political Klan, was mixed. Clearly, the influence of the Empire dominated the elections, from the national to the local scenes. Issues other than Klan influence on candidates obviously helped determine voting patterns. While the *Macon Telegraph* denounced the Klan's violence, had strongly advocated an anti-Klan plank in the Democratic Party platform, and supported Jim Hicks for Bibb County Sheriff, it also continued to support Governor Clifford Walker despite his Klan affiliation. As to the voice of the people at the polls, Maconites and Bibb Countians supported "Klan candidates" Samuel Rutherford, Senator William J. Harris, and the governor, while they strongly supported anti-Klan Sheriff Jim Hicks.

On the *Telegraph's* editorial page there appeared no letters from the people, white or black, raising their voices to protest the power of the Klan in Georgia or Macon's politics. But on primary election day, one lone letter from Alonzo A. Holt seemed to capture the electoral futility of black Maconites. Calling on black voters not to restrict themselves to one party, he criticized the Republican Party for not making "some practical provision to aid the freedmen in gaining economic independence." Likening the black voter to "a flock of sheep" for continuing its loyalty to the party of Lincoln even though "it would gladly get rid of him [the Negro] if it could flirt with the White South." Turning his sights on the Democrats, Holt believed a better name for them would be the "Negrophobic Party," adding: "its attitude to us is just the opposite of what its name signifies.... [Yet] the so-called Democratic Party possesses one admirable trait that the Republican Party hasn't; that trait is frankness of expression. It declares itself a white man's party; it does not want the Negro's vote."[82] In such a context, it is no surprise that black voters in Macon, such as there were, had little from which to choose.

4

The Beginnings of Interracialism

With good reason has historian Dan T. Carter characterized the 1930s and '40s as a turning point, if not a watershed, in the age of segregation. The Great Depression, of course, became a watershed in its own right, shaping the psyche of a generation of Americans and hitting the South particularly hard. In 1937 the region's per capita income of $314 was roughly half that of the rest of the country, and a year later President Franklin D. Roosevelt called the South "the nation's number one economic problem." Roosevelt's efforts to address the ravages of the Depression became a watershed in the nation's political and economic history. The New Deal marked the most important new development in the evolution of government in American life. The size and role of the federal government were greatly enlarged by New Deal liberalism, as the administration's interaction with the economy reduced pure laissez-faire capitalism to a fond memory among the business elite, most of the Republican Party, and a number of conservative Democrats. Despite its mixed reviews on race matters, the Roosevelt administration and its policies slowly began to attract African Americans from the party of Lincoln. Between the 1930s and the mid-1960s, 90 percent of black voters would gravitate to the Democratic Party.[1]

In Macon the 1930s also marked the beginnings of interracial efforts to soften the blows of Jim Crow. Whites and blacks in this decade cautiously began to challenge warnings about "race mixing" to work together to alleviate the harsher aspects of segregation. In instigating the process that eventually accelerated the civil rights movement, these became the first successful efforts to bridge the unutterable separation between white and black Maconites. This interracialism launched both indigenous and transplanted efforts among whites and blacks to take timid half steps toward racial justice. Certain of these cooperative efforts, conducted mostly by Christian denominations, had "made in Macon" stamped on them, while others were imported to Macon from earlier regional organizations of racial uplift. Chief among these organizations were the Commission on Interracial Cooperation (CIC), founded in the wake of Red Summer by Atlanta Methodist minister Will W. Alexander and the spin-off Association of Southern Women for the Prevention of Lynching (ASWPL), founded by Jessie Daniel Ames in 1930.

Interracial work between whites and blacks in Macon took place against the backdrop of political reaction in Georgia against Roosevelt and the New Deal. Racially progressive whites working with African Americans were encouraged by Roosevelt's policies, and especially the sympathetic ear of First Lady Eleanor Roosevelt. At the same time, they worked within a state over which champion race-baiter Governor Eugene Talmadge presided. Linked with the Klan and frequently warning of a "Nigra takeover," Talmadge and his followers, who elected him twice in the '30s and again in the 1940s, made Georgia a dangerous place for any activity that could easily be mischaracterized as "race mixing."[2] This chapter looks at the rise of interracial activities in Macon during the Depression era and the local and state political milieu that made interracial activities difficult and sometimes dangerous.

THE DEPRESSION AND RACIAL DISCRIMINATION

The Depression exacerbated an already tenuous economic picture for the South. In the mid-1920s the boll weevil devastated the entire region's cotton production. One Georgia county saw production plummet from 20,000 bales in 1919 to 333 in 1922. With its eleven textile mills, Macon was suffering even before the market crashed in 1929. Annual income of Southern farmers fell from $206 during the 1920s to a low of $83 during the Depression. As the farm economy weakened, food became scarcer in Macon. Farmers made little profit selling their harvests and planted only enough to feed their families. As national unemployment hit a high of 24.9 percent in 1933, soup kitchens sprung up around town and their lines steadily lengthened.[3]

By 1930 Afro-Maconites numbered 32,906, almost 43 percent of the total Bibb County population of 77,042. Unemployment in the county increased during the decade for both whites and blacks, though growth in black joblessness outpaced that for whites by a factor of almost 2.5. In 1940, 7.29 percent of whites in Bibb County were unemployed, compared with 12.85 percent of blacks. With the number of black owned or operated farms falling by 37.1 percent between 1930 and 1940, compared to only 7.2 percent among whites, black farmers in Bibb County lost their farms during the 1930s at a rate of more than five times that of white farmers.[4]

In the face of such difficulties, blacks received little help from New Deal legislation. The reduction in acreage mandated by the Agricultural Adjustment Act further reduced the meager income of many Georgia tenant farmers, driving them to day labor or unemployment. The codes of the National Recovery Act required higher wage scales and led many businesses to eliminate marginal workers. Not surprisingly, blacks were the first to be displaced. New Deal programs thus, as historian Paul Bolster argued, "produced frustration and a will to dissent" among African Americans.[5]

Throughout the South this increasing competition for jobs made scarcer by the economic upheaval escalated racial tensions. As Clark H. Foreman, a field agent for the Julius Rosenwald Fund and from 1938 to 1967 president of the Southern Conference for Human Welfare, described a situation in which jobs formerly given to blacks were during the Depression being taken by whites. White resentment over having to do "nigger jobs" or seeing blacks with jobs that could have been held by other whites sparked new racial animosities. Foreman wrote, "When you have unemployment in the South, you have race trouble, for it is among the unemployed element, comprising large numbers of under-privileged white unskilled labor in economic competition with Negroes, that race prejudices are most prevalent and most easily stirred."[6]

One group that was stirred up was called the American Order of Fascisti or the "Black Shirts," an American spin-off of Mussolini's organization that drew some 40,000 members in Georgia, with branches in Atlanta, Macon, Savannah, and Columbus.[7] In September 1930, however, in a hint of the interracial efforts that would develop during the decade, an organization of Afro-Maconites named the Forum called a mass meeting at Stewart's Chapel AME Church to discuss employment and other matters affecting them. The audience passed a resolution thanking prominent whites in Macon who had registered their opposition to the Black Shirts:

> Whereas, certain organized forces in Georgia have begun a movement to stir up race hatred and prejudice and oust the men of our race from all gainful employment in the municipalities of this state and elsewhere, making the next a hard winter for the Negroes of Georgia and have him out of every job a white man would care to hold in every city, and town and village in the state, by the middle of next summer; and.... Whereas, many of our white friends in Macon promptly accepted the challenge and have been unremitting in their efforts to make constructive sentiment favorable to us in this present crisis...

The resolution then thanked W. T. Anderson, various civic clubs, and the churches for their "courageous and humanitarian stand...in behalf of our race in this crisis...."[8]

Beyond the economic difficulties of both black and white Maconites, a pair of outsiders observed the troubling racial realities of the city. Studying white-black inequities in education and city services in 1934, Jesse O. Thomas, the Southern field secretary of the National Urban League, concluded that Macon was "one of the most backward cities in the whole South." Five years later, Ila Romola Sircar, associate general secretary of the Student Christian Movement in India, spent several days in Macon as part of a nationwide study of rural and education programs. While in Middle Georgia, she visited projects of the National Youth Administration and the Farm Security Administration. She resigned herself to riding in black sections on trains and buses, and managed only with great difficulty to book a room in a white Macon hotel. Comparing Southern segregation with India's caste system, she told reporters that "more progress has been made in our caste system in the last 20 years than America has made in her racial problem in the past 400 years." She pointed out that the Indian caste system had grown from a race problem similar to that in the South, and advised that giving blacks equal rights would help them develop a race consciousness. "If Negroes lose their slavish mentality and take pride in their race and heritage," she suggested, "they probably would start letting their hair kink up naturally instead of trying to straighten it to emulate the white race." Amazed at Americans' fear of racial intermarriage, he said, "A Negro proud of his own heritage would not want to marry into the white race."[9]

Further progress toward racial equality in Macon and the South would have to wait three or four more decades, however, as the Depression era saw continued discrimination against blacks. While the beginnings of interracial cooperation slowly materialized during the 1930s, there was still plenty of evidence of tension and continued separation. When Mayor G. Glen Toole told a gathering of the junior chamber of commerce that "the Negro is the greatest curse in the community today," blacks rescinded their invitation to the mayor to speak to them regarding black Sunday Schools at a "Harvest Drive." Angered by the insult, white Methodist pastor Walter Anthony called the mayor's comment a "weird and grotesque example of crooked thinking."[10]

Black Maconites also suffered more specific discrimination, especially in voting. In 1920, making up 30.5 percent of Bibb County's registered voters, blacks voted in larger numbers in Macon than in most other Georgia cities. Registrars, however, soon redoubled their disfranchising efforts and by the mid-1940s had managed to decrease black voting to 9.3 percent. In November 1933, the black General Missionary Baptist Convention met in Macon, where delegates adopted a report complaining that "the church has been too much divorced from politics, so that we have today too many demagogues in our legislatures and not enough statesmen." Thus, the Baptists continued, "our people should be taught how to vote, when to vote, and for whom to vote." Still, too few blacks in Macon managed to get on the voter registration lists. On one occasion in the 1930s, a black minister, the Reverend M. E. Moon, sought out a liberal white attorney to take a case involving police brutality. Anticipating a future run for public office, the attorney declined to take the case because blacks did not vote in sufficient numbers.[11]

Reasons for this dearth of black voters were not difficult to ascertain. White registrars exercised inordinate authority to choose who could register. In 1939, a Bibb County tax collector admitted to an interviewer that he asked potential black voters to explain the Supreme Court jurisdiction clause of the Constitution, bragging, "I can keep the president of the United States from registering in Macon if I want to."

That same year H. R. Harris, manager of the Georgia Baptist College, spoke to members of a club in the student activity building at Mercer about the problem of voting among blacks. Un-American groups, he complained, had the right to vote, but "the Negro remains disfranchised." He blamed African Americans' uninterest in voting on poor educational facilities, noting that Bibb County spent more money educating white students than educating blacks. Such conditions gave blacks "little incentive to vote in the South." Still, he argued, blacks were preparing themselves for the opportunity to vote when it came.[12]

A white speaker hit on a similar theme when Buford Boone, managing editor of the *Macon Telegraph,* addressed a Mercer forum on "The Southern Negro in Politics." Boone pointed out the federal government's doctrine that "all men are created free and equal and that no one's right to vote shall be abridged by, among other things, color." With this he contrasted the white primary among Democrats, designed to exclude blacks from the only elections of any consequence in the one-party South. Boone told his audience that the solution of the Negro problem lay "in raising the level of the Negro through recognition of his rights of suffrage," as well as, Boone added significantly, "the admission that he deserves better opportunities."[13]

Discrimination in medical care gave Afro-Maconites additional reason for concern, especially when a black Bibb County farmer named Albert Glover was severely injured when a car crashed into his wagon on Forsyth Road. Taken home by a friend, he was later examined by county physician Dr. Herring Winship, who found Glover able to move only his right arm and leg with great difficulty and his left arm and leg not at all. Winship's request that Glover be admitted to the Macon Hospital was rejected by hospital superintendent Howard V. Williams, who concluded Glover was not sufficiently hurt to be considered "a hospital case." Angered by this decision, Winship took the case before a meeting of the Bibb County Commissioners. Calling for Glover to be admitted, he told the commissioners, "I believe he will die if he is left where he is." The occasion induced another visit by Williams, who commented that Glover was "getting along alright," adding, "if we took in everybody with a sprained shoulder, the hospital would have to be three times as big as it is."[14]

Within a few years this and similar incidents led the Macon Hospital to establish a separate wing for black patients. While this move increased black access to health care, the medical situation for blacks remained tenuous and in some ways the Jim Crow wall was buttressed. Later, Dr. C. W. Dyer, administrator of Macon's black St. Luke's Hospital, wrote a letter to the *Telegraph* suggesting that black doctors and nurses were not getting sufficient training at the Macon Hospital's Negro wing. As a solution, he called on the city to enlarge and take over the funding of Saint Luke's Hospital, while leaving control of it in the hands of Macon's black citizens. Dyer's letter, labeled "The Negro in Macon," ranged beyond discrimination in medical care to address other concerns. Believing that "the South is a great place for blacks," Dyer informed white readers that blacks would find it ideal if the South would address inadequate public education and "justice in the courts."[15]

Such injustice has of course continued over the decades, and Macon blacks in the 1930s also experienced discriminatory treatment by local law enforcement agencies. For example, on 14 January 1933, police raided several black dance halls under "dive and gaming" ordinances passed the previous summer. In what one detective called the largest raid in his recollection, a squad of plainclothes officers led by Chief Detective T. E. Garrett raided a dance hall on Broadway and Hawthorne streets, arresting owner Son Wright for operating a dive and 103 patrons for loitering in a dive. Police Chief Ben T. Watkins had received several complaints about the noise produced by Wright's dances, and used four patrol wagons and all available police cars to transport the "chattering Negroes" to headquarters. On the same afternoon and evening police also raided several other halls, including one owned by C. H. Douglass where eighteen persons were arrested for assembling for purposes of gaming. In all, some 140 blacks were incarcerated in the incidents.[16]

In the following days *Macon Telegraph* publisher W. T. Anderson wrote to Mayor Glen Toole to protest the wholesale arrests. Anderson and other spokespersons from the black community complained that patrons who were not drunk or disorderly or committing any other crime were indiscriminately apprehended in the mass arrests. Such persons, they argued, should be allowed to participate in social events without police interference or intimidation. Toole replied to Anderson that whiskey was reportedly served, in violation of federal prohibition policy, and that Wright had been repeatedly warned to keep order. He added, "I have much sympathy for the Negro, and you may rest assured that I will always see…that they will have the best of the breaks." Toole, Recorder Court Judge M. Felton Hatcher, and Police Chief Watkins conferred with Anderson early in the week, and negotiated the blacks' release after four days in jail. Eventually Hatcher dismissed the charges on all but two of the defendants, but warned the others: "It must be pretty bad if Negroes will call on officers to report complaints on their own race in a matter like this. If you are brought before me again on charges like these, it won't be this way next time."[17]

Wholesale arrests subsided for a while, but later in the decade police began another campaign in which various black homes or "dives" were raided in May 1938. This flare-up saw some fifty black Maconites arrested for drunkenness, public nuisance, or for operating illicit dives.[18] The crusade continued into 1939, when police arrested sixteen-year-old Sara Scott for disorderly conduct and resisting arrest. On 8 February Officer A. J. Millirons ordered a number of black teens to stop roller skating on the Main Street sidewalks. When she refused to take off her skates in accordance with his order, Millirons warned Scott that if she did not comply he would be forced to take her before a judge. "Damn the judge and damn you," came the girl's impertinent reply, followed by her efforts to slap and kick the officer. Claiming to be defending himself, Millirons later admitted striking her, but only after her attacks had begun. Brought to trial on 14 March, Scott claimed the officer had grabbed her and twisted her arm when she could not get her skates off quickly enough. According to her testimony, her resistance to his man-handling led the officer to hit her in the nose. Recorder's Court Judge George M. Nottingham found Scott guilty, but suspended her sentence.[19]

Blacks in Macon became convinced that both the arrest and conviction were unjust. Prominent funeral director Frank J. Hutchings wrote the *Telegraph* calling on the "superior race" to show its supposed superiority by treating the "inferior race" with fairness and justice. Doubting that the 108-pound girl would attack a large, armed police officer without provocation, Hutchings questioned the veracity of the frequent claim that white southerners were blacks' only friends: "We might tell ourselves it is true, but the burden of proof rests with the white man, as actions speak louder than words."[20]

Vouching for Scott's character, Ballard High School assistant principal Lewis H. Mounts told readers of the *Telegraph,* "No member of the family gave any trouble beyond slight matters of normal mischief, nor ever constituted a deportment problem." He further expressed doubts about the negative picture of his former student presented by the prosecution, adding: "I am fully convinced that she would have given no trouble whatsoever if dealt with in any proper fashion. I have had her daily as a pupil in my classroom for over two and a half years and have never found any need of unusual measures for her control. I must state in conclusion that I know personally that serious damage has been done to the Macon Negro's confidence in the white man's justice, and that there is grave need that something be done to retrieve the loss." Singling out of blacks in this manner, Mounts asserted, had hurt black-white relations in Macon. Despite progress accomplished by burgeoning interracial cooperation, the Scott incident and others like it had "done much to undo the work of past years so far as faith in the Southern white man's sense of fair play is concerned."[21]

Discriminatory practices on the local scene, however, were not the only items on a list of factors inhibiting interracial progress in Macon. The political atmosphere across Georgia in the 1930s was poisoned, especially for whites and blacks committed to interracial cooperation, by the state's flamboyant governor, Eugene Talmadge. His demagoguery and race-baiting accusations against Roosevelt's New Deal made interracialists feel particularly unwelcome in Talmadge country.

EUGENE TALMADGE AND THE RACIST RESISTANCE

Born 15 miles north of Macon on a plantation near Forsyth, Eugene Talmadge attended the University of Georgia, practiced law in Atlanta for a year, eventually marrying and settling on a farm in Telfair County. First elected to public office as a state representative in 1920, he rode his strong rural appeal to three terms as commissioner of agriculture beginning in 1926 and to the governorship in 1932. His enthusiastic ruralism and his colorful rhetoric made him one of the most popular politicians in Georgia history. As the state's chief executive Talmadge accepted federal largesse, but came to bitterly oppose Roosevelt's New

Deal for enlarging the federal bureaucracy and its willingness to incur government debt.[22]

By 1935 the governor's distaste for Roosevelt had grown such that Talmadge remarked that "the next president we should have should be able to walk a two-by-four."[23] He also told a gathering of Kiwanis and Rotary Clubs in Rome, Georgia, that the evils of communism were mild compared to the shortcomings of the New Deal. "I've never seen anything in Communism as bad as the New Deal," he said, "and there are things in Communism that are revolting." Hinting that he might challenge FDR for the Democratic nomination, he predicted that 1936 presidential contest would be a matter of "Americanism vs. Communism."[24] By the mid-1930s such associations between Roosevelt or the New Deal with Communism especially resonated with white Southerners. The 1931 Scottsboro Case, handled by the Communist Party's International Defense League, had caused many whites to discern Communist intrigue in even the most timid efforts toward racial equality. Opponents of interracial cooperation now had an additional epithet to fling at racial do-gooders; they were Communists as well as "nigger-lovers."

Just as significantly, elements of the Roosevelt administration also challenged the views of Talmadge's rural constituency, which had less contact with education and educated blacks than city folk and were thereby more susceptible to racial appeals. Besides the administration's modest commitments to racial change, illustrated by a comparatively strong record of appointing African Americans, the activities of Eleanor Roosevelt particularly galled Southerners like Talmadge. The First Lady had publicly supported the Dyer anti-lynching bill in Congress, and often advocated racial equality in many speeches before civic groups. Her acquaintance with black women's groups enabled her to recommend Mary McLeod Bethune to FDR's "black cabinet." She also became friends with Atlanta Methodist leader Dorothy Tilly, a graduate of Macon's Wesleyan College who spearheaded the work of the Association of Southern Women for the Prevention of Lynching and the Commission on Interracial Cooperation in Georgia.[25] Thus Talmadge and many white Southerners eventually came to suspect that Eleanor's husband might utilize his big government mentality to intrude into states' rights on behalf of his meddlesome wife's pet project.

Near the end of 1935, Talmadge traveled to New York to make a radio speech called "Georgia Answers Roosevelt," part of a national effort to deny Roosevelt a second term. In collaboration with wealthy Texas oil man, John Henry Kirby, and author Thomas Dixon, among others, Talmadge formed an organization called the Southern Committee to Uphold the Constitution and made plans to launch the national effort with a "Grass Roots Convention" in Macon.[26] The governor took pains to deny he was seeking to control the convention or to be nominated to run against FDR, but most observers nevertheless saw the meeting as a test of his strength for a possible challenge to the president. As part of a national network, local radio station WMAZ agreed to broadcast Talmadge's speech on 29 January, the opening day of the convention.[27] While the governor fended off questions about a possible presidential run, he also predicted FDR would lose the Democratic nomination that summer. His colleague John Henry Kirby arrived in Macon telling reporters that the anti-Roosevelt efforts would be futile unless someone like Talmadge managed to get his name on preferential primary ballots. If Talmadge were to be selected, Kirby asserted, he was likely to run a strong campaign.[28]

In the days before the meeting, the *Telegraph* replied to requests to get off the fence regarding Talmadge's machinations. Committing themselves, the editors "preferred not to say anything that would appear to be unduly critical of friends within our gates." They nonetheless pointed out the paper's disagreements with FDR. They also scored Senator Richard B. Russell's overly enthusiastic defense of the New Deal. On Talmadge's criticisms, the *Telegraph* held that "practically all of [the governor's] charges against Roosevelt for deserting the Democratic platform and going over to the Socialists and Communists are true." Though rejecting the president's "soak the rich" campaign theme, the editors argued that some of the New Deal programs deserved to survive. Thus, despite associating the New Deal with socialism and communism, the paper oddly declared:

> We want the Democrats re-elected, Roosevelt included.... We want Talmadge to stop running around trying to defeat Roosevelt, and stay home and get Georgia's affairs in order so we can spare him to beat the political life out of "little" Dick

Russell. Roosevelt saved us from one rout and panic and chaos, but he has let brain stormers direct the Government into a hole, and we need as many men as possible like Talmadge with records as to getting out of debt and operating on sound basis.[29]

Also saying his piece as a prelude to the convention, NAACP leader Walter White sent a telegram to Talmadge and Kirby calling on the leaders to declare themselves for black civil rights. Noting that Georgia had violated the Fourteenth and Fifteenth Amendments virtually every day since their ratification, White reminded them: "Disfranchisement, gross discrimination against Negro citizens in apportionment of public moneys for education, violation of constitutional guarantees against illegal search and seizure and suppression of rights of free speech, free assembly and free press, lynching mob violence and other denials of constitutional rights are the rule and not the exception so far as 8,000,000 Negroes are concerned and many white Americans." White concluded by warning that without work to enforce these constitutional rights, the Southern Committee to Uphold the Constitution would prove itself a laughingstock.[30]

The Grass Roots reply to White was unmistakable. Planners greeted the "delegates" with a giant Confederate flag draped behind the platform and an issue of the *Georgia Women's World,* in every seat. Published by the Atlanta-based National Women's Association of the White Race, the magazine pictured Eleanor Roosevelt speaking with a black professor at Howard University. Inside the covers, one article fumed, "Surely no other roamed the country at will as she does.... surely the white women of the nation, at least those of the South, have not shared the cordial comradeship which is so freely bestowed to and among the Negroes of the nation." Another complained about black appointments in the Roosevelt administration. Reading the magazine were some 3,000 partisans, mostly Georgia farmers "united to oppose Negroes, the New Deal and...Karl Marx."[31]

The convention delegates gained permission to enter Talmadge's name on primary ballots, after the governor's speech called on Democrats nationwide to "run that boondoggling crowd out of Washington." In his keynote address, Kirby departed from his prepared text to comment on the importance of the *Georgia Women's World*'s revelatory articles on the Roosevelt's "friendly attitude toward Negroes." Thomas Dixon advised the audience to ignore the NAACP's message, an admonition the convention was pleased to follow. Representing Macon, city attorney E. W. Maynard, chaired local arrangements for the rally and welcomes visitors to Macon. Denouncing the president, Maynard asked, "How can you depend on him to protect this county against Socialism when he is in favor of Socialism? How can you depend on him to protect the rights of the states when he is against states' rights?" Some observers, like Georgia Senator Walter F. George, considered the convention's attendance to be rather small and indicative of strong support for the president in the state. The next day the *Telegraph* analyzed the convention proceedings, registering its qualified support for Roosevelt while predicting his defeat in the general election. "We are for Talmadge for United States Senator, to succeed 'little' Dick Russell," the editors announced, hoping for a new congress that would "keep the Constitution, the Supreme Court, and the country all safe, the President to the contrary notwithstanding."[32]

Macon's general response to Talmadge may be judged by its election results. In 1932 Talmadge received less than 24 percent of the votes in Bibb County, compared to 37 percent two years later in 1934.[33] In these elections, the *Telegraph* voiced its editorial opposition to/support of "the wild man from Sugar Creek." After the Grass Roots Convention, however, while the *Telegraph's* editors remained respectful of the governor's efforts, at least two readers took different perspectives. "A Roosevelt Booster" regarded the convention as a laughingstock, deriding Talmadge with the comment that "every time this clown opens his mouth Mr. Roosevelt gets a vote," adding that as governor Talmadge was "an insult to the voters of Georgia." The following days letters to the editor brought another anonymous comment—indicative of a racially progressive white author who feared racist intimidation enough to avoid signing a name. The writer opined:

> We people of the South have been fortunate in our relations with our Negroes. They did not come here in the first place on their own choice. For years they...made the South the richest spot in the country. During the war they tended the crops and took care of the women and children while their masters were

fighting a war to keep them in slavery. Since the war they have made the best of help on the farms and the best of house servants. They have gotten less and less justice in courts than menials in most countries. They do not try to vote yet pay their taxes and are patriotic.... I think we owe the Negro too great a debt to condemn him because a few of his race have committed the unpardonable crime. I think it is unpardonable in a Governor who will condone the instigation of race prejudice for political purposes or any other cause.[34]

In 1940, Talmadge sought another term as governor after failed U.S. Senate races in 1936 and 1938. Campaigning as what Stephen Tuck has called the "protector of white Georgia," Talmadge made race and the specter of black voting the central issues of his winning campaign. Once back in office, his third term was dominated by his efforts to fire Walter Cocking, dean of education at the University of Georgia, for advocating the racial integration of Georgia's schools. Running for re-election in 1942 against Ellis Arnall, Talmadge again made race and education the central issue of his campaign.[35] Leading up to the primary election, the Georgia State Democratic Committee passed a resolution praising the governor "for his manhood and courage in thus upholding the sacred traditions of this state and the constitution he swore to defend." In the committee discussions, one member said, "I like Negroes. I like 'em in their place. And their place is the cotton field, hoeing and chopping cotton." Regarding support for Talmadge, he added, "In my section you're either for Talmadge or against him. And if you say you're gonna vote against him, we'll ask you whether you're for racial equality, and I can tell you'll have a fight on your hands."[36]

The controversy over racial integration at the University of Georgia spread to the state's other colleges and universities. Talmadge's efforts to dominate the state university system's board of regents eventually led to the loss of accreditation for all the state-sponsored colleges in Georgia and cost him the election. In Bibb County Talmadge received 46 percent of the vote in 1942.[37] The political atmosphere dominated by Talmadge's racist politics, however, guaranteed that anyone in Macon who was involved in interracial work would, indeed, have a fight on his or her hands.

LOCAL ROOTS OF INTERRACIAL COOPERATION

Despite the larger milieu of resistance to racial change in Georgia and the city, blacks and white Maconites worked together to a much greater extent in the 1930s than ever before. Two factors contributed to this birth of interracialism. First, new regional organizations for dealing with racial problems were founded in the post-World War I era. These organizations, most notably the CIC and the ASWPL, established beachheads in a number of Southern cities, including Macon. Making the soil fertile for these interracial organizations in Macon and other cities, however, were cooperative efforts during the Great War, the Depression, and New Deal eras. Such efforts were the second element giving rise to Macon's interracial experiments of the 1930s.

For example, in conjunction with their white counterparts, Afro-Maconites conducted Liberty Bond drives, a War Savings Stamp parade, and Red Cross drives. During the Depression, in the first year of the Roosevelt presidency, the Macon Chamber of Commerce spearheaded the city's campaign to urge businesses to comply with the Blue Eagle Drive of the National Recovery Administration. John L. Morris, head of the local effort, met with black leader Minnie Singleton, to coordinate canvassing of the black sections of the city. Singleton also enlisted the local branch of the National Urban League to participate in the effort. Some 300 citizens fanned out across the city to convince all employers voluntarily to sign a blanket code as a pledge to pay a forty cents an hour minimum wage for a thirty-five hour work week. A second campaign put 800 Maconites to work calling on consumers to patronize only businesses that displayed the Blue Eagle sign and its slogan, "We Do Our Part." Later more than 25,000 participated in a massive NRA parade in Macon.[38]

On at least one occasion during the campaign, Macon blacks held mass meetings at First (black) Baptist Church, where they urged their members to trade only with firms or individuals who not only observed the codes, but were also "giving the Negro a chance to work along with all other people." Along with encouraging such cooperative efforts, however, the leaders also criticized discriminatory administration of the codes and other New Deal projects. For example, H. A. Hunt, principal of the Fort Valley Normal and Industrial School, had called on the New

Deal to become a "Square deal" aiding black relief work projects and lessening the gap between white workers earning ninety cents a day compared to forty cents for black workers. In response a mass meeting led by L. J. May, Dr. C. W. Dyer, A. W. Barrow, Charles H. Douglass, and W. C. Lee adopted a resolution against employers refusing to comply with the codes. Under the law, minimum wage benefits, the resolution asserted, "belong to all wage earners, regardless of race, color or creed.... [T]o deny the Negro equal wages for identical work flouts the program of the administration [and] defeats the great purpose of the NRA."[39]

Macon blacks also volunteered as Red Cross workers in large numbers. In October 1938, for example, black women in Macon formed an auxiliary of the American Red Cross. Mattie Hubbard Jones was elected to chair the auxiliary, and to work closely with Dorothy White, executive secretary of the Macon Red Cross chapter. Meeting at the black section of the Washington Library, White oriented thirty black volunteers to work in "war, disaster, peace, for safety, and other services." They also volunteered to work in campaign a national campaign to fight polio and registered their rejection of communism by participating in a 1938 rally of the American Loyalty League, where a white Catholic priest and two black Protestant ministers warned the audience against communist efforts to recruit black members.[40]

While these activities continued to separate white organizations from their black counterparts, they ran along parallel tracks and showed both whites and blacks in the city that both races were working in similar ways for similar goals. Since blacks worked alongside whites for "white" goals, they also called upon the white community to contribute to their own goals. Chief among these were fund raising campaigns to strengthen certain black institutions.

In fall 1933 Reverend J. H. Gadson, president of the black Baptist Central City College, led a drive to raise funds for capital improvements and an endowment fund to strengthen the school and put it on par with Atlanta University. After a trip to New York in which he induced contributions from the National Baptist Convention, Gadson donated an entire year's salary of $1,800 to the project. That same week he garnered five contributions, including at least one anonymous white Maconite who gave $100 in honor of his two black servants and in memory of his former African-American nurse. While contributions from black church rallies and the annual meeting of the black Georgia Missionary Baptist Convention continued to come in, the turning point in the campaign was the decision of Macon industrialist James H. Porter, head of the school's white advisory board, to pay $5,000 for all the assets of the college. He later turned the college back over to the black Georgia Baptist Convention.[41] When the campaign ended, Frank J. Hutchings, a veteran of the Great War and owner of the Hutchings Funeral Home, wrote a shrewd thank-you note to white Maconites through the *Telegraph* "for showing a Christian spirit in improving the educational facilities of Central City College," which he believed illustrated "a very close bond of friendship" in Macon's black-white relations. Hoping, however, to gain white help on a similar matter, he added: "I am wondering if there isn't some way the same whites cannot be induced, encouraged or implored to say just a few words about the dilapidated, overcrowded 'janitorless' fire traps which we citizens of Macon commonly call the Bibb County Negro Public schools."[42]

In addition to periodic requests that white Macon address inequities in the black public schools, blacks in Macon also sought white help when the Depression hurt the financial base of the privately-funded Ballard Normal School. In February 1933, for the first time in the school's sixty-five year history, Ballard principal Raymond G. von Tobel launched a fund drive to make up for cuts in contributions from its northern benefactor, the Congregationalist Church's American Missionary Association. Hard economic times had reduced Ballard's enrollment from 400 to 215, leading Tobel to write the *Telegraph* to appeal for help. The principal allayed white fears in his assurances that the instruction received at Ballard was safe. Emphasizing a curriculum focused on "manual training" for boys and "domestic arts and science" for girls, Tobel said that the school produced good citizens, asserting, "There is little lawlessness among Ballard students." Noting that Ballard graduates made up 80 percent of the teachers in the black public schools, he assured white Maconites, "Whatever question there may have been…has been answered by the excellent work that the faculty has done in helping to adjust the Negro students to the white viewpoint. The school has served, indeed, a most useful purpose not only in the educational field, but also in the field of race relations." Tobel also recruited George N.

White, a vice-president of the First National Bank to be secretary of the campaign, and Police Chief Ben P. Watkins to help raise funds. Fundraising rallies also included written appeals from Mayor G. Glen Toole and W. T. Anderson. Whites in Macon, however, apparently were not greatly moved to great beneficence, as reports of collection totals at the campaign's end amounted to only $451.80, collected from Ballard students and the African-American churches.[43]

The 1930s also saw efforts of interracial cooperation to improve medical care for Afro-Maconites. Most of the activity centered on St. Luke's Hospital, which began as a clinic treating black patients in 1928, because black physicians were denied access to the wards of the Macon Hospital. On the eighth anniversary of the hospital, administrator C. W. Dyer and other black physicians conducted an open house for both black and white citizens to get acquainted with the facilities. They also invited white surgeons to come and share their knowledge of newer procedures with their black counterparts. Dyer's 250 invitation letters to white Maconites included requests for financial donations, but by the time of the event, only twenty-three contributions had been procured.[44]

The following spring St. Luke's established a plan for affordable hospital insurance at a cost of thirty-five cents a week. As Dyer's brainchild, the plan covered only hospital expenses of twenty-two dollars a week. In one of the first plans of its kind in Georgia, the plan enrolled 400 clients from some 90 black families in its first year. The arrangement trained Macon blacks to look to the hospital in times of illness, contributing to higher cure rates. With his penchant for gently tweaking white sensibilities, Dyer noted, "White people talk about the danger of disease spreading from servants but talking about it is about all they do. We are trying to do what we can to lift the health standards of the Negro race, and a Negro hospital, well supported, together with hospital insurance for those who ordinarily have hospital attention will do something to help us reach that goal."[45]

Dyer's pithy remark may have hit its intended target, because a year later there was some movement in the effort to elevate St. Luke's to full hospital status. In August 1938 Dyer led a group of black leaders to ask the Bibb County Commission to join with the city to sponsor either the building of a new hospital for blacks or for the city or county to take over the privately-run St. Luke's. Aiding their argument with a crucial statistic, Dyer and the others reminded the white leaders that the black death rate in Bibb County was three times that of whites. In addition, he reported that the Macon Hospital's black wings had only twenty-seven beds, a figure later corrected to sixty-two, for a black population of some 32,000. Initially the commissioners referred the matter to the Macon Hospital Commission and the county board of health.[46]

By October the black medical leaders and the Bibb County Medical Society launched a campaign to build a new sixty-bed hospital for blacks, to be staffed by a black staff. Four white doctors lent their vigorous support to the effort. Administrator C. L. Ridley told political leaders that the facilities at Macon Hospital had reached "the end of the row," pointing out that the current situation had been established forty years earlier when Macon had a population of 23,000. Hospital capacity, he argued, was simply inadequate to the current task of caring for a county of some 75,000 potential patients. Joining the argument, was Dr. C. C. Harrold who called on city leaders to help provide a district hospital operated with public funds, from the local to federal level. Harrold sent out letters to the commissioners to meet with all interested parties at the grand jury room of the county courthouse. "We have found that all these groups have been working for the same thing," Harrold explained, "and these letter are to request the entire groups to meet" on 3 November for further discussions. These cooperative efforts successfully led to the incorporation of St. Luke's Hospital in November 1939.[47]

In all these fledgling interracial efforts, usually initiated by black organizations for pragmatic purposes, involved soliciting white financial help to strengthen separate, unequal, and weaker, black institutions in Macon. Or, as in the case of parallel programs during the Great War and Depression, these efforts helped combat the Germans and economic dislocation. In the development of interracialism in Macon, however, they laid the groundwork for cooperative efforts aimed specifically at softening the blows of Jim Crow. In that great struggle, the churches and self-consciously interracial organizations like the Commission Interracial Cooperation (CIC) and the Association of Southern Women for the Prevention of Lynching (ASWPL) would lead the efforts.

INTERRACIAL EFFORTS ON RACIAL ISSUES

One of the earliest interracial religious efforts in twentieth century Macon grew out of the longstanding tradition of Methodism. After Emancipation, Black Methodists in the South were beset with choices. Staying within the Methodist Episcopal Church South with their white co-religionists remained only a short-term possibility, as most blacks wanted church communions where Christian equality and their own African-based religious practices could be honored. Before long, it became clear that they would leave for a black denominational structure. Early on, the only other choice was the African Methodist Episcopal Church, which was rapidly moving into the South and recruiting former slaves who were Methodists. As a Northern-based denomination, however, the AME was considered a dangerous, Yankee influence on Southern blacks. Thus, by 1870 white Methodists helped certain "loyal" (read "uninfluenced by AME radicalism") black members to form a new conference that evolved into the Colored Methodist Episcopal Church. This new denomination, sometimes derided by AMEs as "the slave church," maintained less independence from and thus closer ties with white Methodists in the South. Reflecting this tradition, the educational and missionary convention of the CME met for its annual assembly in Macon on 12 September 1916. Several white ministers from Atlanta's Emory University and from Macon's Wesleyan College and Mulberry Street Methodist Church were invited to instruct their black ministerial brothers. Such Christian mixing, the gathering held, shows that a friendly feeling is in the heart of the best people of both races" and nurtured "the hope of racial adjustment in the South."[48]

By the 1930s some Macon congregations began to participate in Race Relations Day, scheduled for the Sunday nearest to Valentine's Day. But again blacks initiated them. In 1932 the black First Baptist Church observed the occasion by inviting three white laypersons to speak. In the fairly paternalistic affair, Lincoln McConnell, vice president of the City Bank and Trust Company, remarked about the Southern white man's friendship toward blacks. John L. Morris, manager of the chamber of commerce, urged his black audience to educate themselves, advising that "the world pays more for good manners and a pleasing personality than it pays for anything else." Reiterating that theme, Walter P. Jones, superintendent of schools, told the congregation that "education would do more to abolish hatred and prejudice than mere force." Welcoming the white leaders and adding to their comments were black ministers E. G. Thomas of the First Baptist Church and M. A. Fountain, pastor of the Steward Chapel AME Church, as leaders of the ceremonies. Both a black choir and a white quartet provided music for the service. Black-initiated efforts cropped up periodically, beginning late in the decade, such as a 1938 series of services sponsored by a number of black churches held at Macon City Auditorium to express their appreciation to whites who had contributed to the black community in various ways.[49] Still, the white churches stayed away from this sort of activity.

The exceptions to this were Wesleyan College, the Methodist school for women, and the Baptist-run Mercer University. Among white Christians in Macon, these two schools would provide important leadership in more progressive race relations in Macon. Often professors at the schools, and usually at great peril to their permanent employment, surreptitiously subverted their students' racial orthodoxy. An early twentieth-century Mercer professor who became known for both his Christian spirituality and his cross-racial ministry was philosophy professor J. Rufus Moseley. Although resigning his position in 1900 after a short tenure at Mercer, Moseley remained a respected but quirky public figure in Macon. After having a radical spiritual experience that he often likened to Christ's resurrection appearances to his disciples, he left Mercer because of his "radical new developments in religious thought," and wished to avoid involving the school in what, he later wrote, "might prove to be some controversial matters." He then began an unpaid ministry to the poor and imprisoned. From the mid-1920s to his death in 1954, he wrote a regular column for the *Macon Telegraph,* mostly focusing on various spiritual topics. During the heyday of lynching in Macon during the 1920s, an unarmed Moseley once broke up a small lynch mob, who "were filled with fear and fled." Some thirty-five years after his death, an elderly black janitor told a visitor to the *Telegraph* offices everything he could remember about Moseley. "If you had no coat, he would give you his," he reported.[50] Much later, in 1963, when Mercer University drew criticism for the decision to admit black students, its president, Rufus C. Harris received a letter from a supportive alumnus, class of 1911. The Mercerian told Harris: "Your side is sure to win in the final," adding: "This letter is likely due to the seed sown in English class at Mercer where I sat under Professor Carl Steed. He was a great advocate of the rights of the Negro even then, and did not wait until Sunday to say so."[51]

Another way the denominations, working in conjunction with their schools, managed to "integrate" at least the mental universes of their students was by inviting black ministers to speak at meetings of their student organizations. For example, in 1933 the South Georgia Methodist Conference invited W. A. Bell, a black leader of interracial religious work in Atlanta, to speak at its Young People's Assembly at Wesleyan College. Celebrating the work of the black Methodist Paine College in Augusta, Bell told the young audience, "I am confident that your church and mine—and your people and my people—have not caught a glimpse of our possibilities for service—possibilities of wiping out the unnecessary differences between races and building a great Christian brotherhood." Two years later the Mercer Ministerial (Student) Association invited Central City College president J. H. Gadson to address their regular meeting held in Roberts Chapel. In surprisingly frank comments, Gadson told the young ministers that Southern whites were not giving proper attention to the plight of blacks. "Whatever Negroes are in America, whether good or bad, is due to the white man."[52]

Beyond these small-scale efforts, the more significant interracial work in Macon, as in other Southern cities, came from local committees operating under the guidance of the CIC and the ASWPL. The CIC was organized as Will W. Alexander's answer to the post-World War I racial violence. Based in Atlanta, the CIC organized local interracial committees in various towns and cities throughout the South in an effort to bring together the "better element" of both races. In perhaps its most important work, the CIC's interest in social issues and social science evolved into the publication of numerous articles, pamphlets, and books in opposition to lynching. Chief among these was Arthur F. Raper's *The Tragedy of Lynching,* which significantly contributed to reducing such mob violence after its publication in 1933.[53]

The racial ideology and methods of the CIC, however, were a conservative half-step away from the dominant racial views of most white Southerners of the 1920s and '30s. Cautiously progressive, the CIC never challenged segregation itself, taking great pains to avoid appearing to advocate social equality or "race mixing." Generally accepting of "separate but equal," the CIC emphasized its work to insure the equality of the South's racial arrangements, but did not address their separateness. Its chosen pace for racial change was slow and gradual, which often frustrated blacks who participated in CIC activities. Many, such as Morehouse College president Benjamin E. Mays, complained that its white leaders did not encourage frank discussion from black members. At one such meeting, black sociologist E. Franklin Frazier once interrupted a sedate discussion, asking pointedly, "If I am arrested ... what can Dr. Alexander and the rest of you do to see that I get justice and that I am not subjected to the usual brutality of which Negroes are so often the victims?" His question was never answered and, he later reported, "it was found convenient to adjourn."[54] By 1944 the CIC disbanded to make way for its successor organization, the Southern Regional Council.

Founded by Jessie Daniel Ames in 1930, the ASWPL grew out of the Women's Division of the CIC. Ames had been an activist for woman's suffrage until the adoption of the Nineteenth Amendment in 1920, after which she became involved in the Texas affiliate of the CIC. In 1929 she moved to Atlanta to become director of the women's division, but soon became rankled by the male-dominated CIC leadership. Advocating higher profile roles for women in the CIC, she organized the ASWPL as a kind of sister organization to focus attention on the anti-lynching crusade. Numbering some 40,000 members throughout the South, made up mostly of the wives of upper middle-class professionals, the ASWPL pressured local police and politicos to see that no lynchings took place in their communities. In those counties where the ASWPL was most active, lynchings declined from twenty to five a year. Many came to believe that the organization's success had rendered federal anti-lynching legislation unnecessary, leading to the ASWPL's demise in 1940.[55]

By 1936 some forty Macon women, all white, had signed the ASWPL "Declaration and Personal Pledge" to work in the community to create a "new public opinion, which will not condone for any reason whatever acts of mobs or lynchers." Mrs. Marshall J. Ellis led the Macon contingent of ASWPL women and represented Macon on the Executive

Committee of the Georgia Council of the ASWPL. In this capacity she met quarterly with Ames and other CIC members to carry out locally the overall program of the ASWPL. Between May 1936 and early 1937, Ellis began making periodic trips to various Southern venues to participate in workshops on the "American Negro." As part of this campaign to educate whites on the realities of black life, the Macon ASWPL and other branches led their communities in the study of a book entitled, *A Preface to Racial Understanding*. In April 1937 Ellis conferred with Ames and other Georgia leaders on how to build on momentum generated by such study sessions.[56] Apparently serving as the secretary for the Macon branch, Louise Harrold, wife of prominent physician C. C. Harrold corresponded regularly to enlist Jessie Daniel Ames to address various women's church groups in Macon. A member of St. James Episcopal Church, Harrold invited Ames to speak to her Women's Auxiliary on 6 May 1936. Before speaking to some thirty women at St. James, she also gave an address at Wesleyan College.[57]

Over the next several years Ames continued to make contacts in Macon, working either under ASWPL or CIC auspices. One of those contacts was W. Lowry Anderson, a young Methodist minister in Roberta, a town some 30 miles west of Macon. Interested in race matters, Anderson became a part-time field agent for Macon's Committee on Interracial Cooperation, an affiliate of the CIC. In 1941 he sent to Ames a copy of an editorial from the *Macon News* criticizing the ASWPL for supporting the Costigan-Wagner anti-lynching bill in Congress. The column defended the paper's record against lynching as "unequaled by any Southern newspaper," but rejected the bill, believing "that the South was amply able to look after its own affairs. Then in a swipe at the ASWPL and perhaps at Ames's marital status, the commentary concluded, "We cannot, therefore, countenance such calculated propaganda as that released by the Association.... [M]ore men were beaten to death at a recent Detroit auto strike than have been lynched in the South in the last twenty years....for the South's sake, Miss or Mrs. Ames, let's not make this another Scottsboro case."

Along with the clipping, Anderson sent Ames his own commentary: "The editorial, to me, is obviously unfair and based from beginning to end on false assumptions and false interpretations. Knowing something of the prejudicial opinions and petty selfishness of Jack Tarver, it is my guess that he wrote it. And it is like his procedure to try to imply that your letter is an unpatriotic act." Ames in reply suggested that Anderson drop into the *Macon News* offices to "relieve the confusion of the writer…as to my legal title. It seems that he was more disturbed over knowing whether to call me 'Miss' or 'Mrs.' than was necessary."[58]

The most significant interracial work in Macon began in November 1937 when the Reverend George E. Clary, pastor of the Mulberry Street Methodist Church, called together a group white and black Maconites to help build "positive good will in a bi-racial society." This group soon affiliated with the CIC and became known as the Macon District of the Georgia Committee on Interracial Cooperation, sometimes called the Macon Interracial Committee. Before long George Clary began to spearhead CIC activities in Macon, planning the group's first district meeting for 3 November 1938. The state chair of the Georgia Committee invited a number of prominent Maconites to join the group. Blacks who eventually became involved were Dr. C. W. Dyer, Dr. R. S. Smith, Minnie Singleton, Frank Hutchings, and Willis B. Sheftall, along with white members Dice R. Anderson and J. W. Daniel, both of Wesleyan College, attorney Harry S. Strozier, the Reverend Michael M. Warren, pastor of Christ (Episcopal) Church, Louise Harrold, J. Rufus Moseley, and H. N. Massey of Georgia State College for Women.[59]

The 3 November conference focused on "Education in the Macon Area," where Aaron Brown, a professor at nearby Fort Valley State College gave an address titled, "Loopholes in the Education Law." Addressing educational inequities in Georgia according to race, Brown criticized the willingness of the state to tolerate one-teacher schools for black students, citing statistics indicating that one-teacher schools made up 71 percent of all black elementary schools, compared with white elementary schools, only 2 percent of which were one-teacher schools. Brown cited many other inequities: Georgia had state approval for 473 white high schools, compared to 54 black schools. More than 90 percent of white teachers had state certificates, compared to less than 55 percent of black teachers. The average distance from a school was 18 miles for black students, 6 miles for whites, with transportation provided for the white students, but not for the black students. Some 144,000 white students were transported to their schools, compared with less than 2,000 black students. Out of 2,630 buses only 35 served black students, with comparative expenditures for transportation were $188,934 for white children; $16,000 for black children.[60] The committee held three conferences in 1939, at the Mulberry Street Church or at the parish house of Christ (Episcopal) Church, continuing variations on the education theme. Registration for all three meetings totaled thirty-eight whites from eight counties and sixty-six blacks from ten counties.[61]

Between its conference and regular meetings, the Macon Interracial Committee helped develop "racial understanding" through acquaintances and frank discussion. In 1939 the committee hired W. Lowry Anderson as field agent. The disparity between the number of whites and blacks attending the committee's educational conferences suggested a larger Macon community that discouraged interracial work and intimidated many whites who might have attempted it. Lowry Anderson's observations confirm this supposition. "The friendly interest on the part of white people," he noted, "is almost always held in check if not indeed dissipated by fear of group or political disapproval. This is true of your County Commissioners, school teachers, preachers, school superintendents, mayors, businessmen." He criticized as paternalistic the practice of many white organizations that helped pay educational expenses of selected African-American students, but typically felt paralyzed to attempt to change oppressive conditions of his people. Anderson also condemned the air of superiority he had detected in some black members of the Macon Committee for less prosperous members of their race. Anderson believed blacks with such attitudes not only make them aliens from their own people but also make impossible their ever commanding the respect of white friends who would and could do most for their race. Those whites who want Negroes who ask them for cooperation to assume an attitude of superiority toward their fellow blacks are not really interested in equal opportunity.[62]

In 1940 Anderson reported to the Macon Interracial Committee an incident in Roberta. When police beat a young black man, Anderson suggested that the officer's violence had been unnecessary. When police officials and the mayor defended the officer, the young minister addressed the issue of police brutality against blacks and unfair administration of justice in the courts in a sermon. He denounced the police officers assumption that the right to arrest a black man gave him the right to beat him. He told the congregation that "the race prejudice which makes it hard for a colored person to get justice in courts should no longer be tolerated." The sermon received from many in the congregation "a cold and non-committal quietness," and by the end of the year Anderson's bishop had moved him to a new congregation, the Cross Keys Methodist Church in Macon.[63]

By far the most important success of the Macon Interracial Committee in the 1930s was its role in establishing the Booker T. Washington Community Center. The committee combined its work with that of the local Community Chest and the federal Works Progress Administration. In September 1938 the WPA's Recreation Division developed a program to establish black community centers under the sponsorship of local committees in twelve cities. These centers purposed to coordinate welfare programs for blacks, aid local agencies, and to test new WPA programs. After a WPA survey determined the needs of the city, Macon was selected as one of the venues. Bureaucratic tangles slowed the plan's development until spring 1939 when the Macon Interracial Committee discovered other local surveys. These reports coincided with certain statements of needs in the city by the department of health, the board of education, the juvenile court, the city recreation department, and industrial leaders. Chief among these was a report indicating that almost 73 percent of the city's juvenile delinquency came from black children. In addition, young males were responsible for almost 60 percent of black delinquency. The Macon Interracial Committee quickly saw the WPA community center plan as the short-term answer to this cluster of problems and decided to marshal its efforts to make the center a reality.

The committee communicated with WPA officials, along with leaders of the Macon Community Chest, appealing for funding. Eventually, the WPA committed to paying the salary of a director, while the Community Chest put the center in its annual budget. Before the year ended a twenty-four-room house on Broadway was rented, furnished, and prepared for a three-pronged program of health, education, and recreation. The center's health agenda focused on fighting venereal disease and providing general health information to combat fear and superstition regarding local hospital facilities. Its education program emphasized literacy and vocational training, while its recreational

program was designed to counter tendencies toward delinquency by
directing youth toward worthwhile activities.

Willis B. Sheftall, a black Maconite with social work training and
five year's experience, was chosen as the center's first director. In its
first three months of operation the Booker T. Washington Community
Center, as it was eventually named, conducted a camp for 30
underprivileged boys, examined 871 patients through its health clinic,
and formed 3 recreational clubs involving another 36 boys. The Macon
Interracial Council provided leadership, making up the center's first
board of directors. White members included George Clary, George Burt,
executive editor of the *Macon Telegraph,* Methodist laywoman Callie D.
Cutter, Louise Harrold, Reverend C. Logan Landrum, pastor of the
Tattnall Square Presbyterian Church, and Jimmie Wright, a member of
the Junior Chamber of Commerce. Blacks on the board were Matthew L.
Flemming, a local tailor, Frank J. Hutchings, Ruth Hartley Moseley, a
nurse with the Bibb County Board of Heath, Relliford S. Smith, M.D.,
Reverend Douglas L. T. Robinson, pastor of Steward Chapel AME
Church, and Alma Edwina Williams, president of the Progressive
Federated Club. Three board officers, Clary, Landrum, and Harrold were
white, while Hutchings was the only African-American officer.[64]

The Macon Interracial Committee experience acquitted many of the
board members well. Carrying methods and attitudes of the committee
over to the Washington Center board, the members continued to foster a
non-paternalistic ethos of equality and avoided the perception of white
charity for blacks. In its public relations efforts with Macon's white
community, the board emphasized that aiding the black segment would
produce healthy effects for the whole city. A fundraising letter warned
that, if ignored, the problems of the black population could endanger "the
social solemnity of the whole community."[65]

Such strategies suggested the difficulties of interracial work in this
period, as Washington Center leaders feared that most white Maconites
would object to a program aimed almost exclusively at black needs.
WPA guidelines required local funding for the community centers,
making it necessary for board members to tap white support cautiously.
Concerns about attracting white donors to the project, for example, led
the board to scrap its original name, the Interracial Commission Center,
in favor of the safer name of Booker T. Washington.[66]

Booker T. Washington Center, ca. 1940s.
(Courtesy of the Washington Memorial Library.)

These concerns accompanied the decision to seek funding from the Macon Community Chest, which to that date had never contributed to any black organizations. The board thus submitted a proposal filled with statistics regarding the plight of Afro-Maconites. For example, a black Maconite was four times more likely to die of tuberculosis or of murder than a white. Ninety-four percent of Macon's syphilis cases occurred among blacks. Black school attendance was 53 percent of its total enrollment. Blacks were responsible for 66 percent of the city's crime. Nonetheless, the board placed partial blame for this description to white-controlled "environmental conditions" which could be aided by the work of the Center. This cautious appeal carried the day with the Community Chest board, which, fortunately for the center, included Louise Harrold as one of its members.[67]

Historian Robert Burnham has argued that the Washington Center built a strong financial foundation and eventually succeeded in becoming part of the city's establishment. As this process began in the center's first year, the 1940s dawned with two major problems on the horizon. At the state level Governor Talmadge focused his 1940 gubernatorial campaign on race and devoted virtually his entire term to ferreting race-mixers out of the faculties of Georgia colleges and universities. By September 1941, the Macon Interracial Committee scheduled white minister Robert W. Hicks to address one of its meetings on the subject of "Georgia's Problems of Biracial Education and Race Prejudice." Lowry Anderson anticipated that Hicks would "have something to say about our pig-headed Governor." This and a subsequent meeting, however, were poorly attended. Many of those in attendance believed that Talmadge's "recent anti-Negro political moves" had intimidated some members from attending.[68]

Willis B. Sheftall, Director of the Booker T. Washington Center, 1974. (Courtesy of the Washington Memorial Library.)

The other problem lay across the Atlantic, as the United States inched closer to the precipice of involvement in World War II. Even before Pearl Harbor, Lowry Anderson had begun gathering information regarding the issue that had exacerbated race relations during the previous "war to end war"—the treatment of black soldiers at Camp Wheeler. Another war would renew the problem. He discovered poor treatment of blacks by Military Police and that five Northern black soldiers were punished for disciplinary violations by being retained in Southern stations, such as Camp Wheeler or Fort Benning. Anderson sought to bring to the Macon Interracial Committee discussions of the black soldier's status in the new war effort. Even here, however, the intimidating racial milieu scared him away from rhetorical strategies soon to be used by the black press. In a letter to Jessie Daniel Ames, the young minister suggested a more prudent approach: "What we can do is instead of saying anything about the similarity of our treatment of Negroes and Hitler's treatment of the Jew, we have got to discuss the things going on in our community which nullifies [sic] democracy and Christianity."[69]

In the face of these present and approaching problems, and to give Macon's churches and interracial efforts a shot in the arm, several members of the Macon Interracial Committee helped schedule an evangelistic crusade by the renowned Methodist missionary and evangelist, E. Stanley Jones. Because Jones was well known in part for refusing to speak at racially segregated events, Lowry Anderson viewed this event as "one of the most encouraging facts about the interracial prospects in Macon." An interracial group of four white and four black ministers hatched the plan to invite Jones to Macon, then recommended to the white Macon Ministerial Association and the black Ministers' Evangelical Union that they issue the evangelist a joint invitation. The white group initially balked, insisting that Jones be informed that separate seating must prevail at the services even though attendance would be open to both races. The black group agreed to this condition, so long as the Ministerial Association agreed that seating be equally divided between blacks and whites. Albert Grady Harris, pastor of First Presbyterian Church and president of the Ministerial Association, led a small contingent of white ministers in objecting to Jones appearing either at any black churches or schools. The Reverend D. L. T. Robinson, pastor of the Steward Chapel AME Church, dismissed the problem as hypothetical, reminding the white ministers that no black church had even extended an invitation.[70]

After all the ministerial compromises had been effected, Jones spoke in Macon on 19–22 October 1941. In the evenings he spoke at the city auditorium, while addressing chapel services at Mercer, Wesleyan, Central City College, and Ballard Normal School in the mornings. He also spoke at ministers' conferences at the white First Baptist and First Presbyterian churches. Black ministers, however, were welcomed to both churches. In his message at Mercer, Jones seemed to anticipate America's involvement in another European war, heralding America as the "mediator of a new world order based on the central idea of democracy." His definition of democracy, however, no doubt raised some eyebrows when he told the students: "We should give equality of opportunity to everyone within our own borders. Democracy means social and economic democracy as well as political democracy."[71]

While encouraged by Jones's visit to Macon, if only because young ministers love to bask in the glow of more famous preachers, Lowry Anderson showed small signs of disillusionment. The problems of race relations during the coming war bothered him, as did white ministerial wrangling over racial policies during the Jones crusade. A few days before Jones arrived in Macon, Ames wrote Anderson a letter indicating her surprise that Jones sacrificed his previously "inflexible principles" to accept the Macon invitation under racially segregated conditions. She wistfully commented that "this work of race relations is quite the same as clearing a dense forest with heavy under-growth." In reply, the young idealist lamented the fact that too few prominent laypersons had joined the effort. He wrote: "The thing that has limited it [interracial work] so much in Macon—most of them have been preachers who have been interested.... It seems to me that the preachers have fallen down lamentably on the job in failing to interest their boards of stewards and deacons. Of course, we have to confess to that failure."[72] The failures of "unutterable separation," especially within Macon's ministerial class, would continue for a good while longer.

5

Tiptoeing Toward Freedom:
Challenging Jim Crow in War
and Postwar Macon

Through their attendant defense activities and industrial expansion, the World War II and postwar eras did much to transform Macon from an oversized "country town" to a modern metropolitan city. The population of Bibb County grew from 83,783 to 114,079 during the 1940s, while the city of Macon grew from 68,000 to 100,814 in the same period. A number of signs pointed to more vigorous economic health in the period, as bank deposits increased from $14 to $63 million and retail sales went up from $24 to $103 million. Property values grew from $38 to $67 million.[1] Economic progress in Macon, as in the nation at large, turned out to be linked to mobilization for war. In an unexpected way, the same can be said for the progress of the black freedom struggle. Fighting a war against Hitler's Nazi ideology, with its doctrine of Aryan supremacy and its "final solution" to protect against an "inferior people," accentuated the final irony of an America fighting a racist ideology while trying to keep its own racist ideology intact.

During the war the black press discerned this irony long before it showed up on white America's radar screens. Led most notably by the *Pittsburgh Courier*, African-American newspapers launched an editorial offensive called the "Double-V" campaign: The US should press on to victory both abroad and at home, first against Hitler in Europe, then against Jim Crow in the South. Of course, not everyone agreed with this strategy. Many whites, even some who objected to segregation, thought wartime called for a unified front and was no time to point out or exacerbate America's divisions. But that did not stop African Americans from drawing the analogy, as did NAACP Director Walter White, who served in both theaters of the war. His 1945 book, *A Rising Wind*, warned of a new New Negro: "World War II has immeasurably magnified the Negro's awareness of the disparity between the American profession and practice of democracy." This disparity between profession and practice was precisely what Swedish sociologist Gunnar Myrdal had polemically called "the American Dilemma." His best-selling book, *The American Dilemma: The Negro Problem and Modern Democracy*, published a year before White's, suggested that the war-colored glasses that much of America now wore might enable white Americans to see what they had hitherto been unable or unwilling to see. And an increasing number of white American did not like what they were beginning to notice. As historian Peter J. Kellogg noted, Hitler's horrors caused ideas of racial superiority to lose their former "connotations of benevolence," as whites began to compare the Nazi and the American forms of racial superiority.[2]

Thus the war years and the postwar period have rightly been called "the forgotten years" of the African-American struggle for equal rights. Focus on the years after the Supreme Court's *Brown v. Board of Education* ruling had led historians away from the pivotal role played by World War II in setting the stage for the later successes of the civil rights movement. As a result, another generation of historians have for some time now pointed to the years just before and just after the war as the "days of hope" that racial change might truly be in the offing.[3]

Macon provides a serviceable test case for the thesis that the war itself became a catalyst in immediate postwar years for the beginnings of racial change. The war against Hitler helped move Macon's racial progressives, who had worked cautiously and interracially during the 1930s to soften Jim Crow, to a point where they could begin to work even more cautiously to eliminate Jim Crow. In the process they exchanged the Commission on Interracial Cooperation for the less conservative, less gradualist approach of what in 1944 became known as the Southern Regional Council (SRC). That the CIC metamorphosed into the SRC in the years 1943–1944 underscores the transforming effect of the war. The transformation in Macon also began during the war years and continued through the Truman-Dewey-Thurmond-Wallace contest of 1948. By the end of that period, Macon's white progressives had begun to come out of hiding and, though trailing behind Macon's branch of the

NAACP, had begun to tiptoe toward the eventual freedom of all African Americans. Before that goal was reached, however, the progressives in Macon and throughout the South would encounter the fury of "massive resistance."

WARTIME RACIAL TENSIONS

Even before Japan's infamy at Pearl Harbor, black Maconites were organizing to prove their eagerness to defend the community against enemies domestic and foreign. In August 1941, almost four months before the Japanese attack, John W. Summerford, a four-year veteran of the US Army, gathered some 100 fellow black Maconites into the Volunteer Defense Committee of Macon, and them petitioned Governor Talmadge for authority to establish a Colored Home Defense Guard Unit. This unit would help preserve peace and good order by protecting public works, supervising alien activity, and training a civilian defense system. Talmadge never responded to the request, which nevertheless underscored black Macon's loyalty to the US, a question that arises every time the US goes to war.[4] In April 1942, with America having finally entered the war, black soldiers from Camp Wheeler marched in the Army Day parade, causing Lawrence Banister from Perry, Georgia, to write to the *Telegraph* to congratulate the black troops and make a point about their loyalty to America: "American Negroes have never failed you.... The American Negro turned the tide of battle in the first World War and will do it again. We will not fail you at home nor on the battlefield. We are a part of this great America and we will do our part." Lieutenant-Colonel Marcel A. Gillis, commanding officer of the all-black 16th Battalion, concurred, informing the *Telegraph*, "The colored soldier is proud of his uniform, proud of his officers, and proud to be in the service."[5]

In spite of black efforts once again to prove their loyalty, by summer 1942 black military personnel stationed near Macon, along with those affiliated with other auxiliary organizations, began to complain of discrimination. On 16 June a committee of black Maconites complained of discrimination in worker training for war industries. The group filed affidavits that black individuals had been unfairly rejected or given inconclusive responses when they applied for such training. The Macon complaints were part of a larger effort by blacks in Atlanta and Savannah, who protested to M. D. Mobley, director of the state's vocational training program, that his agency had not given blacks equal opportunities in aircraft, shipbuilding, and other facets of the nation's ongoing defense work. Mobley denied that there was any effort "to prevent the training of Negroes," but added that to train blacks for jobs they could not obtain would be a waste of funds. The state program, he noted, had enrolled some 60,000 whites and 12,000 blacks, almost all of whom had been trained to repair and drive tractors or similar farm work. He acknowledged, however, that not much industrial work had been available to the black enrollees.[6]

Appearing on 19 June 1942, at a meeting of FDR's Committee on Fair Labor Practices in Birmingham, Alabama, William Y. Bell, chairman of the Council of Defense Training for blacks, accused officials of systematic discrimination in their training courses, charging that only 12 of 147 courses were open to blacks. Specific complaints regarding Macon's defense plants failed to materialize, when three witnesses failed to appear before the committee. As a result the original complaints were dropped for lack of support.[7] Some months later, however, blacks continued to raise similar complaints. A committee composed of Dr. C. W. Dyer, Y. B. Hooper, Dr. E. M. Calhoun, John A. Jenkins, and Charles Ingram met with War Manpower officials asking for a war industries training program for Negroes. Contrary to reports in the *Macon Telegraph*, most black leaders were unhappy with the city's efforts to utilize black workers. They were particularly angry over the suggestion that no blacks were capable of doing good jobs on such projects. "There are Negroes in all branches of the military," the group told the officials, "and should be given jobs in the production of supplies so that all can feel that they are doing their part in the war."[8]

Weighing into this dispute, black minister Theodore Randall wrote to the *Telegraph* that members of his church had witnessed black women being refused to register for training positions which they were told were not available to Negroes. Black women were, however, allowed to register for typist positions—jobs for which most blacks women would not apply because they required re-locating to Washington, DC. Randall thus surmised that "they are only eligible when the situation makes it impossible for them to take a position." He also speculated whites who hoped to keep blacks working for them as domestics had ulterior motives for such discriminatory policies. "Blacks pray daily," he concluded, "and do not ask for any social equality but to be given the chance to prove they are able to work in war factories and plants that victory may be everyone's."[9]

Contrary to black complaints in Macon, however, statewide the rapidly transforming wartime economy had increased black employment. One journalist had estimated that 80 percent of the 53,000 WPA jobs in Georgia had gone to blacks. Accurate or not, the speculation seemed to anger many whites, and the *Telegraph* blamed the employment of blacks for an upsurge in racial attacks.[10] Complicating racial matters in this period was a series of assaults by black men on white women during the preceding months of April and May. In one of six assault cases, on 10 June, a Bibb County jury convicted J. B. Holmes of the rape and murder of a white Macon woman. Judge A. M. Anderson sentenced him to die in the electric chair one month hence. In white Macon, the outcome seemed uncontroversial, but one reader did complain that the *Telegraph* "found it necessary to portray the big black face of this Negro on the very front page…for young boys and girls to see, read and discuss." Ten days after Holmes's conviction, a black woman who was choked and raped on 7 May positively identified another black man, Sylvester Andrews, as her attacker. After the capture of Holmes and Andrews, the Macon police department marked the cases closed.[11]

Blacks in Macon developed a twofold response to the tensions. One was to step up cooperative work with the Macon Interracial Committee, while a more autonomous action was for the recently organized but still low profile Macon branch of the NAACP to go public. For black Maconites to take this step, despite NAACP's reputation among most white Southerners as an extremist organization, indicates the radicalizing influence of the war effort on Macon's blacks. Earlier efforts to launch a Macon chapter had floundered after field secretary James Weldon Johnson's 1917 organizing trip founded branches in Athens, Atlanta, Augusta, Macon, and Savannah. But the same Volunteer Defense Committee leadership that had sought a colored guard unit now began to inquire into the possibilities of founding a NAACP branch. In October 1941 John Summerford wrote to NAACP offices in New York for information on how to form a local branch, and by the following April the group had applied to the NAACP Board of Directors for a charter. On 24 May, in an ostensibly unrelated event, the Reverend Ralph M. Gilbert, pastor of Savannah's historic First African Baptist Church spoke to graduates of Georgia Baptist College on the subject, "The World's Blackest Hour, The Negro's Opportunity." He told them that "no matter what the complexion of the government…they shall not reach the goal of human welfare, so long as they remain the tools of selfish, prejudiced, godless men." The prevailing racial context suggested a radical message, delivered in code, to black Macon. Also suggesting this was Gilbert's status as president of the very active Savannah NAACP. Within a week, by 1 June the branch had come into being, elected a slate of officers led by Dr. E. M. Calhoun as president, and announced its first membership campaign.[12]

Two other specific incidents in Macon spurred the new NAACP branch to action, further roiling the racial waters. Sometime in the first week of June, Pvt. Alpha Josie, a black soldier stationed at Camp Wheeler, was pistol whipped on a Georgia Power Company bus by the driver and another man. The beating remained unknown to virtually all white Maconites. Many black citizens, however, learned of the incident through the grapevine, leading some to refuse to ride in the rear of the power company bus. The beating also came to the attention of the Macon NAACP, which decided to bring the case to public attention. Secretary John A. Jenkins and publicity director J. T. Collier decided to place on the colored page of the *Macon Telegraph* what turned out to be a controversial advertisement announcing:

JOIN THE NAACP TODAY
Racial Discrimination Must Be Smashed![13]

As the advertisement spawned a public controversy in its own right, a more subterranean element of the story also kept the Macon NAACP on edge. A member of the branch's executive committee, Lucylle McAllister, was replaced as director of Macon's black USO office for not doing her job in a way that was "for the best interests of interracial understandings"—code language for her NAACP efforts to deal with the Alpha Josie incident and the general treatment of blacks at Camp Wheeler. She was ordered to swap venues with Sadye Watson, director of the Atlanta USO, but when the Atlanta office received an anonymous call threatening to lynch McAllister unless she were transferred to New York City, plans quickly changed. By 9 June, two days after the NAACP advertisement appeared in the *Telegraph,* her transfer to New York was announced.[14]

Meanwhile, the NAACP ad had ignited a more public brush fire. White Macon shuddered at the blunt language of the notice, quickly concluding that NAACP activities were responsible for the recent racial incidents and the controversy over the local defense industry. Even some conservative black business and community leaders published a statement critical of the fledgling NAACP branch in the *Telegraph.*[15] The firestorm brought out an immediate denial by the officers of the Macon NAACP disavowing agitation and asserting their desire for racial harmony. The Reverend R. Waite Stennett, pastor of the Washington Avenue Presbyterian Church and member of the NAACP executive committee told reporters that the NAACP's aim was to avoid racial disputes. As a thoroughly American organization, the group did not condone "any subversive or criminal activities among its members" and sought to solve racial disputes rather than to foster racial animosities. Stennett tried to soothe white concerns by rejecting the language of the advertisement as being "at cross-purposes with the organization." In sum, he reassured white Macon that the new branch sought only "the benefits and blessings of the democratic way of life for all Americans."[16]

The next day, W. T. Anderson weighed into the controversy with an editorial that simultaneously congratulated the local leaders while flaying the national organization of which they were a part. "It is no surprise to me," he opined, "that several well-known leaders among Macon Negroes …denied connection with or endorsement of an outside group which has no interest in the Southern Negro except to use him in the North for political purposes…." Calling the NAACP a "carpet-bagger group," Anderson echoed rumors that "Washington officials and certain Negro agitators from outside of Macon" were at work to "'smash' racial discrimination." Anderson advised readers to remember all the interracial projects, like the Booker T. Washington Community Center, that white and black Maconites had built together and to avoid anything that might "promote the purposes of this 'smashing' group." He argued that blacks were uncomfortable in situations of social equality with whites and preferred their own kind. They wanted justice and fairness without being "mixed up and crossed with whites." Prominent blacks from all over the country had spoken to him of Macon's "fine spirit and racial co-operation," which was now being jeopardized by the arrival of "some strange group" demanding the "'smashing' of somebody or something."[17]

On the same day the controversy also reached the halls of justice when the Bibb County Grand Jury summoned NAACP leaders Stennett, Collier, Jenkins, and R. E. Hartley to explain the purposes of the organization, questioning them on their birthplaces and possible foreign influences. When members of the grand jury accused the men of being involved in a "Black Ku Klux Klan," they replied that the NAACP sought only the constitutional rights of their people "and that by Legal Process." Unconvinced, the jury accused them also of inciting blacks to riot among whites who "had always gotten along with the Negro as well as could be expected." Then jury spokesman Michael J. Wittman tried to convince the black leaders to disband the local branch for the duration and that they "think of nothing but winning this War." In addition, he argued that the branch should disband in the interest of interracial understanding in Macon. Wittman also said he and other whites deplored the rumors that Macon might see a resurgent Klan "to cope with Negroes' aggressiveness." The black leaders replied that they were actively supporting the war effort by making every sacrifice.

Of course, the suggestion that blacks sublimate their complaints while pulling together for the war effort had great resonance among white Maconites, as indicated by letters to the *Telegraph.* One writer warned of "enemy propaganda organizations" stirring up trouble among blacks. "At a time like this, when we are engaged in war, our whole population should be united closer than ever," he wrote. "But history will show that we always have more trouble with the Negro during a war, and this is true now." Most blacks were good citizens who "want their own schools and churches." The writer nevertheless saw the irony of "the American dilemma:" "We are fighting a Jew-baiter in Germany and I don't see how we can be consistent if we support a Negro-baiter in Georgia." After the initial flurry of controversy over the Macon NAACP, the *Telegraph* printed an address by its former managing editor, Mark F. Ethridge, who had moved on to a similar position with the *Louisville*

(Kentucky) *Courier-Journal*. While arguing that "no white Southerner can logically challenge" the view that blacks were entitled to full civil rights and economic opportunity, he nonetheless counseled patience and gradualism. By demanding "all or nothing," he asserted, the black press was providing "cruel and disillusioning leadership to their people" and playing into the hands of white demagogues. "There is no power in the world," he continued, "which could now force the Southern white people to the abandonment of the principle of social segregation. It is a cruel disillusionment...and perhaps tragedy, for any other leaders to tell them that they can expect it or that they can exact it as the price for their participation in the war." Occasionally, however, came letters significantly ahead of their time, as evidenced by the writer who compared the argument for racially integrated school systems to "Hitler's argument for proscribing the Jew," adding "segregation means further discrimination; nothing else." Wisely, the writer signed only his initials.[18]

In response to the call for disbanding the local NAACP branch, on 8 June 1942 the Reverend R. Waite Stennett, pastor of the Washington Avenue Presbyterian Church, invited the entire grand jury to a public meeting at his church, where their proposal could be considered by the entire NAACP membership. Before a packed church sanctuary and with the grand jury in reserved seats, the leaders deflected suggestions that their activities had caused the recent attacks on white women. They called on the local newspapers to "play down unimportant incidents," and noted that if other Georgia cities could peacefully co-exist with the NAACP, "surely Macon, with her vaunted peace and harmony between the races, should not fear the Association." They also informed the grand jury of their refusal to cease their activities. Instead, they would redouble efforts to recruit new members. On the crucial question of disbanding the organization, the congregation remained in their seats when Stennett asked all who wished to disband to stand. He then announced, "All in favor of continuing the organization, please stand." When the entire congregation rose to their feet, Stennett turned to the grand jury and replied, "Gentlemen, that is our answer." At that point the grand jury walked out of the meeting.[19]

More secretly, branch leaders alerted the national NAACP office in New York of the situation in Macon. Executive Director Walter White took the grand jury's efforts as a serious attempt to intimidate local branches, similar to efforts after World War I to shut down NAACP branches in Texas, and requested advice from his National Legal Committee.[20] After learning the details of the Macon situation in a letter from John Jenkins, White wrote to encourage the Macon branch: "If the organization...can be intimidated into going out of existence, then Hitler has won the war already, in that totalitarianism rules over Macon, Georgia." In a similar letter, Prentice Thomas, the NAACP's assistant special counsel, wrote, "It is quite important that we continue our work in order that victory may be had at home as well as abroad." The following day Thurgood Marshall, another NAACP special counsel, wrote to a US Justice Department deputy apprising him of the Macon situation and suggesting some action that the Justice Department might take in response.[21]

While unable to convince the members of the Macon NAACP to discontinue their activities, the grand jury did decide to sponsor the formation of a Bibb County Interracial Committee composed of twenty white and twenty black Maconites. Attorney Walter A. Harris was named general chairman of the Citizens' Committee (as it later came to be called), which began meeting on the first Tuesday of each month to "preserve peace" by fostering "a better understanding between the white and colored people of this community." The black membership of this committee included two NAACP members, the Reverend R. Waite Stennett and Frank J. Hutchings.[22] This committee naturally overlapped with the earlier, less official Macon Interracial Committee that had met since the late 1930s. The new committee met regularly over the next year or two, but gradually dissolved after the wartime crisis passed. By contrast, the Macon Interracial Committee would eventually become the Macon Council on Human Relations, an affiliate of the Georgia Council on Human Relations and the Southern Regional Council, and remain a progressive organization through the civil rights years.

As a member of both committees, Lowry Anderson had little confidence in the new group, which he viewed as "made up for the most part of politicians and defenders of the status quo." He bristled at the Citizens' Committee's tendency to play down the "seriousness of the situation," with little interest in addressing even the glaring areas of inequality between whites and blacks in Macon. In his view the white members of the committee argued thus: "Now is no time to correct educational and civic injustices meted out to the Negroes because we have a war to win. Let's all come together and win this war or worse will be the lot of all of us than has ever been the lot of the Negro. Now is not time to insist on rights, it is the time to surrender rights in the interest of our country."[23] In spite of this rivalry and their differing points of view, the two committees continued to work together throughout the current crisis.

The crisis deepened and tensions further increased near the end of a hot Middle Georgia summer when, on 20 August 1942, white police officer Grady "Doc" Favors was shot and killed by Edmund Reed, a black soldier who was AWOL from Fort Benning. Out of uniform and in town to visit his wife and new baby, Reed was caught up in a police sweep of the downtown area in which a large number of blacks were arrested for loitering. When Reed began to scuffle with arresting officer, Military Police Sergeant Marvin Whitmire, Favors went to Whitmire's aid, wielding his billy club. Before he could land a blow, however, Reed grabbed Favors' gun and fired, critically wounding Whitmire and Favors, who died later that night. An angry mob of an estimated several hundred gathered by 9:30, injuring two other black soldiers in the melee, requiring the combined efforts of city and county officers and a large detachment of MPs to disperse. While a posse quickly formed in the city, military officers rounded up all black soldiers at Camp Wheeler, checking their IDs and restricting them to the post "for their protection." What some officials called "the greatest manhunt in Middle Georgia's history," numbering some 150 city and county officers and using bloodhounds, captured Reed the next day in the Tuft Springs area of the city.[24]

At trial Reed's attorneys, T. A. Jacobs and W. T. Walden, argued that Favors had used "unwarranted force" in making the arrest by slipping "up behind the soldier and began beating him on the head with a blackjack." Reed had a right to defend himself against what he believed to be an assault, and had hurt no one and had made no assault until "the unlawful attack" was made upon him. After an hour's deliberation, the jury brought back a guilty verdict, and Judge A. M. Anderson sentenced Reed to death.[25]

A few days after the incident, eight black leaders, led by Frank J. Hutchings, owner of the Hutchings Funeral Home, and Macon dentist D. T. Walton, issued a statement of regret for the incident that was "deplored by the law abiding masses of Negroes of the city." The statement further promised that black citizens would cooperate with whites to maintain "friendship between the races" and would "give their full support to any effort that leads to permanent peace and harmony in Macon."[26] The incident apparently led to another police confrontation when another black soldier, Captain Julian Hannible, suffered a severe concussion. The incidents precipitated a military investigation into alleged brutalities on the part of various police agencies in Bibb County. In early September, a representative of the inspector general's office called on Police Chief Robert Miller as he investigated rumors of harsh treatment of black soldiers that had circulated since the Favors shooting. In response to the investigator's initial visit, John Owings, chairman of the city's police committee, announced he had received no reports of such activities, but promised the city that if any information came to light, "the War Department can rest assured that a sweeping investigation will be made."[27] The Army, however, made no further report on the matter.

Five days after the Favors shooting, the Interracial Committee at the Christ Church parish house to discuss the latest developments. "We took the lid off and looked in the cauldron of race conditions in Macon," Lowry Anderson later wrote to Jessie Daniel Ames, adding, "It looked worse than the witches' brew." An hour's worth of discussion among fifteen blacks and seven whites turned up information that civilian police regularly brutalized black prisoners or suspects. In one case an officer struck a black man for merely looking at a white woman, even before placing him under arrest. Blacks feared to appear in court as witnesses for other blacks. Military police tended to be more respectful than local police in cross-racial arrests. Black soldiers were angry for a number of slights at Camp Wheeler, where they had to wait for their white comrades to be served first. Frank Hutchings, Jr., later recalled that during the war black Maconites deeply resented military officials taking German prisoners into city restaurants where blacks, despite being loyal American citizens, were banned from patronizing. In response, the committee decided to recommend to the Citizens' Committee to request the city council to hire black police. They advised that Camp Wheeler be asked to assign black MPs to work the Macon area, that the Citizens' Committee and city council insist that police give more civil treatment to blacks, and that bus drivers be courteous to all passengers regardless of race.[28]

W. T. Anderson, who served on the Citizens' Committee, remained confident: "To hear some people talk, one would think the Negroes are all armed and ready to rise in rebellion against the white people of this county who been their friends and helpers and well-wishers ever since the first Negro set foot on American soil. In my opinion, such is not the case." Acknowledging that blacks did carry a burden not incumbent upon whites, he wrote: "Frequently on trains, busses, and other places they get less than their money should buy. They have to be more polite, more careful of their conduct. But this is only a part of the Divine plan, as I see it." This was part of the lesson blacks must learn "so he and his children can 'get along' in the white man's country." Yet, he argued, "Patience is a virtue which the Negro has used to better advantage and with more acumen and intelligence than we give him credit for."[29] Such conservative white leadership explains the difficulties a young idealistic minister like Lowry Anderson had with the Citizens' Committee. Nevertheless, though taking different approaches to the local problems, the two interracial committees served as an escape valve for the tensions. Once again black and white Maconites remained separate in their responses, with white concerns gradually giving way to the war effort and blacks sublimating their grievances until the next opportune moment. That moment came on the heels of the Allied victory and was one of the steps by which black disfranchisement would be reversed.

WHITE PRIMARY AND BLACK VOTING

As the tide of war began to turn in the Allies' favor, the stepped-up effort of the national NAACP sparked a period of remarkable growth. Like the black press, the national NAACP was caught up in the "Double-V" crusade, having been invigorated by the ideological war against Hitler. During the 1940s the NAACP boosted its national membership form 50,000 to some 450,000. The NAACP branches became vigorously active in most of Georgia's cities. The Macon branch had been established during this period, and despite its controversial beginnings, was enjoying healthy growth in summer 1942. Naturally this growth created a deepening concern all across white Georgia. By this time, there were also estimates of between 400 and 500 new Klan members in Bibb County, and by January 1944 news reports told of a "state-wide conspiracy" against black voters in for South Georgia counties.[30] Later that year, city leaders sent a resolution to the Georgia delegation in Congress objecting to a War Department ruling against segregation at army camps. Such directives, the Maconites argued, were "calculated to cause race riots, fights, and disorder generally. On the other hand, in early January the Macon Hospital opened fourteen private and semi-private beds for black patients, marking the first time that such rooms were made available to blacks in Macon Hospital.[31] Clearly, the bastion of Jim Crow was under attack, even as Germany and Japan were beginning to wobble.[32]

Another element giving Maconites and other white Southerners pause was the NAACP's legal attack on Jim Crow's educational and suffrage discrimination. On 23 April 1944 the strategy was paying off as the US Supreme Court declared the Texas white primary unconstitutional in its *Smith v. Allwright* ruling. Despite this landmark decision, the Georgia State Democratic Committee nevertheless ruled that blacks would be barred from voting in the 4 July primary election, and the wheels began to turn toward a challenge to Georgia's white primary. Just before election, the recently formed Georgia Council on Human Relations, the state's affiliate of the Southern Regional Council, addressed a letter of concern to the Democratic Committee. Bearing the signatures of Maconites George M. Clary, Reese Griffin, J. Maurice Trimmer, pastor of the white First Baptist Church, Margaret C. Mays, and Mrs. T. J. Stewart, the letter registered its disagreement with the party elite, and urged that all eligible citizens be allowed to participate in the primary regardless of race. "We speak as Georgians," they added, "and citizens of a nation dedicated…to the principles of total democracy and reaffirmed in the Atlantic Charter as an objective of this world struggle.[33]

At the same time a group of black voters called the Georgia Association of Citizens Democratic Clubs met in Macon on 26 June, with representatives from eleven clubs attending. The leadership urged all registered and otherwise qualified Negroes in Georgia to attempt to vote in the 4 July primary election, but emphasized that they maintain order and avoid any trouble in the process. On election day, Georgia blacks were turned away from the polls without incident. One of those denied voting privileges, however, was a Columbus minister named Primus E. King. On 24 August, King who filed suit in US District Court against the Muscogee County Democratic Executive Committee for violation of his civil rights and of the Fourteenth, Fifteenth, and Seventeenth Amendments to the Constitution. Promising to take the case to the Supreme Court if necessary, King's attorney announced that the case was brought in order to ascertain whether the Texas case ruling was applicable in Georgia.[34]

In the following fall, the King case came before Judge Thomas Hoyt Davis, who presided over the US District Court in Macon. An Atlanta native, Davis had graduated from Mercer University, later serving the school's trustee board, and has been US attorney for Middle Georgia. When the district judgeship was vacated in early 1945, in one of his last acts as president, Franklin Roosevelt appointed Davis to the federal bench. For three sweltering days in mid-September, Davis and a racially mixed but segregated audience from all over Georgia heard the arguments. Harry Strozier, progressive attorney and member of the Macon Council on Human Relations (the successor of the Macon Interracial Committee), argued that blacks' right to vote in a primary was as protected by the Constitution as the right to vote in a general election. He further argued that a party's ruling to deny a citizen the right to vote in a primary constituted a "state action through the party," and was thus constitutional. Arguing for the defendants was segregationist attorney, Charles J. Bloch, also from Macon, who argued that the defendants were not bringing a state action, but were rather acting as agents of the Democratic Party and that the primary, unlike that in Texas, was not held according to state laws.

Judge Davis repeatedly pressed the defense to explain, "What alternative do the Negroes have?" In the end, Bloch and his associates were forced to admit that black voters only choice was to form their own party or join a white party where their membership was welcome. Taking the case under advisement, Davis rendered his ruling in *Chipman v. King* a month later. In a twenty-nine-page opinion, the judge awarded King

$100 in damages (he had asked for $5,000), but announced that the denial of his right to vote in a primary solely because of race violated the Constitution.[35]

At the close of the war, therefore, blacks were better off than ever before. The Supreme Court had begun to come to their aid, as had the federal government, most auspiciously in the work of the Fair Employment Practices Committee. More African Americans found work in civil service, and the types of positions open to them also improved. These improvements, buttressed by the euphoria of defeating Hitler in Europe, gave blacks and white progressives a growing hope that the second "V" might eventually be won at home. There was, of course, still work to be done in Georgia and in Macon. Statewide skirmishes over the black vote in the 1946 gubernatorial election erupted as Eugene Talmadge hoped to come out of his unwanted four-year retirement. To do this, he planned to ride white resentment over the loss of the white primary back into office. As for Macon, at war's end segregation continued to reign in rooming houses, restaurants, hotels, theaters, and of course the public schools.[36]

Around this time, the Southern Regional Council sent a memorandum to Governor Ellis Arnall, who, with 54 percent of the vote in Bibb County, had defeated Talmadge in the 1942 governor's race. The SRC noted that some 62,000 black Georgians, including 2,600 from Bibb County, would soon be returning from war, and warned that the state might face "a situation of psychological tension in which even trivial interracial incidents are potentially dangerous to the public peace and morale." While white soldiers may once again have hoped for a "return to normalcy," the black soldier would likely feel that "since he has fought for the preservation of democracy, he deserves a greater share of democracy when he comes home. If his legitimate wants are neglected or repressed, his morale will be extremely low, and he will become hypersensitive and aggressive." The council then suggested that the governor have meetings with police and transportation officials to stress calmness and courtesy. They also called on Arnall to confer with newspaper editors, both white and black, to help shape an atmosphere of tolerance in the state.[37] Although a segregationist, Arnall's relatively progressive stand on race amounted to political suicide, as he gradually came to support black voting on constitutional grounds. He also repealed the poll tax and lowered the voting age to eighteen.[38] Once his constitutionally limited four-year term was over, however, he never again held public office in Georgia.

By contrast, the new Georgia Council on Human Relations was growing to some 500 members, with local committees in Atlanta, Macon, Augusta, and Columbus. In April 1945, the annual meeting of the Georgia Council met in Macon at the Washington Center. A number of new recruits attended an interracial meeting for the first time, including a contingent of faculty and students from Wesleyan College. George M. Clary, former pastor of Mulberry Street Methodist Church now serving in Savannah, was elected chairman. Also elected to offices were V. A. Edwards of Fort Valley (vice chairman) and Louise Harrold of Macon (treasurer). At the Macon meeting, the council, still too cautious to call for the end of segregation, passed resolutions calling for equal facilities and access for citizens regardless of race—in education, in employment, in voting, in access to hospitals and recreational facilities. They also called for Georgia cities to hire black police officers.[39] Over the next year, however, the major battlefield of progressives would prove to be the issue of black voting.

After the court decisions striking down the white primary, through the NAACP's emphases, more than 135,000 black Georgians registered to vote in advance of the 1946 state elections. Two years earlier black registration in Georgia had numbered only some 10,000.[40] Another race-baiting gubernatorial campaign by Eugene Talmadge railed against the rulings and promised to restore both white supremacy and the white primary.[41] Announcing his candidacy in April 1946, Talmadge told his followers:

> The most important issue of all now faces the people of Georgia and of the Southland—the Democratic white primary. Alien influences and communistic influences from the East are agitating social equality in our state. They desire negroes to participate in our white primary in order to destroy the traditions and heritages of our Southland.... If elected governor, I shall see that the traditions which were fought for by our grandparents are maintained and preserved. I shall see that the people of this state

have a Democratic white primary unfettered and unhampered by radical, communistic and alien influences.[42]

Talmadge's also tried to explicate Georgia law that gave any citizen the right to challenge the credentials of any voter considered improperly qualified. Anyone so challenged was to be furnished a copy of the challenge form and given one day's notice before his right to vote was decided upon. Talmadge mailed thousands of challenge forms to supporters around the state. As the controversy unfolded, Maconites did not hesitate to express their views. A Mercer student commented that in light of the court rulings, "there is no way of withholding the privilege of voting from the Negro." A black organization called the Bibb County Progressive Democratic Club issued a statement calling on "the good white people" of the county to use their influence to stop the buying or selling of votes. They also asked that no candidate give money to any voters or to any organization for campaign purposes.[43] Some blacks sought federal help to defeat the vote-challenging plan. In Macon, US Attorney John P. Cowart threatened a full investigation by his office of all complaints of racial discrimination against blacks in the purging of voters' lists. Talmadge counterattacked, calling for a housecleaning of both Cowart and of 3,000 registered black voters with criminal records.

These efforts availed little, however, as the Talmadge forces challenged enough black voters in fifty rural counties and a handful of urban ones to significantly influence the outcome. James V. Carmichael, Arnall's designated successor, won the popular vote, but Talmadge won the election by amassing 242 county unit votes to Carmichael's 146. Talmadge supporters challenged black voters "en masse" and with no specific knowledge of the qualifications of individuals involved. Some were quoted as saying that they did not believe "any nigger was qualified to vote."[44] Cowart's investigation revealed that by applying literacy tests some county registrars had purged all but a small fraction of all black registered voters. For example in Sumter county only 92 of some 650 black registrants were allowed to vote.[45]

Black voters in Bibb County, however, experienced almost no problems in getting to the polls. Black Maconites reveled in their first opportunity to participate in a primary election in Georgia, and held a rally at the Pleasant Hill Playground, where business leader William P.

Randall rallied the troops to vote for Carmichael and against Gene Talmadge. Hearing that Randall had referred to their hero by his first name, the local Klan decided to pay Randall a retaliatory visit. A white electrician who had worked with Randall, however, was grateful to him for helping him pay his wife's hospital bill. The electrician was also a Klansman, and when his hooded fellows proposed an attack on Randall, he intervened with a warning: "If you are going to get that nigger, it'll be over my dead body."[46]

Just before the election, Bibb County Solicitor General Charles H. Garrett published a statement in the *Macon News* reporting that several thousand marked ballots had been sent to black voters to direct them toward the Carmichael campaign. Hoping to generate a groundswell of white votes, the Talmadge campaign paid for a full-page advertisement warning of "outside influences" seeking to generate a bloc vote. There was little doubt, given Talmadge's well-known record, that black voters would go to Carmichael. Most black voters in Bibb County had little difficulty getting to the polls and only fifteen black Maconites were taken into custody after marked sample ballots were found in their possession. In the end, Carmichael polled 56 percent of the vote to Talmadge's 37 percent. Carmichael's claim of Bibb's votes was accomplished by his capturing 5,690 black votes, comparing to the 24 polled by his opponent.[47]

The 1946 election unexpectedly became the governor-elect's swan song, as Talmadge died on 21 December 1946, a few days before his fourth inauguration. Georgia was plunged into political turmoil when Talmadge forces supported Herman Talmadge as the person best qualified to continue their agenda. Talmadge opponents claimed that Lieutenant Governor Melvin Thompson should accede to the governor's seat. In early January 1947 the Georgia legislature elected Herman to serve his father's term, but in March the Georgia Supreme Court ruled his election unconstitutional. Thompson then served as acting governor until a special election in September 1948 in which Talmadge ran against Thompson for the right to serve the remainder of his father's term. But first, Macon had to elect a new mayor, and thanks to Hoyt Davis's ruling in *Chipman v. King*, black Maconites would make the difference in that outcome.

RACE AND MACON'S POSTWAR ELECTIONS

Postwar activism by the NAACP at the national, state, and municipal levels brought race back into Georgia and Macon politics with a significance not experienced since the Hoke Smith-Clark Howell race of 1906. The same month in which the state Supreme Court set up the Talmadge-Thompson contest for the following year, two fresh candidates squared off in the city's 1947 mayoral election. After Mayor Charles L. Bowden opted to retire at the end of his fifth term in office, Lewis B. Wilson, who represented Bibb County in the state General Assembly, announced his candidacy, running against local coal company executive, B. F. Merritt.[48]

If anyone doubted that race would be a crucial factor in the campaign, that uncertainty evaporated three weeks before the election when the Macon Council of Church Women sent a six-point questionnaire to all municipal candidates. The organization of white professional-class women complained that the incumbent city council had not performed admirably in the matters of their concern, telling the candidates, "We will expect a new body of councilmen to rectify these omissions." The Macon Council of Church Women announced they would "gladly support" candidates who conscientiously addressed the following concerns: the abolition of slot machines in the city, a clean-up program for downtown streets and vacant lots, enforcement of fire hazard laws, trained matrons and better quarters for women in city jails.

In addition to these general matters, however, they also addressed two other specific matters: more and better recreational facilities and more paved streets for black Maconites. Lewis Wilson responded to the questionnaire by sending the council a ten-point platform, with an addendum designed generally to answer their concerns without being too specific: "In carrying out the above platform as announced and with reference to your specific questions: We pledge ourselves not to neglect any section of the city nor any group of people and to faithfully perform all the responsibilities of good government." Mrs. T. L. Ross, president of the Council of Church Women, publicly announced her organization's disappointment in Wilson's reply, which she said "did not have a specific answer to any of the questions presented." Clearly hoping to evade the charge of being the candidate of black Maconites, Wilson stuck to his generalities and told reporters, "Our letter to Mrs. Ross was our answer."[49]

Wilson's response turned out to be a shrewd calculation, however, giving him the look of independence from the black vote, which he clearly stood to attract. His confidence in getting black votes lay in his opposition to a disfranchisement bill in the state legislature. Supported by Herman Talmadge as a way to revive the white primary, and ultimately vetoed by Acting Governor Thompson, the bill would have repressed primary voting laws in order to provide a way to stop black voting. One of Bibb's representatives, A. H. S. Weaver, announced, "If that is what it takes, I am for it," and all but one of his legislative colleagues either followed suit or remained noncommittal. Lewis B. Wilson stood alone in opposing the bill, albeit not in order to protect black voting rights, but to restrain "unscrupulous candidates from buying votes openly, stuffing ballot boxes, bribery" and other forms of "rotten politics of the worst sort." Thus, although Wilson's public reasons for opposing the bill did not ring with racial egalitarianism, his negative vote signaled to black Maconites that he was white politician they could trust to be fair.[50]

To his credit, B. F. Merritt did not exploit race during the campaign, and his platform differed little from Wilson's. Interestingly, it was Macon's African-American community that created most of the controversy in the race, apparently developing from a power struggle in its own ranks. The *Macon Voice*, a black newspaper edited by E. M. Calhoun, published a story accusing Larkin Marshall, editor of the rival newspaper, the *Macon World*, of receiving a $500 payment from the Wilson campaign for a promise to deliver a bloc of 4,000 black votes. Other rumors circulated that Marshall had received similar payments from the Merritt campaign. Both candidates, along with Marshall, denied that they had made any such payments or promises. Marshall added, "My paper has never endorsed any candidate for mayor." These allegations were never proven, and the dispute originated in an earlier disagreement between Marshall and Calhoun. Wilson told supporters not to be misled by the many rumors circulating around the city, saying that his administration would be "free of any commitments or promises made in secret with any groups, special interests, cliques or individuals."[51]

By election day, the contest had been transformed from a rather calm affair to a fiery campaign. When compared to the gubernatorial elections before and after it, the Wilson-Merritt race was remarkably free of public race-baiting. Most of the rhetorical fireworks focused on questions of political patronage and support of the previous administration. Clearly, racial dynamics operated during the campaign and final vote, but no Talmadge-like demagoguery marred the proceedings. In the end, however, Wilson was elected with almost 61 percent of the total vote. Even without the black vote, however, he would have eked out a victory, having drawn 51 percent of the white vote. But his overall victory was strengthened by his winning 84 percent of the black vote. The black vote had a more significant effect on the aldermanic races, in which six candidates in three separate wards would have been elected in the absence of the black vote.[52]

The elections of 1948 tapped into racial concerns and feelings on at least three levels. Most significant was the long anticipated Thompson-Talmadge gubernatorial contest, primarily because Herman took a page from his father's strategy book and made civil rights the central issue of the campaign. He was enabled to do this, of course, because of the centrality of civil rights in Harry Truman's bid for election in 1948, which raised racial concerns at a second level. Talmadge's campaign centered on positioning himself as, like his father, the defender of segregation and the continued disfranchisement of blacks. In January 1948 Talmadge publicly supported a new voter-qualification law, to be administered in a discriminatory manner so as to bar blacks from elections. Thompson immediately announced his opposition to such a scheme, asserting, "I will never be the party, by use of trickery, subterfuge, or otherwise, to any attempt to evade the spirit or letter of the law."[53]

Another theme of the Talmadge campaign was to inveigh against federal encroachment on states' rights. His surrogates hammered on this theme in virtually every speech, as did the candidate. Macon attorney and former Bibb County legislator J. Douglas Carlisle gave a radio speech praising Talmadge as "firm, prompt, and vigorous" in advocating Georgia's right to "govern its own affairs." Denouncing the "civil wrongs" bill, he asserted, "The passage and enforcement of such laws would not only violate the rights of the states, but would create discord and disunity enough to gladden the heart of Joe Stalin. The attempt to enforce such laws would create bitterness between peoples who now get along increasingly well." County attorney Ellsworth Hall, Jr., who had defended the Muskogee County Democratic Party in the white primary case, also delivered a radio address citing support of states rights as a compelling reason to elect Talmadge. In response to these arguments, the *Telegraph* countered with an endorsement of Thompson and the counter-argument that "federal encroachments on state rights can never be stopped by state governors, who have absolutely no power to stop them." Earlier, the *Telegraph* criticized the Talmadge forces as having "seized upon the 'civil rights' issue as a means of beclouding the battlefield. They are appealing only to the emotions of the electorate on a matter of segregation of the races. It is a typical Talmadge trick to gain votes. In 1946 the cry was 'white supremacy.' Today it is 'segregation.'"[54]

Just before election day, the Talmadge campaign ran a full-page advertisement in the *Macon Telegraph* and other papers, predicting a landslide victory and announcing: "An Overwhelming Number of Georgians Want a Man Who Will Defend Georgia Against the Civil Rights Program and Preserve Our Southern Way of Life!" Elsewhere, the ad called the election "a Time of Crisis": "Throughout Georgia, citizens by the hundreds of thousands are rallying to the Talmadge cause. There's a tidal wave of resentment against those who would choke the so-called Civil Rights Program down the throats of Southern people."[55]

The campaign generated rivers of ink in the letters to the editor section of the *Telegraph,* both for and against Talmadge. One Thompson supporter wrote, "The Talmadge crowd is so filled with their love for their Herman and hate for Georgia's colored citizens that they can't think hard enough to answer one simple question: Why do you think that Talmadge would make a good governor? ...The only answer that any of his supporters has given is, 'He don't like Negroes, and I don't either.'" A Talmadge backer replied that his was the "only candidate in the governor's race who is making an all-out fight against Communism and its child, the 'civil rights' plan....?"[56] Letters to the editor ran about evenly for both candidates, an outcome that was eventually reflected in the results on primary election day. Thompson won the county's six unit votes and 51.75 percent of the popular vote. In precincts where votes could be separated by race, Thompson polled some 3,770 black votes to

Talmadge's meager 21 votes. Talmadge had, however, won most of the white vote.[57] Despite Thompson's win in Bibb County, Talmadge swept most rural areas of the state for an easy victory.

At the presidential level, by the time Truman began to position himself to make his own 1948 run for the White House, his developing civil rights policy created even more difficulties for Southern progressives. His decision to run on a platform with a strong civil rights plank generated in Macon both another resurgence of Klan activity and the birth of the "Dixiecrats." FDR's diminutive successor signaled a major change in the White House's approach to civil rights when on 29 June 1947, he became the first American president to address a meeting of the NAACP. Speaking from the Lincoln Memorial, with NAACP leader Walter White by his side, Truman called for full civil rights for all Americans: "When I say all American, I mean all Americans. Many of our people still suffer the indignity of insult, the narrowing fear of intimidation, and...the threat of physical and mob violence.... The conscience of our nation, and the legal machinery which enforces it, have not yet secured to each citizen full freedom from fear. We cannot wait another decade or another generation to remedy these evils. We must work, as never before, to cure them now."[58]

Six months later the president returned to the theme in his 1948 State of the Union address. White Maconites had recently been treated to another showing of *Birth of a Nation,* along with Bibb Theater advertisements saying, "This Masterpiece is a must for everyone to see."[59] Now, hearing Truman hawk a different view of race much different from D. W. Griffith or Thomas Dixon, they were not amused. In the address, Truman promised to send Congress a special message on civil rights and announced, "Our first goal is to secure fully the essential human rights of our citizens." Delivered on 2 February, unlike a fortunate groundhog, Truman did not see either his shadow or much sunlight in Dixie when his civil rights messages echoed Gunnar Myrdal's theme: "The serious gap between our ideals and some of our practices must be closed." Then he called on Congress to enact anti-lynching legislation, establish a permanent commission on civil rights and a civil rights division of the Justice Department. He also called for legislation safeguarding voting rights, the establishment of a Fair Employment

Practices Commission (FEPC), and to prohibit discrimination in interstate transportation.[60]

Southern governors immediately blasted the president's program, who said the plan merited extreme measures. Georgia's acting governor M. E. Thompson made cautious, somewhat evasive promise to "stick to my business if the president will tend to his." Looking to get back into the governor's mansion after being ousted by the state Supreme Court, Herman Talmadge announced he was unalterably opposed to any program that would give the FEPC authority over the South. The *Macon Telegraph* doubted that the plan was born of sincere concern for blacks, accusing Truman of "simply bidding for the Negro vote." Truman's message to Congress, the *Telegraph* warned, might give "real momentum to a Southern revolt which at first seemed fantastic, but which…might have historic consequences."[61] Several days later a letter to the editor scored Thompson for not taking a stand: "He wants to soft-pedal the President's Gestapo legislation and at the same time say it's 'unwise' and 'unnecessary.'"[62]

In March an opinion poll of the *Telegraph* indicated that most Maconites continued to support the president.[63] That support, however, would prove soft. One of the blunt instruments softening it was Macon attorney Charles Bloch. A Jewish white supremacist, Bloch had been trained in the law at Mercer, and became senior partner in the firm of Bloch, Hall, Hawkins, and Owens. He became active in politics and was elected to the state general assembly in 1927, where he became friends with future governor and senator, Richard B. Russell, Jr. Bloch held virulently racist views, arguing that blacks and whites could never co-exist as equals. In a letter to Russell, he once compared blacks to farm animals: "It is true that there are laws to protect livestock. And there are customs, too. Hogs and pigs have their separate pens; chickens have their coops; cattle have their barns; horses and mules have their stables; and none of them eat with people." He was also convinced that blacks were contented with segregation until the NAACP had agitated them into their late protests.[64]

Bloch entered a national spotlight that summer at the Democratic National Convention, when he led the Georgia delegation's effort to nominate Russell for president instead of Truman. Tapped to make the crucial nominating speech, Bloch urged delegates to reject the example of the Alabama and Mississippi delegations' bolting the party. He reminded Truman followers that their man owed his position in the White House to Southern pressure on FDR to replace Henry Wallace as vice president. In exchange for serving as Truman's stepping stone, Bloch argued, the president had inflicted upon the South an odious civil rights program.. Adapting a line from William Jennings Bryan's famous 1896 speech, he vowed to his fellow Southerners, "You shall not be crucified on the cross of civil rights."[65]

Such eloquence won Bloch widespread congratulations, but not the nomination for Russell. By August another presidential straw poll conducted by the *Telegraph* revealed that 80 percent of the votes cast preferred the Dixiecrat candidate Strom Thurmond; Truman received only 9 percent of the votes.[66] By the November general election, however, Bibb county voters gave the president the victory with 49 percent of the vote. Thurmond took 28 percent, compared to 21 percent for Dewey and one percent for Henry Wallace. The total number of votes cast, however, was only 14,230, more than 4,000 less than the 18,722 votes cast in the Talmadge-Thompson race.[67] Truman's civil rights policies had thus created a threat to white supremacy and had garnered Macon's black vote in numbers sufficient to offset the loss of white votes to avowed segregationist Strom Thurmond. Truman's policies also fueled Herman Talmadge's gubernatorial victory. In both cases, the anti-civil rights vote was very strong but not decisive in Bibb County voting. A majority of white Maconites opposed the civil rights program, but with a fairly strong minority of whites who backed it. Of course, the growing number of black voters in Georgia, up to some 140,000 by 1948, supported Truman's policies. As a result, in addition to the political firestorm played out in the postwar elections, Macon also saw competing activity from both the black community and the Klan.

COUNTER-ACTIVITIES

The "days of hope" sparked by the war and postwar eras and the rise of the NAACP in Macon set the stage for both increased calls for steps toward and increased opposition to racial equality. During the postwar elections and afterward, black Maconites and a few sympathetic white progressives were emboldened to speak out for improved conditions for blacks. At the same time, the oppositional extreme, the Klan, was also stimulated to more fervent activity in Macon. In this, the opposition anticipated the fevered response to *Brown v. Board of Education* known as "massive resistance."

Perceptions of the Lewis Wilson administration as more receptive to black needs also encouraged progressive voices to speak out. In early 1948, Grover Ables, a correspondent from Warner Robins, noted the many rights denied to blacks. "He [the Negro] has the right to vote," he argued, "but many 'knights' are employed in figuring out ways to keep him from doing it." Blacks also had the right to trials by *white* juries, inferior schools allowed by whites, more poorly paid teachers, the right to be protected by (lynch) law. "Oh yes, the Negro has all the rights a white man has," he concluded, "He just isn't permitted to exercise them." Similarly, NAACP officer John A. Jenkins served notice that postwar black Maconites were restless for racial change: "No, we do not own city busses, but certainly deplore some of the conditions under which we have to use them.... I will not attempt to enumerate the many methods that have been used to intimidate Negroes and deny him his civil rights, but very emphatically insist that 'Southern Negroes are not satisfied,' and have no intention of going North to enjoy these rights we unfortunately inherited."[68]

White realtor Washington Dessau addressed the city council condemning zoning laws that allowed dives and saloons in black residential sections, but not in white sections. "I say it's a crying shame to put these joints where people are trying to raise children," he asserted, adding that he could not name even one saloon in a white residential section compared to a score in black residential sections. "You collect license money from dumps in Negro sections, but you wouldn't allow all that drinking and cutting up in your own neighborhoods." On a similar issue, black Maconite Luke Emmett, Jr., wrote the *Telegraph* concerning "the needs of the Negro" and calling on other blacks to speak up: "I can't see…why we negro voters and taxpayers can be content with so little for our children. Why is it that we have no gyms? Why must our children go to the river or lakes to learn swimming?… Our city has playgrounds and parks with these things provided, but they are only provided for the white children, not the Negroes, and as long as we sit by doing nothing, we won't get any."[69]

Emmett's exhortation apparently bore fruit because less than a week later the Bibb County Citizens Civic Club held a mass meeting at First (black) Baptist Church to discuss problems between law enforcement and the black community. The meeting yielded a seventeen-person committee headed by L. J. May and Ozzie B. McKay, and prepared a public statement calling on the administration to appoint black police to patrol black sections of the city. Arguing that "the detection and punishment of crime would be more easily accomplished" with black patrols, the committee urged that "qualified Negro men be considered and appointed on the regular Macon police force." The next night May spoke for fourteen Civic Club members who accompanied him to a meeting with the city council. May told the council: "If we are, as you say, the largest law violators, then we think we should have our own police." Such, he argued, would not be a new step, as Savannah and forty other Southern cities had so employed African Americans. Both committee chairman Dan Tidwell and Mayor Wilson promised to consider the matter fully and fairly. By the second week in June, two blacks were added to the police department as special officers used at the pleasure of the police chief.[70]

In summer 1949, after the city proposed constructing the pool at Gray's Hill, near Forsyth Street and Hardeman Avenue, 108 whites presented a petition protesting the chosen location. They supported the building the pool, but argued, "Not in our neighborhood." As reasons they cited the depreciation of property values, noise from the recreational area, and possible racial trouble. To counter these arguments a group of ten blacks attended a public hearing on the matter. Topsy Campbell, a resident of East Macon, reminded the alderman and the mayor of their 1947 campaign promise to build a new city swimming pool for blacks. Larkin Marshall, editor and Bibb County Progressive Party leader, warned that blacks would "be mighty disappointed if we don't get one." Several other locations were proposed and for almost two months the controversy raged, until blacks and other supportive whites confronted opponents at another council meeting in late July.[71]

Alderman A. Mack Dodd called a meeting of the city council's recreation committee. Ernest Barfield, accompanied by William A. Bootle and Charles J. Bloch, attorneys representing two other Vineville residents, reiterated the protesters' earlier arguments. Frank J. Hutchings took up the challenge, asserting, "I don't know of anything Mr. Barfield, Mr. Bootle, or Mr. Bloch ever did for the advancement of Negroes." He further noted that most black Maconites favored the original Gray's Hill location. When another black spokesperson said, "If these objections are based on prejudice, then we never will have a pool," Barfield denied the objections were not a matter of prejudice, claiming, "The objections are not to a Negro pool but to its location." Bennie A. Scott arose to demand, "What is more important? Negro youth or property? While we have been arguing about this pool, Negroes have been drowning?" Finally, a white Maconite, Rabbi I. E. Marcuson seemed to win the day, reminding the committee: "These people deserve a swimming pool and its up to you to find a place, even if there is objection…and there always will be." The following night the city council voted eight to four to build the pool at the original Gray's Hill site.[72]

Naturally, activities such as these were met with counterforce, most notably by a renewed Klan in Bibb County. In July 1946, just after Eugene Talmadge's primary victory, seven white youths, ages sixteen to twenty-one, burned a cross in the yard of Z. C. Clay, an organizer of the Progressive Colored Democrats Club of Macon. The young men denied any Klan connections and convinced law enforcement officers that the incident was merely a "malicious joke." They were released with a warning.[73] Later that fall, the activity of the NAACP stimulated and the success of Eugene Talmadge's last gubernatorial campaign encouraged the organization of a new klavern of the Invisible Empire in Macon. Mose F. Byers, a police chief at Payne City, and his son Cyrus, were named by a special state assistant attorney general as the leaders of some fifty textile workers who applied for a Klan charter. Byers denied his and his son's involvement, adding a disclaimer that "There is not any Klan in Macon or the vicinity." Before long, however, Byers' denial of and Macon Klavern was proved wrong, when between 75 and a 100 Maconites met to discuss plans to enlarge the Klan locally. There solicitation cards read: "The Ku Klux Klan is dedicated to the security of America, first, last and forever, and the rehabilitation of a liberal Christian faith as exemplified by our Savior Jesus Christ."[74]

On 5 February 1948, the *Macon Telegraph* carried a front-page photograph of a full-fledged Klan ceremony in Swainsboro, complete with burning cross and, reportedly for the first time since the 1920s, in full regalia. A "naturalization" ceremony was held at Macon's City Auditorium on 10 December 1948, with Georgia Grand Dragon Dr. Samuel Green as main speaker. Green, whose daughter was at student Macon's Wesleyan College, spoke to some 300 persons, including a contingent of Mercer students carrying placards reading: "I am here in protest to the Klan and its principles." Later, Green denounced ministers who, like those in Macon who tried to interfere with the Empire's right of assembly, were "intolerant and communistic." He added: "If such a minister would spend more time in his pulpit preaching the word of God, he would not wonder why his congregational attendance is not what it should be."[75]

The resurgence played to mixed reviews in Macon and vicinity. One letter to the *Telegraph* acknowledged that the "so-called civil rights legislation" sparked the latest Klan demonstration, but claimed, "The people of this state are fed up on the Ku Klux Klan.... We do not propose to allow this evil thing to gain any real strength again, and every good citizens will join in frowning upon these first evidences of a revival." On the other hand, Mrs. Beulah Walker of nearby Byron, Georgia, who wrote to the *Telegraph* regularly to support both Talmadges, also spoke up about the Klan: "I thank God for the KKK, as we have never been dirty, although some men get up and say they belong to the Klan after they had done a dirty deed."[76]

Klansmen, pseudo or otherwise, perpetrated another "dirty deed" just a few weeks later, when an 8-foot cross was burned in the yard of a vacant house on College Street owned by black dentist Dr. D. T. Walton while some 200 persons watched. Walton had purchased the home three years earlier and had rented it to a white family. That spring, however, Walton decided to occupy the home himself and gave a typical sixty-day notice to the occupants. The action led to the cross burning, accompanied by a number of Klan stickers distributed at the scene. Some days later the Macon Committee on Interracial Cooperation issued a statement condemning the incident: "While it can in no way undo the wrong done, perhaps a consideration of these facts will cause all citizens of Macon to resolve that our community will not again experience such a disgrace."[77] Around the same time as the cross burning, Macon businessman W. W. Grant and his wife received a threatening letter from the Klan for unspecified violations of their ethical code. Indicating that they would be closely watched, the letter threatened, "Where the law can[']t do are won[']t do is where this organization takes over. We won[']t be your friends."[78]

Klan recruiting continued into 1949, as Herman Lavender, Exalted Cyclops of the Bibb County Klan No. 1314, announced plans to form the county's first Klan organization for women. To celebrate this new organization, Lavender planned a large rally, complete with barbecue and a speech by Grand Dragon Samuel Green.[79] In May the Bibb County Klan conducted a noisy, horn-blowing motorcade through Bibb and Houston counties, and in June Lavender led "two or three busloads" of Maconites to an initiation ceremony at Stone Mountain. At the Klan's "sacred" space, under the light of 35-foot-high burning cross, accompanied by some 800 persons in robes and hoods, 128 candidates, including about 70 from Macon, were inducted into the Invisible Empire. Responding to this revival of Klan activity in Macon, one sympathizer wrote the *Telegraph* that he always used white corn meal, bought white loaf bread, and a white mule to ploy his garden. He added, "Yes, the more white things are the better I like them. There will always be a Ku Klux Klan by statute or otherwise. And…the torch of white supremacy will always burn in the Southland."[80]

Racial progress after World War II had moved America and Macon toward equality. Even the association of the Klan with Nazi racism was becoming commonplace in the South. In the midst of the 1948 elections, so focused on race and civil rights, the *Telegraph* printed a cartoon depicting a hooded Klansman (representing "Ku Klux-Race-Religious baiter") shaking hands with Hitler as the "Spirit of the Nazi Brute." Beneath it ran the caption, "Not Dead—Of Course." But as shown by the revived Klan, strong racist attitudes remained. "We feel toward them [blacks] like the affection one has for a dog," explained a Macon railroad mechanic, "we love 'em in their place…. Sometimes we have to keep them there."[81] Thus ended the postwar period in Macon, with all sides energized for the battle that would come over the next two decades.

6

Macon and Massive Resistance

In 1952, after a number of years away from the segregated South, black journalist Carl Rowan got off a train in Macon on his way to Milledgeville. Seeing no newspapers in the black waiting room, he entered the white area to find one. Just as he offered a nickel to a woman at the newsstand, he heard a voice behind him call out, "Boy! This ain't the colored waiting room! What are you doing in here?"

"I'm buying a paper," Rowan told the stationmaster.

"Don't take his money," he barked to the woman. Turning back to the troublemaker, he told Rowan to go back to the colored area and have the black attendant buy a paper for him. The reporter, however, continued to challenge Macon's mores with his questions: "He's darker than I am and I've got the nickel. Where's the logic in that?"

"He's in uniform."

"What if I were in uniform—of the United States Navy?"

"You'd still have to go where niggers belong. Goddamit, I just follow orders here. You ain't in New York. You're just another black nigger in Georgia!"

Rowan then exploded: "Anybody who would say that he 'just follows orders' and can't explain those orders to his own conscience...can't be any more than a low, scurrilous sonofabitch!"

At that, the stationmaster retreated to his office and made a call to police. Rowan quickly found a taxi and headed for his destination, still mumbling to himself, "Georgia is still a police state and any white man who decides to be is a policeman where a Negro is involved."[1]

If white Maconites were sensitive about black challenges to racial orthodoxy in 1952, such concerns naturally became more pressing after that orthodoxy received the ultimate challenge in the *Brown v. Topeka*

Board of Education rulings of 1954 and 1955. Led by future Supreme Court justice Thurgood Marshall, the NAACP legal team argued that segregation psychologically harmed black children even if their separate facilities were equal in quality. Accepting his argument, on 17 May 1954, the Supreme Court ruled segregation in public schools "inherently unequal" and thus unconstitutional. Over the following year, opponents of the ruling raised concerns about the practical difficulties of its immediate implementation. The high court eventually heard arguments on such concerns and in what historians have called *Brown II* and sent the cases back to their original district courts. The Supreme Court instructed the lower courts, however, to execute *Brown* "with all deliberate speed."

Brown II thus set up a long-term battle in the South between the federal courts, and occasionally the executive branch, and whites who vowed never to allow racial mixing in their public schools. Historians have used the term "massive resistance" to describe the conservative white South's rhetorical and political war against desegregation.[2] Led by a succession of governors beginning with Herman Talmadge and ending in 1970 with Jimmy Carter, Georgia was at the heart of this racial counterrevolution. In central Georgia, the citizens of Macon were understandably divided over the Supreme Court's desegregation rulings and over Southern resistance to them. At the official level of city administration, however, Macon's political leadership was decidedly moderate compared to other politicians from other sections of Georgia. While the administration of B. F. Merritt, elected mayor in 1953, did not hurry to accede to the courts' desegregation rulings, neither did it engage in the "bitter end," race-baiting rhetoric of Georgia's governors during the era. At the people's level, moreover, Macon saw healthy activism on both sides of the controversy.

MASSIVE RESISTANCE: LINES OF ATTACK

Most of the initial white reactions to *Brown* reflected a mixture of disbelief and defiance. Georgia's highest political leaders denounced the ruling. Leading the pack was Herman Talmadge, who vowed that mixed schools would never become reality while he was governor, adding, "Georgia is going to resist mixing the races in the schools if it is the sole state in the nation to do so." The following year Talmadge attacked the decision in a full-length book entitled, *You and Segregation*. Attorney General Eugene Cook, a former president of the Mercer University Alumni Association and member of the school's board of trustees, denied the court's allegation that segregation gave to blacks feelings of inferiority, warning of even more serious reactions in racially mixed classes where blacks would have "a constant reminder that they are not up to par with the average white person." Along with the attorneys general of Mississippi and South Carolina, Cook immediately began to look for loopholes that would preserve segregation.[3]

An unscientific poll of Maconites and middle Georgians conducted by the *Macon Telegraph* indicated an overwhelming majority strongly disapproved of the ruling. Most whites and blacks, argued the majority, were content with things as they stood. "I don't think they can legislate brotherhood, which is what they are trying to do," suggested one Macon woman. Bibb County's State Senator J. Douglas Carlisle called the ruling the "most radical thing the Supreme Court has done in my lifetime," while state representative Denmark Groover denounced the ruling as based "purely and simply on sociological issues." He also predicted that the Georgia legislature would take some action to maintain segregation and at the same time provide educational opportunities for all its citizens." Some city officials, most prominently Mayor B. F. Merritt, avoided immediate comment, but one anonymous city leader said the ruling had violated states' rights and "taken away the meaning of the word democracy." Another expressed the hope that, "Maybe my children can finish school before they bring in the Negroes." Superintendent of Schools Dr. Mark A. Smith said the ruling would pose serious problems in Macon, while fifth grade teacher June Wood offered, "I still think Georgia and the South will find some way to work around this ruling." Bibb County Sheriff James I. Wood expected the decision to destroy the South's public school systems and degrade race relations to their worst conditions since the post-Reconstruction era.[4]

By the time the Supreme Court issued *Brown II* on 31 May 1955 a new governor had been elected by billing himself as "the white man's candidate." Vowing to resist desegregation "Come Hell or high water," Marvin Griffin rejected the high court's implementation decree, saying, "No matter how much the Supreme Court seeks to sugarcoat its bitter pill of tyranny, the people of Georgia and the South will not swallow it."[5] In November 1954, Griffin defeated racial moderate M. E. Thompson not only statewide, but also in traditionally anti-Talmadge Bibb County. Losing Bibb County for the first time, Thompson received 5,935 votes to Griffin's 6,765. On the way to his election, Griffin had supported a proposal by Herman Talmadge to circumvent *Brown* by amending the state constitution to allow public funds to subsidize private education in Georgia. This Private School Amendment, as it came to be called, envisioned state, county, or municipal funds going for direct grants to parents wishing to send their children to segregated private schools. Along with Attorney General Cook, Bibb County School Superintendent Mark Smith voted with the 14-4 majority on the Georgia Commission on Education to support the plan.[6]

Bibb County and Macon were divided over the plan, with most educators opposing it. The Bibb Education Association's voted 290 to 10 against the plan, and attorney Charles W. Walker told a meeting at city hall that the proposed amendment was an effort to "hope away" the *Brown* ruling. In a similar vein, a writer to *Telegraph* opined that the public schools were "a great example of democracy," and that Georgia could and should find other ways of dealing with segregation.[7] Mattie Hubbard Jones, a black Maconite who often voiced her opinions in the *Telegraph's* Letters section, asked, "[H]ow can children learn to be obedient and respectful to a law when many grown-ups are opposing the Supreme Court?" On the other hand, another writer argued that voters should support the amendment because it would keep the schools "free and segregated even if they are not public." Another accused the federal government of being more concerned with the will of blacks than with the concerns of Georgians, admonishing readers to support the amendment as "the only way to avoid integration in the schools in Georgia."[8]

Despite the opposition of Macon's two dailies, which joined most other Georgia newspapers in rejecting the amendment, almost 54 percent of Georgians voted for it. The *Macon News*, while supporting segregation, attacked the amendment as "dangerous to democracy." The *Telegraph* reminded readers that "Georgians did not give the Griffin administration an overwhelming mandate to abolish their public schools." These doubts were somewhat reflected in the local vote, which unlike the state at large, opposed the amendment by a narrow 52 percent margin. Given the nearly universal opposition of black voters, it appeared that most white Maconites agreed with other white Georgians in supporting the amendment. For his part, the governor-elect told voters he would not ask the legislature to act on any private school plans until the schools were actually closed because of integration.[9]

The next year, a few weeks after the *Brown II* ruling, a number of Maconites weighed in on a new controversy sparked by Attorney General Eugene Cook's proposal that the State Board of Education permanently to revoke the certificate of any teacher who "supports, encourages, condones, or agrees to teach [racially] mixed grades." Later, a resolution by the board broadened its ban to include teachers affiliated with the NAACP, which according to one estimate would have involved 90 percent of the black teachers in Bibb County. Maconite George Daniel wrote the *Telegraph* to support the effort and called on fellow citizens to support Cook "and outlaw the NAACP from Georgia." Another opponent, Douglas L. Garrett, accused the NAACP of "trying to undermine our American way of life through trickery by first getting non-segregated schools. Then would come other public spots, such as cafes, hotels, movie theaters, swimming pools, etc., until finally they move into the city, county, and state governments and also into interracial marriage, which I believe to be their ultimate goal." Still another white Maconite expressed the fervent conviction that "this organization is far more a threat to our national freedom than is the KKK, or any other organization that I have ever heard about." Mattie Hubbard Jones countered by comparing the device as reminiscent of Hitler. The same sort of division marked the debate of the state board itself, as lengthy wrangling eventually led the board to replace the controversial resolution with a more generic one requiring that teachers support the Georgia Constitution.[10]

Still, NAACP affiliation remained a sign of radicalism among most white Georgians, many of whom hoped to see their state follow the example of Alabama, which outlawed the organization in May 1956. Two months later, Attorney General Cook devised another effort to strike at integration forces in Georgia. Supported by Governor Griffin, Cook proposed that the general assembly set up a six-member legislative committee to investigate the activities of the NAACP. Cook himself averred, "I think they ought to be investigated. I think we ought to run them out of Georgia if we can, and I think we can." Bibb County's representatives supported the idea, with J. Douglas Carlisle saying, "I want racial harmony and if such an investigation would discover that the NAACP is destroying such harmony, I would see no objection to it."[11]

Cook took another line of attack in fall 1955 with a major address titled, "The Ugly Truth About the NAACP." Speaking to the Peace Officers Association of Georgia, he sought to unmask "the subversive designs behind the current crusade of the misnamed National Association for the Advancement of Colored People and its fellow-traveling fronts to force upon the South the Communist-inspired doctrine of racial integration and amalgamation.... totally disrobe the NAACP and to present this sinister and subtle organization in all its nakedness." Using information from the staff of Mississippi Senator James O. Eastland's internal security subcommittee and other such sources, Cook accused the NAACP of seizing on the race issue to "dupe naive do-gooders, fuzzy-minded intellectuals, misguided clergymen, and radical journalists to be their pawns." He "reported" that twenty-eight of the organization's forty-seven-member board of directors had been cited for un-American activities. Included in this number were Georgians Benjamin E. Mays, president of Atlanta's Morehouse College, and Savannah NAACP president Wesley W. Law. By calling for "full racial equality" and the abolition of all segregation laws, Cook argued, the NAACP shared the "racial aims" of the Communist Party. Cook also denounced the Southern Regional Council (SRC) and the Georgia Committee on Interracial Cooperation as "front organizations" aiding the NAACP in its "fomenting strife and discord" between the races "which heretofore—and at present are—harmonious and friendly in every respect."[12]

"McCarthyism has come to Georgia," announced the *Macon Telegraph* editorial comment on Cook's address. Disclaiming any support for the NAACP, which the editors believed was "well on its way to discrediting itself by its own radical and unreasoning actions," the commentary accused Cook of resorting to half truths. Ralph Bunche, for example, had been "cited" by investigative committees, but Cook failed to note that he had also been cleared of any un-American activities. Cook's tactic thus "smacks too loudly of political opportunism." The SRC rejoinder to Cook noted that neither it nor the Georgia Committee on Interracial Cooperation had ever been accused of disloyalty to the United States. The statement defended the prominent Georgia clergy on the Georgia Committee and its executive director (and Mercer graduate) Dr. Guy H. Wells. The SRC argued that the Communists were indeed trying to convert the dark-skinned peoples of the world with the claim that American democracy was "available only to white persons." Cook and his fellow demagogues, concluded the SRC statement, were doing "a great service to the cause of communism every time they raise their voices on behalf of 'white supremacy.'" For its part, the NAACP challenged Cook's advice to local school board not to move toward desegregation, arguing that the Supreme Court had "said unmistakably that all state laws requiring or permitting racial segregation in education are unconstitutional."[13]

Cook responded in public statement on 28 September in which he rejected the Macon NAACP's interpretation of the *Brown II* ruling as "nefarious, vicious, and erroneous.... just another subtle approach typical of NAACP leadership." Carefully parsing *Brown II's* legal language, Cook cleverly argued that segregation could be maintained on the basis of "factors wholly unrelated to race or color." Later, when a succession of NAACP spokespersons, including Executive Director Roy Wilkins, denounced the Attorney General's speech, Cook reiterated his criticisms of the organization, commenting, "The hit dog always hollers." He also criticized the *Telegraph* for its rejection of his arguments. Throughout the controversy, Cook held that by not being party to its decisions, Georgia was not bound by the Supreme Court. It would take, he noted, separate suits in each of the state's 201 school systems to end segregation because "only the specific county involved in the suit" would be affected.[14]

In 1956 the Georgia General Assembly continued its massive resistance to *Brown* by passing an appropriations bill that rendered racially mixed schools (which at that time did not exist) ineligible for state funds. The legislators also adopted an interposition resolution declaring the *Brown* rulings null and void. In an important symbolic line of attack, the state senate signaled its rejection of integration and its allegiance to the Southern way of life by voting 41 to 3 to replace the Georgia flag's three vertical stripes with the Confederate St. Andrew's Cross on a red background. Criticizing the vote, the *Macon Telegraph* argued that the state flag should not be changed "without an overwhelming expression from the people that they want it changed." There was, however, no overwhelming outcry from the Georgia populace denouncing the change or the undemocratic manner by which the flag was changed.[15]

Thus, when the measure reached the House, Macon's representative Denmark Groover, serving as Governor Griffin's floor leader, vigorously supported changing the flag, which he believed would "perpetuate the memory of the Confederacy," and "leave no doubt in anyone's mind that Georgia will not forget the teachings of Lee and Stonewall Jackson." Atlanta representative John Sammons Bell said he was proud of the new flag, adding that "all true Georgians ought to be." With only 4 more votes than were needed, the House passed the bill by a 107 to 32 tally. In the only public criticism to surface in the *Telegraph,* one writer denounced the paper's opposition to the measure and advocated adopting the "complete stars and bars" as the state flag as "one way of telling the government…that we will never surrender our sovereignty and principles of life to any Supreme Court." His concluding admonition called on the paper to stop condoning the "mongrelization of the white race": "Try God for a change and tell about his separation of the races when He made man."[16]

Although views were increasingly mixed as the civil rights era wore on, the bulk of white Maconites who expressed their views in the *Telegraph* shared such religio-racial views. Reading of an interracial ministers' meeting, one reader complained, "[I]f the Macon preachers want to live with them, mix with them, they have my permission. But get out of my race and church and do it. And you had better get out of the South. Go on up north where you belong." Another wrote, "We can not mix races without violating the laws of God with out stirring up a lot of trouble." Still another denounced the ministers for reading only the New Testament, while ignoring Old Testament passage that called for separation of the Israelites from their neighbors. His mother had taught him to believe "every last page" of "the Old-Time Bible, not a Sociological Bible," and he refused to send his children to any church that did not believe likewise. Yet another opined that the "South was very happy as things stood, without having the Negroes crammed down our throat," adding, "Those that do read the Bible should know, without a shadow of a doubt, that our Lord and Savior is not pleased with race mixing."[17]

More prominent white Maconites advanced decidedly more political arguments against integration. State Senator Douglas Carlisle denounced 312 Atlanta ministers as "quislings" for their publication of a manifesto on race relations and called upon other legislators to follow his lead. Attorney Charles J. Bloch announced in a speech that he preferred "no schools to those run by Chief Justice Earl Warren and Associate Justices Black, Douglas, Frankfurter, and other advisors of the NAACP." State Representative Denmark Groover blasted the *Telegraph* for claiming to support continued segregation while rejecting all recent proposals for doing so. Accusing the Supreme Court of disregarding "long-established legal precedents" in favor of arguments of the Communist Party, he demanded that the *Telegraph* fully support segregation and any means of maintaining it.[18]

Although likely shared by the majority of white Maconites, this opposition to integration hardly had the public stage to itself. Not quite as cautious as they had been in the World War II period, Macon's white and black progressives found themselves buoyed by the Supreme Court's rulings. When added to earlier civil rights policies of the Truman administration, blacks began to see in the federal government signs that their "God of the Oppressed" was moving to change the racial status quo and expel Jim Crow from the body politic. With somewhat more caution and less fervor, white progressives in Macon raised their voices against segregation.

ACADEMIA AND RACIAL SUBVERSION

At the height of the gubernatorial controversy of 1947, before the legislature elected Herman Talmadge, Mercer University President Spright Dowell received a letter asking him to use his influence to lobby for continuing the Talmadge program by electing Herman to replace his father. Working for the Talmadge campaign, Reid H. Cox wrote, "Knowing that you have always stood for the County unit system, the white primary and many other fine principles of Mr. Talmadge's program, I would consider it a personal favor if you will immediately advise your State Legislators if you feel that Herman Talmadge...is the only one fully qualified to carry through his father's program." Dowell made no reply to the appeal.[19] From 1928 to 1953 Dowell presided over a university that was becoming central to Macon's educational, cultural, and economic development. His quiet non-response to the Talmadge program illustrates the way Mercer University and Wesleyan College began unobtrusively, often inconsistently, to subvert the racial arrangements in the mental universes of their students. While that mission seems to have been on the agendas of early twentieth-century faculty members like Carl Steed and J. R. Moseley, the postwar World War era enlarged the roster of progressive double agents on the Macon campuses.

At least since Socrates ran afoul of the ancient Athenian authorities, teaching has often proven to be a subversive calling. There have always been those who view education as a matter of pouring orthodoxy into the empty heads of students. But as the twentieth century unfolded and the mission of colleges shifted from moral instruction to the search for truth wherever it might lead, college teaching gradually became as much inspiring students to think critically as communicating a body of knowledge. In ways much less visible than Socrates, a minority of college professors in Macon worked gently to prod their charges to think differently about segregation and race.

Mercer and Wesleyan could hardly have been mistaken for schools of radicalism—twentieth-century Oberlins sending abolitionist students out into the Jim Crow South. Their records on race matters were mixed. At the same time that radical egalitarian J. R. Moseley taught philosophy at Mercer, Christianity professor and later fundamentalist leader John Roach Straton taught that the evolution of blacks was far behind that of whites. Blacks were suffering from "ethical and even physical decay" that even education could not stave off.[20] A look at the persons given honorary doctorates by Mercer over the years suggests the university's willingness to honor both the advocates of change and the protectors of order. Among the defenders of the status quo honored by the university were United Daughter of the Confederacy leader Dorothy Blount Lamar (1940), conservative Senators Walter F. George (1957) and Richard B. Russell, Jr. (1957). On the other hand, the university also honored Guy H. Wells, executive director of the Georgia Committee on Interracial Cooperation (1934), anti-lynching managing editor of the *Macon*

Telegraph and *Louisville Courier-Journal* Mark Ethridge (1942), and racially progressive Arkansas congressman Brooks Hays (1958).[21] In addition, the schools attendance policies were products of their times. Until the 1960s neither school allowed blacks to enroll. Wesleyan allowed occasional black speakers, but did not allow them in the audience, whereas Mercer allowed blacks to attend public events (though with segregated seating) but allowed no black speakers to be officially invited by the college administration.[22]

E. Dorothy Blount Lamar, ca. 1950, was an official prominent historian of the United Daughters of the Confederacy. (Courtesy of the Washington Memorial Library.)

While these policies matched the racial views of most of the schools' Baptist and Methodist constituencies, Mercer presidents had a tradition of working both sides of the street on racial issues. In the 1920s president Rufus Weaver was appointed by Governor Clifford M. Walker, a member of the Klan, to serve on the Georgia Literacy Committee. At the same time he wrote letters to Mercer alumnus Guy M. Wells, encouraging him to work toward a Ph.D. In response, Wells wrote Weaver from Columbia University to tell him, "You doubtless are the cause of my coming here. I am now more determined than ever to complete my education." Wells' study of "educational democracy" under John Dewey would eventually bring him to leadership in the interracial movement.[23]

Leading Mercer from the just before the Great Depression to just before the Supreme Court's *Brown* ruling against school segregation, Spright Dowell managed to keep the preachers of the Georgia Baptist Convention happy with the school—most of the time. In 1939 a student named John Birch challenged the theological orthodoxy of five Christianity professors and a trustee committee that included future Judge Hoyt Davis. Dowell, the professors, and academic freedom weathered the storm when the committee acquitted them of heresy. Their statement on the issue, however, recognized the need for caution in the classroom and especially on the part of the administrator who put them there.[24]

Occasionally, he also spoke directly on questions of race. Though not widely publicized to the wider Macon community, Dowell guardedly traveled to Tuskegee Institute in 1949 to speak at a memorial service for President Robert Russa Moton. Quoting a speech by Moton, Dowell told the congregation, "Here in America these two races are charged under God with the responsibility of showing to the world how individuals, as well as races, may differ most widely in color and inheritance and at the same time make themselves helpful and even indispensable to each other's progress and prosperity." He also praised the Southern Sociological Congress and the Southern Regional Council as believers in "the gospel of cooperation between the races," who rightly decided "it's up to us as Southerners to join together, face up to the South's problems honestly, and work to solve them." In Dowell's mind and temper, however, solutions meant gradualism and compromise. Whites must cease thinking of blacks as a "servant race," and grant them "the rights granted to him under the Constitution," including the franchise, jury responsibilities, justice in the courts, freedom from mob violence, and equal educational opportunity. For their part, African Americans should dispense with impatience and radicalism—"the demand for all or nothing." He added, "[W]e must not let the traditions of Tuskegee and of the other best Southern institutions and agencies be lost by reason of a revival of reactionaries and prejudiced Southern leaders of the white race, or by the bitterness and radicalism of the leaders of the Negro race and their friends."[25]

These are not the words of a social revolutionary, to be sure. Like most Southern whites born in the late nineteenth century, Dowell shared a basic view of African Americans as inferior. He could use word "nigger" in private conversations. To a great extent his personal fondness for blacks was conditioned upon their willingness to accept their inferiority. Like most white Southerners, his interactions with blacks was characterized by paternalism, perhaps best illustrated by his and his university's response to the 1939 death of Lee Battle, a black Maconite who served Mercer as a janitor and other capacities for forty years. Dowell allowed Battle's body to lie in state in the Faculty Trustee Room of the university, an honor typically restricted to school presidents or others similarly situated. Members of the university community attended his funeral at the Unionville Baptist Church. Dowell and university trustee Louie D. Newton presided over graveside ceremonies in Forsyth. The two also spearheaded efforts to erect a Lee Battle Memorial on the campus, eventually settling on naming the school's infirmary after him. Later, a student organization established a marker in Battle's honor on the campus near Sherwood Hall.[26] From a post-civil rights, post-Black Power perspective, such devotion may be dismissed as maudlin kindness for a "mascot" who was loved partly because he always knew his place. Nevertheless, the degree to which Mercer honored a black janitor was remarkable. And the bare facts that Dowell spoke at Tuskegee at a time when the Talmadges still shaped the political landscape and his Baptist constituency in Georgia remained vigilant to ferret out unorthodoxy wherever they could find it, places Dowell among those who were tiptoeing toward freedom.

One quiet, gradual way to do this was to continue to hire a handful of racial progressives, mostly educated at Northern universities, to join his faculty and widen Mercerian horizons. A number of these young subversives, Southerners who had been educated in the North and who returned to launch quiet attacks on the staid worldviews of their students, arrived at Mercer even before the postwar era. English professor Talmadge Smalley slyly informed Mercer students, "If you're going to keep the nigra on his back, you'll have to stay on your face to do it."[27]

A small swarm of professorial gadflies arrived in Macon after the war. In 1946, Christianity professor Howard G. McClain, a member of the progressive Fellowship of Southern Churchmen, sought out SRC Executive Director Guy B. Johnson to collaborate on a program of providing research materials on the South to local churches. On another occasion, he arranged to take a class in race relations to a seminar and the black Atlanta University, along with a tour of black businesses, and a visit to the SRC offices. McClain was particularly eager to have his "born-and-bred Georgian" students to interact with SRC stalwart Dorothy Tilly, also a Wesleyan alumna, and member of President Truman's Civil Rights Committee. His charges, McClain told Tilly, had "come along very encouragingly in their work and experiences in this class so far and we are confident that this trip to Atlanta will...be an experience they will never be able to get away from."[28]

Another professor hired by Dowell who undermined his students' conventional wisdom on race was Das Kelly Barnett. Arriving at Mercer in the late 1940s with a doctorate in theology from the Southern Baptist Theological Seminary in Louisville, Kentucky, Barnett was a gifted preacher and idealistic enough to believe his oratory could change Southern Baptists. Besides filling Georgia Baptist pulpits on occasional Sundays, he taught courses in Christian and biblical ethics in the Mercer Christianity department. From his lectern he informed students that "basic civil rights are essentially spiritual, and to deny these rights to one is to endanger the same rights for others." In another 1947 course, he gave a great proportion of his lectures to explaining the Social Gospel to his students, highlighting all the major works of the leading spokesperson for the movement, Walter Rauschenbusch. He told students that in the previous forty years the labor movement had done the most good for people in the United States, while "churches have just passed a few resolutions. The more un-Christian," he noted, "have upheld the Christian principles." He called the god of the Ku Klux Klan "a tribal god," and informed students that the biblical book of Ruth refutes "racial intolerance." Barnett was later known for deliberately riding in the "Negro" sections of Macon buses. Eventually, however, Barnett grew weary of trying to change Baptists. Always ambitious for bigger things, he left the denomination when he was overlooked for a prestigious position at his seminary alma mater in Kentucky. Becoming an Episcopalian, partly for that tradition's social progressive and partly for its more liberal views on alcohol, he finished his career teaching in a seminary in Texas.[29]

Like most Southern college presidents in the era of Jim Crow, Spright Dowell's record on race was mixed. At times these gadfly professors went farther than Dowell could safely tolerate. When they did, Dowell had to fire them or encourage them to move on, as became the case after *Brown* caused the institutional caretaker to take a harder line against radical, racial activism. Despite Dowell's wavering, he nevertheless showed sympathy for the interracial cause, a cause that was slowly catching on at Mercer within a small group of students and faculty. In April 1947, R. L. Russell, director of the Georgia Committee on Interracial Cooperation, requested that Dowell recommend a Mercer student to speak to an upcoming meeting of the committee in Macon. Dowell referred the request to professor of Christianity Hansford D. Johnson, who recommended World War II veteran and then Mercer ministerial student, Virgil Colson. At the meeting, Colson spoke on the topic, "A Better Race Understanding for Better Living in Georgia." The following year another ministerial student, Jack Singletary and his wife, joined the African American Tremont Temple Baptist Church. Controversy erupted over whether this violated any law and whether Singletary's Mercer education had influenced such a radical action. City attorney Ed S. Sell, Jr., assured citizens that no law had been broken, while Professor Hansford D. Johnson told reporters that the student's decision "doesn't grow out of any instructions he has received at Mercer." Despite Johnson's disingenuous claim to the contrary, the teaching of Mercer's subversives was apparently hitting some of its targets.[30]

Aiming most eagerly at these young targets was Spright Dowell's most prophetic professorial hire, G. McLeod Bryan. Educated at Yale as a firebrand ethicist, Bryan became steeped in the teachings of the biblical prophets and began teaching his students, inside and outside of the classroom, in 1949. With a Jeremiah-like "fire in his bones" to confront the racial status quo with biblical truth, Bryan's bravado developed a relatively small group of preacher-boy followers who came to be disparagingly known as the "Bryanites." Most Mercer students remained in the grip of Southern racial mores, as was indicated by a 1958 survey conducted by the student newspaper, the *Mercer Cluster*. Of the 637 students who cast ballots, 61 percent opted for continuing segregation at Mercer. An even larger majority, 73 percent, believed that segregation was not unchristian.[31] Bryan, campus minister Ray Brewster, and the other academic gadflies could not convert the majority of their charges, but they made a deep impression upon a small, activist minority—what the Hebrew Bible called "a remnant" of progressive ministerial students who gloried in challenging the fundamentalist, racist mores of Macon.

One of Bryan's converts, and later dean of students at Mercer, Joseph M. Hendricks later described Brewster, who arrived on campus in 1952, as cautiously leading students "into a freedom they didn't want," while Bryan was the sort to wave a red flag in front of a bull.[32] One of Bryan's more radical techniques was to take students on field trips to visit Koinonia Farm in Americus. Koinonia was an interracial commune founded by Clarence Jordan, a Georgia farmer with a Ph.D. in New Testament Greek from the Southern Baptist Theological Seminary. At Koinonia and in their mentor's home the Bryanites participated in theological bull sessions that influenced their thinking as much as their classroom work. Bryan also took students to conferences at the historically black Morehouse College and Fort Valley State College. He published an underground newspaper called *Combustible/Burn*, which advised its young clientele to burn it pages after they had perused them. The paper expressed a statement of principles shared by the teacher and his pupils:

We stand for the break-down of all things that create prestige-seeking class-consciousness: secret clubs, fraternities and sororities, ostentatious behavior and possessions. We stand for a minimum standard of living based on the necessities, rather than the luxuries of life, complete sharing, beginning in our homes, of the things we own with our brethren who sacrifice and our neighbors who need. We stand for the free, honest, and rigorous pursuit of Truth and the exchange of ideas in a fearless forum. We stand for the ecumenical fellowship of Christians as over against narrow creeds and a self-centered concern for institutional denominations. We stand for alternatives to war, iron-curtain propaganda, nationalistic patriotism, and armaments: this may be the path of all-out pacifism or lesser degrees of variation upon that. We stand for the complete integration of all people, with equal opportunities beginning in our homes and for every new-born child. We stand for the sense of Christian vocation in its deepest and widest implications. We will accept each person for what he or she is.[33]

In the classroom, where more cautious colleagues occasionally warned him not to address certain topics, he charged ahead. As a prophetic spirit, given not so much to "foretelling," but to the "forth telling" of the Hebrew prophets, he was galled by the "conspiracy of silence" he perceived in Southern race relations, and particularly the fearful, muted voices of the Southern and Georgia Baptist Conventions. Noticing the avoidance of race in denominational teaching materials and sermons, students approached Bryan wondering, "Why is our denomination—the largest and most prominent denomination in the South—not saying a word about this issue?" Thus propelled by his students' queries as much as his own impulses, Bryan ignored warnings about losing promotions or even his job and dealt openly with race in both formal and informal settings.[34]

In 1953 a student named Hinse Houser, whose diving accident had left him paralyzed and confined to a wheelchair, matriculated at Mercer and studied with Bryan. Houser was attended by a black aide who pushed his wheelchair from classroom to classroom. While Houser sat in a class in Christian ethics, his aide remained out in the hallway eavesdropping on Bryan's lectures. The professor and students began to strike up conversations with the bright young black man before and after class, eventually leading Bryan, with the class's approval, to invite him to sit in on the class as an auditor. Within twenty hours, Bryan later recalled, word had reached university administrators who instructed the would-be student not to return to the classroom again.[35]

The next year, just after the *Brown* ruling, Bryan responded with a letter to the *Macon Telegraph* calling on Maconites to display "intelligence and democracy and Christianity," all of which the world might rightly question if white Southerners continued to deplore the Court's decision. "Now is the time for the really constructive forces, level-headed people to go to work and plan for the solution of this problem, instead of allowing the reactionaries to take over."[36] A few weeks later a Bryanite student named Clifford York ran afoul of Macon's racial mores and of the police when he invited Richard Scott, a black friend from Talladega College in Alabama, into his home. When a white neighbor saw Scott and the others playing croquet and grilling hamburgers, York received an irate phone call, beginning "Get that nigger out of there."

"First, of all, he's not a nigger," came York's quick reply. "He is a Ne-gro. And he is my guest."

"Well, you better get him out or I'm going to call the police."

"Well, you do whatever you have to do."

After a while, two officers from the sheriff's office arrived and, without a warrant, proposed to arrest Scott and York for violating segregation laws. At one point one of the officers privately told York, "Look, just give me the nigger, and we'll just drop everything against you." Fearing that his friend would be beaten on the way to the station, York declined the offer and was also arrested. The two were released a short time later, however, as there was no law against whites and blacks visiting each other. The officers had acted on the "authority" of an "unwritten law," and later Bibb County Sheriff James Wood defended the arrest: "An act legal within itself may become illegal if coupled with factors tending to produce a breach of the peace...."[37]

The following year Governor Marvin Griffin demanded that Georgia Tech's football team boycott the Sugar Bowl rather than play against a team with black players. Angered by the governor's decision, some fifty Mercer students began a demonstration on their campus, then proceeded to march to the offices of the *Macon Telegraph*. The protesters picked up supporters along the way, as they sang the Tech fight song and hanged the governor in effigy. Their placards read, "Mercer Backs Tech, Here Hangs Gov. Griffin."[38]

Bryan's radicalism had proceeded apace, as he joined the Montgomery Improvement Association during its famous bus boycott and had appeared with Martin Luther King on a program at Fort Valley State. At the same time, the more cautious George B. Connell had succeeded Spright Dowell as Mercer president. Bryan had long chafed at Macon's repressive racial ethos, such as that displayed by a neighbor with whom the professor occasionally watched the World Series on television. When his neighbor, a Baptist and a Macon police officer, ceremoniously left the room whenever Jackie Robinson came to bat, Bryan grew weary of the effect of race and prejudice on the most mundane of activities.

Up to that point, he had ignored offers to leave Mercer, but in the more cautious atmosphere at the university since Connell's arrival and since the Brown ruling, Bryan began to reconsider. By the summer of 1956 his associations with King led the administration without any warning to replace him as the teacher of a course on "Human Relations." Angered by the administration's betrayal, he accepted an invitation to move to Wake Forest College. Later, he reminisced about his leaving Macon: "When I left Georgia I left because I said there's no way you can breathe in Georgia. You can't go to get a hamburger, you can't go to the drugstore, you can't take a bus-ride, you can't go to a ballgame, you can't go to church, can't go anywhere, without race. And I said that's stifling. Who wants to spend your life in a place in which every single moment of your existence had to do with race."[39]

The professor-prophet was gone, but the parade of subversive professors at Mercer continued. Bryan's quieter colleague, Harold McManus, continued to stimulate critical thinking in the minds of Mercerians, as did Bryan's successor, Robert Otto. Historian Willis B. Glover played a prominent role in the Macon Council on Human Relations, and in 1957 told a chapel audience that in the face of the Supreme Court's desegregation rulings, "nonsense is all we've got out of our political leaders."[40] Ray Brewster persisted in his progressive pedagogy into the late 1970s, and former Bryanite Joseph Hendricks would become a major force in aiding both Mercer and its first black students adjust to integration. In the meantime, across town a cadre of professors at Wesleyan College similarly challenged their students' racial assumptions.

Founded in 1836 as the first college for women in America, Wesleyan College in some ways had progressive social thought in its genes. With some 350 students and a few professorial gadflies of its own, Wesleyan added to the list of academic subversives the names of Emmett Johnson, William Hinson, Carl Bennett, and Thomas Gossett. Somewhat more conservative on race than his cross-town presidential colleague Spright Dowell, school president B. Joseph Martin once ordered his faculty not to tell him that refusing admission to blacks was unchristian. He also was reported to have promised the trustee board that any blacks admitted to the school would be "over his dead body."[41]

Such warnings, however, did not deter English professors Bennett and Gossett, who participated in the Macon Council on Human Relations. A "Quakerized Baptist" who grew up in Waycross, Georgia, Carl Bennett began a fifteen-year teaching stint at Wesleyan in 1944, while he finished his Ph.D. in English at Atlanta's Emory University. After holding membership in the Ingleside Baptist Church for a year, Bennett and his wife Margaret discovered that the recently formed congregation's by-laws prescribed that its pastors not preach on "race, politics, or any other controversial subject." At the minister's insistence the clause was moved from a section on "The Pastor's Duties," to a preamble suggesting that all church schoolteachers avoid such subjects. In response, Bennett resigned his teaching assignment. Several years later, Bennett argued with his fellow Baptists when conservatives defeated an effort to have the state convention's Social Service Commission study the forthcoming *Brown* ruling. An incredulous Bennett wrote the state Baptist newspaper, the *Christian Index,* asking, "What more pressing need in the field of human relations do we face in Georgia... than the current issue of segregation in the public schools?"[42]

Besides his own progressive religious convictions, Bennett's relationships with Afro-Maconites also spurred him to action in the Macon Council on Human Relations. A black friend and his family had gone for a Sunday drive out in the vicinity of the city's segregated Baconsfield Park. As they saw white children across the park riding in a miniature train, the man's eight-year-old son asked, "Daddy, if I scald myself white, will they let me ride it?" Sometime after the end of the war, Bennett learned that a black friend was going to move into a house owned by his family but previously rented to a white family. Before his family could move into the home, however, they discovered a burning cross in their yards. In response, they were frightened away from living in their own house.[43]

Such experiences turned Bennett into even more of a crusader than his colleagues at Mercer. In 1947 he addressed a radio forum, denouncing a bill in the Georgia legislature to restore the white primary. Responding to a radio appeal to the "good white people" of Georgia to support the bill, Bennett told his audience: "I should like to speak for some 'good' white people who are opposed to the iniquity that will be perpetrated by this so-called white-primary legislation.... I oppose the so-called white primary legislation for at least four reasons. In purpose it is immoral, in form it is illegal, in content it is undemocratic, in practice it is unworkable.... No appeals to prejudice or ignorance should be allowed to abridge or destroy the individual rights of any American citizen."[44]

On another occasion, Bennett invited Benjamin E. Mays, president of Atlanta's Morehouse College, to speak at Wesleyan, but knew the college would not allow Mays to eat in the school cafeteria. Arranging a small luncheon, Bennett led Mays and a small group of students and faculty to their accommodations at the city YWCA. As they approached the dining hall, May's asked bluntly, "Are we going to eat at the same table?" A relieved Bennett happily assured him that they were. Later, in the 1950s, when Koinonia Farm was suffering from an economic boycott, Bennett and his colleague Tom Gossett came to the rescue. They searched Bibb County for one proprietor who would sell supplies to Koinonia. The Wesleyan professors found one store owner willing to do so, but only provided the Koinonians meet him halfway, at a neutral site well away from the Sumter County line. The merchant feared that snipers on the way into the county might shoot his driver.[45]

Both professors also entered the fray with their pens. Bennett occasionally took on white supremacy in letters to the *Telegraph*. In 1946 he countered an earlier letter from "a Christian woman," who referred to the nineteenth-century myth of Ham. He submitted a six-point refutation of the argument that Noah's curse of his son Ham's descendants caused God to relegating "the Negro race" to a permanent servant status, concluding that "it is abundantly clear that God had no more a part in the event than he had in Noah's getting drunk and exposing himself in the first place.... The false tradition of 'Bible authority' for racial domination was built up by a loose and false interpretation of the Scriptural account. We have used this racial myth in order to rationalize our disgraceful subjection of a whole people."[46]

Later, in a more scholarly vein, Bennett wrote a report for the Southern Regional Council called, "Race in the News," in which he analyzed the way Southern newspapers editors treated blacks in their stories. Basing his research on four and a half months of stories in the Macon newspapers, he found that the word "Negro" appeared in 153 headlines. Only twelve identified them by name rather than by race. In sum, 270 articles identified blacks with violence and lawbreaking, while in contrast there were 801 accounts of white violence or law breaking, with only four mentions of their color. Crimes of blacks against white got much more attention than those involving blacks against blacks or whites against blacks. By contrast, most Southern dailies dismissed black murders in a paragraph or in routine roundups of court news. He concluded, "This pattern of explicit versus implicit handling of the color angle...serves to perpetuate the popular notion that the Negro is characteristically a sorry, low-down, good-for-nothing, trifling troublemaker." Both *Time* and *Newsweek* magazines ran stories about Bennett's study in their 3 October 1949 issues. For his part, Thomas Gossett's research produced a widely read and highly regarded book called, *Race: The History of an Idea in America.*[47]

WHITE PROGRESSIVES OUTSIDE ACADEME

White progressives outside the not-so-cloistered halls of Mercer and Wesley also responded to the *Brown* ruling. Their efforts strained to keep a lid on the segregationist extreme while slowly trying to win the hearts and minds of more moderate whites. But this strategy emerged only gradually, not taking a high public profile until the latter part of the 1950s. Led mostly by a few of the city's white ministers, the initial reaction to both rulings combined four parts silence and one part caution. In his immediate response to the 1954 decision, C. DeWitt Matthews, pastor of the Vineville Baptist Church and president of the Macon Ministerial Association, hoped for time for the South to adjust, saying: "In eliminating segregation...however right it may be, the actual change is psychological and sociological, and these processes may never come to pass quickly." The Macon Committee on Interracial Cooperation (MCIC), soon to be recast as the Macon Council on Human Relations (MCHR), was more positive, praising the ruling and urging the community to "see that the moral and legal implications of this historic ruling are honored and respected.[48]

White ministers said little after this until October 1955, five months after *Brown II,* when the Macon Baptist Association issued a report accepting "the fact of the recent Supreme Court ruling." The report carefully noted, however, that the association "doesn't endorse the decision but only acknowledges it." Beyond this, the resolution merely advised preaching the gospel, studying the facts, and extending courtesy to African Americans. The Baptists also warned that immediate desegregation would likely result in greater problems.[49] Continuing its low-key educational approach, the MCIC met regularly at Christ Episcopal Church, the only white church at which they were allowed to gather. At the same time the Baptist Association issued its statement, the MCIC brought in Atlanta University sociologist Mozell C. Hill to advise them on conducting a human relations survey of the community.[50]

This first major public forum on the integration issue brought together the white Macon Ministerial Association with the black Evangelical Ministers' Union. Some fifty black ministers and twenty-five white ministers gathered again at Christ Church in February 1956 to discuss the topic "We Are One in Christ." Most of the larger Protestant churches were represented at the meeting, as the group called for "a Christian searching for solutions to ease racial tension in the community." The ministers, however, reached no agreement on what to do next, and the discussion degenerated into a debate on interracial marriage. Two white ministers viewed the possibility as "completely abhorrent," while the Reverend Charles W. Ward, minister of the black First Baptist Church, assured his white brothers that intermarriage was not part of his people's agenda. Ward also condemned white usage of the Bible to defend segregation. Henry Stokes, pastor of Macon's white First Baptist Church agreed, complaining that such misinterpretations too heavily depended on Old Testament passage, adding that a Christian view of race relations should be based upon the New Testament.

At the end of the meeting, the black ministers called for more frequent meetings of that kind, and the Reverend J. T. Saxon issued the white ministers a pointed challenge: "The things that we say here won't amount to much until the white ministers can say the same things to their congregations and stay in Macon. The ministers of the gospel can settle this thing more quickly than anyone else. Will we do it?"[51] A few days after the meeting, a *Macon Telegraph* reader penned a letter to the editors dismissing racial intermarriage as a red herring. "I doubt seriously," he suggested, "that if and when complete racial integration is realized, people will tend generally to marry persons they do not choose to marry." Beside, he argued, biblical injunctions against intermarriage were based on religious rather than racial grounds. Complimenting the ministers for their meeting, he called upon the board of education, civic clubs, and other community organizations to follow suit.[52]

Of growing importance in providing a moderate voice within Macon's white community was the Macon Council on Human Relations (MCHR). An affiliate of the Georgia Council on Human Relations and its parent group, the Southern Regional Council, the MCHR stepped up its efforts to continue the tradition of interracial cooperation in Macon. Members admitted that the angry atmosphere in Georgia forced them to work "slowly and cautiously, sometimes ineffectively." Statewide, the GCHR had affiliates in Atlanta, LaGrange, Albany, Augusta, Savannah, and Macon, some 350 members who overcame widespread fear among whites about improving race relations. Along with sponsoring fellowship and informational meetings, both the Macon and state councils sought to educate law enforcement officials, civic, college, and church groups on the problems of human relations.[53]

Nevertheless, the most radical strategy of the MCHR was to hold its regular meetings and occasionally host the statewide annual meeting of the GCHR in Macon. Sometimes these meetings invited "controversial" speakers to address them, as when the Reverend William Holmes Borders told the group to "hurl the torch of democracy around the world to prove that Christianity does work." A native of Macon and pastor of Atlanta's prestigious Wheat Street Baptist Church, Borders had recently challenged segregation on city buses by riding in the front seats. Still, white and black Maconites held high the torch of interracial cooperation. But although it had begun merely advocating that blacks' separate facilities be truly equalized, the Supreme Court rulings had transformed its agenda to helping their white neighbors comply with *Brown* more speedily and with less deliberation. White leaders of the group included businessman Gus B. Kaufman and Mercer professors Marguerite Woodruff, Willis B. Glover, and Joseph Hendricks. Black leaders included mortician Frank J. Hutchings, Daniel O'Hemmigan, pastor of the Washington Avenue Presbyterian Church, nurse Ruth Hartley Mosley, and Willis Sheftall, director of the Booker T. Washington Community Center.[54]

Frank J. Hutchings, 1962, a member of the Macon Council on Human Relations and a well respected voice of Macon's black community. (Courtesy of the Washington Memorial Library.)

Naturally, the NAACP and other black groups mounted the most vigorous and courageous efforts to protest the continuing reign of Jim Crow. Emboldened by recent events that convinced them that both God and the Supreme Court were allies in their struggle for racial equality, black groups strengthened the work begun by the NAACP during the war years until it became the foundation for a major assault during the 1960s.

BROWN AND BLACK PROTEST

From both his involvement with the NAACP and the MCHR, Frank J. Hutchings seemed a likely spokesperson for Macon's black community as word of the *Brown* hit the newswire. In a monumental understatement, he suggested, "I don't think we are going to have any hullabaloo. I think the colored people and the white people are gong to put their heads together and come up with a wise solution."[55] Hutchings apparently did not anticipate massive resistance, but the NAACP quickly generated its own hullabaloo by moving past public rhetoric to immediate action. Within a week of "Black Monday," as segregationists called the day of the *Brown* decision, the Macon NAACP followed the blueprint of the national office and petitioned the local school board for the immediate end of segregation. The school desegregation effort was coupled with an earlier petition by the Macon Negro Golfers Association requesting that the city allow blacks to use the Bowden Municipal Golf Course twice a week. Both petitions received noncommittal responses from Mayor B. F. Merritt, who announced no meeting on the petitions could be scheduled for at least a week. Six months later both petitions were still pending. By early November the golf petition still languished in the city council's public property committee, while Superintendent of Schools Mark A. Smith and board president J. D. Crump declined comment on the desegregation of the Bibb County schools.[56]

In due course the silence of white officials sparked NAACP action, as the Macon branch voted to submit another petition to the board asking that "immediate steps" toward integrating the schools be taken. The group also voted to support the golfers' petition. Citing the *Brown* ruling, the petition asked the school board to schedule a hearing with black leadership and offered "to be of whatever assistance we can to devising and implementing a program of desegregation. The petition was signed by forty-two black parents and endorsed by a prominent black civic organization known as the Homosphian Club. To avoid any economic reprisals on the signers, NAACP President J. S. Williams recruited only blacks employed by the federal government or other blacks. Ignoring the NAACP efforts, the board shelved the request until "a constructive and proper" time.[57]

On the eve of the next academic year, however, the board had been unable to find a proper time to discuss the matter with the city's black parents. In early summer Williams announced that "Every locality will get at least one test," as the NAACP sought at least one "good victory" in the state. Such, he told reporters, "would show that no state can successfully and indefinitely defy the supreme law of the land." By mid-summer 1955 NAACP leadership in Georgia had planned to file petitions in Atlanta, Macon, and Savannah. At the same time the national, state, and local NAACP organizations countered the state's efforts to ban NAACP-affiliated teachers. In Macon, Williams vowed to burn the group's membership rolls before he would allow teachers to be singled out. He compared Attorney General Cook's efforts to Nazi tactics, and asked, "[W]hat's to stop him from extending it to other groups such as

Catholics, Republicans, and members of labor unions?...When you restrict liberty and narrow freedoms of a group of people, it does not only affect that group but all people." He also challenged state officials to try to revoke his physician's license: "I don't know how the teachers will react, but they would get a fight from me."[58]

In a conference held in Macon state NAACP heads announced the group's intention to continue it petitions and to support its teachers. In its public statement after their meeting the NAACP reminded the public of its support for the law and democratic principles, adding: "Our teachers...form an army of devoted public servants who should certainly not be intimidated by other officials who are sworn to uphold the Constitution of the United States.... Our membership, including teachers, is composed of the best type of citizens and our program has the support of labor, business, professional and religious institutions. We are not in this fight alone, and have been pledged the aid of other organizations in this fight for freedom."[59]

Williams and thirteen black parents later signed this second petition, submitting it to the school board on 25 August 1955. Citing the *Brown II* ruling, the statement asserted that "the time for delay, evasion or procrastination is past." Reminding the board that black Maconites had not previously insisted on immediate desegregation, the group now put added pressure on the board to integrate the schools a year hence. At the same time, however, Williams also asked that the board open the Dudley M. Hughes Vocational School to blacks during the coming academic year. "A school child can wait," he argued, "but a veteran who comes home has had it—it's time for him to go to work." Blacks coming from the service "ought to be able to take a course in the machinist trade, or radio or air conditioning or sheet metal work or anything else offered to whites this year." He also reminded the public that blacks had become convinced that integration was the only way to get "equal educational opportunities," despite recent efforts to improve the black schools. In reply, the board set a date of 8 September for a discussion of the petition. On that date, however, after Superintendent Mark Smith announced the agenda would only deal with "routine matters," Williams declined even to send a delegation to the meeting. The board did, however, form a committee to study the petition, but did not set a specific date for the committee to issue a report or make any recommendation.[60]

Two days after the meeting, the NAACP made public a letter to the board requesting a definite yes-or-no answer by 15 October. Hoping merely to get the board's intentions on record, the letter warned that failure to give an answer by the deadline would be taken as a negative and "we would feel no restraint in taking the matter directly into federal court." The *Macon Telegraph* then weighed into the matter, admonishing the board to make a candid reply to the NAACP, even though it called the 15 October deadline "immaterial." The editors recommended the board follow the example of Savannah board of education, which directed a subcommittee to launch a full study of the effects and problems of desegregation. One day before the deadline, the board committee announced its decision to study further "all of the complexities and ramifications" of the petition. To act without such a study would be "inappropriate, unwise, and entirely out of harmony with the intent of the Supreme Court decision." The Bibb board of education thus succumbed to "passive resistance," selectively parsing *Brown II* and choosing deliberation over a speedy implementation.[61]

These activities led to a spike in NAACP membership in Georgia in the middle of the decade. As national leadership challenged all local branches to begin new membership drives with a goal of ending all vestiges of segregation and completing the full emancipation of African Americans on by the Emancipation Proclamation centennial on 1 January 1963. Less than a week after *Brown I*, the Macon branch launched a high profile drive. Over the next two years, total membership in Georgia increased from 5,426 in 1954 to 7,855 in 1956. By 1958, however, white intimidation of NAACP members had caused the membership to drop to a ten-year low of 4,347. Morale within the state was low, leading field director Amos O. Holmes to step up recruiting efforts and to mount another membership drive in a "Statewide Freedom Dinner" in Macon on 14 November. By the end of the decade state memberships had again risen to 5,598.[62]

The Macon branch saw a modest growth spurt in late 1959 as the result of an acquittal of Tommy Paul Daniels, who had been accused of raping a virginal fifteen-year-old black girl who had been his babysitter. The victim had testified that Daniels had threatened to kill her if she spoke of the incident. Other witnesses had testified of Daniels's bragging about the matter and even offering the girl to his brother. Daniels claimed the liaison was consensual. Fifty or sixty black Maconites had attended the day and a half long trial, many of them weeping as the verdict was announced. When the jury reached its verdict after less than an hour's deliberation, a black minister called the acquittal "a disgrace to the state of Georgia." Reporting on the trial for the prominent black newspaper, the *Pittsburgh Courier,* Trezzvant Anderson wrote, "My stomach is still nauseated from the reading of that rape trial verdict.... And I am informed that this is nothing new here. There are reports that any early morning excursion into Pleasant Hill will find many Negro women jumping out of white men's cars and dashing into their houses after rendezvous." Later that fall, however, black voters received a small measure of revenge, delivering enough votes to defeat Daniels's attorney Abe Crosby in his campaign for the state legislature.[63]

Minor controversy over bloc voting by black Maconites erupted in the 1956 elections as well. Blacks formed the Middle Georgia Democratic Club, led by Thomas Hooper, who sent out letters endorsing candidates to members of the black electorate. The club endorsed James I. Wood for reelection as Bibb County Sheriff, despite questions about his deputies' 1954 arrests of Clifford York and Richard Scott.[64] Mostly, their vote for Wood amounted to a vote against his opponent W. L. "Rock" Robertson, who boasted during the campaign that the NAACP would never "hang a flag on the courthouse" if he were elected. The club also endorsed Mercer law professor Edgar H. Wilson over Denmark Groover in the race for state representative.

Both Wood and Wilson would soon be drawn into even larger controversy over bloc voting in 1960, an omen of which appeared in the letters to the *Macon Telegraph.* Just before the election an anonymous writer noted the Wood campaigns exploitation of Robertson's anti-NAACP statement. The NAACP's bloc vote, he asserted, "speaks for itself and I am satisfied that if Wood is reelected, the NAACP will have a definite foothold in policy of the sheriff's office. I shudder to think this." A few days after the election came a rejoinder from Frank J. Hutchings, who noted that the NAACP had only once dealt with the courthouse, and that in regard to school integration. If Wood was the choice of black Maconites, Hutchings asserted, it was rather because of the Middle Georgia Democratic Club had convinced them that he was the better candidate. The NAACP had never, he pointed out, been involved in any political campaign. He added, "I think that when a candidate brings the racial issue into a political campaign, he must feel that all other planks in his platform are rather weak. I hope the day will come when a man is elected to public office on the basis of what he can do for the progress of his community, the state and the nation, rather than what he promises to do against the Negro."[65]

Edgar H. Wilson, 1964, progressive mayor of Macon, 1959-1963, whose leadership during the bus boycott kept violence to a minimum. (Courtesy of the Washington Memorial Library.)

The 1950s saw Macon make some concessions to black concerns, both within the city government and in private organizations. In 1952 five black physicians were admitted to full membership in the Bibb County Medical Society, giving them the right to vote on society matters and hold office, as well as to attend its meetings. Admitted to membership were Drs. C. W. Dyer, R. S. Smith, G. A. Johnson, J. S. Williams, Jr., and W. A. Davis.[66] In October 1955 Macon Hospital removed racial bars on the respective assignments of white and black nursing students. With no fanfare the hospital administration began allowing black students to work with white patients in almost every section of the hospital. The black students comprised a class of twenty young women in the hospital's first reactivated division for blacks. Administrators also planned a nursing intern program. When a black student submitted an application, announced hospital director Arthur Smith, "it will be processed like the others."[67]

In another sort of victory for the black community, Mayor B. F. Merritt led the city council to decline a request by the Bibb County Klan 115 to lease the city auditorium. In February 1957, Merritt argued that a Klan meeting would "not conform to the recommended uses of public property." The city council's auditorium committee canceled an earlier reservation, leading the Empire to file suit against the city. In response to the suit, Bibb Superior Court Judge Oscar L. Long issued a restraining order to keep the city from leasing the auditorium on the requested date, pending a hearing on 8 March. Eventually Judge Long the contract invalid on the grounds that auditorium manager had not been authorized by the city to sign contracts in its stead. In reply, Lee Davidson, Grand Klokard of the local Klan, denounced the city council for discriminating against his organization. "It is high time," he complained, "for the white people to wake up to the things that are going on in their city." When the Klan met for their rally, meeting south of the city with over 2000 in attendance, Imperial Wizard E. L. Edwards of Atlanta again denounced the city council for its "yellow streak," and warned, "Communists and Communist Jews have infiltrated the government.... Jews will be dictators in twenty years!"[68]

Thus, while certain segments of white Macon resonated with the themes of massive resistance that were echoing across the South, cautious white progressives in some of the churches and in the Macon Council on Human Relations followed behind the efforts of the Macon NAACP. The black community had seen some minor victories in the latter part of the decade, but the Bibb County Board of Education was still studying school integration. In early 1957, Atlanta saw an attempt to integrate the buses and Maconites wondered how the matter would be handled in their city. Mayor Merritt and Police Chief Ben T. Watkins told reporters they would handle the situation in the best way possible. Bibb Transit Company President Linton Baggs declined comment altogether. One of the city's black clergy warned that the city did not exist in a vacuum, and that developments elsewhere would have an effect in Macon. A few days later an otherwise anonymous black Maconite named Houston Johnson wrote the *Telegraph* to "predict" a smooth transition on the buses: "The bus company officials, our beloved mayor, our court officials, our different representatives, all of our white ministers, educators, businessmen, and etc., being the God fearing people that they are, I don't think that they will find bus integrating so hard to bear. No sir, this mess that happened in Montgomery will not happen in Macon. Our white citizens are much too intelligent and Christian hearted to allow such."[69]

7

Bloc Votes, Boycotts, and Baptists:
Disintegrating Jim Crow in 1960s Macon

For some time now historians have been moving away from Great Man depictions of the civil rights movement. Because of Martin Luther King, Jr.'s prominence in the struggle for racial equality in America—and also because of his martyrdom in that struggle—historians have been attracted to the charisma of King's personality and the drama of his life and death. But as civil rights histories have become more detailed, the indigenous quality of the movement has become the focus of their narratives. John Dittmer has led a train of historians emphasizing the role of "local people" in "homegrown" movements in their own particular venues. In some of these venues, such as Birmingham or Selma, the Southern Christian Leadership Conference (SCLC), the Congress of Racial Equality (CORE), the Student Nonviolent Coordinating Committee (SNCC), or other national organizations played a role, though not the central one. They aided, but did not direct, the local movements. In Georgia, as Stephen N. G. Tuck has shown, the efforts to disintegrate Jim Crow were almost exclusively local, indigenous movements.[1]

Macon's civil rights story is quintessentially local, in which, other than the NAACP, national civil rights organizations played little or no role. Inspired by the success of the movement in other parts of the South, Black Maconites gradually stepped up the pace and the fervor of their protests against segregation. Their efforts reached a critical mass by the 1961 bus boycott that sparked the beginnings of rapid racial change. These successful efforts built upon the organization of the Macon NAACP branch in the 1940s and its calm, but steady pressure on the city in the aftermath of *Brown*. Other than following the nonviolent methods they viewed from afar in the Montgomery bus boycott, the leaders of the movement in Macon did not call on SCLC or other groups for additional aid. As one of the ministerial leaders of the Macon movement, the Reverend Van J. Malone, later told an interviewer, "We didn't feel that we needed anyone to come in and help us. We thought that we were doing a pretty good job ourselves. And the Lord gave us guidance and direction, and we followed it."[2]

One important reason, however, for the success of black protest in the 1960s, and for the relative absence of violent white response to it, was white Macon's tradition of racial moderation. Unlike some Southern cities where social paroxysms accompanied the disintegration of Jim Crow, Macon had a racially moderate professional class large and strong enough to shape the city government's reasonable response to black protest. The moderate professionals also managed to control more volatile working class white reactions to desegregation and keep violence to a minimum. Two strong and respected pillars propped up this protective canopy of white moderation. One was the longstanding moderate, anti-lynching, anti-Klan editorial stance of the *Macon Telegraph*. The other was the influence of Mercer University.

Of course, violence and volatility did not completely absent themselves from Macon in the 1960s. There were angry demonstrations and hard feelings, but there were no fatalities, and white gradually came to share power with blacks. Nor, as has been outlined earlier, were the records of the *Telegraph* or of Mercer University purely on the progressive side of the ledger. The *Telegraph's* editorial stance was often critical of the NAACP and continued to advocate states' rights in the political debates surrounding civil rights. Yet the race-baiting of Georgia state politics was eschewed by editors Mark Ethridge, W. T. Anderson, and C. R. Pendleton going back to the Hoke Smith-Clark Howell gubernatorial race of 1906. The paper had been cool toward both Eugene and Herman Talmadge from the 1930s to the era of *Brown*. As a result, far right-wing reactions to race issues were not fueled by incendiary rhetoric from the city's most important public medium.

Mercer University had its own racial shortcomings. It was, after all, a Baptist institution of higher learning. As such, university presidents like Spright Dowell, George B. Connell, and Rufus C. Harris were often called upon to fend off the conservative constituency of the Georgia

Baptist Convention. The democratic polity of Southern and Georgia Baptist institutions often put the university at the mercy of conservative denominational bureaucrats, pastors, and laypersons. Free to denounce various unorthodoxies at will, the cultural and biblical fundamentalism of any Georgia Baptist individual or congregation of Georgia Baptists could put Mercer in the bull's eye at any given moment. Thus, Mercer presidents and professors kept a wary eye on Baptist opinion, and did not look for occasions to disagree with it. Still, the racially prophetic strain of thought at Mercer not only slowly converted many of the students, but also slowly infiltrated white society in Macon. Mercer's moderating influence on the city made itself felt in three ways: The leadership of President Rufus C. Harris, the role of Mercer professors in the Macon Council on Human Relations, and the election of Mercer law professor Edgar H. Wilson as mayor.

The civil rights movement flowed into Macon from two but converging separate streams. Inspired by earlier events like *Brown,* Montgomery, and Little Rock, black Maconites continued to organize and keep the pressure on Jim Crow. At the same time, a prophetic religious tradition in the classroom and a courageous leadership in the president's office helped end segregation at one of Macon's key institutions. Macon's white moderates also managed to put a racially moderate Mercerian in the mayor's office at the crucial time when black protest pressed its hardest.

Edgar H. Wilson, a young law professor at Mercer followed his uncle, Lewis B. Wilson, in being elected mayor in June 1959. Like his uncle, Ed Wilson was a racial moderate, clinging to segregation publicly while willing to negotiate in good faith with Macon's black leaders. Like his uncle, his willingness to give ear to black concerns was born of political pragmatism, as he owed his election as mayor, and his 1956 defeat of Denmark Groover for the state House, to the city's burgeoning black vote. Wilson and his campaign manager attorney Buckner Melton worked the black community unapologetically, developing ties with successful building contractor William P. Randall, a successful building contractor, who had effectively replaced J. S. Williams as black Macon's most influential leader.[3] Randall and other leaders turned out the black vote solidly for Wilson and expected progress from the new mayor once in office. The relations between Randall and the Wilson administration

would come into play as blacks began to press for the desegregation of
Macon in the early 1960s.[4] Their first controversy, however, surrounded
the Wilson campaign's recruitment of the black vote.

William P. Randall, 1963,
a prominent black
business man, emerged as
Macon's most influential
leader in the Civil Rights
era. (Courtesy of the
Washington Memorial
Library.)

BLACK VOTE, BLOC VOTE

In response to the 1945 *Primus v. King* case that ended the white primary
in Georgia, the NAACP's voter registration drives had significantly
increased the electoral power of black Maconites. Before 1944 blacks
made up only 9.3 percent of all Bibb County voters, but within two years
had skyrocketed to over 10,000, about a third of the total.[5] As a result,
the black vote had been instrumental in the elections of mayors Lewis
and Ed Wilson. Other local figures angered by the rise of black political
power in the county began to devise means of weakening the black vote.
The chief means of doing so was to attack what they called the "Negro
bloc vote." On 6 June 1960 the issue boiled over in Macon when
Superior Court Judge Oscar L. Long charged the Bibb County Grand
Jury to investigate black bloc voting in recent county elections. Long had

developed a reputation for being tough on African Americans who found themselves in his courtroom. He had once sentenced a Fort Valley physician to a year on a public works camp for insulting a white woman over the phone. In 1958 he had presided over the trial of Tommy Paul Daniels, who was acquitted of the charge of raping his fifteen-year-old black babysitter.[6]

Long told the grand jury to investigate "the inane and inexplicable pattern of Negro bloc voting" in every election in Bibb County for the previous several years. He estimated that 80 to 85 percent of black voters had engaged in bloc voting, to which he acknowledged they had a right. He argued, however, that voters had no right to barter their franchise "at the whim of domineering individuals or conspiratorial organizations." Issuing a rather hysterical warning that the practice could "ultimately destroy this country and its system of government," he indicated that two laws, both misdemeanors, may have been violated by recent election practices. One prohibited the buying or selling of votes, making it unlawful to hire campaign workers to influence votes on behalf of any candidate. The other prohibited the use of facsimile ballots in polling places. Long directed the jury to look into how candidates were soliciting the black vote. Specifically, they were to look into rumors of the buying and selling of votes, asking what sort of contact was made between candidates and black leaders, what money was involved, and what promises were made in exchange for the bloc vote. Long also indicated that his purpose for the "probe" was to insure fair and honest elections, and that two other Superior Court judges, A. M. Anderson and Hal Bess, had sanctioned his charge to the grand jury.[7]

The following day Bibb County Sheriff James I. Wood publicly denounced Long's charge to the grand jury as overlooking "the mountain of white candidates and campaign workers who have violated this old law, to investigate the mole hill of a few Negro campaign workers." He dismissed the probe as a ploy and described it as "the height of hypocrisy to dust off an old blue law that has been ignored for fifty years and suddenly order its rigid enforcement against a minority group of voters." He charged that Long's actions were more dangerous than that which he sought to investigate. He also characterized the probes as "political persecution in the guise of law enforcement," predicting that the action "will be considered one of the most deplorable examples of race agitation to come out of Middle Georgia in recent years." He added, "At a time when all thinking people want to preserve the good will and cooperation between the races in Bibb County, this action appears either a crude attempt at judicial intimidation of Negro voters and leaders, or at best, as agitation for a Negro vote issue on local politics." Wood had received large numbers of black votes in his previous campaign, but had recently joined the Republican Party and opted not to run for re-election. In a final shot at Long, Wood likened the judge's judicial intimidation to the physical intimidation of the Klan.[8]

Immediately, however, Neal D. McKenney, president of the Macon Bar Association, joined the fray, calling Wood's criticisms "deplorable," and defending the judge's investigation as applying to white voters as well as black. Instead of criticizing the judge, McKenney argued, Wood, as an officer of the court charged with enforcing the law, should have offered his full cooperation with the probe. Wood was also denounced by Lee Davidson, grand dragon of the Georgia Klan, who called for the sheriff to be impeached. Davidson led a thirty-minute demonstration by 150 Klansmen, burning a cross in protest against Wood, who, Davidson argued, "has continually tried to destroy our Southern way of life." At the same time, the *Macon Telegraph* editorially supported the investigation, saying Long deserved "public congratulations." The probe, wrote the editors, was "not only desirable, but essential," but, "Bloc voting is insidious. Insofar as it exists in this community, bloc-voting should be identified and stamped out." The paper also rejected Wood's criticism of the probe, charging that his comments had "done far more to worsen race relations" than Long's actions. Bloc voting "injects racial issues into elections where none existed before and ...is an enemy to the very racial harmony he professes to desire."[9]

On the first day of its proceedings, the jury heard from five witnesses under subpoena. City Alderman Gus Bernd, who had polled 1,001 black votes and 300 white votes in his successful campaign, was questioned for two full hours, along with two of his opponents, Joe V. Kennedy and William K. Stanley. Gus B. Kaufman, a successful business leader who had actually joined the Macon branch of the NAACP and became a leader in the Macon Council on Human Relations, testified about his progressive political activities and his efforts in support of both of Ed Wilson political campaigns. A proud secular Jew (and theological agnostic) who described himself as "imbued with a sense of fairness," Kaufman proudly wore a nonconformist badge and testified matter-of-factly about his eagerness to turn Macon away from the race-baiting Talmadge legacy in Georgia. He had been recruited by Buck Melton to work in the Wilson mayoral campaign in 1959. Melton had made contact with blacks leaders who along with Kaufman, extracted a promise from Wilson to integrate the public library in exchange for recruiting support in the black community. He also testified to having received $150 from the Wilson campaign to pay for his expenses during two days of canvassing. Last to testify on the first day was William P. Randall, who was questioned about his activities as president of the Associated Democratic Clubs of Georgia.[10]

For his part, Mayor Wilson early on called the probe "the worst blow to race relations in Bibb County in recent years." His testimony before the grand jury lasted some twenty minutes, while Sheriff Wood responded to a half hour's worth of questioning. By the end of the month-long proceeding, the jury had called some fifty witnesses, but brought no indictments. Nonetheless, it issued a lengthy presentment against black leaders Thomas B. Hooper and William Randall. As president of the Middle Georgia Democratic Club, Hooper gave four hours of testimony, receiving criticism for making no records of money received from various candidates. Randall was particularly singled out not only for receiving payments without adequate records and for allegedly taking money from two candidates while supporting only one.[11] In its final report, the grand jury disclosed that both black and white individuals had sought out and received money "solely for the purpose of influencing voters." They accused Hooper and Randall of using their influence for personal gain and that their organizations were "formed solely for the purpose of influencing Negro voters." The jury further believed that had the facts been known by the black community there would have been no bloc vote for particular candidates. The grand jury also called criticisms of Wilson and Wood "insulting and unfounded."[12]

Deliberately choosing to hold his response on 4 July, Randall called a press conference to refute the charges against him point by point. In supporting the grand jury, the *Telegraph* had implied that Randall and Hooper were "so-called leaders whose real interest is the almighty dollar." An angry Randall denounced the failure of the grand jury to indict, an action challengeable in court. Rather, it chose to make its bogus charges in a public presentment, which he said must be answered in kind. He denied that he had received any money from Taylor Phillips, whom he had supported in a 1958 election for the Georgia House. Nor had he received money or supported Phillips's opponent, Denmark Groover. He further argued that during fourteen years of political activity he had received less than $2,000, all of which had gone for expenses without any hint of misappropriation. "What I have done politically," he replied, "has been done for 'personal gain' only in the sense that I have firmly believed that the candidates for whom I have worked without personal compensation would give us a better government and a better community."[13]

Later, Randall mocked the investigation, arguing that white Maconites had considered the city to have had good race relations until the late 1950s when, as a result of increased black voting, "the Courthouse crowd became incensed or afraid enough for a Superior Court judge" to investigate bloc voting. He continued to point out the grand jury's failure to indict him or anyone else and was heartened when five different white attorneys volunteered to represent him without cost in any forthcoming indictment. He privately believed that Long had merely used the probe to help "create a white bloc vote." Years later, Randall told an interviewer that near the end of his life Long had approached him to apologize for his harassment. Having earlier thought of Randall as "the biggest son of a bitch in the world," the retired judge told him, "We were extremely lucky to have you here to lead the movement." Randall told Long not to worry, because he had thought Long was also the "biggest son of a bitch in the world."[14]

The Macon NAACP looked into the possibility of legal action against members of the grand jury and called on Georgia Field Secretary Amos O. Holmes and National Director of NAACP Branches Gloster B. Current for advice. Meeting with Holmes on 7 July, the Macon branch's executive committee discussed the constitutionality of the laws on which Long's investigation had been based. They also discussed a possible Justice Department inquiry and the legality of requiring voters to explain their political affiliations. Holmes's report on the meeting denounced the probe for slandering and defaming all whom it had investigated. Without returning any indictments the grand jury had publicized "untrue charges as though these persons were guilty. Holmes also charged that the investigation, backed by a Denmark Groover still smarting over two electoral defeats at the hands of black voters, was an effort "to destroy all Negro political organizations in Macon and Bibb County" or at least minimize their voting power. The grand jury investigation, he believed, was being used to discourage blacks from voting in a 20 July special election for sheriff. With the advice of Holmes and others national NAACP leaders, the Macon branch decided to form a political action committee to redouble and coordinate political efforts in Macon. More specifically, Randall himself began spearheading a new black voter registration drive in the county. This effort, conducted as part of the Southern Christian Leadership Council and NAACP's regional Voter Education Project, yielded some 6,000 new black voters in 1962 (which more than doubled the number from the previous year), 3,000 in 1963, and 1,432 in 1964. The project would continue into the 1970s and greatly increase black political power in Macon.[15]

Of course, Long's investigation would not be the last effort to try to neutralize the black vote. Once again elected to the state House of Representatives, in January 1963, Denmark Groover introduced a bill requiring a majority rather than a plurality to elect any candidate to local and state offices in both primary and general elections. Candidates failing to receive majority votes would be forced into runoff elections, in which the influence of bloc voting would be reduced. The bill was eventually passed by the general assembly in May 1964. Historian J. Morgan Kousser has rightly pointed out the Bibb County Grand Jury investigation focused only on the 1958 Groover-Phillips race. Just as Groover had supported the grand jury effort, he clearly advocated the majority rule law in the aftermath of his earlier electoral defeats. In a 1984 deposition in a federal case investigating the restriction of black voting rights in the South, Groover admitted that the phrase "bloc vote" was a euphemism for the black vote. As something of a racial convert, he also testified: "I was a segregationist.... I had many prejudices, and I don't mind admitting it.... If you want to establish that some of my political activity was racially motivated, it was.... It would have been a major miracle, or taken a modern case of absolute blindness, for blacks to have supported me in 1958."[16]

Blacks did and still do, of course, vote in "blocs," much as there has often been a "labor vote" or a "farm vote." Certainly, in rallying white support against civil rights advances politicians who played the race card did, as Randall charged, seek in essence to marshal a conservative white bloc vote. As noted by black political historian, Clarence A. Bacote, blacks quite naturally have voted against candidates who disregarded black rights and for those who have been sympathetic. The bloc vote, he noted, "has been merely the Negro's inevitable reaction to the vicious race baiting of some politicians.... Negroes will vote in a bloc only when white supremacy is the issue."[17] The hysteria over "Negro bloc voting" was a bogus issue, another of white conservatives' many efforts to keep white supremacy alive in one form or another. In Macon the failed effort backfired, goading black Maconites into pressing even more vigorously for their full civil rights.

DOWNTOWN DESEGREGATION

A month into the new Kennedy administration, the Macon Council on Human Relations (MCHR) called on Macon officials to re-examine its policies regarding racial discrimination as enunciated by the Supreme Court. Reminding the public that compliance with federal courts was inevitable, the MCHR complimented local officials for promoting racial harmony in the city, or for at least not doing anything "to stir ill feeling." Macon had thus far preserved the status quo, which the MCHR argued, "cannot continue unchallenged." Noting that it had been "essentially conservative" in its approach, the MCHR acknowledged, "that our Negro citizens soon will make new demands for compliance," and concluded, "We call upon our mayor and council, the board of county commissioners, all county officials, the board of education, our state and local judges, and our state legislators to join immediately in planning to meet the new era with sense and realism on the local scene." Soon after the statement was released, MCHR co-chairs Joseph M. Hendricks and the Reverend Elisha B. Paschal found crosses burned in their lawns, suggesting that the transition would be more difficult than these progressives were hoping.[18]

A few weeks later, black Maconites reopened the discussions on desegregation at the Bowden Golf Course. Partly the result of black patience and partly because the NAACP's focus was elsewhere, the petition for desegregating the golf course had lain dormant since late 1955. On 4 April 1961 the Bibb County Coordinating Committee (BCCC), a new black protest organization led by Randall, filed another request that the city council once again take up the golf course issue. Over the next two months, as Robert L. Anderson has shown, the Randall slowly and quietly negotiated with the Wilson administration. At the same time, negotiations also focused on integrating the lunch counters at downtown department stores. Anderson correctly noted that blacks were able to act patiently because of their "faith" that they could work within a political system that would work. Such faith had been borne out by the mayoral records of both Wilsons. On 6 June 1961, the city council voted to desegregate the golf course, the first venue where Jim Crow was run out of town. Still, most Maconites did not know of the decision, which was not mentioned in the *Telegraph* until 1 November, when blacks had moved on to push for the integration of downtown lunch counters.[19]

In February 1960 news reports told of student efforts to desegregate department store lunch counters in Greensboro, North Carolina. After Martin Luther King's Southern Christian Leadership Conference endorsed and encouraged the tactic, black students throughout the South began taking up the challenge. Most observers fully anticipated similar efforts shortly to appear in Macon. In May, the MCHR held a panel discussion on the subject in Macon. By 1960 the organization numbered some 165 black and white members, largely dominated by members affiliated with Mercer. At the meeting on sit-ins, history professor Willis B. Glover presided, while editor of the *Mercer Cluster*, Cliff Hendrix traced the history of the sit-in movement. He held that sit-ins made clear that blacks were not content with segregation and could promote discussions that could lead to breaking racial barriers. On the other hand, he feared many would be antagonized if the technique were used as an economic bludgeon. In a later column Hendrix wrote that "unless the real desire on the part of 'sit-in' participants is to effect such community and not merely to win the rights of a certain special interest group, valid though their demands may be, the real goal of understanding and fellowship between races may be impaired rather than enhanced through such activity." Joseph M. Hendricks, the new director of religious education at the university, seemed to agree, telling the group that sit-ins might bring equality, but were also likely to harm Christian community. The meeting closed with the council voting to meet with Mayor Wilson to discuss courses of action in the event of sit-ins in Macon. In addition, MCHR chairman Gus B. Kaufmann suggested the group try to convince the mayor to appoint an interracial council for the city.[20]

The comments of Mercerians Hendrix and Hendricks suggest an important reality in the realm of white-black relations in Macon as in America at large. For most of the history of their interaction with the dominant white majority, African Americans have typically faced assumptions that as a group whites were in a position of justified superiority. Under this assumption conservative whites believed that as long as blacks deferred to them in accordance with a lower social standing all was right with their racial world. As long as blacks conformed to this assumption and accepted their inferior place, good race relations could result. Refusing to conform to this assumption, however, meant sacrificing "good" race relations in exchange for grudging steps toward equality. The more vigorously and loudly blacks pressed for equality, the angrier the white response became. Thus the civil rights era, many whites believed, fundamentally hurt "good" race relations because social interaction between races was based on the assumption of "rightful white over black." Having been a part of the cultural landscape at the beginning of the American experiment, assumptions such as these were very difficult to dislodge. If seen as elements in our nation's birth or "genesis"—as opposed to being viewed as a set of immutable inherited traits—these assumptions can be understood as part of America's "genetic" make up.

Sit-ins did not surface in Macon, however, until a year later, when on 2 June 1961, teams of black teenagers took seats at five department store lunch counters. In one encounter, sixty-seven-year-old Floyd Prince punched seventeen-year-old Benjamin Snead as he sat on a stool in Woolworth's. Police officers arrested both of them on charges of disorderly conduct, while all five stores immediately closed the lunch counters, but did not ask the students to leave. No other students were arrested in connection with the incident. Mercer Professor Carlos T. Flick, who had served as an observer of the sit-ins, was surprised that the demonstrations were barely noticed by customers who little excitement over the matter. Flick commented to reporters, "Macon must be more progressive than I thought." Black leaders had recruited Flick and professor Robert Otto, whom they trusted to be sympathetic to their cause, to be on hand to make note of the proceedings. One of the white men who gathered at Newberry's was Flick's barber. Discerning that Flick was there in support of the sit-in, the man loosed a torrent of profanity at his customer, adding the threat that if he ever returned to his barber shop he would learn just what a razor could do.[21]

A month later cases against Prince and Snead were both dismissed by Recorder's Court Judge William W. Hemingway for lack of evidence." Once again low-profile discussions between the mayor, city and county officials, a committee of twelve white business leaders, and black leaders continued over the next months, leading in November to the successful integration of ten stores in downtown Macon. The peaceful reaction of whites prompted Mayor Wilson to comment: "Macon has once again proved that it is a city of law abiding people. I am proud that our city has not been the scene of race strife and turmoil such as has occurred in other cities."[22]

By January 1962 Macon had impressed the national news media with its willingness to desegregate many of its facilities. "Perhaps nowhere in the Deep South," noted the *Wall Street Journal,* "has desegregation been carried out at a more rapid pace than in Macon." The article outlined the end of the Jim Crow golf course, public library, and lunch counters. Macon's white business elite had deliberately sought to avoid the confrontations of other Georgia cities like Atlanta, Savannah, and Albany. A white member of a secret committee of business leaders explained: "In Savannah we learned that a Negro boycott cut retail sales was much as 50% in some places. Stores weren't the only one hurt, either. Bankers, insurance men, small loan companies—all of them felt it." Assessing the impact of black efforts to speed up integration by the use of public protests, Mayor Wilson told the reporter, "We've been watching these freedom rides and boycotts in other cities and we're getting the picture. Even Robert E. Lee finally had to surrender, didn't he?"[23]

In spite of such an outlook, the new year would disprove the black Maconite's tongue-in-cheek "prediction" that whites were too "intelligent and Christian hearted" to allow "the mess that happened in

Montgomery" to happen in their city. The run-up to an all-out boycott lasted a full year, as in early 1961 city officials met with representatives of the Bibb Transit Company, advising them to ignore any attempts to desegregate the buses. Company drivers balked, however, and although the law in question had already been declared unconstitutional by federal judge Frank Hooper, city attorney Wallace Miller, Jr. advised city officials to prosecute offenders under its jurisdiction. The next day, 25 February, officers arrested twelve black youths who sat in white sections of the buses. Authorities soon called William Randall, now the president of the BCCC, which had taken over leadership of black concerns in Macon, to come bail the students out of jail. Randall later recalled that the incarcerated students sang so long and loudly that he was asked to come bond them out as soon as possible. Randall, Ruth Hartley Mosley, and Frank Hutchings quickly provided the funds to do so. Eventually, one of the twelve riders, nineteen-year-old John Elisha Glover, was convicted of violating state bus laws and was given a twelve-month suspended sentence and a $100 fine.[24]

The students received public support from Macon's black ministers when the Evangelical Ministers Alliance issued a statement acknowledging that the "rising tide of the cry for freedom and equality" had reached Macon. "As messengers of God," the ministers announced, "we take the stand that rights of equality and human dignity should be afforded to every citizen, regardless of race, creed, or color." In addition, Walter Davis, prominent NAACP member, wrote the *Macon News* that he "felt a shout of acclamation, for at last the Negroes of Macon had joined the ranks of those fighting for human dignity." Saying the time had come to end all forms of segregation and white supremacy, Davis made a sharp appeal: "…if there be any whites of good will: to rid your souls of this sin and shame, join ranks of any that work to eliminate this evil." In the same edition, the *News* in essence advised the transit company to get the matter over with and avoid the legal costs and the detrimental affects such a fight could cause. "People are not dumb," the *News* opined, "They know what the outcome will be…. Why shouldn't the community avoid this potential trouble spot in race relations by going ahead and complying with the law now?"[25]

In August, Glover's attorney, Donald Hollowell, filed a motion for a new trial, arguing that Glover had been convicted of disobeying a law that was unconstitutional. Hollowell argued that the law clearly discriminated against blacks in violation of the Fourteenth Amendment, having thus been nullified by federal courts. On 18 January, the Appeals Court upheld the Glover conviction. Hollowell then indicated his intention to appeal the case to the US Supreme Court, but events soon rendered that effort unnecessary.[26]

Since the February 1961 arrests of Glover and the other students, Randall had negotiated with city officials and with transit company president Linton D. Baggs seeking an agreement to end segregated seating on the buses. On 7 February 1962, Randall, NAACP President Walter Davis, the Reverend A. J. Shaw, president of the Macon Evangelical Ministers' Alliance, and Ruby Williams, president of the City Federation of Women's Clubs, sent a letter to Baggs requesting the end of segregated seating and the employment of black drivers and mechanics. When Baggs ignored their requests, Randall began to advocate a boycott in regular mass meetings in the black community. During the 1956 Montgomery bus boycott Randall visited serval mass meetings, returning to Macon convinced that local clergy could be useful to local protests.[27]

Many of the more conservative black clergy in the city had criticized Randall's challenge of segregation laws as "sowing confusion," and reminding members that "God is not the author of confusion." He countered by admonishing mass meeting congregations, "Don't give a preacher money who won't support you in your fight against oppression." Accordingly, he suggested they put buttons in the offering plates instead of coins. Within three weeks, he later recalled, a number of erstwhile clerical critics had come around volunteering their church sanctuaries for mass meetings. But it took a bit more convincing to get them to volunteer to risk jail in challenging the transit company's seating arrangements. Having become friends with Joseph Hendricks, Mercer's seminary-trained director of religious life, Randall asked Hendricks to come to a mass meeting to help convince local black ministers to take the lead in challenging the bus seating arrangements. Hendricks made a short speech at a mass meeting warning the ministers that if they did not get on the buses, they would be "as sorry as the white preachers." One of them exclaimed, "Oh my God!" and another of them, the Reverend Elisha B. Paschal, pastor of the Tremont Temple Baptist

Church, told his brothers, "Nothing is going to happen until some of these preachers get arrested and I'm going to go now." Three others decided to join him on the buses. [28]

The next day, Saturday, 9 February, four Baptist pastors, Paschal, and the Reverends Van J. Malone (First African), Ellis S. Evans (Macedonia), and H. R. Rancifer (Center Hill) rode one bus without incident, then boarded a second bus heading back into the downtown area. "Thank you, but we're quite comfortable where we are," answered Malone when driver Hugh Jennings asked them to move to the rear, leading him to stop the bus and phone the police. Minutes later Officers C. H. Sauls and J. F. Huff arrested the ministers, who were shortly bonded out of jail by Randall. Efforts to meet with Bibb Transit Company President Baggs or with attorney Wallace Miller came to nothing, as Miller informed Randall they could not meet until Monday.[29]

On Sunday Paschal represented the black community at a televised news conference. From a prepared statement, he informed the city:

> Four ministers rode up front on a bus and were arrested. We immediately notified the general public that unless we could have a conference with officials to resolve the matter we would refrain from paying to be segregated on the buses. We were informed by the attorney for the Bibb Transit Company on…Saturday, February 9, that…he had a dinner party for that night. We then asked for a conference for the next day, which was Sunday. He said that he would try to see us on Monday. We informed him that would be too late, as we had already asked Negroes to refrain from paying to be segregated. His answer was "Well, let 'er rip."[30]

That night at the Allen Chapel AME Church, Randall told a congregation of some 3,000 persons that inasmuch as Miller had said a meeting might be held "if we can get to it," that time had run out and a boycott was being launched on Monday morning and would continue "until we can ride in dignity and without risk of arrest." Specifically, the effort would continue until black passengers could sit anywhere on the buses and until the company agreed to hire black drivers and mechanics. Randall implored all who owned cars to participate in a motor pool, while Robert Byas, who chaired the transportation committee, had young girls record the names of volunteers. Warming to the crowd, Randall admonished them, "Don't ride the buses. Walk if you have to. We don't want no half-baked cracker telling us to move to the rear of a bus." At the end of the meeting the gathering approved a letter to Baggs announcing that after eight years of requests to meet with the company with no results, blacks were prepared to boycott the buses, but remained "willing to talk at any time." Baggs replied that he had wanted Mayor Wilson to attend any negotiations with the group, but that Wilson was out of the city until Monday.[31]

On the first day of the boycott, black youths threw rocks at buses near Ballard-Hudson High School, leading Baggs to cancel selected routes into black sections of the city. By the second day the boycott was virtually 100 percent observed, with almost no black riders on the buses. There were, however, reports of intimidation against those who did ride. In one incident a young man jumped on a bus and hit a lone black woman onboard. Within three days over 200 cars had been volunteered for the motor pool, and leaders had developed effective tactics for getting passengers to their destinations. Police harassed drivers, handing out over 700 traffic citations in a few days time, for violations like carrying more than five passengers in a taxi.[32] Some 5,000 attended the mass meeting on the first night of the effort, leading *Pittsburgh Courier* reporter Trezzvant Anderson to heap praise on the indigenous Macon movement:

> This is probably the largest turnout of Negroes at any single Georgia rights meeting and is a tribute to the local leadership and the sincere interest of Macon Negroes in their own welfare. No single church here can hold the huge crowds....this is strictly a LOCAL affair, with no guidance or direction from ANY outside force or source. Macon Negro leaders said they were fully able to run their own affairs and were not inviting any outsiders to come in try to direct what is going on here. This is good, for it keeps down the Caucasian battle cry about "outside agitators coming in."

Anderson also denounced the transit company, writing that "in no other Southern city have I encountered bus operators who were more uncivil, insulting, discourteous and uncultured than these in Macon. The Macon situation…is absolutely the creation of the Caucasians: they have only themselves to blame, here specifically Bibb Transit Co. president Linton Baggs, Jr."[33]

Early on, a group of some fifty whites acted to ease the transit company's financial burden by boarding a bus, paying the fare, and riding for only one block. Another man reportedly bought $1,000 worth of tokens. Meanwhile, the *Telegraph* sought to push black leaders, city officials, and Baggs into negotiations, editorializing that a federal court's recent ruling that Georgia's segregated bus laws were unconstitutional gave the company an easy opportunity to drop its policies. At the same time, Paschal made public new demands that charges be dropped against the four ministers and the twelve students arrested a year earlier. Noting that the white community had not yet approached black leaders for negotiations, Paschal reiterated their availability, adding, "We still pray our Christian white friends will support us in this move."[34]

On Thursday, 15 February, four days into the boycott, black leadership recruited two more ministers to ride the buses again in order to establish a test case. The Reverends Cameron Alexander and Booker W. Chambers took front seats on a Vineville bus, then moved to the rear when instructed by the driver. That afternoon they conferred with attorney Donald Hollowell, who prepared to file for an injunction against the bus company in Judge W. A. Bootle's US District Court. That night Mayor Ed Wilson held a news conference to announce his attempts to bring the parties together for negotiations and to try to dampen outbreaks of violence that had occurred during the day.

At the same time Linton Baggs used television and radio spots to urge white Maconites to "ride a bus and help break the boycott." He told of one drivers, who, fearful that a shutdown that might cost him his job, sold $63 worth of bus tokens door-to-door in four hours. The following day Hollowell presented the two ministers' case against the transit company and Police Chief L. B. McCallum, asking for a temporary injunction against them. Judge Bootle, who earlier had denied a request for a temporary restraining order to stop the boycott, set a 28 February date for a hearing. Learning of Bootle's decision to allow the boycott to continue and of the shooting of two blacks in the downtown area, Wilson issued another invitation to both parties to meet with him the next day. He also invited Bibb County Sheriff Jimmie Bloodworth and County Commission Chair Kenneth Dunwoody to attend the session. Once again Baggs refused to meet, commenting that could not "negotiate with someone holding a gun at my back."[35]

A four-hour meeting attended by the mayor, Wallace Miller, city attorney Buckner Melton, Dunwoody, Randall, Paschal, and Hollowell ended with no solution. Sheriff Bloodworth sent a telegram to Wilson sharply indicating his refusal to participate. "I am a law enforcement officer of the State of Georgia," the message began, "and until the courts order otherwise, I could not agree to permit a violation of its laws and since the bus company is a private concern, I would not attempt to tell it how to run its internal affairs...." Melton later recalled that a number of prominent white business leaders attended these meetings, largely under duress and disgruntled at the prospect of negotiating as equals with black leaders. The next day the *Telegraph* expressed its concern that continuing the boycott without a solution would encourage more incidents of violence, which the editors viewed as "only a prelude to more lawlessness if the calming influence of responsible individuals and organizations does not make itself felt." They also criticized Bloodworth's decision to avoid the negotiating session.[36]

During the boycott's second week Bibb County Superior Court Judge Oscar Long issued a temporary injunction against the NAACP, the BCCC, and other black organizations from intimidating blacks who might ride the buses and from damaging the buses. The suit by the transit company asked for $100,000 in damages from the defendants. The petition cited fourteen cases of alleged rock, brick, and bottle throwing by blacks objecting to others riding the buses. The injunction, however, failed to restrain whites who had engaged in shootings and other forms of violence to intimidate boycotting blacks.[37]

White response to the boycott was predictably mixed. Mercer Dean of the Chapel F. Robert Otto, who had also succeeded Mac Bryan as professor in the Christianity department, wrote the *Telegraph* to critique Linton Baggs's position on the boycott. Reminding readers that both the Supreme Court and federal district courts had declared segregation unconstitutional, Otto mocked Baggs's apparent view that "what is unconstitutional in one district is constitutional in another, as though the distinction…were a matter of geography." He also attacked Baggs' suggestion that boycotts were outside "the Christian way" of settling disputes, asserting that the Christian way proceeded from an uncompromising commitment to the "Lordship of Christ over all of life, including seating arrangements on buses." In stark contrast, James B. Wade's letter denouncing what "organizations supposedly claiming to be of a religious nature are doing to destroy a society built upon the moral integrity of a white race with little or no help from Negroes or any foreign country." Arguing that the transit company was a private concern, he argued that Baggs "should have the right to say how the business is to be run, and if he desires to seat races separately or deny service to anyone, that should be his God-given privilege." Buoyed by such support, a still-stubborn Baggs announced that the boycott "would never end" if its end depended on the hiring of black drivers or mechanics. He also indicated, however, that without increased usage by white Maconites, bus operation in the city would cease by 1 April.[38]

On Monday, 26 February, three days before Judge Bootle was scheduled to hear arguments on the two-week-old boycott, black leaders received aid from Washington, when the Supreme Court ruled on a Mississippi bus segregation case. Ruling that it had settled "beyond question that no state may require racial segregation of interstate or intrastate transportation facilities," the high court also directed the federal district court in Jackson, Mississippi, to "make such corrective order as may be appropriate to the enforcement" of its ruling. Citing three earlier rulings, the Court bluntly asserted, "The question is no longer open. It is foreclosed."[39] On the rainy afternoon of 1 March, Bootle concurred with the high court's argument and ruled unconstitutional all forms of racial segregation in city transportation. After a twenty-day boycott, the transit company capitulated as Mayor Wilson and city attorney Buckner Melton finally convinced Baggs to attend a negotiating session and attorney Wallace Miller announced compliance with Bootle's order beginning the next day. Only one minor pushing incident was reported when on 2 March blacks began to ride in the front sections of city buses. In addition, the bus company began negotiations on the employment of black drivers and mechanics, while jubilant black Maconites continued to hold mass meetings to celebrate

their victory. Across the state NAACP leader Wesley W. Law of
Savannah told *Pittsburgh Courier* reporter Trezzvant Anderson, "We
here are proud of Macon's success. My hat is off to Paschal, Randall,
Malone, Davies, etc. Tell them to keep it up." Indeed, black Maconites
fully intended to follow that advice.[40]

Not everyone's hat was off to the movement leaders, however.
Opponents of the movement staged a drive-by shooting at a house owned
by Randall. Unfortunately for them, their information was faulty and
they fired on a vacant home rather than the leader's primary residence.
Randall would take no chances with his family, ordering his wife and
daughter from their front bedrooms to another room at the rear of their
home. Randall's wife asked her husband in reply, "Are *you* going to
move to the back bedroom, too?" When he answered negatively, she shot
back, "If you're going to stay up front, I will too."[41]

WHITE BAPTISTS AND THE INTEGRATION OF BLACKS

Just after black Maconites were being led into their bus boycott by four
of their Baptist preachers, white Baptists found themselves challenged by
efforts to banish Jim Crow from their institutions in Macon. Both
controversies centered on changing times at Mercer. In 1959 times had
definitely begun to change when Mercer's presidential search committee
called Rufus C. Harris, the retiring president of New Orleans' Tulane
University home to lead his alma mater. A Baptist and a lawyer, Harris
was a strong-minded president who joined the white First Baptist Church
for its decorous spirituality and its political connections in Macon. In a
sea change from his predecessor George B. Connell, he cared little for
the pretensions of super-piety by the ministerial types within the Georgia
Baptist Convention. Just as he had no aspirations to tell ministers how to
administer their churches, he intended—as much as possible for a
denominational school—for them to leave university administration to
him.

Harris kept a wary eye on racial developments around the South,
and occasionally commented publicly on them. In 1962, after Governor
Ross Barnett sought to stop James Meredith from matriculating at the
University of Mississippi, Harris included a blistering critique in a chapel
address. Rejecting Barnett's efforts at interposition as "die-hard

sentimentality," adding, "It is a basic confusion of nostalgia with fact. Like the Confederate flag, it is beautiful in sentiment. It reflects a desire to forget the twentieth century." Responding to news reports of the speech, a local critic suggested that Harris and his kind would "go down in the burning lake as sinners for setting yourself up as a Living God for the Black race." The writer added his opinion that "if the American Negro should be deprived of the association and leadership of the white race within a generation the innate urge to savagery would destroy the thin veneer of civilization acquired from contact with the white race....."[42]

The president also kept abreast of changing attitudes on his campus. In spring 1958 Mercer students Marty Layfield and Beverly Bates debated integration on thirteen Northern campuses, returning to Macon to inform their fellow students, "If we don't take responsibility for the problem, then we will have other people taking it for us." The student body, 61 percent of which had supported segregation in a poll earlier that year, by 1961 had reversed its opinion by a 63 to 37 percent margin. Editorially, the *Mercer Cluster* took a pro-integration stance late that same year, and a year later the faculty of the college of liberal arts expressed their willingness to accept blacks by a vote of fifty-six to three, with four abstentions.[43]

Perhaps sensing that the Macon community, which had accepted the end of Jim Crow golf courses, lunch counters, and buses with a minimum of violence, could now withstand the integration of one of its largest private institutions, Harris told the Georgia Baptist newspaper, the *Christian Index,* that some academically unqualified black applicants had already been considered for admission. He added that any forthcoming application from a qualified black student would be submitted to the trustees for a decision. Indicating that he personally favored the admission of blacks to Mercer, he nonetheless made clear he would abide by the decision of the trustees. Even before this disclosure, Harris's mail had grown thick with commentary both criticizing and commending his stance. One fellow Maconite informed Harris, "It is my earnest wish that you may live long enough to have the joy of bouncing your mulatto grandchild upon your knee. You are, sir, in my opinion 'white trash.'" Macon realtor Crockett Odom advised him to "fight to maintain the strength, dignity, and preservation of the white race at islands like

Mercer than to bow to public pressures and diseased sentiment by becoming embroiled in this racial struggle."[44]

Harris also received a letter from the pastor of the Black Jack Baptist Church in Bainbridge, Georgia, not only opposing the integration of Mercer, but also suggesting he should not have made his personal views public without first polling "the people who support the institution." Not passing up the opportunity for a good argument, Harris noted that taking a poll of his congregation would likely hinder his exercise of "the freedom of the pulpit under the leadership of the Holy Spirit." He concluded with his standard reply, given to virtually similar inquiries: "The reason I personally favor admitting qualified Negroes to Mercer is that I believe the law requires it of us, since the Supreme Court's decision outlawing segregation…until the decision is changed, it is the law of the land, in my view. It being the law I do not wish to be defiant.… Besides, as a Christian, there is a matter of conscience involved, I think, in the seemingly unchristian act of drawing a color line in education." In more private conversations with his secretary, Amelia Barclay, and other confidants, the Georgia native who had been away from his home state at Tulane for many years said, "I never knew that Baptists could be so mean."[45]

On 18 October 1962, Harris warned that students and faculty would become dispirited unless Mercer dropped its racial barriers, and appealed to the trustees that "for the good of Mercer, for the progress of Mercer, for the future existence of Mercer, I believe the barrier should be removed. All of us know that the removal of the racial barrier is inevitable. If we wish to postpone its removal, however, in the hope that in a few years it will be more palatable; i.e., that in a few years we may not personally be criticized by anyone for doing so, that seems scarcely fair. In those few years Mercer will have suffered great loss."[46]

Moved by the president's words, the Mercer trustees unanimously approved Harris's motion to form a special committee that would study "the matter of admissions to the University without regard to race or color." The committee was chaired by Walter Moore, pastor of Macon's Vineville Baptist Church, and included Maconites T. Baldwin Martin and J. Warren Timmerman. Renewed levels of controversy immediately erupted in Macon and across the state. Ben Bloodworth, leader of a new white Citizen's Council in Macon, circulated leaflets in an effort to recruit 10 million new members. Also, the Mercer Law School alumni passed a resolution 27-17 opposing the admission of black students, as did the Alumni Senate of the Delta Theta Phi Law Fraternity. Harris himself took additional abuse, receiving a hand-scrawled letter addressed to "Race Mixer Harris" and a letter from a former Mercer trustee who announced, "I am through with helping Mercer until Dr. Harris and his views are removed." In November the Georgia Baptist Convention's integration opponents hired an airplane to circle the church where the meeting was held pulling the message, "Keep Mercer Segregated." An angry Mercer student wrote the student newspaper:

> It is the "White Negro" that makes my stomach crawl. What is a white Negro? A white Negro is, embarrassingly to say, a white man with "black" blood, who loves a Negro more than a member of the white race. Who are these white Negroes?... Now that Kennedy has taken over our country; Sanders, our state; Wilson, our city; and Harris, our historical institution: the Negro can now safely say, "Scram white man. This is my country now, and I finally have gained control over you."[47]

Finally, in early January 1963, the trustees study committee unanimously agreed not to proceed with the admission of blacks "at this time." As historian Alan Scot Willis correctly noted, however, "everything changed" when Sam Jerry Oni, a convert of Baptist missionaries in Ghana, applied for admission.[48]

Oni's journey to Mercer began in 1955 with a Mercerian's missionary journey to Africa. Harris Mobley had been a "Bryanite" ministerial student who, when his mentor visited him in Ghana four years later, colluded with Bryan to challenge what they regarded as "Southern Baptist hypocrisy." Recognizing that the application of an African convert would put Georgia Baptists in a dilemma between their missionary zeal and their commitment to Jim Crow, Mobley and Bryan began looking for someone to recommend to Mercer. In December 1962, Sam Oni applied for admission, with Mobley's full support. Director of Admission John T. Mitchell wrote Harris that except for his color, Oni's academic credentials would have gained him acceptance "without question." He then asked, "Would this young Christian understand that the doors to the University which prepared the missionary who brought the Gospel are closed to his converts?"[49]

In February the Mercer University Ministerial Association, assured Harris, "[Y]ou may depend upon our support in the effort to eliminate the racial discrimination in Mercer University's admission policy, and passed a resolution supporting the admission of Oni, who planned to study for the ministry. Buttressed by such support, Harris approached the spring meeting of the trustees with the recommendation that Oni be admitted. After months of difficult debate, Chairman Walter Moore announced the admission committee's decision to recommend the racial bar be dropped, initiating an emotional two-hour discussion that included two substitute motions. One proposed to delay the committee's report by sixty days, while a second suggested Oni be admitted as a foreign student without changing the admission policy concerning American blacks. Both were defeated. Harris's report to the trustees had included this appeal: "Now, I would ask you to do a brave thing. I would ask you to remove the barrier because I believe it is the right and Christian course to take. I ask it also because the discrimination is, I believe, a barrier to Mercer's progress." When, at last, the vote was called for, Harris's comments carried the day. The momentous vote was thirteen in favor, five in opposition, with three abstentions. Nine days later Mac Bryan wrote Harris from his office in North Carolina, "The hearts of all Christians troubled about the defect in our witness where and when we are involved in the idolatry of racism were lightened by your actions at Mercer University.... I know that your leadership was required, a God-send. For while both Dowell and Connell were thoroughly convinced and ready, their hands were tied. It took forceful leadership like your own to break the final barrier."[50]

That same April, while 275 miles away Birmingham, Alabama, was becoming an international embarrassment for its use of police dogs and fire hoses to avoid integration, Macon's largest institution of higher education voluntarily voted to desegregate itself without court orders or massive demonstrations. That fall, while school integration in Birmingham led to the bombing of Sixteenth Street Baptist Church and the deaths of four young black Birminghamians, Sam Oni and two black Maconites, Cecil Dewberry and Bennie Stephens, broke the color barrier at Mercer. The editor of the *Mercer Cluster* proudly told the story: "No governor stood in the doorway...or conveniently called out the state militia which the president could federalize. Rather, of her own accord, Mercer chose to remain no longer a detour on the road to social justice." There were, of course, a few minor incidents to spoil Oni's arrival. There were bomb threats and Oni and his white roommate, Don Baxter, received their share of hostile looks when they first entered the dining hall. A member of the Mercer basketball team, Baxter spent the better part of a season fighting with a teammate who harassed him and called him a "nigger lover." Then when the coach put the two on the same squad, he refused to pass the ball to Baxter.[51] But on the whole, the story was a peaceful one, and led by Dean of Students Joseph M. Hendricks, Mercer would develop programs to support black students' financial and academic adjustments to their new environment. At one time, Mercer would go on to have three times more black students enrolled than the University of Georgia, whose overall enrollment was five times that of Mercer's.[52]

The integration of another Baptist institution in Macon, however, was not as successful. As a ministerial student, Sam Oni naturally sought membership in a Baptist church. Within a month of his arrival in Macon, Oni decided to join the Vineville Baptist Church, whose pastor, Walter Moore, had chaired the committee that opened Mercer's doors to the African. Having been warned that Oni would not be accepted at Tattnall Square Baptist Church, built on the Mercer campus itself, Baxter and Oni were invited to worship at Vineville by Moore. Unsure whether his congregation would accept Oni, Moore proceeded through the service in the customary manner, inviting those interested in membership to walk to the front during the closing hymn. Baxter and Oni did so, along with a dozen or so other students. Calling on the congregation to vote for the white students separately, Moore then presented Oni. "We are very blessed to have in our midst this morning Sam Oni, a young man who came to know the Lord through our missionary efforts in Africa." Interrupting the proceedings, one man rose to his feet and said, "Reverend Moore I am *not* going to sit here and watch you destroy this church by bringing niggers into the congregation! My grandfather helped found this church and I'm not going to allow you to bring niggers into the congregation!" Another complained, "Outsiders are tryin' to integrate our church. Mercer couldn't be satisfied to go out on the streets and get a

Macon nigger. They had to go all the way to Africa." After two separate
ballots, some 70 percent of the congregation voted to accept Oni into the
membership.[53]

Since Baptist church votes on new members are virtually always
unanimous, this split vote tally portended a mixed reception for the
young African. The widow of a former Mercer professor often invited
him to eat in her home and hired him for frequent odd jobs. When he
later attended her funeral, however, a wealthy white Maconite, and a
member of the Vineville church, watched Oni take a seat in the mortuary
chapel, and commented to another, "He looks like a monkey, doesn't
he?" He also received anonymous letters saying only those members
connected with Mercer accepted him. [54]

Soon one of the members at the Vineville church who had supported
Oni's membership became drawn into an even larger controversy. In
1964 Thomas J. Holmes, a minister who served on the Mercer staff as a
liaison to Georgia Baptist churches, was invited to become the new
pastor of the Tattnall Square Baptist Church. Since 1891 this
congregation had become the college church, having been founded
specifically to minister to the Mercer community and built on land
deeded by the university. During Holmes's discussions with church
leaders, some deacons admitted regretting the church's not allowing Oni
to visit told Holmes the time had come to accept black students, provided
"they really come to worship, not to create a disturbance." Thinking the
times had indeed changed at Tattnall, Holmes accepted their offer,
making clear his personal conviction that blacks should be allowed in
worship at the church.[55]

During the next two years Mercer students returned to Tattnall for
worship. Eventually, however, the growing number of black students
would make integration an issue for the church once again. Holmes and
his two associate ministers, Douglas Johnson and Jack W. Jones, wanted
to invite blacks, while the deacons hoped the matter would go away. One
Saturday night Johnson received a call from a Mercer contact warning
him that black students would be attending worship at Tattnall the next
day. Alerting Holmes of the impending visit, the senior pastor planned to
proceed normally. On Sunday, 26 June 1966, for the first time two black
students with three white companions attended worship at Tattnall. Grace
Holmes, the pastor's wife, and her friend Annette Highsmith warmly

greeted them with handshakes before and sat with them during the service. That afternoon she received an embittered phone call asking her how it felt to shake the hand of a "nigra." "I felt liberated," was her reply. Later, she and her husband found themselves the target of increasing hostility. "I went to the grocery store," she later told a reporter, "and the man who used to be so nice to serve me now didn't seem to want to serve me. We felt unacceptable most everywhere we went."[56]

That night after the evening worship a deacon vented his wrath on Holmes, promising, "You'll be voted out for lettin' them niggers in here this mornin.' You're lower down than any dog. You knew last night them niggers was comin.' Why didn't you call one of us and we would've had 'em thrown out."

"That's exactly why I didn't call you," he replied, fighting to maintain his calm. "I didn't want pictures of the church I pastor spread over the front pages of the world tomorrow morning showing deacons turning away God's children from God's house. Nor did I want those nice young men so embarrassed."

"Well, you're through here. I'm goin' to have you voted out."

"You may vote me out," Holmes said, "but you called me here to preach the gospel, and as long as I'm here I will preach it.... And while I'm your pastor, we'll not turn away any person who seeks to worship."

"I intend to get up here next Sunday morning," retorted the deacon, "and make the biggest fuss ever made in this church. I intend to have you fired, you and your associate pastor, and that music director too."

"You've got one vote." Holmes answered.

"I've just got one vote, and I'm just a little man, but…

"You certainly *are* a little man, just about as little as any man I ever saw."[57]

Angry members had already begun a telephone campaign both to stop further visits by blacks and to fire the ministerial staff. In mid-July a special committee on the seating of blacks voted three to two to bring a resolution to the entire diaconate, which voted fourteen to eight to call on the congregation to vote on the question of seating blacks. On the next Sunday, 24 July 1966, an estimated 100 members who had not been to church in over a year showed up to cast their votes with the majority. The congregation voted against seating African Americans by 286 to

109. By late September the majority had marshaled their forces again, this time to oust the pastor and his colleagues. On 25 September, on the day the congregation was set to vote on the fate of its ministerial staff, Sam Oni attempted to visit Tattnall Square Baptist Church. In part to support Holmes, in part to try to convince the congregation of the negative effect of their policy on Southern Baptist missionary efforts, in part simply to be a thorn in the side of racists, Oni was met by two deacons on sentry duty, commissioned to stop any blacks, and especially the troublemaker from Ghana, from gaining entrance. Reminding him of the church's policy, they put Oni in a headlock and pulled him down the front stairs to a police car stationed nearby. Inside the sanctuary, matters were just as tense, as the congregation voted 259 to 189 to fire all three of the ministers. Afterward, Holmes, Johnson, and Jones issued a public statement: "We can feel only sorrow at this action of the Tattnall Square Baptist Church in discharging us from our positions. Not sorrow for ourselves but sorrow that a church with such a distinguished history of Christian service..., has allowed itself to be shattered over the issue of the seating of all persons who desire to worship in our sanctuary."[58]

In the aftermath of the controversy, famed Atlanta columnist Ralph McGill editorialized, "If this were not so ineffably sad it would be hysterically funny." Holmes later told the *Christian Index* that his ouster had had the fortunate result of causing at least four other Baptist churches to adopt open door policies. The black Baptist Ministers Brotherhood of Macon issued a statement on the Tattnall decision to fire the ministers, condemning it for making "a mockery of Christian ethics." By contrast, the white Macon Baptist Pastors' Conference debated the right of pastors to interfere in the autonomous actions of a Baptist congregation before finally deciding not to issue any public statement. The Reverend Tommy Stowe, secretary of the white group, did follow the request of the other pastors to write a letter assuring the Tattnall ministers of their prayers as they faced the controversy. Mercer students mocked the church's decision with placards that read, "TATTNALL SQUARE ~~BAPTIST CHURCH~~ PRIVATE CLUB. PASTOR WANTED. NEED NOT BE A CHRISTIAN." Another read, "If God is Dead, It's Churches Like Tattnall That Killed Him." Rufus Harris called the ouster "not only an act of savagery, but also a denial of the relevancy of Jesus

Christ as Savior in twentieth century life," and re-hired Thomas Holmes as his special assistant.

As for the Tattnall Church itself, some 100 members of the congregation left after the controversy, and in 1972 the church reaffirmed its stance against integration. The following year the church had another opportunity to turn away more black worshippers, as twenty-seven black Mercerians visited worship services. After the students refused to leave, the congregation deliberately ignored their presence, even to the point of refusing to accept their contributions to the offering plate. Three years earlier, the church had opened the Tattnall Square Academy, a private school ostensibly established to provide a Christian education to students from kindergarten through high school, but also clearly a rejection of the possibility of integrated public schools. Eventually the congregation tired of confrontations over race and the "community in transition," a euphemism for a rising population of African Americans. In 1974 Tattnall sold its building back to Mercer and three years later moved to a new location in the wealthier, whiter section of North Macon. Looking back on its own racial troubles and the firing of Holmes and the other ministers, the church's centennial history sanitized its interpretation of the events in one misleading sentence: "The widespread and far-reaching social changes of this period had their effects on this church, and on 25 September 1966, the pastor, associate pastor, and minister of music ended their association with the church."[59]

On the other hand, doubtless many white Maconites shared the views of a writer to the *Macon Telegraph* whose letter praised the Tattnall church for being "a combatant force against sin and her beguiling enemies." Castigating the white First Baptist Church for voting to accept black worshippers, the writer attributed the decision to conformity to "the spirit of communism." He concluded, "I think Tattnall Square Baptist Church should be applauded rather than condemned, for standing by her convictions. The congregation can take heart in the knowledge that they are not in the minority—not even in Macon."[60]

Subsequent developments appeared to bear out such assessments. Over the next thirty years an exodus of white Maconites—including a number of churches—would follow Tattnall's example, leaving the city to relocate in North Macon. In effect, Tattnall Square Baptist Church had blessed whites' decisions to evade their black neighbors, and led them to a new promised land.

Thus, by the mid-1960s black-white relations grew more tense as blacks stepped up their protests and made significant progress in disintegrating Jim Crow at least in facilities controlled by the more progressive city government. One early sign of increased tensions was in October 1962, when hundreds of black Maconites wore armbands in a march around city hall to protest the shooting of seventeen-year-old A. C. Hall, the third such incident in the previous eighteen months.[61] The moderate administration of Ed Wilson ended after one-term, and more conservative mayors B. F. Merritt in 1963 and Ronnie Thompson in 1967 succeeded him. Meanwhile, as the decade ended, Macon's public schools had yet to begin desegregating. Since those schools were controlled by a countywide board of education, the political influence of blacks in the city of Macon was more diluted and less effective. City facilities more susceptible to black political power managed to eliminate segregation with relative ease. The battle to expel Jim Crow from the county's public schools would be more difficult and more divisive.

8

A New Nadir:
Macon's Race Relations in the
Era of Black Power

Blessed is the historian influential enough to name an entire period of history. Thus whenever later generations of historians discuss the turn-of-the-nineteenth-century South, they will henceforth echo Rayford W. Logan's description of the period as the "nadir" of African American life in the United States.[1] None will doubt that the early twentieth century, with its unutterable, Jim Crow separation, defended by peonage, disfranchisement, and lynching, was indisputably the low point of black life in Macon as well as the rest of the South. To speak of race relations, however, is to address not the status of the black minority to the relative white majority, but the level of harmony felt by both groups toward each other. By this definition, at least in Macon the early twentieth century cannot be considered the nadir of racial harmony.

To say this is to argue that while blacks found earlier periods more difficult or dangerous, their public complaints were quiet or infrequent enough for whites to continue the self-deception that blacks were content and race relations were harmonious. However inwardly disgruntled blacks may have been, whites continued to rest securely in the protective cocoon of white supremacy and apparent black acquiescence to it. Most black complaints were not shared with whites, who were thus able to believe that all was right in the world of black-white relations. Living in survival mode, blacks were wise enough not to bite the hand that often fed them. This absence of *overt* disgruntlement massaged the white will to believe in racial harmony.

By the end of the 1960s, however, Southern whites could no longer convince themselves that "our colored people" had been content until "outside agitators" stirred them up with radical, Communist ideas. Especially not in Macon, where the first wave of the civil rights movement had proceeded from the indigenous, middle-class leadership of the NAACP, the Bibb County Coordinating Committee, and local African-American churches. The first phase of the civil rights movement across the South had yielded the end of Jim Crow, protected by the Civil Rights Act of 1964 and the Voting Rights Act of the following year. In Macon the racial bars to public accommodations had been lifted by surreptitious negotiations between the city administration and black leaders, by a three-week bus boycott, and, compared to other parts of Georgia and the South, with minimal racial violence. While black Maconites entered the 1970s recognizing their status was improving, their progress sparked both a hunger for further economic and political gains and an angry backlash from white neighbors. Many whites throughout the South, and of course in Macon also, come to believe that political liberalism had allowed blacks to move too far too fast and given them too much too soon. Hence racial antagonism and anger between black and white Maconites erupted periodically in Macon after 1970, bringing racial tension to its peak and racial harmony to a new nadir.

In large measure this increasing tension reflected the unfolding of the civil rights movement at large. As the movement turned north, King's Southern Christian Leadership Conference found rougher sledding as it tried to build on its mid-1960s triumphs. The 1964 Civil Rights Act had effectively ended segregation in public accommodations, while the Voting Rights Act of 1965 put the federal government to work protecting the black franchise in the South. Moving into the urban north, King found economic discrimination, in housing and employment, for example, more resistant to change. Increased resistance sparked more anger as alienated urban blacks came to reject King's nonviolent and interracial tactics as too dependent on white good will and increasingly expressed their anger through the "Black Power" slogan of Stokely Carmichael, the young leader of the Student Nonviolent Coordinating Committee. The more militant rhetoric of this Second Civil Rights Movement, its focus on economic equality, its association with the Black Nationalism of Malcolm X, and its rejection of nonviolence combined to form a Black Radicalism that leveled a more thoroughgoing critique of American society.

Throughout the nation, whites began to view these developments and the urban riots that followed King's assassination with alarm and anger. They worried about what they perceived as the black turn toward violence and they fumed at what they interpreted as African-American ingratitude. In the 1964 Civil Rights Act and the 1965 Voting Rights Act, white America, represented by Congress, had "given" to blacks the end of segregated public accommodations and federal protection of the right to vote. Now, they reasoned, racial equality had been reached. Never mind that the achievements of the movement had only belatedly "given" African Americans those benefits that they should have received in 1789 when the Constitution was ratified, or at least Emancipation. Moreover, other than their white supremacist pride, integration had cost white Americans nothing. Now that the movement was seeking economic and political equality—which through affirmative action or other federal programs might actually have a price tag for the nation—white support for the movement began to dissipate across the nation.

In Macon, white support for movement was always tenuous and certainly dissipated further when Black Power emphases arose in the form of a new organization of younger African Americans known as the Black Liberation Front (BLF). Challenging the leadership of the local NAACP and BCCC, which had dealt mostly with middle-class issues, this new, more militant phase of the Macon movement focused on concerns that more directly affected poor blacks. The competition over leadership in the black community added to the increased tensions, as both whites and the more established black leaders viewed the BLF as too radical. For whites, however, this alarm was built upon a foundation of concern about the integration of the Bibb County schools. Since the *Brown* ruling whites in the South had sought to delay racial mixing of school children as long as possible. After attempts to integrate Macon's schools in 1954, 1955, 1961, and 1963, were ignored by the Bibb County Board of Education, the city saw small-scale desegregation in 1964, and prepared itself for a full dosage. Macon's federal district judge, William Augustus Bootle, would write that prescription, first with regard to the University of Georgia, and finally with the Bibb County schools.

Anticipating these developments, white Maconites stiffened their resistance.

WHITE RETRENCHMENT

On 26 January 1970, the United States Supreme Court issued a ruling that symbolized not only white Macon's almost century-long commitment to the separation of the races, but also its recommitment to it even when challenged by the civil rights movement. In *Evans v. Abney* the high court resolved a long-simmering controversy over Macon's Baconsfield Park. Wending its way to the Supreme Court twice since 1963, the *Evans* ruling judicially ratified what has been described as Macon's "sacrifice to Jim Crow."[2]

Baconsfield Park pond and scenery, March 1949. The Park has been called "Macon's sacrifice to Jim Crow." (Courtesy of the Washington Memorial Library.)

In late March 1963 Macon's Tattnall Square and Baconsfield Parks were desegregated. While violence flared when blacks began to use Tattnall Square Park, the courtroom battles over Baconsfield were longer lived and more significant. On Sunday, 31 March, blacks were evicted from Baconsfield by a pistol-waving caretaker. NAACP leaders William P. Randall and Walter Davis were called to the scene, along with police officers. The incident ended peacefully with no arrests. Some time earlier, at the suggestion of Mayor Ed Wilson, city attorney Buckner Melton and Mitchell House had expunged from the city code all segregation laws prohibiting integrated activities in municipal facilities.[3] Under ordinary circumstances, this would have ended the matter, but Baconsfield Park had been segregated not only by city statute, but also by the last will and testament of Macon's Senator Augustus O. Bacon.

In 1911 Bacon's will had bequeathed 117 acres of land to the city of Macon for a "park and pleasure ground" to be used by the city's "white women, white girls, white boys and white children." The will highlighted the senator's view that black and white races should remain forever separate and specifically stipulated that park was not "to be used or enjoyed together or in common." Just as precisely, however, Bacon also stipulated that the park continue as a park in perpetuity: "…in no case and under no circumstances shall any part of the property herein conveyed…be ever sold or otherwise alienated or practically disposed of by any person or authority whatsoever."[4]

On 9 April 1963 attorneys C. E. Newton and A. O. B. Sparks Jr., Bacon's great-grandson, represented the Baconsfield Board of Managers in a meeting with city attorney Buckner Melton to discuss whether the terms of the will, if violated, might result in the reversion of the property to the Bacon heirs. Sparks recommended that the city voluntarily resign as trustee of the park, that private trustees be appointed, and that the park's swimming pool contract with the city be cancelled. Believing that the public interest was best served by city control of the park, Wilson and Melton refused to resign as trustee. As a result, in May the Baconsfield Board of Managers sued the city for allowing blacks to use the park "in direct contravention of the terms of the trust." Newton argued that the city be replaced as trustee, citing the will's terms empowering the board to "exclude at any time [from the park] any person or persons…who may be deemed objectionable." Arguing for the city, Melton contended that under recent Supreme Court rulings the city had no authority to enforce racially discriminatory restrictions. Meanwhile, a contingent of black leaders including the Reverends Ellis S. Evans, J. L. Key, Booker W. Chambers, and Van J. Malone, along with NAACP leaders Louis H. Wynne and William P. Randall, intervened in the suit hoping to desegregate the park. Their attorneys argued that the board's suit had not been filed with "clean hands," but rather with the purpose of violating the Fourteenth Amendment and thus the constitutional rights of black Maconites.[5]

A new city administration, however, would come into power before the suit could be decided. While running for mayor in 1963, B. F. Merritt's sympathies appeared to lay with the Baconsfield board and heirs. Then, two months after taking office, the Merritt administration resigned as trustee of the park. On 10 March 1964, Bibb Superior Court Judge Oscar Long announced that he would appoint new trustees who would carry out Bacon's intent of keeping the park segregated, or failing that, to allow the property to revert to the heirs.[6] Macon's blacks intervened again, appealing Long's judgment to the Georgia Supreme Court, where attorneys argued that the court should allow the park to continue its existence on an integrated basis. According to the doctrine of *cy pres,* they contended that when a valid bequest was incapable of being executed exactly as specified by the donor, the court could lawfully "carry it into effect in such a way as will as nearly as possible effectuate his intention." On 28 September 1964 the Georgia Supreme Court rejected the blacks' argument and upheld Long's ruling.[7] An appeal to the US Supreme Court reversed *Evans v. Newton,* ruling in January 1966 that the park could not remain segregated and remanding the case back to the Georgia Supreme Court "for further proceeding not inconsistent with the opinion of this court.[8]

Two months later the Georgia high court declared the Bacon trust null and void because its "sole purpose" (a segregated park), was "impossible of accomplishment." The court further instructed Judge Long to rule on the "intentions of the trustees of the Bacon estate and intervening heirs." In late 1967 and early 1968, Long terminated the Bacon trust, judging it to be unenforceable. He further ruled that *cy pres* did not apply because there was no general charitable intent in the will, and appointed Guyton G. Abney and Willis B. Sparks, Jr., as receivers for the property for the heirs. In 1968, led by the Reverend Ellis S. Evans, blacks appealed to the Georgia Supreme Court in *Evans v. Abney,* in which the Georgia court upheld Long's ruling, explaining that whites were the "objects of his [Bacon's] bounty" and that black Maconites had "not been deprived of their rights to inherit because they were given no inheritance.[9]

In one last appeal on 12 and 13 November 1969, the NAACP lawyers argued the *cy pres* doctrine, asking the US Supreme Court "to amend the terms of the will by striking the racial restrictions and opening Baconsfield to all the citizens of Macon without regard to race or color." In January 1970, however, *Evans* received a 5-4 decision upholding the Georgia Supreme Court, agreeing that the whites-only character was an "inseparable part of the testator's plan" and that "the Senator's charitable intent was not 'general' but extended only to the...benefit of white people." As such, wrote Justice Hugo Black for the majority, *cy pres* did not apply. The Georgia court therefore had no alternative "but to end the Baconsfield trust and return the property to the Senator's heirs." In a dissenting opinion, Justice William O. Douglas argued that Bacon's will had also stipulated that the property was "under no circumstances" to be used for any purpose "excepting so far as herein specifically authorized." Douglas further noted that since the will intended to donate land for the city's use, ending its municipal use did "as much violence to Bacon's purpose" as would integrating the park. "Letting both races share the facility," Douglas held, "is closer to a realization of Bacon's desire than a complete destruction of the will and the abandonment of Bacon's desire that the property be used for some municipal purpose."[10]

The next year a group of citizens formed an organization named "Save Old Baconsfield Incorporated," which pressed the city to buy the land outright from the heirs and re-open it as an integrated park. The heirs, however, believing that such a sale would violate the senator's intention, insisted on a sales contract that prohibited the property from being used as a park. In 1972 a group of investors purchased the land for $1.5 million, and over the next ten years the former "pleasure ground" was replaced by an office park, apartments, a McDonald's restaurant, and a shopping center. Thus, many in the white community colluded with the Bacon heirs, who stood to gain financially in the reversion of the property, and sacrificed the general welfare of the city and the park to the gods of greed and Jim Crow. As Mary Ann Berg Richardson summed up the incident: "Bacon's voice, spoken through his will, had been manipulated to dam the rampant stream of the civil rights movement, even if at just this one place, Baconsfield Park."[11]

A less symbolic, more overt way for white Macon to dam up what Martin Luther King, borrowing from the biblical prophet Amos, called the "ever-flowing stream" of racial justice was its turn away from political moderation. In three of four racially freighted elections during the mid-1960s, white Macon voted to oppose the gains of the civil rights movement. In 1963, when Ed Wilson was prohibited by law from running for re-election, B. F. Merritt sought to regain the mayor's office that he had previously held from 1953 to 1959. Facing off against Kenneth Carswell, Merritt played the race card when campaign workers brought him copies of letters from black leaders William Randall and Thomas B. Hooper. As chairman of the Bibb County Democratic Club, Randall had indicated to Carswell that he and Hooper had intended not to endorse either candidate. When, however, Merritt raised the issue of bloc voting, Randall decided indirectly to endorse Carswell. He wrote another letter to the black community arguing that "in order to be sure that the next city administration will not be racist and that the streets of Macon will not become a battleground where police dogs and high pressure water hoses will be our adversaries, we urge you to vote tomorrow and vote for...candidates who have not raised the race issue."

In response, Merritt traded salvos with Carswell, claiming the letters proved conclusively that his opponent had made "a deal with the bloc vote." Merritt denied that he had played the race card, saying he had not attacked "the Negro race." Resorting to the code-word politics that would become common among conservatives in the post-civil rights South, the former and future mayor argued that he had only "attacked those voters who blindly vote according to the dictates of self-appointed leaders whose support is for sale in the market place." Exposed as the candidate of black Maconites, Carswell was forced to go on the offensive, charging that if the "extremists now in control of my opponent's campaign have their way, our racial problem will be met with violence and riot." He accused Merritt of selling out to "the radical racist group" and having "dumped the colored voters in my lap." Defending himself against Merritt's specific charges, Carswell denied making "any promises to Negro leaders or voters." Then he added, "Macon cannot afford a mayor who loses his head when the going gets tough. Macon must not become another Birmingham." [12]

Two days later, with the largest voter turnout in the city's history, white voters rallied to give Merritt a twenty percentage point margin of victory over Carswell. This was the first election since a 1961 annexation had greatly expanded the city's boundaries to include more white voters in the outlying areas of Bibb County. The larger percentage of white voters, a larger percentage of whom were angry about the Wilson administration's racial moderation, clearly chose the candidate with the harder line against further black advances.[13] The trend continued the following year in the presidential election, when for the first time in history the state of Georgia voted for a Republican. Campaigning against the Civil Rights Act of 1964 and the president who signed it, Barry Goldwater swept twenty-four of twenty-seven Middle Georgia counties and polled 24,717 (59 percent) Bibb County votes to Lyndon Johnson's 17,141. Years later, Herbert Dennard, editor of the *Georgia Informer*, saw such polarized voting patterns—most blacks voting for Democratic presidential candidates; most whites voting for Republicans—as an important signal that race relations were worsening.[14]

In 1966 Georgia experienced what an Atlanta reporter called "the most hectic, confusing, complex election in the history of the state." The six-candidate race for governor included former governors Ellis Arnall and Ernest Vandiver, along with future governor and president, Jimmy Carter. Also running was the unlikely candidate and Atlanta restaurateur, Lester G. Maddox, who by 1964 had built a national reputation for bigotry. As owner of the successful Pickrick Restaurant, Maddox defied the recently enacted Civil Rights Act, using a pistol to drive away three potential black customers. When he eventually closed his restaurant rather than submit to the law's requirement to serve black patrons, he came to rival Alabama's Governor George Wallace as a national symbol of racist reaction. During his campaign Maddox vowed to run Martin Luther King out of the state and invite Wallace in. He finished second to Arnall in the 14 September primary, forcing a runoff election two weeks later. In the primary only 1,916 Maconites voted for him, giving him a fourth place finish behind Arnall (3,061), Albany journalist James Gray (2,451), and Jimmy Carter (2,163). In the runoff Arnall managed to win Bibb County by a slim 243-vote margin. While taking only 49.54 percent of the vote in the county, Maddox took 54 percent of the statewide vote to win the Democratic nomination.[15]

Thus, while Macon's vote ran counter to the state at large, a significant portion of the city's white voters had again supported the segregationist hard-liner. In November, Republican candidate Howard

"Bo" Callaway barely edged Maddox in the popular vote. Nevertheless, because a write-in campaign for Arnall garnered some 50,000 votes, neither was able to win a majority. In Macon, however, Callaway drew almost 62 percent of the vote. Eventually, the Democrat-controlled general assembly elected Maddox governor by a vote of 182 to 66, with 11 abstentions.[16]

The 1967 mayoral campaign, however, played the most prominent role in setting up the racial tensions of the 1970s. Political observers were surprised when the race resulted in the city's first Republican administration. After a bruising Democratic primary battle between Ed Wilson and B. F. Merritt, the incumbent faced off against thirty-three-year-old Republican challenger Ronnie Thompson. Merritt had brought a successful court challenge against the law that barred him from succeeding himself, giving some voters the impression that he felt entitled to the office for life. Having alienated Wilson's supporters (especially his black supporters) during the primary campaign, Merritt mounted a low-energy effort and underestimated Thompson, whose youth and good looks attracted many voters. In addition, his service on the city council and notoriety as a Gospel music singer on a local television program that had aired for eight years aided his name recognition.

Merritt was also hurt by the race issue, which took some odd turns in this contest. Thompson's campaign received an unexpected boost when Clarence L. Townes, Jr., a black member of the Republican National Committee, sent a telegram of support. In addition, black Maconites were divided over the two candidates. While William Randall endorsed Merritt, the Reverend Booker Chambers and the Baptist Ministers Brotherhood endorsed Thompson. Aiming his real criticisms toward Randall, whom he derided as "Mr. Big," Chambers said: "I, for one, am tired of the ill-guidance and misrepresentation given to the present administration and their dogmatic machine running this city's government and omitting the working people of this community."[17]

Black disenchantment was deepened in the last week of the campaign, when both candidates accused the other of injecting the race issue into the campaign. When Merritt denounced Thompson's campaign as having been directed by a black representative of the GOP, Thompson countered by calling the mayor a racist. In addition, Thompson

successfully linked Merritt with President Lyndon Johnson and the civil
rights agenda by distributing photographs of the mayor at Johnson
headquarters during the 1964 election. With the caption, "Lest We
Forget," Thompson reminded voters that Merritt had served as co-
chairman of the president's Bibb County re-election effort. Not
surprisingly, voter turnout in the heaviest black precincts decreased by
453. Thompson won the election by just over 53 percent of the vote.[18]

Within four months of taking office, Thompson's responses to the
grief and anger of the black community sparked by the assassination of
Martin Luther King brought race back onto center stage in Macon.
Thompson's immediate statement regarding the assassination expressed
shock and concern, along with regret that racist feelings "lead to such
useless tragedies." The next day the mayor met with two civic groups to
discuss local reaction to the assassination. In a lengthy statement after the
meetings, Thompson took King's visit to Macon two weeks earlier,
which occurred without incident, as a sign of the city's good race
relations. He further noted the emotions stirred by King's death and the
anxiety created by it. He called on all Maconites to observe President
Johnson's designated day of prayer, concluding, "As mayor, it is my duty
to enforce the law, protect lives and property, promote a better
environment in which to live. I call on every Maconite to aid me in this
most worthwhile cause, and I am confident you will."[19]

In the first hours after the news hit the wires, William Randall made
a public statement calling for understanding and hoping that "hot heads
will not take the lead." Later, he added to his earlier comments,
confessing, "I am afraid that those who advocate and practice violence
will take the tragic murder of Dr. King as a signal to plunge our country
into an insane strike." Around midnight the next night, however, police
broke up a number of disturbances by blacks angered by the killing.
Young blacks threw trash cans through a number of department store
windows. Uncivil disturbances such as these had spread across the
country in the wake of King's murder and during the first two days after
the assassination resulted in nineteen deaths in Chicago, Washington,
Detroit, Tallahassee, Memphis, and Minneapolis. Similar incidents
plagued Macon the following night, when the downtown area saw a fire
bombing and more shattered windows.

Civil rights marchers, May 10, 1968. (Courtesy of
the Washington Memorial Library.)

Participating in a disturbance on Poplar Street was Billy Randall,
the son of Macon's most prominent black leader. A law student at Emory
University, the younger Randall had grown angry since the mid-1960s
and King's murder enraged the young man further. Mounting a garbage
can, he admonished his fellow rioters and called for retaliation. Before
his speech got very far, however, his father—now just as angry as his
son—drove up, snatched him off his makeshift dais and threw him in the
car. "Have you gone crazy!" the elder Randall asked, "I'm ashamed of
you. You know this ain't the way!"[20]

Another group of some twenty-five blacks commandeered a city
bus, which police eventually stopped on its way toward the Westgate
Shopping Center. Police also stopped a car with nine fire bombs arrayed
on the back seat. Some sixty persons were arrested in connection with
the disturbances. Thompson responded by issuing a 12:30 A.M. to dawn
curfew, telling a television and radio audience, "Unless you have
business, please stay off the downtown streets as we have emergency
vehicles operating in that area."[21]

That same day a predominantly-black group of some 300 Maconites
marched down Cherry Street and Cotton Avenue toward city hall for a
memorial service to honor King. Led by the elder Randall, attorney
Thomas Jackson, and Joseph Hendricks, one of a sprinkling of whites in
the assembly, the marchers carried placards calling for the continuation

of King's nonviolent methods. Mayor Thompson greeted the marchers, expressing his sympathy to the mourners and telling the crowd would "depend on your influence" to help keep peace in the city. Hoping to steer blacks away from more militant leaders like Stokely Carmichael, Hendricks told the gathering that in such troubled times King had been "the best friend the white man ever had," reminding the mostly black audience that many whites in Macon and throughout the nation who were willing to "reach out their hand" to help blacks achieve equality. Now with his anger more subdued the younger Randall called on blacks to continue King's nonviolence, although he admitted that "nonviolence is often very difficult to use."[22]

The deep grief and anger generated in African-American youth by the King assassination indeed made nonviolence a more difficult path to follow. The pent-up frustrations of 300 years of slavery and segregation, so slowly and grudgingly and incompletely remedied by white America, had been kept in check for fourteen years since *Brown*. King's admonitions and successes had helped control growing black rage as whites continued to drag their feet, giving as little as possible to black demands. Now the voice of nonviolence had been silenced. If this was to be white America's answer to a nonviolent approach, many young blacks concluded it was time to try another method. Billy Randall's comments foreshadowed the growing anger of black America, and in this period the elder Randall did much to keep a lid on matters in Macon. Shortly after King's death Joe Hendricks commented about how lucky Macon was that local blacks had shown relatively little anger. Randall gently corrected Hendricks, lamenting that whites had no idea how much desperation and anger were mounting among younger blacks.[23]

Thus Macon's young mayor had performed admirably in his first brush with a civil rights movement beginning to grow more militant. Macon's outbreaks of violence after the King assassination were minor compared to those in larger cities, but they were the first fruits of a more pervasive anger to be harvested over the next few years. As the frustrations of black Maconites grew, and their demands grew louder, white tensions escalated and Thompson's responses stiffened as they reflected the frayed feelings of the city. Concerns about the possibility of black rioting around the country, coupled with a similar upsurge in Macon, gave the edge to "law and order" candidates in the 1968 election cycle. In George Wallace's third party campaign for the presidency, 47 percent of Georgians found a hero. Along with winning the state, Wallace also carried Bibb County with almost 43 percent of the vote.[24] Clearly, the racial tensions of the era were driving a large swath of white Maconites toward hard-line segregationist politicians.

All of these tensions, of course, built to a crescendo as the specter of school desegregation hovered over Macon as the 1970s approached. A central figure in those events was Judge William Augustus Bootle of the US District Court. Having earned his undergraduate and law degrees, and later serving as interim dean of Mercer's law school, Bootle had been appointed Bibb County district attorney in 1929 at the age of twenty-six. Just days before the *Brown* ruling, the conservative Republican lawyer was appointed by President Eisenhower to the federal bench. Like most conservative white Southerners, Bootle had accepted segregation and during a 1949 dispute he and arch-segregationist Charles J. Bloch represented white Maconites who objected to a swimming pool for blacks being built in their neighborhoods. On that occasion, black leader Frank Hutchings publicly pointed out that Bootle was not known to have ever done anything for black advancement. As such, he was an unlikely candidate to order the desegregation of Bibb County's schools. But after *Brown* he came to see desegregation as the law of the land, which he had sworn to uphold.[25]

Bootle's historic opportunity to do so came ten years before the Bibb public school debacle when NAACP attorney Donald Hollowell brought before him arguments to allow Hamilton E. Holmes and Charlayne Hunter to integrate the University of Georgia. The UGA experience foreshadowed things to come. During the 1958 gubernatorial campaign Bootle was invited to a meeting of the Macon Rotary Club to hear a speech by soon-to-be-governor Ernest Vandiver. Seated at the speaker's table next to the candidate, the judge listened to Vandiver's standard stump speech that "No Not One" black student would attend a white school if he were elected governor. As Vandiver finished with a rhetorical flourish the audience gave him an extended ovation. Not wishing to join in the applause, Bootle chose that moment to take several sips from a glass of water. Catching him as he left the building, a Rotarian told the judge, "I hope you heard what he said." Later, he got a phone call from a former client who ribbed him, noting, "Gus, I noticed you got mighty thirsty during the program." "Yes, a glass of water never came in so handily," came Bootle's judicious reply.[26]

Hearing the arguments of Attorney General and Mercerian Eugene Cook and Donald Hollowell in September 1960, Bootle took the UGA matter under advisement, not reaching a decision until 6 January 1961. After he ordered the university to admit Holmes and Hunter, he quickly issued a stay of his own order, hoping that the US Court of Appeals and Supreme Court would back up his original ruling and reverse his stay. The plan worked, as Appeals Court Judge Elbert Tuttle reversed the stay. Both Tuttle the Supreme Court handed down their rulings upholding Bootle's earlier desegregation ruling on the same day the stay was issued, prompting a clever journalist to write the headline, "From Bootle to Tuttle to Black and Back." By this time, Holmes, Hunter, and Bootle had all been hanged in effigy on the UGA and the Mercer campuses. Governor Vandiver had also denounced the judge's additional decision to block the state from closing the university.[27]

Not surprisingly, closer to home Bootle's ruling re-energized the Klan in Macon. A group of Klan-affiliated women, a number of whom were Maconites, picketed the state capital with placards reading, "We mothers want segregation. We will not accept integration" and "White People Have Rights Too." A few days later 100 Klansmen burned a cross at a gathering on Old Columbus Road in Macon. Imperial Wizard Lee Davidson denounced the ruling, saying "it would be better to close the university" rather than allow it to be integrated. "White people must unite," he declared, "if racial segregation in the South is to survive." Davidson ended the occasion with an appeal to the teens present to join the Klan and a prayer.[28] On the Sunday after Bootle's ruling, a fellow member of the First Baptist Church huffed, "He's got his nerve," when she saw the judge enter the sanctuary. Years later, the woman's son, a prominent Macon lawyer, told the judge, "Mother never could forgive you for those rulings."[29]

On the other side of the ledger, Bootle received support for his decision. That same Sunday, Bootle visited his longtime friend and former Mercer president Spright Dowell in the hospital. Before Bootle could even utter a greeting, Dowell sat up in his bed and implored him, "Boode, you've got the knowledge, you've got the power, you've got the courage. Make them do it," before lying back down. In response to the ruling, Mercer professor Robert Otto began sending friends postcards bearing a picture of the federal courthouse in Macon where Bootle presided. Beneath the photograph, Otto wrote the caption, "This is where church is being held." In the midst of the controversy, Mrs. J. R. Miller wrote to the *Macon Telegraph* to support Bootle as Georgia's "Man of the Year." She wrote: "There always comes a time in history where one individual must be heroic enough to step out and stand alone for awhile, in the march of progress.... This one act can only be appreciated at full value years from now, as is true with all historic events."[30] While most Maconites of the present have fulfilled this writer's prophecy, Bootle nevertheless rankled large numbers of white Maconites with his 1970 rulings to desegregate the city's public schools.

Token integration began for Macon in June 1963, when the Bibb County Board of Education admitted Bert Bivins III to a federally-funded electronics course at the Dudley M. Hughes Vocational School. The board of education claimed that as a federal program Hughes did not fall under any segregation provision. Later that summer the board voted eleven to four not to desegregate the Bibb County public schools without a court order, a resolution that William P. Simmons, one of the four dissenters on the board, called "the most irresponsible act" in the board's ninety-one year history. On 12 August 1964, Judge Bootle issued an order that desegregation begin that fall. On 1 September the board of education's gradual desegregation plan went into effect, as sixteen blacks students were transferred to previously all white schools. This amounted to a statistically insignificant .0009 percent of the white students in Bibb County, but racial progressives like the MCHR saw an importance beyond the numbers. Through those particular students, the MCHR asserted, would "be tested our readiness to deal independently with a new situation, ... and our ability to plan for the future." Reflecting on the upcoming desegregation, the MCHR issued a statement calling on all Maconites to work together to "build an educational system which best serves the needs of all children." The group acknowledged that black students had been deprived of educational opportunities available to white students. Noting that many black students were "behind their grade level in several subjects," the MCHR advocated tutorial programs to help close the gap.[31]

School and NAACP officials asked a number of the best, most mature black students to enroll in the white schools. William P. Randall later recalled, "They had to be militant and yet not go around with a chip on their shoulders. We gave them a lot of advice about what to expect and what not to expect. They did a beautiful job. They laid groundwork for others." The sixteen students joined white classmates at Miller Junior High, along with Lanier, and Willingham High Schools. Feeling that someone had to be the first, Wilfred Anderson agreed to spend that year as the only black at Willingham. Playing on the football team, Anderson found a surprising level of support from his teammates. Other white students who associated with Anderson were occasionally beaten up by students aggrieved by Anderson's presence.[32]

Throughout the mid-1960s, black Maconites continued to petition the courts to quicken the pace of desegregation in Bibb County, while the board of education proceeded slowly through a Freedom of Choice plan. Despite higher court rulings outlawing such plans, in late 1969 Bootle reaffirmed Freedom of Choice, only to be reversed on 1 December 1969 by the US Fifth Circuit Court of Appeals, which ordered full integration and a full faculty merger by September 1970. A week later the Macon NAACP asked the US Supreme Court to stay the Appeals Court ruling and force full integration with no further delay. On 14 January the Supreme Court ruled in black Maconites' favor, ordering the Bibb County schools to be fully integrated two weeks hence, by 1 February. Board of education and city officials expressed dejection and resignation to the inevitable and appealed for reason and calm. County Commissioner and ex-officio board member Emory Greene disagreed with the ruling but noted that the public had no choice but to comply. "We have got to think of people who can't afford private education," he told reporters, "and do everything we can to save public education. We must think of the alternative." State Representative Marshall Keen accused the Court of being uninterested in education, and complained that the mid-year transfers would "cause an irreparable educational loss and emotional harm."[33]

Just after the Supreme Court's ruling students assembled at city hall where Mayor Thompson commiserated with them, complaining "Central government is taking away the rights of the people." He also led a smaller contingent of students to the board of education office, where they convinced the board to drop its plans to suspend students who left school to participate in the protests. That night the judge's wife Virginia took a call from a committee asking to come over to talk with her husband. Assuring them of their welcome, at dusk the judge and his wife were surprised to find a large protest of some 1,500 students and adults outside his home, chanting "We Want Bootle" and "We Want Freedom of Choice." Their signs read, "We Want Neighborhood Schools" and "Give the schools back to the people." As Bootle was expected to make a new ruling on the specific integration plan to put into effect, the protesters asked the judge to come out to speak with them. Advised by police officers not to speak with the crowd because some in the crowd had been drinking, Bootle instead invited a small contingent of three protesters into his home, where they presented him a petition favoring a Freedom of Choice plan. After about an hour and a half, the protesters left the premises, but the police continued to guard Bootle's home for another two days.[34]

On Saturday, 18 February, 4,000 whites gathered at the Macon Coliseum to rally against the desegregation ruling. Thompson and board of education president W. Earl Lewis led a succession of student speakers demanding a freedom of choice plan. Thompson had withdrawn an invitation to Governor Lester Maddox, fearing that the governor would follow through on his promise to advise students to withdraw from school to protest the court order. The mayor charged, however, that the schools had been sold to the highest bidder, namely the federal government. Speaking to scattered boos, Fredicia Raines, a black high schooler, told the audience that they had blamed everybody but themselves. The Supreme Court, she asserted, "simply ruled in favor of the national law which Georgia and sister states have knowingly delayed for over a hundred years." Whites had had "ninety-nine years to prepare for the Supreme Court decision of '54 and fifteen additional years since then" to act on this matter. She then challenged the white audience, pointedly asserting, "Now you are in the 114-year grace period, [and] we blacks would really like to know what did you did with the time." The boos grew louder until the moderator, another student named Paul Fountain, stood and raised his hand to quiet the crowd. Later, Fountain's speech criticized the local press for referring to the meeting as a "racial rally" rather than a rally for rights. The following day a letter to the

Macon Telegraph punctuated the tension rife in the city: "Can anyone deny the fact that friction between the black man and the white is at an all time high?"[35]

Three days later, on 21 January Bootle ruled in favor of a freedom of choice desegregation plan that aimed at a 60-40 white to black ratio in the system. Bootle held that such a plan, which he had earlier approved in his 12 August 1969 ruling, would abolish all-black schools and put the Bibb schools in a unitary system, as mandated by the Appeals Court. He further argued, however, that a teacher transfer and a 60-40 ratio were sufficient because the Appeals Court had not specified full racial balance in each school. Calling freedom of choice "the only wise, safe and correct constitutional principle," Bootle said he could not deny freedom of choice to black or white students to achieve racial balance unless "some court of higher authority is willing to hold specifically and unequivocally that the Constitution requires it."[36]

Blacks were naturally angered by the judge's ruling. The plaintiffs attorney, Thomas M. Jackson, immediately asked that the US 5th Circuit Court of Appeals reverse Bootle's freedom of choice order just as it had reversed Bootle's 12 August ruling. The following day Billy Randall, the son of the NAACP president, blasted white Macon in the *Telegraph*:

> I have read with utter amazement and great disgust the many letters from the "good white folks" and their "angelic" little children as they rant and rave over the recent ruling of the Supreme Court ordering Bibb County school officials to implement now a decision that was handed down not yesterday, but fifteen years ago.... These are the same people who scream for "law and order," but they mean law and order without justice.... The day has come for white people to stop being the hypocrites and to stop trying to turn back the clock of time to a period that will never be seen again.[37]

In reply, a writer identified himself as one of Randall's "good white folks" who resented being called a hypocrite "just because I do not want my children going to schools not of my or their choice." He did not, however, wish to be dictated to "just to satisfy the whims of a minority group," adding, "[W]e scream for law and order to be administered to all people instead of letting a few of the civil rights groups violate the law just because one of the so-called leaders told them that the law didn't apply to them because it violates their civil rights." Another white reader denounced the editorial stance of the *Telegraph*: "Rather than stating 'we have had 16 years to prepare for this' I would have thought you would stand for freedom—rather than force. This latest 'decision' of the Supreme Court denied freedom to all—black as well as white." Still another white spoke out to denounce the uproar over freedom of choice.

> Has one thought been given to the many decades the Negro was denied freedom of choice? When he wanted to attend school better equipped than the Negro schools, he was denied. When he wanted to ride on a school bus he was denied.... When he wanted to attend the University of Georgia to study medicine, law, etc., he was denied. Instead, he had to leave his home state to seek his education in other state universities. White people are responsible for the dilemma now facing them. For 15 years they employed every possible means of evading all-out integration of the schools. The basic cause of it all is prejudice and hatred. It is time to wake up.[38]

On Monday, 2 February students returned to their classes after a three-day weekend. Many found new teachers of the opposite race upon their return, as 376 teachers were transferred on the previous Friday. Some black teachers complained of hostile receptions at their new, formerly all-white schools, while at Ballard-Hudson students greeted white teachers with applause when introduced by the principal. Only seven teachers in the system opted to resign rather than accept reassignment. The relative tranquility of that occasion, however, evaporated two days later when a two-to-one ruling by the Fifth Circuit Court of Appeals reversed Bootle's freedom of choice plan and ordered him to implement a more thoroughgoing desegregation plan by 16 February. The ruling voided the earlier teacher transfers and required more racial balance in the Bibb and Houston County schools.[39]

Soon Thompson called a press conference to announce another motion by attorneys for a rehearing of the case before a fourteen judge panel in the Fifth Circuit Court in Houston, Texas. The mayor called on citizens to "maintain the tranquility that has always marked their actions," adding that "prejudices and hatred can only penalize our efforts." In Atlanta, however, Maddox countered Thompson's words by urging students and teachers to defy the most recent court order and continue reporting to their present schools. Billy Evans, Bibb County representative in the state House, concurred with the governor. School officials nevertheless worked feverishly over the weekend to reassign 35,000 students and 2,000 teachers into a unitary system, a task that normally took an entire summer to accomplish. Meanwhile, attorney Thomas M. Jackson met with Bootle and school board attorneys and officials who tried in vain to convince Jackson and the plaintiffs to accept a delay until the fall. Afterward, Jackson commented that opinions at the meeting were so split that no position could be taken. The Reverend Edsel Davis spoke for the Macon NAACP in calling for immediate integration, saying, "We do not favor delay in any kind of way. We believe the plans are workable." Eventually two black members of the Bibb County board of education, William S. Hutchings and Dr. D. T. Walton, helped broker a compromise plan, moving forward with the integration of the elementary schools while allowing the secondary to desegregate by the end of the current school year. On 13 February, Judge Bootle put the authority of his court behind the compromise agreement, officially allowing more time for the desegregation of Bibb's secondary schools.[40]

On Friday, 13 February, Representative Marshall Keen, serving as chairman of a pro-Freedom of Choice organization called Citizens for Quality Education, invited Governor Maddox to speak at a rally in Macon two days hence. Keen announced that Maddox was considering using a state riot prevention law to close the Bibb County schools rather than integrated them according to the current plan. Maddox agreed to address the rally and told a news conference that the Bibb board of education was "betraying" students in its efforts to implement the court order. The following day Maddox announced he planned to suspend Georgia's compulsory attendance laws in Bibb County schools rather than allow the state to prosecute parents who refuse to send their children to school against their will. Such action was necessary, Maddox asserted, because "these ungodly and cruel and criminal edicts threaten the peace, safety, liberty and property of the citizens." By the day of the scheduled rally, however, no Macon official had notified the governor that they expected a breach of the peace. In editorials on consecutive days, the *Macon Telegraph* denounced Maddox's "ruinous pronouncements" and mused, "What irony if his visit here and his own conduct help create conditions justifying the suspension of compulsory attendance when, if left alone, this community could resolve its own problems."[41]

At the Sunday rally, some 4,000 Maconites gathered at Porter Stadium to hear the governor and mayor urge parents not to submit to the transfer. Thompson told the crowd he planned to take his son to his old school. He also discouraged anyone from "laying a hand" on the students, "because if they do I am going to accept it as a declaration of war and send our troops in there." Still considering the option of closing the schools, Maddox told the audience, "better than closing schools, you ought not let one little boy or girl be transferred tomorrow," which he said would send "a message across Georgia and the nation." Marshall Keen concurred with the governor and mayor, and Clarence Knight, Jr., pastor of Hillcrest United Methodist Church and member of the Citizens for Quality Education, declared, "If freedom of choice is good enough for Almighty God, it is good enough for me, and it had to be good enough for the Supreme Court of the United States." Again, the *Telegraph* dissented: "Both of these men are a discredit to the office they hold.... [T]hey have no conception of the dangerous forces they are setting into motion when they tell people to violate the law or regulations made under court orders. We hope and believe the people of Bibb County will display a maturity so sadly lacking in the mayor and governor." On the same page, Janis Heard, a high school student called on school superintendent Julius Gholson to defy the federal courts, even if it meant sacrificing federal funds. "We have done without them before," she wrote, "and we can do without them again."[42]

The 16 February transfers of an estimated 5,500 elementary school students took place with few incidents. Parent escorted some 500 students to their original schools. Among these parents was Mayor Thompson, who took his son, Johnny, back to Neel Elementary School. Claiming his defiance of the court order was a non-racial decision, Thompson noted that his son's teacher at Neel was an African American. He also announced that he would file suit in federal court against the school board and the federal government "for violating my son's civil rights." He promised also to defy any future transfer of his daughter, Ronita, from McEvoy to Ballard-Hudson High School.[43]

Over the next week, many white parents continued to take their children to their old schools, with reports that some interfered with instruction by sitting-in the classrooms. In response school superintendent Gholson warned that the students could not indefinitely absent themselves from their new schools without academic penalty. A week after the desegregation order, however, a large protest almost closed down the Morgan Elementary School in West Macon, as mothers protested black students being bussed there from a recently-closed black school. Blocking school buses, the protesters implored other parents to withhold their children from their classes. That same day school officials evacuated students from Morgan and Neel schools after receiving bomb threats. These incidents finally prompted Judge Bootle to issue a restraining order against parents protesting the integration order. He ordered school officials to withhold academic credit from students not attending their assigned classes and warned that violation of his order could result in fines or imprisonment. Bootle also extended the restraining order to the forthcoming integration of Bibb high schools.[44]

The 17 February issue of the *Mercer Cluster* reflected the racial tensions sparked by the school controversy. Given that the university setting was the most racially progressive white institution in Macon other than the MCHR, the polarization illustrated on the "Letter" pages suggests how divided was the city at large. A black Mercerian argued that America had historically attempted to destroy the "racial integrity" of blacks, constantly reminding them that they owed everything to the good graces of whites. With its institutional racism, wrote the student, whites could invite blacks into the system "because it means that the evils of the existing institution need not be changed, because the Blacks who do enter will be thinking white." A white Mercerian addressed the "'thinking' colored people" on the next page:

> [W]e're getting sick to our stomachs at your rioting, protesting, demanding, and your race's famous quote, "Burn, Baby, Burn".... I, and others will not accept you as an "equal" as long as your colored mentality believes in violence and militancy as means of gaining admission into the flow of society. It seems

that all you people want is to be given everything on a silver platter.... I am sick with your demands. In 1964 you were given more than an inch and through more "civil rights" acts you have taken fifteen miles! You have the same, and possibly more rights than the whites and you're still complaining.[45]

The *Telegraph* carried similar letters. One writer lamented parents who continued to instill "the same hatreds and biases" that were creating the "ridiculous activities" in the Bibb County schools. "It saddens me to think of how little progress we have made in the field of brotherly love," he concluded. Another offered the insight that "a lot of 'good Christians' are complaining about going to school with Negroes when all men are created by God." At the other end of the spectrum, another writer complained that "these 'people' have been equal and are presently, but are still unsatisfied." A Macon woman registered her resentful compliance with Bootle's order, noting her agreement with a local pastor who viewed the current school situation as "the beginning of the end of our Constitutional Government." Bert Bivins, the first black Maconite to attend an integrated school, sharply denounced those advocates of "Quality Education," which he rejected as another euphemism for segregation born of "an intent to deceive." To have sought "quality education" before *Brown* would have been a noble effort, he argued. To do so in 1970 was merely an effort "to degrade or get rid of Negro teachers by requiring standardized testing." One white teacher, apparently concerned with quality and surprised to find her new black colleague "so articulate," commented that she must have gone to school "up North." Controlling her resentment, Palmyra Braswell, who had studied at Columbia University, summoned her best Southern accent and replied, "Well Ah spec Ah did."[46]

The day after Bootle's restraining order, Thompson called a press conference to announce his decision to obey the court. He advised other parents to do likewise, saying he would continue to fight for freedom of choice in his suit. He indicated that he obeyed the order against the will of the entire Thompson family, but affirmed, "I must abide by the law if I am going to enforce it on others." He ended his press conference by saying, "God save America."[47] Bootle's order had a similar effect on other white Maconites as schools quickly returned to nearly normal operations, although a group of seventy-five parents visited Thompson at city hall asking to be included in his suit. That suit was filed on behalf of Johnny Thompson and thirty other students on the following day.[48]

Criticism of Bootle from Georgians high and low continued for three weeks after his restraining order. Flirting with contempt of court, Governor Maddox told a meeting of the Macon Optimist Club that "the actions of the court were contemptible. With one fell swoop," he fumed, "this federal judge, who transformed himself as a federal dictator, denied the citizens of Georgia their constitutional rights of assembly and freedom of speech in complete violation of the very Constitution he is supposed to be upholding." Later, Thompson called Bootle a "weakling judge" who "put his federal paycheck above his constitutional principles," and provided a police escort for a group of twenty-five women who marched to the federal building to protest Bootle's decrees. Six of the protesters carried a mock coffin made of cardboard and draped in black crepe paper. The "coffin" contained an American flag covered with dozens of roses. On its sides, were signs asking, "Does your flag still stand for justice for all?" and "Will we be forced to bury our freedom?" Upon arrival at the courthouse, three members of the contingent met with Bootle, who reminded them that his earlier ruling for freedom of choice had been reversed by a higher court.[49]

That summer another letter to the *Telegraph* suggested that emotions remained frayed. Signed by eleven white Maconites, the missive pointed out that the right to peaceably assemble "does not mean rioting, burning, and looting," adding, "Thank God we have a few leaders who realize this and are not afraid to say so and do something about it. One such man is our beloved Mayor, Ronnie Thompson." Tensions continued during the next school year, breaking out in a fight between white and black students at a Willingham High School football game. Willie Goolsby ignored taunts from white teammates, while coaches and peers from predominantly black schools called him a "traitor" for playing for a mostly white school.[50]

As tempers slowly cooled, black attorney Thomas M. Jackson warned that black Maconites would continue to press for advancement in the area of political power. City- and county-wide elections, he noted, diluted black electoral strength. In sounding a note that was destined to become a cliché in the nation's the race struggles over the next three decades, Jackson pointed out, "It's a sophisticated discrimination we are dealing with now. It's hard to get the masses emotionally involved because they can't put their finger on it." He indicated that, as a result, the civil rights movement would focus more on instilling racial pride and increasing black political power.[51]

Recording Artist James Brown receiving key to the city from Mayor Ronnie Thompson. (Courtesy of the Washington Memorial Library.)

BLACK LIBERATION AND BLACK POWER

The growing frustration and militancy of the black freedom struggle after 1968 combined with growing white resistance to black demands, resulting in the greatest tension and least harmony between the races in twentieth-century Macon. Symbolizing that volatile combination was the relation of Ronnie Thompson with a new organization of younger black leaders known as the Black Liberation Front. Thompson had antagonized blacks Maconites early on in his administration by announcing that demonstrators in Ralph David Abernathy's Poor People's March were not welcome in the city. He created a controversy with demonstration leaders by refusing to allow the march to proceed along its preferred route down Vineville Avenue through the central business district toward Central City Park. He suggested two alternate routes through black sections of the city in order to give the march less visibility. Finally, Thompson warned that any attempt to proceed down Vineville Avenue would result in marchers being "mowed down and stacked like cordwood." Machine guns were the mayor's weapons of choice, prompting friend and foe alike to begin referring to the him as "Machine Gun Ronnie Thompson."[52]

His performance in the school desegregation crisis weakened his stature among blacks even more. A few weeks later Bert Bivins wrote the *Telegraph* another letter accusing Thompson of "working toward discord than togetherness" and showing "open contempt" for African Americans. William P. Randall told reporters that keeping communications with Thompson had been more difficult than with previous administrations, noting "We have had to pressure this administration much harder than others to keep up with the changes that are going on elsewhere in the country."[53]

Beyond their dislike for Thompson, blacks in Macon, as elsewhere around the country, had been driven to despair and rage by the King assassination and the slow pace of racial equality in America. Even with the successes of the Southern civil rights movement, black Maconites lagged behind whites in economic strength. The 1970 census revealed that in Macon blacks, while 40 percent of Macon's population, made up 57 percent of service workers, mostly in cleaning and food service; 72 percent of Macon's laborers; 49 percent of manufacturing employees; 24 percent of the city's craftsmen, mostly in construction work. But blacks only comprised 13 percent of the clerical positions; 8 percent of managerial and administrative jobs; 7 percent of sales positions. Black average income was $4,455, compared with $10,110 for whites. Almost 40 percent of black families in Macon lived below the poverty line.[54]

In addition, by 1970 black Maconites grew dissatisfied with electing sympathetic white politicians to city and state offices. They wanted black representation in city, county, and state government. Thus, black leaders like William Randall began to push for district rather than at-large elections. Randall pointed out to white officials that Macon's relatively peaceful civil rights gains had been born of both white concessions *and* responsible black leadership. "But unless we find more acceptance in employment, housing, and city government," he warned, the people could be expected "to turn to more militant leadership."[55]

Randall did not have to look far to verify his predictions, as his son William C. "Billy" Randall, was radicalized by the King assassination. Never fully committed to nonviolence, his grief and rage after 1968 pushed him in a more militant direction. He and a number of other younger blacks organized the Black Liberation Front (BLF), more influenced by the Black Power philosophy of Stokely Carmichael. When some of the leaders began to criticize the Old Guard black leadership as "Uncle Toms," including "Daddy Bill" Randall, the younger Randall distanced himself from the BLF. Eventually Curtis Gassaway surfaced as the new organization's point man.[56] Gassaway and other leaders of the BLF, including Herbert Dennard and Robert Brown, voiced the concerns of working class blacks in direct encounters with the city council. Their philosophy focused on black empowerment by attacking systemic discrimination in Macon's economic and political structure.[57]

The first major confrontation between the BLF and the Thompson administration came on 9 June 1970, when a group of young blacks arrived to address city council a few minutes after its regular meeting adjourned. Turned away and angered, they called out to Thompson, "You don't want to hear from the people. We demand that you hear us. You have pulled the same trick before." Several council members commented that the black group should have been on time for the meeting. Billy Randall accused the mayor of discriminating against blacks, promising, "We're going to get rid of Mayor Thompson." Vowing also to "put a muzzle on some of these cop pigs and strike racist businesses," Randall added, "Anyone with any conscience knows the black folks of Macon have been abused." Eventually, the group departed with a warning: "Keep on, and you won't have a city."[58]

Threats of that sort were unlikely to win them a hearing from Thompson, who in the atmosphere of the time was driven to a more rigid stance. The next week, on 16 June, Gassaway led group of some forty young blacks to a meeting of the city council, this time arriving ten minutes early. Identifying himself as "Malkie X," Gassaway claimed to be carrying a list of six demands signed by 1,500 black Maconites. Seeking an immediate response from city officials, Gassaway called for the hiring of twenty-five black firefighters and five blacks in clerical positions in each city department and the Macon Water Board. They also demanded the paving of all streets and sidewalks in black neighborhood, the enforcement of city housing codes, the cessation of police brutality and disrespect toward blacks, and the provision of adequate recreational facilities in black communities.

Two other spokespersons for the black community appeared. Frank Hutchings, Jr., accused the city bi-racial committee of doing nothing to address racial tensions in the city. Calling the committee a "political front" for the white and black middle-class, he advocated the establishment of a more representative committee. Johnny Morris addressed the issue of at-large elections of members of the council, calling on the city to consider district voting in an effort to help elect blacks to represent their constituencies on the council.[59]

To that point Macon's older black leaders had not managed to wring concessions from city officials on most of these matters. In 1970 many of Macon's black neighborhoods remained unpaved, and recreation facilities in black areas had long since fallen into disrepair. Almost 32 percent of the city's housing, most of which was property rented to African Americans, was judged substandard by the state building inspector. The city employed 7 black police officers on a force numbering 177 and 1 black among 192 firefighters. Further, black leaders like William Randall and the more militant Gassaway argued that police promotions for blacks had been largely stymied by culturally-biased testing procedures.[60]

Three days after Gassaway's appearance at the city council meeting, both the BLF and Thompson turned up the heat on an already boiling kettle. When the mayor made no response to their demands, the BLF launched an immediate boycott of several downtown stores. Around twenty-five protesters picketed the stores, vowing to continue their protests until their six demands were met. In reply, particularly to earlier black threats of violence, Thompson issued an order to police to shoot to kill any citizen engaged in "lawlessness and anarchy." The mayor protected himself from charges that he had aimed his order only at blacks by emphasizing, "*Anyone* trying to cause violence in the city of Macon must be dealt with accordingly. People engaged in burning, looting, and killing and the destruction of the city of Macon will not be tolerated.... Those people engaged in lawlessness and anarchy must be stopped. Shoot to kill." Thompson also said he would swear in and arm 1,000 volunteer police officers.[61]

Except for one store that reported the intimidating of black customers, the boycotts proceeded without arrests or other incidents. Thompson's reaction grew out of his prejudices and fears, and many stepped up their criticism of the mayor. William Randall quickly made a public statement denouncing Thompson's order, saying he knew of no one in Macon who had advocated violence or destruction. "This kind of rhetoric has produced violence and killing over the country. This kind of talk preceded the death of six persons shot in the back in Augusta. I pray to God that it will not happen here." City Alderman Burton Lee also criticized Thompson for aggravating the city's racial problems with his order, saying the mayor seemed "intent on creating a racial confrontation." The following day the mostly white Macon Ministerial Association also rejected Thompson's order as "arbitrary and impulsive." The association pointed out other of the mayor's alternatives, noting that his shoot to kill order "will only add to the grief and sorrow which already exist among all of us." In Savannah for a meeting, a radio interviewer asked whether the mayor saw the order as extreme, Thompson defended the policy: "If it takes using firearms, if it takes shooting people and killing people in order to enforce the law... that's exactly what I'm going to do. And I'm not going to put up with burners and looters and killers and stealers and thugs." He also accused blacks of being communist influence because of their use of the term "liberation front" or the slogan, "Down with the establishment."[62]

On 30 June the city council defended itself against charges of discrimination and answered the BLF's demands, saying that there was, however, a communication breakdown between the council and the black community. Answering each demand in series, most of the council's responses were greeted with laughter from BLF members in attendance. Fire committee chairman Tom Ivey said he had seen only one application from a black Maconite in more than six years as an alderman. Eight applications from blacks were pending among a total of thirty-one, but there were no openings in the department. Carl Parker reached an agreement with Gassaway and Billy Randall for a list of black street paving priorities to be considered in the next street paving contract. During the meeting the council approved eleven streets for paving, eight of which were in black neighborhoods. Other committee chairmen similarly sidestepped accusations of discrimination by noting earlier minor concessions. As Robert L. Anderson correctly analyzed, while BLF efforts in 1970 made little headway in the short run, the organization had lasting importance in sensitizing the white power structure to the level of black frustration. He noted, for example, that the term "Negro" disappeared from the council minutes after its encounter with BLF in June 1970. In addition, the BLF began to win over middle-class blacks to the idea of mass mobilization and actual black political power. Getting black Maconites elected in city hall became the new goal.[63]

After the initial crisis over BLF demands had passed, the *Macon Telegraph* brought together seven representative black leaders for a round table discussion of black concerns. Five of the contingent were women, and in an effort to draw out different perspectives, the paper excluded the usual Old Guard and BLF leaders. The Negroes were selected as well-informed, respected members of the Negro community. Others who are generally termed "Negro leaders" and who often claim to speak for the Negro community were purposefully omitted, as were younger, more militant Negroes whose views have been well publicized in recent weeks. Ruth Robinson noted the city's lack of consideration of black needs in paving projects, citing dead ends on First through Fifth Avenues that hindered movement into Pleasant Hill without going down Walnut or Forsyth Streets. Alonzo Leroy Epps argued that blacks should be consulted in the planning of any decisions affecting the total community. He also complained that the lower end of Astor Street, where he and other blacks lived, was unpaved, although it *was* paved at the upper end where white resided. Louise Rives launched a perceptive lecture on the role of history and black poverty:

> I've heard white people say "Oh, these old Negroes don't want bath tubs in their houses, they don't know what they're for." Negroes are just as clean as anybody else. We've always been on a double standard and who's responsible for it? We're not. That's the reason we can't pull ourselves up by our boot strings, when one group is trying to put us on one level, and yet they want us to come up to their level when they have all the money. How can we do it? We have to go back into history when our parents weren't even allowed to have a book. Negroes

weren't even allowed to go many places the white man could go. Now all at once he wants us to pull ourselves up. He [the white man] has always pulled us down, and he's pulling us down now.[64]

The next day, a *Telegraph* editorial announced, "Macon Makes Headway In Its Race Relations." Accomplishing certain of the BLF's demands, the editors argued, was impossible. Some city departments did not even have five employees altogether. Paving *all* streets in black residential areas was not economically feasible. But the editors agreed with the BLF that far more streets in black areas should be paved. City employment of blacks was below its proper level, and the *Telegraph* called for "a more diligent search for qualified Negroes to fill vacancies." Other black concerns like building code enforcement, police brutality, and unequal recreational facilities also deserved the city's full attention. The editorial concluded, "The people do not want preferential treatment for any individual or group. Nor do they want problems brushed aside until a major crisis erupts."[65]

Ten days later Macon felt a minor eruption emanating again from the mayor's office. Thompson had publicly accused the *Telegraph* of "deliberately trying to create racial unrest and possible bloodshed in the city of Macon." The mayor based this charge on the discovery that several months earlier Curtis Gassaway had been employed by the paper as a circulation solicitor. *Telegraph* general manager Bert Struby parried Thompson's accusation with a statement to that effect, adding that he had not been employed by the paper at the time of his BLF activities, and "we would not condone any employee…conducting himself as Gassaway has done recently." Struby also acknowledged that Gassaway's mother continued to work for the paper, but did not "condone or participate in activist affairs." He added the countercharge, "He well knows that…the [paper's] editorial urging of racial calm has helped maintain racial stability in Macon while his own irresponsible and irrational statements have created crisis after crisis." In a parting shot, Struby declined to "become engaged in a braying contest with a jackass." Interestingly, the same issue of the *Telegraph* carried a front page article on the loose handling of thousands of expense fund dollars by the city. An editorial the following day noted, "It is hardly a coincidence that only hours later, the mayor comes out with his blast against the newspapers." In the meantime, the "Letters" section of the paper received strong support for Thompson's "shoot to kill" approach to urban rioting, the possibility of which the mayor believed to be very high.[66]

An even larger controversy erupted the next summer when on 24 June 1971 a black man named Jimmy Lee White was shot to death in an altercation with white police officer John R. Beck. While the NAACP requested a review board of both blacks and whites to investigate the shooting, Thompson refused to suspend Beck or even consider a review board, judging that the shooting "was necessary. It was kill or be killed." The mayor cited witnesses who reportedly saw the officer being beaten and choked by White and his brother. The new leader of the Macon NAACP, the Reverend Julius C. Hope, had arrived in 1970 to pastor the black First Baptist Church after years of activism in Brunswick, Georgia. Now he led the NAACP to weigh in on the issue of police brutality as it never had before. Picketing the grand jury's investigation of Beck, who had been charged in involuntary manslaughter, NAACP members called for Beck's immediate suspension. Hope told his followers, "If the grand jury turns this man loose, we must plan to do something, but we want to stay within the law."[67]

Several fire bombings over the Fourth of July holiday indicated rising tensions in the black community. Hope made a public statement rejecting "taking the law into our own hands," and warned that law breakers would find no comfort in the NAACP. At the same time, Mayor Thompson established another curfew. In response, some BLF leaders advocated a large march on the downtown area to break the curfew; others called for small congregations of blacks on street corners to pester police. Older leaders like Hope and Randall urged blacks to avoid confrontations with the police or the Thompson administration.[68] Confrontations flared up again after the 15 July dismissal of the Beck case by the Bibb County Grand Jury. Several hours later Thompson ordered all police, fire, and civil defense employees to be on alert and put extra police on duty in case of violence. In the early morning hours of the next day he ordered a police officer to test fire his machine gun so that he could hear the weapon over the police radio. When told the shooting had taken place in the woods, he joked that it should have been test fired in the neighborhoods where "a lot of unpatriotic people and radicals" resided. In addition, he said he would give the officer a medal for every one he shot.[69]

Pickets protesting police slaying at Macon City
Hall. In foreground, Rev. Julius Hope.
(Courtesy of the Washington Memorial
Library.)

At the same time NAACP leaders held mass meetings at Hope's First Baptist Church to keep emotions under control. Hope implored the several hundred in attendance not to take to the streets over the grand jury's decision and called on the federal government to bring a civil rights charge against Beck. He also called on the congregation to meet the following night to rally for improved employment opportunities for black Maconites. "I know you are mad," he told them, "I too am mad. We all agree that Beck should have been suspended and he should have been given some type of sentence. We are continually being misused by the system, it's just not Beck or the mayor, or anyone—it's the system, the power structure, that is committed to destroying black people."[70]

The following day saw a small march of some 250 participants and a rally at city hall protesting the failure to indict Beck, but quickly modulating to efforts to increase black employment and elective representation in the city. "We are tired of paying taxes," declared the Reverend J. L. Key, "without being represented, and the only way we can stop it is to vote the right people into office." That afternoon, however, leaders Randall and Hope met with chamber of commerce president-elect Charlie Jones to deal with employment questions. The meeting succeeded in establishing a series of additional meetings with the city, county, Downtown Council of the Chamber, Manufacturer's Bureau, and an organized association of Macon personnel managers. In addition, Sears manager Pat Galloway told reporters that his store would begin hiring without reference to race, adding, "We do need to be more aware of the racial problems that we are facing as it relates to business." Black leaders were heartened enough by the response to cancel plans for another boycott of Macon businesses. Attending the meeting, state NAACP Field Director Bob Flanagan commented, "I am impressed with the sincerity of this particular meeting. It appears we are dealing with people who can do something—and who are committed to do something."[71]

Meanwhile, white progressives of the Macon Council on Human Relations published a statement denouncing Thompson's bizarre order to test fire a machine gun and his comments about it. Questioning his fitness "to continue in command of our city's police department," the MCHR said, "When an elected official violates these rules so flagrantly, ...he loses his rightful authority to command obedience." Signed by MCHR officers Aaron O. Cook Jr., William A. Lane, and Joseph M. Hendricks, the statement also commended police sergeant Ray Foster for finding a deserted area in which to carry out Thompson's order. The criticism did not deter Thompson from continuing his hard-line appeal to the angry white voters of Macon. A few months later he ran for re-election sporting campaign buttons with a picture of a machine gun and the slogan "Keep on Ducking." In the November general election, he defeated challenger Emory Green with 58 percent of the vote.[72]

Outside Macon and the state of Georgia, Thompson's tough-guy image was becoming something of an embarrassment. In summer 1971, the *New York Times* ran an article announcing, "Macon Mayor Led Assault Armed with Machine-Gun." Three years later, when Thompson began considering a run for governor, the *Times* referred to him as Macon's "Machine-Gun Mayor." Years later black Maconites Henry Ficklin and Robert L. Scott, Jr., both reported being teased about their hometown's mayor as far away as Texas and Chicago.[73]

Civil rights rally sponsored by the NAACP crowd in
front of Macon City Hall. July 17, 1971. (Courtesy of
the Washington Memorial Library.)

During Thompson's second term many of the racial tensions
continued. In 1974 a new black college student wrote to the *Mercer
Cluster* complaining that Macon was "one of the most racist towns any
person would want to encounter." He noted "the Gestapo-like rule"
where a police officer threatened him with jail for "acting cute," saying
he hurriedly left the school-sponsored dance for fear that "in Macon, Ga.
that may be a felony." He also told of a friend who was arrested "because
he looked like a robber," although he was out of town when the robbery
occurred.[74]

Despite these recurring problems, racial tensions between 1971 and
1975 decreased somewhat as private businesses began to hire more
African Americans, who also made gradual inroads into elective power.
Monitored by the US Department of Justice, district voting became a
reality in 1972 after district lines were redrawn. Delores Cook was thus
able to become the first black to win elective office in Bibb County since
Reconstruction, taking a place on the Bibb County school board. Two
years later William S. Hutchings won another seat on the school board,
becoming the first black to win a county-wide seat in Bibb County.

William C. "Billy" Randall and David Lucas became the first blacks in the twentieth century to serve Bibb County in the state House of Representatives. Randall and Lucas submitted a redistricting plan for Macon City Council elections calling for five at-large members and ten members chosen by districts. When the Justice Department chose to support their plan, the 1975 elections saw five blacks elected to the city council.[75]

That same election saw a black leader run a credible campaign for mayor. Reverend Julius C. Hope gave frontrunner Buckner Melton and four other candidates a strong run. Most of the fireworks came from fissures in the black community over Hope's sometimes divisive leadership style and the larger issue of electability. Herbert Dennard later told interviewer Robert Anderson that black Macon simply did not have enough registered voters or the get-out-the-vote apparatus to elect a mayor in 1975. When William Randall came to the same conclusion, he opted to support Melton rather than Hope. Part of this decision stemmed from something of a leadership rivalry between Randall and Hope. But Randall also felt a political debt to Melton, who had worked to gain black support for Ed Wilson and later spearheaded the effort to remove segregation ordinances from the city code during the Wilson administration. A political realism that suggested Melton as the candidate most likely to prevail also figured in Randall's choice.[76]

Announcing his candidacy at his church, Hope told parishioners and followers, "I'm running for mayor and incidentally I'm black." A flock of other black pastors attended the campaign kickoff and pledged their support. Attorney Thomas Jackson gave a rousing speech calling Hope the "only candidate truly concerned about the people." He further observed, "Whites must come around and overcome racism to vote for Hope." Surprisingly free of the racial politics, the campaign saw the candidates agree on almost every pressing issue, and one *Telegraph* reporter, doubtless sharing the views of many other Maconites, called the mayor's race dull. No candidate raised the issue of race, but outgoing mayor Thompson, who was prohibited by the city charter to serve more than two four-year terms, did venture an eleventh-hour evaluation of the contestants. Calling Melton the most qualified, Thompson did exclaim concerning the black candidate, "If he's our last hope, then God help us." Virtually the only racial concern to surface in the race was charge by

BLF member Herbert Dennard, who claimed that Melton disingenuously told a radio audience that "anyone would be welcome in the private Idle Hour Country Club." Melton knew, asserted Dennard, that many chamber of commerce and government functions had been held at the club "to which the entire black community were not invited and could not get in." The accusation barely made a ripple.[77]

On election day Hope drew 75 percent of the black vote, and just over 22.5 percent of the total, to finish second and force a runoff with Melton, who drew 32.7 percent of the total, but just under 10 percent of the black vote. Of Hope's 6,203 votes, only some 200 were from white voters. As in the primary campaign, the runoff contest produced no racial sparks. Asked if he would make race an issue, Melton replied, "Heavens, no." During the two-week interval, Hope brought in singer James Brown and US Representative Andrew Young to campaign for him. In the runoff election, however, Hope did not draw additional white votes and lost to Melton by a three-to-one margin. While neither candidate played the race card, the racial dynamic was nonetheless felt in the voting patterns: Melton received few black votes and Hope took few white votes. Herbert Dennard noted, "The whites voted more down racial lines than the blacks. More blacks voted for Melton than whites voted for Hope." As a result, he reasoned that an outspoken black candidate could not win a city-wide election. "Daddy Bill" Randall demurred, arguing that Macon remained about eight years away from being able to elect a black mayor. Hope did not blame race for his defeat, but three years later told a reporter, "I lost not because I wasn't ready but because the community wasn't ready. I had hoped they [the white community] had grown up. I was wrong."[78]

The Melton administration would prove relatively untroubled by racial concerns, although he was forced to deal with charges of discriminatory hiring early in his term. Near the end of his tenure, a Klan rally in Macon earned his denunciation. Melton said, "Citizens should remember Macon is a city which draws strength from different races and religious perspectives. No violence is anticipated and none will be tolerated."[79] Despite seeing race relations reach a tense nadir, Macon emerged from the 1970s without major explosions of violence. Macon's low point in black-white relations managed not to sink as low as those in many other Southern cities. The angry white Maconite, however, would flourish in the Reagan-Bush era. The culture wars of turn-of-the-twentieth-century America, with racial and cultural diversity at their core, would continue Macon's unutterable racial separation.

9

Macon, Race, and the Culture Wars

American racism today is more subtle than in the past. During the past twenty years or so this point has gone from insight to truism to cliché. Yet the point also obscures the truth that American racism has always been characterized by a number of polarities—subtle versus blatant, institutional versus individual, political versus relational. Up to the 1964 Civil Rights Act and the 1965 Voting Rights Act, the civil rights movement focused its attention on the most blatant forms of racism, which generally entailed individualistic and relational expressions. The movement succeeded in dragging American democracy and the South kicking and screaming toward virtually eliminating the most egregious of our racist behaviors. Anyone who presides over a college classroom today has regular occasion to hear the complaints of some African-American students complain that nothing much has changed since the civil rights movement. Despite the cynicism or simple ignorance behind such assertions, the United States *has* made significant progress toward racial equality. The fact that state and municipal laws no longer give moral and legal legitimacy to segregation is a development that millions of African Americans prayed for throughout the Jim Crow era. Denying racism and discrimination the legal sanction it enjoyed in earlier eras is unquestionably a major step toward genuine racial equality

Even if it has not achieved its ideal goal of full racial equality, the black freedom struggle did result in an improved status quo where mainstream voices can no longer spout racist bilge with impunity. Today only the fringe elements of the radical right still condone the use of the N-word or begrudge black access to public accommodations or the voting booth. Slips of the lip by public figures, such as Ross Perot's addressing a 1992 NAACP audience as "you people" are generally condemned as lapses into the social etiquette of a racist past, although the uproar about them is also dismissed as the verbal nitpicking of the "politically correct." Either way, the contemporary situation is such that everyone, be they politically liberal or conservative, seeks to avoid being accused of racism. Even if America's commitment to racial equality and tolerance is sometimes incomplete, a hypocritical commitment is better than no commitment at all. As the French writer Francois La Rouchfoucald once noted, hypocrisy is the tribute that vice pays to virtue.

By accepting the end of Jim Crow, the United States was converted to the virtuous gospel of racial equality. Thus no contemporary politician can be successful without embracing this ideal, at least rhetorically. That is giant step forward. Only those Americans too young or too ignorant of history to remember the race-baiting success of Thomas Watson, Eugene Talmadge, and George Wallace can say that there has been no progress in this area. Since the civil rights movement, *overtly* racist rhetoric has become a formula for political failure. To say this is to note an important step toward true democracy and equality that should never be dismissed as meaningless.

The successes of the civil rights movement, however, centered on racism's most egregious forms, and those that were most susceptible to moral suasion. These successes were certainly far from easy. After all, they did cost the lives of a large number blacks and a few white activists. But inasmuch as the movement focused on laws denying blacks equal access to public accommodations and the ballot, it dealt with the more individualistic or relational aspects of racial discrimination. Once the onerous segregation laws were removed, white Americans could grow to believe they could exorcise the demon by saying "black" or "African American" instead of "nigger," "colored," or "Negro," or by avoiding racist stereotypes, or by having a few black friends. Since most whites have learned to avoid the most obvious forms of racism, and treat individual black persons as equals, they have come to view the status quo, in the words of conservative pundit Dinesh D'Souza, as "the end of racism."[1] Accordingly, since Jim Crow laws are extinct, since consciousness has been raised enough for most whites to avoid the use of racial slurs or stereotypes, since black-white friendships are now considered normal and socially acceptable, since no one publicly advocates racial discrimination, and since everyone now salutes the flag of racial equality, one can say, as most whites do, that racism is no longer a major problem in America. Admittedly, examples of the old style racism do occasionally arise, like the dragging murder of James Byrd in Midland, Texas, but most white Americans dismiss these as historical anomalies or heinous exceptions to the rule.

Unfortunately, however, the racism that D'Souza and other neo-conservatives believe has ended is only part of the racism that has infected the American body politic. It is the part most easily noticed, most easily targeted, and most easily eradicated. It focuses exclusively on the relations between white and black individuals. According to neo-conservative reasoning, as long as there is equal protection under the law, race is only a problem in America because blacks and other liberal agitators won't "get over it." Perhaps, on the contrary, America's current race problem is of another sort, one that is invisible to those who recognize only the individualistic, relational forms as racism. Perhaps racism is deeper than merely the interpersonal relationships between blacks and whites.

Most white Americans appear to be oblivious to a continuing national reality known as "white privilege." That reality whereby Americans with white skin have statistically better chances of success than those with black skin corresponds to a more intractable form that sociologists call "institutional racism." The fruits of this racism are cultural and economic disadvantages that remain a part of African-American life in spite of civil rights advances. To political conservatives, these cultural and economic disadvantages are rather inconsequential facts of life that the political process need not and should not address. To do so would take politics beyond the conservative bounds of "limited government." From this perspective, government's only role is to protect all Americans equally regardless of race. With regard to racial and cultural diversity, conservatives see government's role as that of establishing a "colorblind" society, where in Ronald Reagan's words, "things will be done neither because of nor in spite of any of the differences between us—ethnic differences or racial differences, whatever they may be—that we will have total equal opportunity for all people."[2]

Using the words of Martin Luther King's "Dream" speech, many conservatives say they want for Americans what King wanted for his children, that persons be judged "not by the color of their skin, but by the content of their character." They want a society that ignores racial identity. Many a Caucasian has paid a black friend what they thought was a compliment by saying, "I don't think of you as black; I just think of you as a person." While blacks typically do recognize the complimentary elements in the statement, many accept the comment with a wince. They often hear in it an unconscious and certainly unintended assumption that black culture is inferior to more "normal" white culture. Although whites sincerely mean it as a compliment, blacks often understand it to mean, "You'll be accepted by whites as long as you don't act too 'black.'" After almost 400 years of history in the Americas, most of which has denigrated and devalued their color and their culture, African Americans are more likely to prosper in a society that accepts them despite the differentness of their color and culture than in one that is blind to that differentness.

As a result most civil rights advocates of the early twenty-first century are inclined to say, in another cliché, "We've come a long way, but there is still a long way to go." The contemporary question is whether or not government still has an active role to play in moving American society further along that way. Since 1980 the perspective holding sway in America has been the political minimalism of Ronald Reagan and the Republican Party he left behind. Since the Barry Goldwater candidacy of 1964, and since the Religious Right helped make Ronald Reagan the dominant political figure in the last quarter century, hard-line conservative Republicanism has come to sweep the once-solidly Democratic South. Its social, cultural, religious, and racial conservatism has dominated the South in national elections, and is increasingly doing so at the local level.

In what has been called the "culture wars," the Republican Party has successfully turned "big government," "liberal," "welfare," and "affirmative-action" into four-letter words. At times the party has felt the tension between "movement conservatism" and "big-tent" (or "compassionate") conservatism. Both wings of the party have claimed to believe in the goal of racial equality, but neither wing believes in the use of government programs to work toward that goal. Further, since 1964 both wings have resorted to the use of racial code words to rally former opponents of the civil rights movement into their ranks. They have done so while claiming to be a culturally and racially inclusive party running on a platform dedicated to equality. In doing so, they have proven a contemporary political maxim: Politicians cannot overtly appeal to racial prejudice, but they can and do successfully play the race card in *covert* ways.[3]

They have done so covertly by waging a sort of racial, guerilla, culture war. That warfare is between Americans whose goal is a colorblind society and those who aim for a color/culture accepting society. Advocating a colorblind society is the contemporary equivalent of the early nineteenth-century image of America as a "melting pot." This particular process of Americanization melts down differences of nationality in order to create a "new race" of "just plain Americans," as opposed to "hyphenate" Americans. Over against this, their adversaries opt for a multicultural America and prefer the image of a tossed salad to that of the melting pot. Both sides in this racial culture war preach an anti-racist gospel, but like American religion more generally, they are divided between an individualist and a social gospel. The Conservatives prefer a "relational anti-racism" that depends on individuals to avoid the old-style, individualistic aspects of racism. Liberals, like the social gospelers of a century ago, choose a "political anti-racism" aiming at eradicating the deeper, institutional forms of racism.

Black-white relations in Macon during the last two decades of the twentieth century have been played out against this larger American backdrop. Clearly, this survey of a century has shown that events outside of Macon have shaped race relations as much as, and sometimes more than, events inside Bibb County. One is hard put to isolate particular events in Macon that influenced local black-white interactions in the period between 1980 and 2000. National events, however, such as the political dominance of Ronald Reagan and the Republican Party, the presidential campaigns of Jesse Jackson, the Martin Luther King Holiday, the Rodney King verdict, and the rise of multiculturalism did much to shape the period. In these events one can see how the culture war, and especially its racial aspects, played out in Macon, Georgia. One can also see how efforts to improve race relations were divided between the modes of relational and political anti-racism.

CULTURE WAR AND BLACK CULTURE

The racial culture war of the 1980s and '90s, which continues into the present, pitts against each other two powerful images of America. One can be called "Colorblind America," which aims to create good, loyal, unhyphenated Americans, and generally worried that efforts emphasizing cultural, racial, or ethnic differences among citizens might "disunite" the United States. The other image, called "Multicultural America," sees the nation as a "democracy of nationalities," and exalted America's cultural pluralism.[4] These perspectives take predictably divergent views of African-American culture or concerns such as Black Studies, Multiculturalism, Black History Month, affirmative action, and the use of the term of "African American." To Colorblind America such movements focusing on the black or African heritage encourage divisions between whites and blacks by continually reminding Americans of the heritage of racial discrimination in America. These emphases are thought to endanger America's unity by keeping racial tensions stirred up and are thus steps away from the goal of a colorblind society. Multicultural America views such elements as enriching the nation and celebrates the distinctive ways African Americans had historically forced the nation to come to terms with its pluralism.

Both reactions surfaced in Macon even before the dawn of the 1980s, with the 1978 *Bakke* decision. After the ruling announced its limits on affirmative action programs, one Maconite wrote the *Telegraph* to express his renewed faith in the court by its strike against what he considered "reverse discrimination." Calling for a colorblind policy where "regardless if you are white, black, Indian, or whoever, if you want to sit in the front of the bus, be first in line.... If you want to go to medical school, study more than the next man, mold a good character, and make the highest grades."[5] A similar reaction yearning for American colorblindness was a 1980 survey conducted by historian Edward Cashin to assess how Georgians viewed their past. Whites continued to view the NAACP as "the favorite modern villain in history," believing Georgia blacks would be satisfied apart from the organization's agitation.[6] Were the association less concerned with *black* advancement, so the argument ran, race relations would be more harmonious. This finding suggests that whites saw blacks as too conscious, and thus too sensitive, of race as a factor in human relations.

By the mid-1980s the rise of black enrollment and the establishment of a Black Studies program at Mercer had generated something of a white backlash. Of the school's observance of Black History Month, a white student named Jay Vitalian complained of being "deluged" by the black emphasis: "It is a struggle...of which I desire to have no part. If it is a sense of identity that the blacks seek, then let them find it on their own time and their own expenses." Many who shared his views, he believed, allowed "themselves to be led down this unwilling path."[7] Other white Mercerians called on black students to avoid segregating themselves into their own organizations. One wrote, "Blacks should seek membership in groups other than the Organization of Black Students.... Racism does exist here as white versus black, but also as black versus white." A corollary of this view, which grew to prominence among whites during these two decades, held that racism was the same, whether expressed by a white or black American. Rather than viewing black organizations or fraternities as support mechanisms for students dealing with the stress of minority status in a hostile environment, whites dismissed them as examples of black hypocrisy or reverse (black against white) racism.[8]

By contrast, Joyce Evans, an assistant metro editor for the *Telegraph*, represented Multicultural America when she wrote, "When I hear whites talk negatively about affirmative action... I just feel sick. Being black has closed more doors in my face than it has opened, and I've documented the times." She then told of a ranking editor at another paper denying her a position as assistant news editor in order not to antagonize whites who had more seniority. Yet he hired a white female with five years less than Evans, who noted that "those guys didn't say anything. They had to accept it." On the matter of Mercer's black history emphasis, a black student replied to Jay Vitalian's criticism: "Why an intelligent being, who is part of the majority, would feel threatened by the humble expressions of a minority is beyond me. If this individual feels threatened by the periodic expression of a culture different from his own, it would be most interesting to see how he would hold up under the constant pressure of culture by a majority, as is the case with the Black man in America." Another Mercerian defended the university's black

Greek system, which was being criticized "because we do not conduct our organizations in a way that would be considered normal—normal being defined as a method similar to the white Greek system." Her reply came in an article titled, "It's a Black Thing: You Wouldn't Understand," which asserted, "Ours is a system which is deeply rooted in our heritage and standing firm in tradition."[9]

The multiculturalists' biggest success in this period was its push to establish the Martin Luther King, Jr. National Holiday. The push by entertainer Stevie Wonder and civil rights organizations, of course, sparked vigorous debate in Congress and the nation, with strong opposition from President Reagan, North Carolina Senator Jesse Helms, and other prominent national Republicans. Since its passage by Congress, prominent politicians of both parties have added the third Monday in January to their civic calendars and made obligatory tips of the hat to King and the "dream" of racial equality. Since its first national observance in 1986, King Holiday celebrations in Macon and most other venues have settled into affairs attended mostly by African Americans and a sprinkling of white liberals. Ironically, apart from the politically motivated observances designed to help politicians attract liberal white and African American votes, the King Holiday, conceived in order to exalt a multicultural America, has largely become a holiday for African Americans.

In 1980 black state representative Tyrone Brooks spoke at Macon's Macedonia Baptist Church calling for King's birthday to be named a national holiday. Three hundred black Maconites in attendance roared their approval. In the following year the *Mercer Cluster* asked, "Should King's Birthday Be a National Holiday?" Black Mercer students answered affirmatively. Herman Ivey noted that because a black American had never been singled out in this manner, "The holiday would be a tremendous motivation for black people." Sophomore Jerlena Griffen called on blacks to be outspoken in support of the holiday, adding, "There always seems to be some kind of static when it comes to recognizing our devout black leaders."[10]

Indeed, there was a great deal of "static" before Congress finally passed legislation establishing the King Holiday in 1983. By that time the Reagan administration was antagonizing blacks by advocating tax exemptions for Bob Jones University and other segregated schools, by delaying the extension of the 1965 Voting Rights Act, and attacking affirmative action programs as "quotas." Largely as political cover for such policies, President Reagan eventually distanced himself from North Carolina Senator Jesse Helms's vigorous opposition to the holiday, reluctantly deciding to sign the bill.[11]

Once it went into effect, black Maconites celebrated the holiday enthusiastically, as for example in 1988, when over a thousand persons packed the Macon City Auditorium. A four-hour service praised King's "dream and vision of a world free of hate and prejudice." Several marches spread across the city, leading persons to the service, where William Randall preached the gospel of voter registration. By then a member of the Bibb County Commission, Randall told the audience, "A new day is coming and we have to work for it, vote for it, and pay for it." The following year black Mercer student Jonathan Miller lauded the significance of the King holiday. As Washington had fought to free America from the British, King had fought for "freedom *within* America. He argued further that whites "have benefited from his life, whether they realize it or not. America has become a much better place due to his efforts."[12]

More locally, the most prominent multiculturalist success took the form of the Tubman African American Museum. In 1976 the Catholic parish of St. Peter Claver was assigned a new priest, Father Richard Keil. A thoughtful but feisty Irishman from Wisconsin, Keil had been reared in a working class family and grown disillusioned with secular life after participating in the Korean War. After entering the priesthood he worked in parishes in rural Alabama, where he became appalled by the treatment of African Americans both inside and outside the Church. Studying the writings of Martin Luther King and the liberation theologians, he became committed to the goals of the civil rights movement, and actively involved in it where circumstance allowed. He brought his theological concern for liberation to Macon, eagerly building the black leadership of the parish.

The same concern for liberation inspired Keil to envision a museum where both blacks and whites could learn about African-American art, history, and culture. Blacks could be liberated from America's negative images by seeing depictions of their culture. The museum would enable them to say to themselves and to whites, "We are here. We have accomplishments. You're going to have to look at us as persons." At the same time, whites could learn about black accomplishments and liberate themselves from negative stereotypes and their sense of superiority over blacks."[13]

In 1981 Keil discovered an abandoned building on Walnut Street in downtown Macon. After four years of fundraising and building, the museum opened in 1985. In its first year, Keil and other members of the museum board sought to raise $250,000 in corporate donations and $50,000 in private gifts. In 1987 the Bibb County Commission approved a grant of $25,000, helping the museum to weather a storm of financial difficulties during it first few years in operation. The museum also saw a rapid turnover in leadership, with its first three directors resigning in its first three years, a situation that was stabilized when Carey A. Pickard became director in 1992.[14]

In February 1998, after the county commission donated another abandoned property in downtown Macon, the Macon-Bibb County Urban Development Authority voted 5-0 to give a three-quarter acre plot of land at Cherry and Fifth Streets for a new, 48,000-square-foot facility. Later that year, the commission agreed to provide financial backing to allow the Authority to buy additional parcels of land for some $525,000. Supplemental actions raised the commission's support to $739,000, which included paying half the cost of building a plaza to connect the new museum to the Georgia Sports Hall of Fame.[15]

Construction on the new museum began in April 2001. Later that year the Macon City Council approved a $10 million revenue bond package that included $1 million for the museum, and in 2002 fundraising efforts received a major boost from $464,000 in two grants from the US Department of Housing and Urban Development. A downturn in the national economy, however, slowed fund-raising efforts and delayed the opening of the new Tubman Museum beyond its original 2003 target date to sometime in 2005. By 2004 the Tubman had become one of the premier museums of its kind in the Southeast. It housed fourteen galleries including the world-class Noel Collection of African Art. Other galleries depict African and African-American cuisine, local history, and black military history. Each year the museum now hosts more than 65,000 visitors from all over the world.[16]

MACON'S ANTI-RACISMS

The two combatants in America's racial, culture war both claimed to exalt the ideal of racial equality and eschew racism in American life. As has been argued, however, their differing images of America and differing goals for America, created divergent forms of anti-racism. More conservative and individualistic in strategy, Colorblind America's relational anti-racism focused on decreasing tensions in interpersonal relations among black and white Maconites.

At the beginning of the 1980–1981 school year a new Bibb County racial troubleshooting team received a $70,000 federal grant in order to hold a series of workshops on ways to reduce racial conflict in the public schools. After receiving training at the University of Miami's Desegregation Assistance Center, the team held eight such sessions, bringing together teachers, students, administrators, school board members, and community leaders. In 1983 three white and two black churches established the Community Advocacy Ministry (CAM), a short-lived organization designed to foster fellowship and pool social service resources. In June 1984 the black Holsey Temple Christian Methodist Episcopal and the Washington Avenue Presbyterian churches, along with the St. Paul's, St. James, and St. Francis Episcopal churches, held a fellowship outing in Washington Park to publicize CAM's work in the community. On this occasion members of all five churches ate, prayed, and sang together, with the organization's vice-president, Reverend Earnest Pettigrew, calling on members to join hands with someone of the other race. In addition to fellowship, the organization helped provided medical and financial help to local indigents.[17]

In 1986 Mercer sponsored a special course to help white and black students debunk myths about each other. While still dealing exclusively with interpersonal relations, teacher Bobby Jones edged somewhat toward multicultural terminology by telling students, "People are not culturally deprived. They are culturally different." Yet the individualism of Colorblind America remained a part of the course's goal. "The whole essence of this course," Jones said, "is to teach people to start treating people as individuals." In one session Jones brought four other black speakers—a law student, a social studies teacher, a part-time cook, and a Mercer undergraduate—to answer "no-holds-barred" questions. Among these were "Why are blacks' morals so low?" or "Why do blacks wait a week to bury their dead?"[18]

The following year concerned citizens launched another effort to form a biracial committee after a black woman named Bronica Collier moved into a predominantly white rental property near Pio Nono Avenue and found herself the target of an angry white neighbor. Firing a 12-gauge shotgun and a handgun at Collier's house, Alton Rowell was charged with aggravated assault, making terrorist threats, and criminal damage to property. In the aftermath of the incident, NAACP leaders met with city and county officials to discuss forming a committee to put out such brush fires and inform the community that local law enforcement would not merely give such perpetrators "a slap on the wrist." A month later, the committee's organizing meeting, led by Bibb County Commission Chair Emory Greene, drew only ten persons and a dismissive comment from Unionville activist Frank Johnson. "We're talking ourselves to death and where are we going? Nowhere." He fumed, "You can sit here all night and get nothing done." Despite promises to keep the committee intact, the effort soon fizzled.[19]

Church burnings in the mid-1990s sparked another attempt by white and black churches to foster interracial understanding between congregations. Concerned about these developments, the Reverend Ben Haygood, pastor of the white Vineville Baptist Church, began going to weekly breakfast meetings with the Reverend Eddie Smith of the predominantly black Macedonia Baptist Church. Flowing from their pastors' friendship, the two churches each hosted fellowship meals with the other congregation in the summer of 1996. For Haygood, Macon's racial tensions were rooted in ignorance: "Black and white people don't really know each other." After eating together, the intermingling congregations broke out into racially mixed small groups to discuss strained relationships between the races. Although, his weekly breakfast meetings with Smith continued until Haygood left his Vineville pastorate in 2001, the congregations only met together some six times (three times at each church). As congregations prepared to erect new buildings, both "got too busy" to continue the interracial relationships. Smith later said that the blame for letting the efforts drop lay equally with both congregations.[20]

Two years later, Jack Ellis, the future first black mayor of Macon, hosted a two-and-a-half hour forum on race relations on King's birthday. Then the host of a local cable television talk show called *Community Forum*, Ellis had run unsuccessfully for mayor in 1995, but was elected by a narrow margin in 1999. Ellis's town hall meeting at the Douglass Theatre drew a capacity crowd that participated in panel discussions aired live on WGXA-TV. During the audience discussion the Reverend Jim Walker, priest at the St. Peter Claver Catholic Church, said racism in America existed as much as ever, though it was now "covered with white whipped cream." His only advice, however, was to encourage people to love one another. Black spokesperson Alex Habersham criticized blacks for continuing to blame whites for their difficulties. He also noted, however, that white needed to acknowledge that blacks "still suffer because of the vestiges of slavery." Panelist Palmyra Braswell, a member of the Bibb County school board, called for Maconites to continue the dialogue. The conversations continued the next month when the Macon Area Ministerial Alliance held another forum on race relations in Macon. On 2 February, Mercer professor Catherine Meeks led discussions, telling the audience, "We need to get over being so afraid of each other, of people who are different." A third meeting the following weeks brought together for further discussions Meeks, *Macon Telegraph* reporter Charles E. Richardson, Reverend Laura Dunham, pastor of the St. Andrews Presbyterian Church, Frank Broome, moderator of the Georgia Cooperative Baptist Fellowship, Nancy Anderson of the Museum of Arts & Sciences, and Judge Thomas M. Jackson.[21]

This series of meetings culminated in a major *Telegraph* article dealing with race relations to commemorate the thirtieth anniversary of King's assassination. The overall tenor of the piece pointed up the limitations of relational anti-racism and the need for deeper, more political efforts. Frank Johnson told the writer that Macon's race relations were "very subtle, very traditional." He frowned upon the city's continuing the practice of putting black neighborhoods last on the list for infrastructure improvements. "We're still the last hired, the first fired, and the least upgraded," Johnson noted. Commenting on Macon's residential segregation, he observed, "It's an unwritten law that white folks don't want to live with blacks, ... not 100 percent of them, but 99 and nine-tenths." Mayor Jim Marshall called racism the city's greatest weakness, while Warner Robins businessman and civil rights advocate Jack O. Davis reminded readers of the serious economic disparities between blacks and whites, which he believed most Americans did not wish to talk about. "It's a dilemma for the country as a whole," he suggested, "because many of the problems feed off of this racial chasm that has never fully been addressed."[22] Out of similar perspectives came also efforts to address race matters in more institutional, less individualistic ways, as during the 1980s and '90s Macon saw its share of political anti-racism.

As a strategy, political anti-racism assumes that a relational approach alone is impotent to touch the deeper institutional or economic aspects of the race problem. By focusing almost entirely on developing interpersonal relations between black and white individuals, relational anti-racism does not address the deep wells of hopelessness and anger still latent in black America. Such anger remains potent because of the conviction among many African Americans that white Americans refuse to acknowledge the economic inequality that continues to exist between the two groups. Such anger continues to collect in black consciousness because whites either cannot or refuse to see that white privilege remains a part of American culture. Such anger is generated by the widely held white belief that the end of segregation also ended racism and effectively leveled the American playing field. From that point in American history, conservative whites came to believe government action toward racial equality was no longer necessary. Such anger persists because, to use the language of theologian Dietrich Bonhoeffer, white Americans opted for "cheap grace" by accepting the end of Jim Crow. But since that acceptance did not really cost them anything, white Americans have not yet fully repented of the sin of racism. Political anti-racism is a latter-day social gospel working to effect such a repentance in the public square. During the 1980s and '90s the public square was dominated by the conservative ideology of Ronald Reagan, and thus the hard right policies of the Republican Party became the enemy of political anti-racism.

By the 1980s the civil rights leadership of the city had moved into mainstream municipal and state politics. Blacks increasingly were elected to offices in city government, partly because of the ward system and partly because of a significant white exodus outside the city limits. Leading the way were the father and son team of William P. and William

C. "Billy" Randall. The elder Randall and Albert Billingslea were the first blacks elected to the Bibb County Commission in 1980, while the Billy Randall and David Lucas became the first blacks elected to the state House of Representatives since Reconstruction. The younger Randall later served as judge of Bibb County Civil Court. Robert Brown was later elected to the state senate in 1991. Locally, black Maconites had been elected to five of fifteen city council seats, two of five seats on the county commission, three seats on the school board, three of eight seats on the water board, and one member of the Macon-Bibb County Planning and Zoning board. In 1980 many predicted the city would elect a black mayor within ten years, although that development would not occur until 1999. In spring 1981, prominent blacks on the county commission discussed the merits of city-county government consolidation. While Commissioners Albert Billingslea and William Randall both supported consolidation, they also warned that blacks would view consolidation as a way of diluting their voting strength. Blacks made up 44 percent of Macon's population, but only 39 percent of the county's. "Of course I think consolidation is what we need," Billingslea stated, "If blacks could get equal treatment, then consolidation could be sold to the community."[23]

As the 1980 election neared, black Maconites rallied with Joseph Lowery and the Southern Christian Leadership Conference, harking back to the glory days of the 1960s and hoping to stave off the dawn of the Reagan era. Speaking at the Steward Chapel AME Church, Lowery denounced the country's "insidious individualism," which had rendered blacks apathetic. Joined by state senator Julian Bond and David Lucas, he urged them to get out the vote for Jimmy Carter. He also criticized the "rise of the religious right wing," which had been galvanized by the Reverend Jerry Falwell's Moral Majority to support Reagan's candidacy. Two months later, just days before the beginning of the "Reagan Revolution," Lowery spoke again in Perry, Georgia, charging that "a Klan-mentality in the Republican-controlled U. S. Senate poses a bigger threat to blacks and poor whites than overt racist activity. He criticized Senators Strom Thurmond (SC), Jesse Helms (NC), and Orrin Hatch (UT) for eliminating busing, repealing voting rights legislation, and increasing defense spending at the expense of social programs for the poor.[24]

Opposition to Reagan's budget cuts and his administration's opposition to renewing the Voting Rights Act generated strong criticism in Macon as it did across much of the nation. Sandra Robertson of the Georgia Citizens Coalition on Hunger warned the Reagan program would result in more hunger, malnutrition, and deprivation in Georgia. Cuts would imperil the food stamp program, Aid to Families with Dependent Children, the Women, Infants, and Children program, and school nutrition programs. "The administration is saying the cuts will not affect the truly needy," Robertson said, "but they will." Henry Ficklin, president of the Macon SCLC, participated in a Washington, DC, demonstration, protesting the president's economic proposals and his failure to support extending the Voting Rights Act. Calling on Congress to continue protecting black voting rights won during the civil rights movement, Joseph Lowery vowed that "black rights groups will seek a coalition with labor interests and others to challenge the Reagan program." By the first summer of the Reagan era, County Commissioner William Randall was predicting greater black involvement in politics because Reagan's economic cutbacks unfairly targeted black Americans. Two months later, at a memorial service honoring longtime NAACP leader Roy Wilkins, Randall called upon blacks to fight "President Reagan's attempts to roll back civil rights gains and social programs" through exercising their right to vote. "If Roy was here," Randall admonished, "he would say 'Shame on you for being too lazy to exercise a right that cost people blood, sweat and tears for you to gain.'"[25]

In fall 1981, the Macon SCLC, NAACP, and the Unionville Improvement Association combined to launch a selective buying campaign against white businesses that did not hire blacks. NAACP chairman Ronnie Miley connected the action to Reagan administration policies, which advocated the private sector taking up the slack in unemployment. "But with attempted rollbacks in affirmative action programs and civil rights laws," he noted, "I have little faith in private industry doing much to ensure fair employment practices." At a 24 October Black Summit meeting, organizer Herbert Dennard urged black Maconites to support only black-owned businesses or those white businesses that hired African Americans. "There are still places in Macon," he advised, "that refuse to hire black people. If we do not apply any pressure, they will continue not to hire black people."[26]

Reagan's White House had thus generated significant, though largely unsuccessful, opposition from black voters who resisted the president's efforts to turn back the clock on African-Americans' civil rights gains. Nevertheless, their efforts coalesced around the Democrats' feeble attempts to deny him re-election. Macon's blacks saw hope rising in the presidential candidacy of the Reverend Jesse Jackson.

MACON AND REAGAN'S REPUBLICAN PARTY

At least three conservative backlashes against 1960s liberalism converged to generate Ronald Reagan's rise to the presidency. An anti-Communist reaction rejected the Nixon-Ford, and later Carter, policies of *detente* as too soft on the Soviet Union, which Reagan viewed as an "evil empire." The Religious Right railed against the secularization and de-moralization of American popular culture—seen in the removal of prayer in public schools, the *Roe v. Wade* ruling, the feminist and gay rights movements—as undermining America's status as a "Christian Nation." A white backlash increasing denounced a federal government that had taken up the civil rights agenda, "given" African Americans enough, and coddled their continuing complaints. These strands of reaction resonated deeply with the political traditions of the white South. All three viewed the liberal movements of the 1960s as an unpatriotic, faultfinding, "Blame America First" crowd. All three strands found their hero in Ronald Reagan. During his two terms in office, white Maconites, along with the majority of white Southerners, grew to find him and his party more favorable to their views.

Individually and in combination, these three conservative backlashes attracted white Southern voters sufficient to convert the region, at least in national elections, into the "Solid Republican South." In the long view of history, however, racial concerns have dominated the South since before the Civil War. Over the course of the twentieth century race shaped politics in Macon as much as in any other Southern city. Thus, while anti-communism and the concerns of the Religious Right have had their appeal, historic racial fears made the white backlash against the civil rights movement the key ingredient in the South's late twentieth-century political realignment.

Such fears have historically been most potent in places like Macon, which have a large population of blacks. As a result, since the 1964 Goldwater campaign the Republican "Southern strategy" has centered on the use of carefully chosen code words (e.g. "law and order," "welfare cheats," and affirmative action "quotas") that stimulate white Southerners' racial concerns without resorting to overt racial invective. Symbolically Reagan showed himself a master of this approach by launching his 1980 general election campaign by advocating "states rights" (a powerful codeword for white Southerners) at a rally in Philadelphia, Mississippi, where three civil rights workers were murdered in 1964. He continued it in his opposition to the King holiday. His successor, George H. W. Bush, built on this technique with his 1988 campaign commercials, focusing on prison programs that furloughed the black rapist Willie Horton. Other conservatives concerns, but centrally those concerns about race, contributed to the culture war of the era and drew growing numbers of white voters in Macon and the South into GOP ranks.

Because his opponent was a former governor of Georgia, Reagan managed to gain only 31.8 percent of the Bibb County vote in 1980.[27] A majority of Macon's white voters gravitated toward the president by the time of his 1984 re-election campaign, while a majority of black Maconites flocked to the anti-Reagan, pro-black self-esteem candidacy of Jesse Jackson. Considering a presidential run, Jackson visited Macon in 1983 to encourage blacks to enter the political process. Taking aim at Southern techniques such as gerrymandering, annexation, runoff elections, the former Martin Luther King aide denounced "a conspiracy to undercut the Voting Rights Act of 1965." During his visit Jackson charged that the Macon-Bibb County Board of Elections discouraged black participation by providing too few registrars and registration sites. "Schemes used to make it difficult for blacks to win an election," Jackson asserted, "are disincentives for blacks to register to vote." Apathy, he argued, was not the central reason why less than half of Bibb County's voting age blacks were registered. In addition to these comments, he also called on blacks to run for office at every level, including the presidency.[28]

Not all of Macon's black voters moved toward the Jackson crusade. Early in the Reagan era, Melvin White, president of the Georgia Black

Republican Council, celebrated growing interest among blacks in the Republican Party. Fifteen black Maconites formed a local branch, naming it the Jefferson Long Republican Council, after the former slave who represented Macon in Congress during the Reconstruction era. Nationally the Black Republican Council had grown from 1,500 members in 1976 to 8,000 by February 1981. By the president's 1984 re-election campaign, a "Blacks for Reagan" organization had been formed, earning the praise of three black Maconites. Walter Davis, a former NAACP leader, liked Reagan's emphasis on self-reliance, and criticized both the Democratic Party and black ministers for failing to advocate it. Lonzy Edwards, a Republican attorney and pastor of the Mt. Moriah Baptist Church, argued that years of promises by the Democrats had led too many blacks to expect the government to provide for them. Charles Tatmon, a Republican city council candidate and pastor of the Bethel AME Church, agreed, saying Democrats had "dangled a carrot in front of black faces and provided jobs that were obsolete even before the training was finished. Blacks have too long been encouraged to sit back and wait for the welfare check."[29]

Even some committed black Democrats were caught up in the growing conservative philosophy of the era. State representative William C. "Billy" Randall told 250 delegates of the Georgia Federation of Colored Women's and Girls' Clubs that blacks should accept responsibility for their own futures. "It is up to us and no one else to solve the problems of black people," he asserted, excoriating black apathy toward education. Calling for blacks to "learn English, not Black English," he also called on black parents to exercise discipline in their homes: "If we do it at home, it'll be less of a problem at school."[30]

Still, even Macon's black Republicans like Edwards and Tatmon doubted that many African Americans would be converted to Reagan's gospel. Indeed, a CBS-*New York Times* poll indicated only 10 percent of blacks supported Reagan, while 83 percent supported his opponents. Thus, once Jesse Jackson began to campaign in earnest for the White House, most black Maconites rallied to his support. County Commissioner William Randall, a Jackson supporter, observed, "I have never seen this much enthusiasm in [Macon's] black community since the bus boycott of 1962." Most supported Jackson as a matter of black pride, like the elderly man who tearfully told a group, "I haven't felt this proud since Joe Louis." A number of Macon blacks, including Randall's son Billy, chose to support former vice president Walter Mondale, whom they considered more electable, but virtually all black Maconites agreed that they would support either Democratic candidate against Reagan, who, according to Jackson campaign chairwoman Elaine Lucas, had "hurt blacks and poor people too much."[31]

In the 13 March primary election the elder Randall proclaimed "victory" for Jackson despite his close second-place finish to Mondale. "Tonight we proved that Jesse Jackson was a viable candidate for all people," he exulted. "We have won a great, marvelous, tremendous victory, and they will have to talk to us at the convention." Winning just under 30 percent of the vote in Bibb County, Jackson trailed the eventual nominee by only three points, guaranteeing a significant slice of the convention delegates. This, Randall explained, meant "for the first time blacks will have some genuine power in the presidential process." The Jackson campaign galvanized Macon's black voters and reversed the city's usual voting patterns, as the majority black precincts turned out the heaviest vote. Even after their candidate's narrow loss, Jackson's supporters in Macon and across Georgia continued the push to register greater numbers of black voters.[32]

During the general election, Reagan made a Southern swing in his campaign itinerary, hopping over to Macon after a rally at the University of Alabama. Carrying over the football analogies he had used in Tuscaloosa, he lauded both the Georgia Bulldogs and his administration, because of which "America is scoring touchdowns again." Looking out over a predominantly white crowd of 15,000 to 22,000 and a placard that claimed, "Macon is Reagan Country," the president blasted Mondale's "tax and spend" policies and called for Congress to grant him a line-item veto, "an idea favored by a leader named Jefferson Davis." Continuing his appeal to white Southerners, Reagan concluded his twenty-minute speech by promising, "The South will rise again, and you will help lead this nation to a new golden age of growth and opportunity." Lingering long after the president had left the dais, three fifteen-year-old sophomores at First Presbyterian Day School giggled as they told a reporter, "He's gonna whip Mondale's butt." Referring to Mondale's running mate, New York representative Geraldine Ferraro, the teens added, "We don't want a woman vice president. She'll get up there and mess things up."[33]

Some days later Reagan's visit spawned a controversy in the *Macon Telegraph*, whose "Letters" section bristled with charges and countercharges. One writer told of Reagan partisans cursing and pushing Mondale supporters in the crowd and confiscating their posters. The writer said that those who shoved her "wore the faces and suits of Macon businessmen," and asked, "Is this a return to the 'good old days?'" Another writer claimed there was no abuse anywhere to be seen at the rally. A third was "sickened" by a minister's linking of Reagan supporters with the Klan and demanded an apology.[34]

Days before America went to the polls, however, Mercer students foreshadowed the ultimate outcome with a mock election. A portion of the university's predominantly white student body gave Reagan a resounding victory with 346 votes to Mondale's 106. On the election that counted, Reagan swept Georgia and the nation in a landslide victory. In Bibb County, however, some 95 percent of Mondale's vote came from black voters. While Mondale managed to add enough white voters to his black base to carry Bibb County by 52.6 percent, it was clear that *white* Macon *was* Reagan country. By garnering 80 percent of the county's white votes, the Republican had increased his support in Macon to 47.4 percent, fifteen points higher than his 1980 totals. Four years later, George H. W. Bush continued this trend, by capturing 50.1 percent of the Bibb County vote to Michael Dukakis's 49.9 percent.[35]

This trend among Macon's white voters away from the Democratic Party continued in presidential elections for the rest of the twentieth century, with Bush and H. Ross Perot taking a combined 48 percent of the 1992 vote, and Robert Dole and Perot taking 49 percent of the 1996 vote against Bill Clinton. In 2000 George W. Bush lost Bibb County by an eyelash, garnering 49.1 percent of the vote to Al Gore's 50.9 percent. Despite losing Bibb County's overall vote in 1984, 1992, 1996, and 2000, the Republican Party received the majority of the white vote in every presidential election since 1984. While many conservative issues contributed, race issues were central to this realignment, leaving black-white relations in Macon as polarized as ever.[36] Such racial polarization continued to harden during the 1990s, caused partly by the "culture war" over Bill Clinton, but more importantly, by Macon's reaction to the controversy over the Rodney King verdict.

RODNEY KING AND MACON'S FLAG FLAPS

On 29 April 1992, a Simi Valley, California, jury with no African-American members rendered verdicts of not guilty on Lawrence M. Powell and three other officers of the California Highway Patrol. Almost fourteen months earlier they had arrested and beaten a black motorist named Rodney King. On probation after a two-year prison sentence for armed robbery, King was drinking and high on marijuana when Powell's patrol car attempted to stop him for speeding on Interstate 210 in Los Angeles. Fearing his parole violation would return him to jail, King led a chase at speeds of up to 115 miles per hour. By the time King was apprehended, twenty-one officers had arrived at the scene, where King lay handcuffed and face down. Claiming he had lunged at them, the officers used a stun gun on him, and hurled taunts of "What's up, killer?" or "What's up, nigger?" (King's dazed condition rendered his later testimony uncertain on that point.) Then, during the next eighty-one seconds a nearby resident videotaped the officers deliver fifty-six blows with night sticks and six kicks to the prostrate King.

The acquittal of the officers touched off several days of riots in South Central Los Angeles. Blacks angered by the verdict launched a cataclysm of violence on their own neighborhood. By the time calm had been restored rioters had damaged more than $1 billion worth of property and killed some fifty people. Most dramatically, another videotape had captured the images of black youths nearly beating to death a white truck driver named Reginald Denny. Journalist David K. Shipler aptly summarized the racial explosion as "a convulsion in a simmering fever of rage among people too abused by the police, too impoverished by the economy, too marginalized by the society to have much stake in the preservation of neighborhood or system."[37]

The riots also sparked incidents across the country. In Beaufort, South Carolina, Macon native Carl W. "Will" Schultze, Jr., a member of the Army National Guard, was attacked by a group of angry blacks, who fractured his skull and broke his nose and left eye socket. Rumors of a similar beating of a white student in one of Macon's high schools circulated during the days after the King riots.[38] The tragic events also sparked a renewed public discussion of race in American life, both in Macon and across the nation. The result was a polarized dialogue unheard since the 1968 Kerner Commission report warned of separate Americas, black and white, separate and unequal. Once again, in commenting on the King verdict and its aftermath, the racial culture war between Colorblind America and Multicultural America raged more fervently than ever.

The *Macon Telegraph* deplored "the whole rampaging collective madness of the mob." Dubious about the jury's verdict, the editors admitted, "it *was* their call. That's the system. It works more often than not, but could have worked better in this case." This, of course, marked a major dividing line between white and black assumptions in America and in Macon. Whites trust the legal system to dispense relatively just outcomes, while, given their sad experience with the white-controlled courts, blacks have reason to be much less confident. The *Telegraph* did aver that if the officers did not use "excessive force" on King, the term needs redefining. "Mob mentality answers mob mentality," ran the editors' summary of the incidents. In a second editorial, the *Telegraph* commented on the nation's anger. Many blacks *and* whites were incensed over the "blindness of [the] jurors. Many others, the editors noted, were angry with the "opportunistic and sadistic criminals who don't deserve the freedom they claim to be seeking." Warning of a "dangerous turning point in human relations," the *Telegraph* pointed up the racial element of the culture war: "Black society remains oppressed, despite thirty years of progress, but the white middle class is hurting—and resentful—too."[39]

On 2 May black leaders held a "Rally For Peace" at City Hall, principally to help young black Maconites process their anger and frustration over the King verdict. They urged local ministers to address the matter in their forthcoming church services. Jack Ellis, Leroy Thomas, host of the *Ebony Speaks* television show, city council member Elaine Lucas, Herbert Dennard, and Minister Stanley Muhammad of the Nation of Islam addressed a slim gathering of some fifty persons. Former NAACP president Anne Moore told the audience, "We cannot sit back silently and be complacent, letting things go on that are not right."[40]

Many black and other Multicultural Americans wrote the *Telegraph* to warn of the nation's deep chasm on race matters. One writer, a young adult of twenty during the bus boycott of 1962, noted that the King verdict had touched off more rage than at any time in his lifetime. He explained, "No jobs, or low-paying ones, cause low self-esteem, bad housing, poor education. That leads to drugs to forget the situation that they're in, which in turn leads to robbing and killing to get them." Central High School sophomore Dana L. Zellner pointed out "a definite problem of racism in America today" and then heaped up adjectives to describe the verdict: "absolutely ludicrous, ridiculous, unfair, immoral, unjust, prejudiced and racist. How could those twelve people view that videotape of the barbaric beating of Rodney King and not see it as it was?... I can understand the hurt and humiliation felt by the minority race following this verdict."[41]

Another black writer scolded the *Telegraph* for its lurid headline, "Blacks Attack Whites in Atlanta," reminding the editors, "White people have been beating, attacking, hanging, and killing our people and other non-whites for over 200 years and I am sure you never printed 'Whites Attack Blacks' the way you did on that Friday." Such journalism left the impression, she noted, "that white lives are more important than Afro-Americans." Lorenza Davis viewed the verdict and riots as a rallying point for activism, saying, "The handwriting is on the wall, black America. It's time to get off the stool of do-nothingism....Let the burnings be a triumphant blaze to our unification." H. Lee Perdue, voicing a less dramatic version of relational anti-racism, called on leaders to renew Teen Partners, a defunct youth program begun by the Macon-Bibb Interracial Council during the 1988–1989 school year. "One-to-one contact could dispel stereotypes," he suggested, adding, "We need to put our egos aside and move beyond our ethnocentric comfort zones.... If not, progress regarding the races will continue to retard."[42]

By the following fall, race concerns and the King incidents continued to roil the waters at Mercer. One well-traveled student wrote the *Mercer Cluster*, "I have lived in several states across the nation, but I don't recall having lived anywhere that racial slurring was so pronounced, almost to the point of being culturally acceptable. It's not uncommon in Macon to hear open references to 'niggers' or white

supremacy, for instance." A classmate pointed out that common
sociological definitions of racism involved prejudice plus political
power. Blacks might be prejudiced against or dislike whites, but have
insufficient or no political power to weaken white privilege. He
concluded with a comment by sociologist Jenny Yamato, "People who
have not thought about or refuse to acknowledge this imbalance of
power/privilege often want to talk about the racism of people of color."[43]

Other letters focused on the infamy of the rioters. Resisting being
called "rednecks and racists," one writer believed the "totally
inexcusable" riots had set race relations back twenty-five years. While
the King verdict was wrong, he suggested that similar miscarriages of
justice often happen to whites as well. Opining that "blacks have a
problem co-existing and accepting others," he fumed, "I am sick and
tired of listening to black leaders and two-faced white liberals blaming
poverty, crime, illegitimacy and every other problem in the black
community on whites."[44] Another seemed simply to throw up his hands
at the racial impasse:

> Blacks claim that whites are able to get a better education
> and have better job opportunities than blacks. Whites claim free
> minority summer enhancement programs, college grants,
> scholarships, free tutors, legally padded scores, job quotas and
> affirmative action actually stack the deck in favor of blacks....
> Blacks claim they are not making economic strides in this
> country because they are systemically "locked out" by whites.
> Whites claims that blacks are not making economic strides
> because blacks have trouble coexisting with other races, polarize
> themselves and actually have the system "locked in."...Blacks
> claim they are not getting their share of power "as a people."
> Whites claim that empowering "separatist" race, sex or religious
> groups, as such, splinters the concept of unity, and that the needs
> of America are more than just the sum of the needs of all the
> groups that make up the whole.[45]

In the aftermath of the King verdict, a symbolic action by black
members of the city council attracted similar response from whites,
bringing the racial culture war home to Macon. At the 5 May meeting

council member Charles Dudley led seven other members to remain silent rather than recite the council's customary Pledge of Allegiance to the American flag. Calling on the council members to join his silent protest America's failure to provide "justice for all," Dudley wanted "to show a sign that work needs to be done." White council members Theron Ussery and Jim Lee, declined to join the protest, saying that they abhorred the King verdict, but nonetheless wished to maintain their loyalty to the flag. While Dudley and fellow member Lonnie Miley had declined to repeat the pledge since the council began the practice several years earlier, the refusal to say the pledge only became divisive after the King controversy. The entire council did support reading Elaine Lucas' statement expressing "concern and displeasure" into the minutes. In the end, six black members of the council—Dudley, Miley, Lucas, Delores Brooks, Thelma Dillard, and Henry Ficklin—along with white members Dee Shields and Rodney Smith, remained silent during the pledge.[46]

Before long Dudley and the others had drawn a barrage of criticism. A *Telegraph* reader wrote that the action made her sick and accused them of "a mean spirit and a lack of thankfulness for sitting where they sit." Another launched the oft-invoked implication that Americans should show their gratitude for the right to protest by not protesting: "If a person refused to pledge allegiance to the country where he lived, that person would probably be put in prison." Another professed his faith in America and willingness to salute the flag despite the nation's faults. He noted that the flag he would not salute "guarantees their freedom of speech and protects the right to vote which placed them on the council in the first place." It was also the flag carried by Will Schultze when he was beaten in South Carolina. He called on the entire council to begin its next meeting with the pledge and a prayer for the young Maconite attacked "by young thugs simply because of the color of his skin."[47]

The political heat eventually led council member Rodney Smith to issue an apology for implying he did not love America and its flag. Explaining that in his actions he had hoped "to bring our citizens together in harmony at a time of shock and unrest"—a rather naive miscalculation, to say the least, Smith asked the forgiveness of those he had offended.[48] This mea culpa served only to offend Gary Len Solomon, a black Maconite whose open letter virtually branded Smith a political coward: "[A]s soon as a few white people didn't agree with you, you wrote back begging and pleading." He added a pointed tirade:

> I think that when a person pledges allegiance to the American flag he is only standing and telling a lie that has been told far too long.... That is the same flag that flew over the battleground in World War II, when black men fought side by side with the whites but couldn't use the same bathrooms. So excuse me if I don't stand a pledge allegiance with you. I would hate to stand and tell a lie by saying this is one nation under God, because it is clear that there is a double standard in America: one for whites and one for people of color. The part about "justice for all," well, we all know there's not an ounce of truth to that. We haven't seen justice for 400 years.[49]

The stakes were raised in the flag furor when Robert F. Cunningham, a candidate for the US House, and other Republicans called on council members to apologize. Echoing President George H. W. Bush's successful 1992 efforts to challenge the loyalty of opponent Michael Dukakis, Cunningham took the moralistic and patriotic high ground. "It's a moral issue," he asserted, asking, "Are we going to support this country?" Speaking for his fellow council members and the Macon NAACP, which had joined the fray, Ronnie Miley defended their action as an exercise of their free speech and denounced Cunningham's effort as to boost his campaign. He also called on citizens to attend the upcoming council meeting "to voice their displeasure toward such racial tactics."[50]

Before the council meeting scheduled for 2 June, both the *Macon Telegraph* and the Macon Ministerial Association tried to calm the tensions. On Sunday, 31 May, the editors criticized Cunningham's efforts, along with the council members' protests. They wrote, "Trying to turn a local controversy into a flag waving issue reeks of the politics of division. If council members involved in the protest were guilty of bad judgment, so are those running for national office who seem bent on making hay with it." That same day, dabbling once again in relational anti-racism, the Reverend Chuck Conner, pastor of the Lutheran Church of the Holy Trinity and president of the Macon Ministerial Association, joined with the Reverend Lonzy Edwards, pastor of the Mt. Moriah Baptist Church, in sponsoring an interracial baccalaureate service for graduating high school seniors. In an effort to unite the divided community, the service brought together some 150 worshippers at the Grand Opera House. Summing up the purpose of the service, Conner told the congregation, "We have to learn to rise above all the differences in race and religion that we have allowed to become walls. We have to tear those walls down."[51]

Tempers continued to flare, however, despite the ministers' unifying efforts, and by the Tuesday meeting Cunningham's crusade was joined by a citizen group bearing a petition signed by 700 Maconites demanding that the offending members apologize, resign, or face a recall effort. In response, all of the protesting council members except Elaine Lucas issued a defensive public statement claiming that their action had been misinterpreted. They explained their action as necessary to express their concern for "the equality and justice of the criminal justice system. Reaffirming their love for America, they called on Maconites to respect the principles of free speech. Unsatisfied with less than complete capitulation to their threats, leader Bill Hudson said he wanted to hear unrepentant members recant their protests. "The infamous behavior of these eight council members," he charged, "is helping to pull this nation apart." Defending Lucas in her continued refusal, activist Frank Johnson, retorted that no one was being disloyal, adding, "If anyone is recalled, we'll elect them right back just as fast." About 100 Maconites attended the meeting, with blacks supporting the no-pledge protesters and whites vocal in their opposition.[52] Since in their statement all but one of the protesters had at least leaned toward an actual apology, the furor eventually subsided, while Elaine Lucas' seat on the council remained safe within her district.

Letters to the *Telegraph* continued to address the pledge controversy through mid-June. Lucy Harrison wrote to defend Robert Cunningham against the editors' criticism, arguing that as a good citizen he had a right to both free speech and to involve himself in the local debate. "These rights," she added with the fervor of a culture warrior, "are not exclusively the domain of the media and leftist protesters." Just under her letter, the *Telegraph* printed Bert Bivins' defense of the non-pledging council members. He wrote that he would have joined their silent protest had he been on the council, adding, "It would not have been because I do not respect the pledge. It would have been because I do not appreciate the ritualistic recitation of the pledge of allegiance, or those who make a mockery of the principle of 'liberty and justice for all.' That's what the Rodney King case did, and I think that's what those eight members of the council were protesting."[53] Still another writer denounced Gary Len Solomon's earlier letter calling the pledge a lie. He called for a Colorblind America and rejected Solomon's hyphenated Americanism:

> I am sick at my stomach from reading such letters. He says he is Afro-American. If he was born in America, he is an American. My ancestors came from Germany...but I'm an American, not a German-American.... Discrimination or racism is definitely prevalent in America. But open your eyes, if you dare. It's practiced between blacks and practiced between whites as well as between blacks and whites. Arrogance, screaming discrimination or racism and riots will not solve our problems but only irritate people.[54]

An even more symbolic flag flap, however, helped divert the attention of culture warriors away from Macon's City Council. In Atlanta, on 28 May 1992, in a frontal attack almost sufficient to ruin his re-election chances, Governor Zell Miller said it was time to remove the Confederate emblem from the Georgia state flag. Couching his arguments in terms of the state's image as it prepared to host the 1994 Super Bowl and the 1996 Summer Olympics, Miller's effort, intended or otherwise, would also help defuse some of black Georgians' rage after the Rodney King paroxysm. The continued use of the stars and bars, he argued, did not comport with the image of a progressive, new Georgia. He called the post-1956 banner "the fighting flag of those who wanted to preserve a segregated South in the face of the civil rights movement.... It's a time now when I think we should shake completely free from that era." Of course, Macon's delegation in the state House divided over the proposal. Macon's Republican Representative Wayne Elliott immediately announced, "I'm going to fight him like hell. That is a part of history that cannot be erased. The next thing there will be other things they don't like. If you start that, where do you stop?" Similarly, Denmark

Groover, still representing Macon in the state House, as he did when he engineered the 1956 change in the state flag, announced he would oppose changing the flag again. Acknowledging that black Georgians were offended by the Confederate emblem, he argued that the Civil War had been fought over a state's right to secede, rather than slavery, adding: "[T]hat is simply not what it [the Confederate flag] meant when it was flown in the 1860s."[55]

On the same day as Miller's flag proposal, Atlanta representative Newt Gingrich told the delegates at the Georgia Republican convention that he supported the flag change. Later, D. Mark Baxter wrote the *Telegraph* to say that most Georgia Republicans who, like himself, had heard the speech rejected Gingrich's position on the flag. Noting that Gingrich's views on the flag generated boos and catcalls by the 1,500 persons in attendance, he observed, "Perhaps some GOP leaders are not listening. Perhaps they will not continue long as GOP leaders."[56]

Representative Billy Randall announced his full support of the governor, noting accurately that the legislature had changed the state flag in 1956 "in an act of defiance which was racially motivated, no matter what some people might say."[57] Others Maconites agreed with the governor's proposal, including state Senator Robert Brown and Bob Ensley, a top aide to Mayor Tommy Olmstead. Breaking ranks with many other Georgia Republicans, however, Attorney General Michael Bowers agreed with Miller, adding that in the wake of the Rodney King riots "the state should drop a symbol that divides Georgians along racial lines." In so doing, Bowers distinguished himself as one of the few prominent Georgia politicians to connect the flag change with efforts to damp down racial tensions caused by the Rodney King verdict and riots. At the level of private citizens, Timothy Bagwell registered his displeasure over Elliott's pro-flag stance. "Why does Elliott," he asked, "wish to retain a symbol born out of racist reaction?" The flag issue reflected issues of "moral sensitivity and character," Bagwell argued, and citizens should reject leaders who could not see those large issues.[58] By the next legislative session in 1993, Miller's support across the state dwindled. The governor lost his effort to change the state flag, leaving the volatile issue to his two successors, Roy Barnes and Sonny Perdue.

Through the mid-1990s both national and local events kept the racial pot boiling in Macon. The issue of black control of the city surfaced in February 1995, when the city council asked the Georgia General Assembly for a referendum on reducing its number from fifteen to seven members. The local delegation, however, dominated by black members and fearful that with two at-large seats a seven-member council would block blacks from gaining the majority of seats, refused to support the request. The following month, tempers flared along racial lines when the council approved a redistricting plan that created three black majority wards and two white majority wards. Four white members voted against the plan. At the same time, the members battled over a proposal to reduce the council to eleven members. Council president Willie Hill voted with eight white members to defeat the proposal that would have included two members from each of the five wards, plus one seat for a council president elected citywide. The other black members voted for the plan because it would also have eliminated four at-large seats, thereby making possible a black majority on the council. White members supported it as a means of maintaining the white majority.

Another racial issue was raised over consolidation of city and county law enforcement, which black members denounced as a plot to keep the council in the control of the white majority. Council member Delores Brooks fumed that the council looked "like a bunch of clowns," as relations between black and white members were "as bad as they have ever been." Accused of racist plots to protect white power, white council members displayed their anger. "I resent that we are being called racist," said council member Dee Shields, "or are involved in some kind of plot because of some position we take. I've been down here a long time, and you know me better than that…. I am not a racist."[59]

Similar concerns arose that year when Jack Ellis sought to become Macon's first black mayor in a campaign against Mercer law professor Jim Marshall. While neither candidate overtly played the race card, the tensions of the era and the long term concern about "black rule" kept the issue before the voters. With a low turnout Macon gave Marshall a slim victory.[60] By the time Marshall took office late that year, another national *cause celebre* brought racial tensions back to the surface. When football star and sports commentator O. J. Simpson was acquitted of charges of murdering his ex-wife, questions of race in the American judicial system sharply divided white and black Americans.

In his 1997 State of the City address, Marshall bluntly denounced racial divisions and called racism "the city's biggest weakness." Urging Maconites to think of their city as a single community, he admonished an audience of civic and business leaders to help bridge racial, social, and economic gaps by volunteering in children's causes. Tying racial divisions to the problems of economic development, Marshall minced few words: "You look at us from a national perspective, and we're way behind the times.... People are not going to put their money in a place that does not have its act together, and we don't have our act together in the way we should.... It's a big mistake to be a racist, and too many of us are."[61]

A month later a Gallup poll revealed that the racial chasm being felt in Macon was, unsurprisingly, shared by the nation at large. Whites were shown to be little concerned about job, education, and housing opportunities for blacks. Compared to the 59 percent of African Americans who saw a greater need for government remedies for racial inequality, only 34 percent of whites agreed. Frank Newport, vice president of the Gallup organization observed, "White Americans don't see a major problem. Ergo, they don't see a need for governmental intervention." Other measures pointed toward a weakening of white prejudice against blacks. White approval of racially-mixed marriages had increased from 4 percent to 61 percent since 1958. In that year 80 percent of whites said they would move out of a neighborhood if large numbers of blacks moved in; by 1997 those willing to engage in "white flight" had decreased to just 18 percent.[62] Commenting on the survey, the *Telegraph* agreed with the poll that race relations remained a significant problem in America. "Race relations in a community is like a marriage—unless each party is happy, no one is happy." The polls simply pointed to what everyone knew from the Rodney King and the O. J. Simpson experiences. Recalling the ways the Simpson verdict divided blacks and whites, the editors concluded, "If we have such a different take on the actions of one man whose life was publicly documented and scrutinized, is it any wonder we disagree on how the rest of us black and white are treating each other every day? The gulf was with us all along; we ignored it. Do we believe all that has faded just because the Juice isn't on television anymore?"[63]

The economic gaps, the racially divided perceptions of the playing field, the impulse to ignore them, and the unutterable separation between black and white Maconites were all poised to persist into a new century. On the eve of a new millennium the election of the city's first black mayor tested test Macon's willingness to bridge the chasm, while the public comments of a Macon-bred baseball player brought the city's race relations into a national spotlight.

10

Still Unutterable, Still Separate: Blacks and Whites in the Ellis Years

On 14 December 1999, Macon, Georgia, inaugurated its fortieth, and its first African-American, mayor. Earlier that year, in the primary election—tantamount to a general election because there were no Republican opponents—former Army paratrooper, car salesman, and talk show host, C. Jack Ellis defeated former mayor Buckner Melton with 53 percent of the popular vote. The campaign was fairly matter of fact, with racial tension at a minimum. Neither candidate overtly played the race card nor did the outcome generate any great hue or cry from the white population. As might naturally be expected, the black population celebrated having "come this far by faith"—clearly, a long, long way since the days of disfranchisement and lynching.

One might like to say that in the campaign race was non-existent and that the Ellis years represent a new era as well as a new millennium for Macon. But the color line that W. E. B. Du Bois saw as the key "problem of the twentieth century" remains for the twenty-first a major factor in Macon as in all of America.[1] If, as many have suggested, racism is America's "original sin," an Augustinian or Calvinistic theology would confess that basic human frailty as impossible to eradicate completely. Race, as the poor, we have with us always. So while in the mayoral election of 1999, Macon saw neither candidate play the race card overtly, only the historically and politically naive could miss the shadow of race.

For instance, several newspaper reports reminded readers that by 1999, within the city limits, Macon had 1,957 more blacks registered to vote than whites. On election night, while staying on message that

Macon "is not for white people and not for blacks people. It's for all people," the mayor-elect nonetheless had to admit race had still been a factor: "Of course. I got more black votes than him and he got more white votes than me." Two days later, while making the rounds of Georgia's major news outlets, early on interviewers asked questions such as "What will you do to allay fears in the white community?" He gave his standard answer: "There shouldn't be any fears. I'm a Maconite. I'm an American. I've been in the military, and I was willing to die for my country. Why should there be any fears?"[2]

Thanks to a black community fervently hoping to make history this time around and a strong "get-out-the-vote" campaign led by Bibb County legislators Robert Brown and David Lucas, Ellis mounted an energetic campaign. Even Republican County Commissioner Dennis Dorsey agreed that Ellis had generated an ardent following, noting, "Melton raised more money, but it didn't translate into votes. Ellis translated his support into votes."[3] Within a few days of taking office, Macon and its new African-American mayor entered a national spotlight over the public comments by another of the city's native sons, Atlanta Braves pitcher John Rocker.

JOHN ROCKER AND MACON'S IMAGE

In October 1999 the New York Mets swept the Atlanta Braves in the National League Championship Series, during which Braves' twenty-five-year-old ace-reliever John Rocker developed a testy relationship with New Yorkers. On one occasion, he booed the fans as he was forced to leave the game. All was in fun until two months later, when a major article in *Sports Illustrated* quoted Rocker's candid assessment of New York. In an extended tirade, he told reporter Jeff Pearlman:

> The biggest thing I don't like about New York are the foreigners. I'm not a very big fan of foreigners. You can walk an entire block in Times Square and not hear anybody speaking English. Asians and Koreans and Vietnamese and Indians and Russians and Spanish people and everything up there. How the hell did they get in this country?... Imagine having to take the [Number] 7 train to the ballpark, looking like you're riding

through Beirut next to some kid with purple hair next to some queer with AIDS right next to some dude who just got out of jail for the fourth time right next to some 20-year-old mom with four kids. It's depressing.

Quoted as referring to an African-American teammate as a "fat monkey," he then added, "I'm not a racist or prejudiced person, but certain people bother me."[4]

Thus began a national rhubarb about how major league baseball and the Atlanta Braves should deal with what was now a public relations problem. Before the furor dissipated some two months later, only to re-surface during baseball's 2000 spring training season, Rocker's attitudes had drawn comments from New York mayor Rudy Giuliani, former Atlanta mayor Andrew Young, gay rights and civil rights groups, newspaper editors and writers across the country, including nationally-syndicated columnists Carl Rowan and Cal Thomas, and comedians Jay Leno and David Letterman. Braves general manager John Schuerholz distanced himself from Rocker's comments, while baseball commissioner Bud Selig ordered the pitcher to undergo psychological testing. Within a week after the story broke, *Telegraph* editor Ron Woodgeard had seen more than 300 articles and broadcast pieces on Rocker, with headlines from as far away as Scotland. For his part, Rocker issued an initial apology, saying his comments had "gone too far" and that the article had misrepresented him as a racist.[5]

Virtually everyone in Macon seemed to weigh in on the controversy, as the *Macon Telegraph* ran a full-page of reader reactions on both 26 December 1999 and 2 January 2000. Those two pages, presumably representative of the avalanche of reactions spanning the two-month controversy, printed sixty-seven letters or emails from readers, 61.2 percent of which defended John Rocker. One reader lamented that 40 percent of the respondents to the *Telegraph's* online poll believed that major league baseball should do nothing to punish Rocker. This result, however, differed little from the poll of an Atlanta television station in which 19,960 viewers voted against punishment to 9,827 for punishment, or an ESPN poll in which almost 45 percent of 35,499 votes called for no further action against Rocker beyond his psychological evaluations.[6]

Several Maconites who wrote the *Telegraph* in Rocker's defense argued that if he had been black, or more specifically, if he were Jesse Jackson or Louis Farrakhan, "he wouldn't be catching all the crap being thrown at him. His persecution for making racist remarks is in itself racist." Regarding Rocker's remarks themselves, another added, "But I think he got it about right." Still another complained, "The way gays and minorities will exploit this is a much greater crime than anything Rocker said." On the other hand, a Rocker detractor opined, "'Local boy makes good' and with too much money and too much ego humiliates his community, team, and state. He should be banned from baseball." Another wrote, "[C]an we really fault him for is views? He is a product of Macon.... Now he is exposed to people other than those he was 'sheltered' with in the lovely town of Macon. He has unfortunately reconfirmed to the country that the 'true South' is alive and well."[7]

As the firestorm raged into its third week, national media outlets began to request interviews from the first black mayor of Rocker's hometown. Ellis told ESPN that Rocker was young, had made a big mistake, and owed apologies to Macon, major league baseball, and the nation. He added, however, that though Maconites should dissociate themselves from his comments, they should not distance themselves from Rocker himself. On Friday, 7 January, Ellis flew around the country as a guest on talk radio programs from Las Vegas to New York City, gave interviews to cable news channels CNN and MSNBC, returned back to Atlanta to appear on CNN's afternoon *Talk Back Live* program. Returning to Macon that evening, he appeared on the syndicated tabloid show *Extra*. Most Maconites seemed to believe the mayor did the city rather proud, with council member Jim Lee commenting, "I do think it puts Jack in an unusual circumstance. But I think Jack is able to handle himself. I don't envy him at all, but he seems to be up to it." Others no doubt agreed with the *Telegraph* reader who saw more sinister ambitions in the new mayor: "Does Mayor Jack Ellis honestly believe that the people of this country would automatically assume that the views of John Rocker reflect the collective views of the citizens of Macon? Or could it be that the new mayor saw a perfect opportunity to bask in the national spotlight, however briefly?" In addition to these media appearances, Ellis also scored points by phoning New York mayor Giuliani to apologize for the player's remarks, and by meeting with Jake Rocker, the beleaguered pitcher's father.[8]

On the same day, the *Telegraph* ran an article on Jake Rocker's reactions. Calling the imbroglio the "worst [character] assassination" he'd ever seen, he told reporters, "They're saying worse things about John than they did about Timothy McVeigh, and he killed people, including minorities and babies in diapers." Noting that minority teammates had occasionally lived with John in the Rocker home, he defended his son against media accusations: "The kid's not a racist. He sees some things he doesn't like." Finally, Rocker himself came home to Macon, where he granted an interview to ESPN's Peter Gammons. While he claimed to have been "grossly misrepresented" by *Sports Illustrated,* he issued a second apology for his remarks. He also put his feelings in the context of the heat of competition during which New Yorkers poured beer on him, spit in his face, and hit him in the back with a battery. After the ESPN interview, Rocker and his father visited the mayor's home, where Ellis accepted his apology as sincere and told reporters he did not believe Rocker was a racist. Eventually, on 1 March 2000 major league baseball reduced its penalties on the young pitcher, cutting his suspension in half to the first two weeks of the 2000 season and his fine from $20,000 to $500.[9]

In the midst of the controversy, however, *Macon Telegraph* editors Ron Woodgeard and Charles Richardson raised the issue of John Rocker's educational background. Woodgeard noted, "It was not lost on me or anyone else that he went to a private school. It doesn't matter which one. With one exception, they got started well after the Legislature put the Confederate battle emblem on the state flag in 1956." Wary of hitting this "touchy subject" too hard, Woodgeard described his discussions of diversity with his public-school-educated sons and speculated that those conversations would never had occurred had they "attended an all-white school." Two days later Richardson addressed the same issue in an open letter to Rocker. He advised Rocker to concern himself with fellow Maconites who heard tales of his tantrums in little league or who wondered whether the apple had fallen near the parental tree. More pointedly, Richardson told Rocker he should worry about "others who say, 'I knew they were teaching little racists out there,' referring to your alma mater, First Presbyterian Day School."

Richardson's comment elicited a defense from an angry *Telegraph* reader from Cochran, Georgia, who castigated the editor for his not-so-veiled criticism of Rocker's upbringing and private school education and demanded that Richardson issue an immediate apology. This column on an obviously racially-sensitive topic likely caused a spike in Richardson's communications from readers, some 75 percent of whom brought racially tinged reactions. Although he made no apology for his column on Rocker, he later mused, "We've hidden from any meaningful dialogue too long."[10] Even in the first two weeks of the twenty-first century, the separation between Macon's blacks and whites was apparently still unutterable.

WHITE FLIGHT AND RE-SEGREGATED SCHOOLS

The columns of Woodgeard and Richardson raised the private school issue because those schools had, like the rebel-dominated Georgia state flag, been born in the context of the South's massive resistance against public school integration. Across the South such schools were often called "segregation academies" because most of them were clearly founded by white parents determined to prevent their children from attending schools with black students. If the federal government would no longer allow Southern states to segregate their children into all-white schools, parents decided to allow the economic limitations of most black families to do so. The official journal of the Citizens Councils commented in September 1969 that private schools would flourish because parents "want their children educated, not integrated." That fall the parents of some 300,000 students had chosen to send their children to some 200 segregated private schools that had sprung up throughout the South between 1954 and 1967. Most of these institutions had opened after the passage of the 1964 Civil Rights Act. An unofficial survey indicated that with the encouragement of Governor Lester Maddox, who had hoped to see at least 100 more private schools, some 155 private schools were operating in Georgia by 1969.[11]

Even those critical of the private school movement acknowledged parents' legitimate concern that the inferior education previously provided black students might depress achievement levels in integrated and predominantly black schools. Rather than take the steps necessary to avoid temporary declines in public education, however, many parents chose to flee such responsibilities, abandoning public education for their children altogether. Educators across the South and in Bibb County expressed concern that the private school exodus would hurt the local public schools. Decreasing student populations typically led to diminishing budget allocations. In addition, "white flight" to wealthier suburbs left poorer families in the majority in the inner city schools and severely reduced the tax base for the public schools. The general loss of public support also hurt the public schools. In the South, the region of the country that historically supported public education the least, the result would be devastating.[12] These developments became realities in Macon after 1970.

Others chose private schools because of court-ordered busing to achieve racial balance. Previously, however, few, if any, of these parents had complained about the busing of *black* children to maintain racial segregation. Moreover, a 1969 report indicated that Southern private schools were generally busing a larger percentage of students, and busing them longer distances, than public schools in the region. "Many of those who cry the loudest about the busing involved in integration plans," asserted the report, "have no fear of busing if it is to maintain segregation." In the states of Alabama, Florida, Georgia, Louisiana, Mississippi, North Carolina, South Carolina, and Virginia, public schools bused an average of 49.5 percent of their students, compared to 62 percent of private school students. Public schools in those states bused their students an average of 10.1 miles each way per day (in Georgia the average was 10 miles), while private school students were bused an average of 17.7 miles per day.[13]

In Macon, with the exception of Catholic parochial schools, private education had fared poorly throughout the twentieth century until the specter of desegregation cast its shadow in the mid- to late 1950s. One of Macon's premier private schools, Stratford Academy was clearly a part of the massive resistance movement in the South. Some thirty white Maconites met on 10 March 1960 to discuss establishing a private school, according to the conveners, "because of what many of us consider to be an impending crisis affecting not only the education of our children but the children generally of Bibb county and the State of Georgia." If this were not enough to establish the school's origins as devoted to segregation, the choice of its name would. Officials chose Stratford because of associations with both Shakespeare and Robert E. Lee.[14]

After the first wave of school desegregation swept over Macon in 1964, plans to establish private schools increased significantly. Between 1959 and 1969 Macon saw a 200 percent increase in the number of private schools.[15] By April 1969, Bibb County School Superintendent Julius Gholson indicated that because of rising private school enrollment in Bibb and Monroe Counties, for the first time in fifteen years, Bibb public school enrollment figures had dropped enough to result in the loss of at least $500,000 in state funding. Assistant superintendent Allan Gurley suggested that interest in private schools would wane once "people adjust to some things they don't like." Asked what those things were, Gurley and other public and private school officials commonly answered, "Well, you know what the real reason for private schools is."

Two new private schools, Tattnall Square Academy and Macon Christian Academy, were both established by Baptist churches citing increased secularism in the public schools as reasons for their founding. But their founding congregations, Tattnall Square Baptist Church and Gilead Baptist Church, also had racial reasons for their schools. Tattnall headmaster Durwood Souther acknowledged that given the church's firing of its ministers in 1966 integration was likely a main factor in its founding a school. As an independent Baptist church, the Gilead congregation also rejected racial mixing on what they believed were biblical grounds. Thus the Gilead congregation founded Macon Christian Academy for both religious and racial reasons. In February 1970, Macon's downtown First Presbyterian Church announced its plans to establish the First Presbyterian Day School in the North Macon area. While emphasizing "academic excellence within a Christian Atmosphere" in its college preparatory program, the school's timing and location suggested some additional racial concerns. When a church establishes a private school away from its location in downtown Macon, with its high concentration of blacks, and chooses a site in a virtually lily-white area of the city at the same time that Judge W. A. Bootle was ordering the desegregation of the Bibb County schools, only the very gullible could deny that race was a factor.[16]

By September 1969 public school enrollment in Bibb County had dropped by 589 (1.7 percent) to 35,032, while almost 2,000 students were enrolled in Macon's private and parochial schools. The following year public school enrollment dropped another 1,742 students, which added to a total of 3,224 students lost between 1967 and 1970. In the same period, private school enrollment in Bibb County grew by 1,874 students. Between October 1969 and July 1970 fifty-eight new private schools were opened in Georgia. In September 1970, seven months after Judge Bootle desegregated the county's public schools, five new private schools opened their doors in Macon—Cochran Field Christian Academy, First Presbyterian Day School, Jonesco Academy, Macedonia Christian School, and Windsor Academy. That same fall Stratford Academy, which opened in 1960, added 285 new students (a 44.5 percent increase).[17]

This dramatic increase in the county's private school enrollment began a trend that persists into the Ellis era. In 1960 only 2.2 percent of Bibb County students attended private schools, while the precipitous 1970 jump more than doubled that figure to 5.4 percent. By 1990 private school enrollment had climbed to 15.3 percent, although in 2000 the percentage had declined slightly to 13.7 percent. By 2004 estimates put private school enrollment in Bibb County at somewhere between 15 and 20 percent, compared to 6 percent statewide. The number of private schools also rose from eight (counting Catholic schools) in 1970 to twenty in 2002. In the early 1990s, when Charles Richardson joined the *Macon Telegraph*, all of the paper's editorial board members sent their children to private schools—a powerful symbol of white rejection of the public schools and the majority black students who are educated there.[18]

Although Macon's private schools were not established solely because of resistance to integration, the proliferation of such schools would not have happened without it. Race continued to be a factor through the first generation of private school students. In 1975, a front-page article on the city's private schools in the *Macon Telegraph* signaled the continuing racial element by observing: "Virtually every white child, if he is not mentally retarded, can win admission to at least two Macon area private schools." Two days later another article in a series quoted Bibb superintendent Thomas Lott, who opined that private schools proliferated because of parents rather than their children. "It's the adults that have the hang-ups, social, racial, and otherwise."[19]

Some of those adults have continued to have racial "hang-ups" into the nineties. "Susie," a Macon State College freshman who attended private schools, tells of her friendship with an African-American girl named "Vanessa." Although she and Vanessa became very close, Susie picked up signals of her family's discomfort with the relationship. She was never allowed to sleep over at Vanessa's or to go on outings with Vanessa's family. On one occasion, after much pleading, Susie was allowed to attend a birthday party sleepover—but only until 10:00. Not until she reached high school was she allowed to include black friends in her own sleepovers. Regarding her mother's reaction to Vanessa, Susie concluded, "It took me a long time to accept that my mother must have seen something in her family that I didn't.... Maybe [Vanessa's] family just rubbed my mom the wrong way."[20]

Prominent white Maconites, like Councilmen F. Stebin Horne III and Cole Thomason, indicated their plans to send their children to private schools even though they know the high percentage of students in private education hurts the county's ability to attract new businesses. Although Thomason dislikes what he calls "sterilization"—the attempt to keep people away from certain kinds of people—he cites "nauseating" low test scores and high teen pregnancy rates in the public schools as necessitating his decision. As a parent he says he cannot gamble on his children's education, admitting, "I wish it wasn't the case. I wish it wasn't necessary."[21]

One must also acknowledge that gradual cultural change in the nation over racism has weeded out much of the overt racism in the founding of the South's "segregation academies." As such intolerance has become increasingly frowned upon, those schools have downplayed or denied the racial factor in their origins, along with redoubling efforts to highlight cultural diversity and teach racial tolerance. Further, particularly in the Protestant private schools, the perception of rising secularism in American culture and public education has led officials and parents to view their schools as incubators of a "Christian counterculture" that does include racial amity. Thus many private schools have sought in recent years to bolster their racial diversity. As a group, the five largest private schools in Bibb County are around 92 percent white. One of those is 84 percent white. Edward England, headmaster at Stratford Academy in 2002, announced financial grants of up to $7,200 to attract minority students to its 93-percent white student body. Tattnall Square Academy remained 97 percent white.[22]

Despite attempts to diversify both the makeup and the curriculum of the county's private schools, the drift of white students toward private education or home schooling has resulted in a largely re-segregated Bibb County public school system, particularly when coupled with the well-documented national trend of whites leaving central urban areas to live in outlying suburban areas. These trends have hurt the public school system by diminishing its overall support and siphoning off students from wealthier families and stronger educational backgrounds. Alex C. Habersham, a black business leader and former public school teacher, commented that too many whites with educational and financial resources "are either neutral or anti-public education. But public education can't make it without community support. Everybody's support.... That's our responsibility to the community and to society is to see to it that we've got an educated population. Not just my Billy and my Joe and my Jane, but everybody." He suggested that paying double (taxes plus tuition) for private education generates a white resentment toward both public education and their black neighbors that further weakens the city's racial harmony. Habersham further asserted that "although that one individual may receive a 'better' education (and that's arguable) from the private school, the big picture is that...from a community perspective that hurts us because we...need those resources committed to public education." He called on whites and middle-class blacks to become active in volunteering their time and human capital at inner city schools or for white-owned businesses to adopt some of those schools as part of a growing culture of support for public education. For Habersham the consequences of not doing so are almost apocalyptic: "That separation and segregation is *history*. We can't make it with that racism and that prejudice. We are going to melt and float down the Ocmulgee if this community doesn't do something about trying to come together from a racial perspective and build this community with all these natural resources we already have."[23]

In addition, white flight to the county and to private schools has polarized relations between the increasingly black and poorer central city and the whiter and wealthier county. The decision by such a large segment of white Maconites to reject the integrated public school system has left a deep chasm of resentment that cuts across blacks of all ages. Albert Billingslea, one of the first African Americans elected to an at-large seat on the county commission, believed that if whites of power and influence had accepted integration "and moved to make it work, we would not have the bitterness that lingers still to this day." Billingslea notes that white flight amounts to "[b]asically one half of the community saying, 'We don't care about you. We're out of here. We're going to take our children, we're going to take our spiritual and financial support and put it into a set of segregation academies.' I think that has hurt this community tremendously." The sentiment sadly penetrates into the youth as well, evidenced by the black high schooler who commented to a white student he perceived as intellectually advanced: "Oh, you must go to private school."[24]

A 2001 study by Harvard University's Civil Rights Project noted the nationwide trend toward white flight, which has resulted in 70 percent of black students nationwide between 1988 and 1998 attending mostly minority schools and a third went to schools with minority populations of upwards of 90 percent. Figures for Bibb County followed suit as during the 1990s white population decreased by 15,800 and the African-American population rose by 5,100. At the same time, white enrollments dropped significantly at nine elementary, middle, and high schools. Union Elementary, to take the most dramatic example, went from 64 percent white in the 1991-1992 school year to 64 percent black by the end of 2000–2001.[25]

In the existing court-approved integration plan for Bibb County, majority-to-minority transfers allow students to move from zones where they are in the majority to one where they are in the minority. In October 2000 there were only seven majority white schools in the system into which black students could transfer. That year only 511 of 24,500 students transferred under this policy. At two elementary schools, Springdale and Taylor, both of which had over 150 black student transfers, white parents quietly complained that the results were overcrowding the schools. The Reverend James Louis Bumpus, pastor of the Tremont Temple Baptist Church, noticed the refusal of white parents to send their children to predominantly black schools, even where those neighborhood schools had strong leadership, discipline, and academic achievement. He asked:

> Why wouldn't white parents transfer their children into a Burke Elementary, where Vivian Hatcher is principal. The school has excellent test scores, atmosphere, faculty, principal. But what we see more of is black families sending their children to Springdale or Sonny Carter—minority to majority transfer—and those schools scores are not necessarily any better than the scores of students at Burke. And it's almost unthinkable—even the most liberal of white parents would not think of transferring their child from their community school—from a Springdale or Sonny Carter—to Burke Elementary. Race plays a great part, I think.[26]

Thus, many community leaders note the problem, but beyond calling for dialogue, few Maconites see any solutions. "Our community is just so divided." "We are just so fragmented in so many ways," said Martha Jones, former principal at Miller Middle School. "It doesn't matter whether we're talking about education, whether we're talking about politics.... We polarize. "We tend to forget that we have shared vested interests." Bibb County Board of Education vice president Betty Phillips, a former public school teacher, worried about the polarized school system's impact on Macon's economic development, pointing out, "Anytime your school system doesn't reflect in some way the demographics of the county as a whole, businesses will look at that.... That immediately sends up a red flag." A frequent public critic of Macon's all but non-existent racial dialogue, the Reverend Lonzy Edwards, lamented, "We can't even talk about the problem, and if we can't talk about it, we can't solve it.... Not talking about race issues is a sign of a closed community that is slowly withering and dying."[27]

By 2002 nearly 60 percent of Bibb County's black students attended schools that were more than 85 percent black, up from 45 percent in 1997 and 35 percent in 1992. In the same period white students in schools more than 85 percent white rose from 13 to 15 percent. White-black student ratios thus widened during the last decade of the twentieth century. The system's 38-62 white-black ratio of 1990 widened to a situation in 2000 where the public schools had twenty-eight white students for every seventy blacks. This statistic raised the specter of the Bibb public system becoming what Peter C. Brown, director of the Mercer Center for Community Development, called "an urban system"—a euphemism for an all-black public system. Another controversy arose in 2000 when parents of the predominantly white Porter Elementary School complained that their school's "family like atmosphere" and strong standardized test performance would be lost if Porter added large numbers of students from the 80-percent-black Weir Elementary. More than 400 parents of Porter students said they were "very likely" to switch to a private school if Weir Elementary Students were sent to Porter. While these parents had legitimate concerns about the academic performance of their children's school, veiled racial concerns were no doubt a component of their worries.[28]

In February 2002 another major controversy arose over a new redistricting plan that would have closed four schools and combined four others to better integrated white and blacks students. When parents at Taylor, Porter, and Hunt Magnet schools protested, approval of the plan was postponed before eventually being approved with some changes on 19 December 2002.[29] Race in the schools therefore remains a persistently intractable, and only surreptitiously discussed, problem in Macon and Bibb County.

RACE AND THE MAYOR'S RE-ELECTION

After performing admirably during the John Rocker incident, Jack Ellis' grades on job performance took a precipitous plunge as a result of a string of high profile, sometimes embarrassing miscues. A novice in public office, some of his blunders were born of mere inexperience. Many of his troubles, however, stemmed from his personal life, which to many of his detractors seemed to cast a Clintonesque pall over the city administration. In March 2001 Ellis filed for divorce from his mercurial wife, Margarethia. By this time, unsubstantiated rumors circulated about an affair between the mayor and a white woman, as well as the announced separation, set tongues once again to wagging.[30] After this, Margarethia Ellis began a series of bizarre behaviors that sparked ridicule. The former First Couple squabbled over their property division, and the former Mrs. Ellis was sued for backing out of a deal to sell the house she had gained in the divorce. As the buyers sought possession of the home, they eventually asked a local judge to evict the recalcitrant former First Lady. In September 2002, after sheriff's officers seized her property to satisfy a lien on the house, Margarethia Ellis was evicted from the home. Commenting on what he called "one of the more bizarre things" he had ever been involved with, Superior Court Judge S. Phillip Brown, said, "It's gotten to the point of ridiculous. She is in the same position as a trespasser."[31]

Finally, on 9 September 2002, Margarethia Ellis agreed to pay some $17,000 in attorney's fees and drop her claims on the home in exchange of dismissal of a contempt petition. The melodrama's end brought a handshake between the buyers and Mrs. Ellis, whose comments celebrated being able to avoid legal proceedings in the dispute: "In our talking today, the most important thing to me was the opportunity to talk about the love of Jesus to everyone involved in the case and ask them to see that first beyond the house, whether or not it's the law. 'What would God do?' is the question I kept asking." By the time this episode ended, Margarethia Ellis had reconciled with and remarried the mayor and announced that she was launching a new Christian women's magazine named *ME*. The *Macon Telegraph* headline, full of journalistic pun and derision, announced, "It's All About 'ME,'" noting that the magazine bore Mrs. Ellis's initials as its title. She also found herself in a dispute with the dress shop over an unpaid bill for her inauguration gown, saying she thought the dress had been a donation by the shop to the new First Lady. Although the mayor himself was only indirectly involved in these escapades, none of this gave the administration the look of competence.[32]

The mayor's personal troubles exacerbated an earlier controversy over the eventual firing of Police Chief John Vasquez. Many picked up troubled vibes between Ellis and Vasquez even before the new mayor took office. During his campaign he consistently refused to answer reporters' question as to whether he intended to retain Vasquez as chief. In Ellis's first ten months as mayor, Ellis and Vasquez butted heads several times, although Ellis downplayed the rift. In May 2000 Vasquez was angered when the mayor asked the Georgia Bureau of Investigation to look into a police shooting of a man in the Fort Hill area of the city. Two months later the two disagreed over the mayor's decision to disband mounted patrols in the downtown area, with Vasquez charging Ellis with making police decisions without consultation. They disagreed again over Ellis's decision, again made without consultation, to buy only from gun companies that agreed to a national safety policy. In October 2000 they feuded over Ellis's negative evaluation of Vasquez's job performance.

At this point the professional dispute seemed to have become entangled with Ellis's personal woes. Vasquez claimed that the mayor's driver, Sgt. Raymond Reynolds, had on two occasions indicated to the chief that he had embarrassing information about the mayor's "personal problems." On 7 November Ellis called Vasquez into his office to present him a letter from Reynolds accusing the chief of asking personal questions about the mayor. When Vasquez refused to resign, Ellis fired him the next day, citing Vasquez's unspecified "gross misconduct." Later, Reynolds publicly supported the mayor and wrote the *Telegraph* to assure Maconites that he had no damaging information about Ellis. Some police officers, however, were embittered by the manner of Vasquez's removal. When Ellis eventually replaced Vasquez with Rodney Monroe, an African-American assistant chief of police with the Washington, DC department, many Maconites speculated that all along Ellis had wanted to replace Vasquez with a black police chief.[33]

Other fiascoes followed for the mayor. When Ellis put up a privacy fence at his new home, there were concerns in city council that he had submitted an invoice to the city for payment. Refusing to give specifics about his consultations with the police department and city attorneys, he seemed to stonewall, saying "I have no comment on security measures I take to protect my safety." Unnamed city officials informed council members Jim Lee and Dick Dickey of the mayor's requests. Eventually, after city attorneys advised Ellis that such a purchase was illegal, the mayor paid for the fence himself. A month later, matters modulated into a new controversy over whether or not Ellis had ordered a special security detail and round-the-clock patrols of his home. Ellis complained that he had received threatening phone calls with racial slurs, along with instances of vandalism. Many Maconites doubted the veracity of the claims, when Ellis did not give details of the alleged vandalism. Further, Ellis's neighbors told reporters they had seen no evidence of vandalism.[34] A trip by Ellis and other officials to explore a sister city relationship in Ghana generated more debate. So did an 8 May 2001 incident in which

Ellis spotted a reckless driver and called upon Officer Andrew Dawson, who had not witnessed the violation, to issue a ticket.[35]

All the while, Ellis's errors gradually became fodder for ridicule on right-wing talk radio. Comments by Atlanta host Neal Boortz created a stir when he told his audience that Ellis had

> infuriated some members of the Macon city council by actually appointing a (gasp!) white guy to a seat on a joint city-county authority. Didn't Ellis know that this was a black slot? How dare he appoint a white guy to a black position? Pretty gutsy, wasn't it? ...Now, the other comments about Jack Ellis had to do with persistent rumors in Macon about his having a little tête-à-tête with some Macon lass, which, it is rumored, has resulted in a pregnancy. That information did not come from *The Macon Telegraph,* though I might have given that impression on the air. In retrospect, those are some pretty nasty rumors to repeat if you don't have any more substantiation than I did—and I freely admit that I was wrong. Mea culpa, mea culpa, mea maxima culpa. So, in this regard at least, we'll have to draw a differentiation between Jack Ellis and Jesse Jackson.[36]

In Macon talk-meisters "Kenny B and Jami G" regaled listeners to WMAC-Radio with anti-Ellis comments, especially after council member Jim Lee revealed a private conversation in which the mayor told him, "I just don't like to see so many black people arrested." Lee took the comment as a signal that Ellis wanted the police department to go easier on black citizens, explaining, "I could not help consider the racial overtones.... It indicated to me he was more concerned about the arrest of black people than about crime." Lee also seemed to blame the mayor's attitude for a later string of robberies in the black community. Ellis charged Lee with taking the comment out of context, saying he was only expressing his concern about the contemporary crisis regarding black males and crime. In response to this controversy, the Reverend Eddie Smith, pastor of the Macedonia Baptist Church, and John Hiscox, director of the Macon Housing Authority, came to Ellis's defense, while hosts Kenny Burgamy and Jami Gaudet continued their frivolity with snippets of the classic Ray Charles song, "Hit the Road Jack," dedicated to the mayor.[37] A local website, related to WMAC, continued the levity by featuring a photo of an inebriated black man outside a bar with an Ellis campaign poster. The photo's caption read: "Jack must have *really* wanted my vote. Wow! That 10th boilermaker is really going to my head. I-I-I c-c-can't f-feel my feet...and the street is tilting."[38]

Such pointed social commentary on the public airwaves struck many as continuing a long tradition of white derision of African Americans. Contemporary racism, argued Palmyra Braswell, a former teacher in her eighties, "comes out in a demeaning manner in conversations that you hear on radio. The way it's presented by the media. I think the worst thing is the Kenny B Show.... if you talk about Council, it's the Little Rascals. If you talk about the mayor, it's in a demeaning way.... And people hear it, they believe it. They internalize it and it becomes a part of their thinking." Often a lightning rod because of her blunt manner of addressing race issues in Macon politics, Elaine Lucas reflected similar resentment about this popular program. "Their constant poking fun at black leaders spreads much ill will," she argued, adding, "So for a lot of whites that's reinforcing for them, 'Well, blacks can't lead. Blacks are incompetent. They're inept. They can't talk. They don't understand. All of those stereotypes are reinforced, which translates into more disrespect, more lack of regard.... And I think all of that keeps us drifting apart."[39]

On 20 August 2001 the *Macon Telegraph* ran an editorial written by African-American columnist Charles Richardson, who complained of the mayor's penchant for public relations blunders. He continued, "It's good that he accepts responsibility, but he should have learned by now, with all of the scrutiny that he has been under, that when you're the mayor—every little thing, from extra police patrols to cameras to fences to travel plans—ends up as an issue waiting to spoil any good that is accomplished. While it can be debated that the intense glare of the spotlight is fair, there is no debate that the spotlight exists and must be dealt with."[40]

There is little question that Ellis's troubles were mostly self-inflicted and any even-handed observer would have to admit his early incompetence at public relations. Gradually, however, Ellis showed himself capable of learning on the job, and the latter half of his term was not marred by similar gaffes. Still, one might justifiably ask if the mayor's race heightened the normal level of scrutiny for a new office holder. Successful African Americans, particularly those who pioneer as firsts in various areas, are often held up as representatives of their race. Perceptions of ineptitude regarding the presidency of Jimmy Carter, for example, did not cast doubt on the competency of other whites to be president. But it is not difficult to imagine Ellis's mistakes, or those of his wife, raising questions about the abilities of future black mayors. More important, the "good natured ribbing" of Macon's talk radio hosts clearly suggested a certain racial insensitivity or misunderstanding.

Nor can it be denied that Ellis's accomplishments were overshadowed by his foibles. During his first term, his administration received more than $3 million in grants to assist youth in job training, mentoring, tutoring, after-school programs, and other crime reduction programs such as midnight basketball, boxing, and other athletic programs. The crime rate dropped by 7 percent. The administration partnered with the Bibb County school system to build a new community center in the Pleasant Hill area at L. H. Williams School. Under Ellis's leadership, the city was awarded $2 million in federal and state grants to purchase and develop the historical downtown terminal station. With the assistance of various non-profit partners, the Ellis administration helped build over forty affordable houses that were sold to first-time buyers in South Macon, Tindall Heights, and West Macon. In Ellis's first term, the city began a $5.5 million renovation of the Macon Airport.[41]

In addition, in November 2000, in the wake of the Vasquez controversy and complaints of "reverse discrimination" among some white firefighters, Ellis also set up a Diversity Committee to help bridge racial divisions in the city. Eventually composed of nearly 100 members from the black, white, Indian, Chinese, Hispanic, Korean, Nigerian, disabled, and gay and lesbian communities were commissioned by the mayor to address a number of diversity issues including family status, ethnicity, religious beliefs, education, age and mental and physical abilities. Over the next two years, however, the committee only met a handful of times with little to show for its efforts, largely due to schedule conflicts and changing personnel. In November 2002, the mayor and committee chair Chester Fontenot moved to breathe new life into the committee, with plans to regularize its meetings and launch a magazine and cable television program to highlight the city's growing cultural, as well as racial, diversity.[42] A re-election campaign, however, seemed to take the mayor's eye off the diversity ball, and by early 2004 the best that could be said about the Diversity Committee was that it was dormant.

Ellis's primary campaign for re-election easily dispensed of three Democratic opponents, two black and one white, garnering 57 percent of the vote and carrying twenty-six precincts. Teacher and twenty-year veteran on the Macon City Council Thelma Dillard managed to attract only 3.3 percent of the voters, while Robert Ensley, who had served in a number of government jobs, including working for the Justice Department and as the executive assistant to two Macon mayors, took 6.2 percent. Ellis's white opponent, Dominick Andrews, drew 33.5 percent of the vote and won twelve heavily white precincts in North Macon. A police officer who moved to Macon in 1993, Andrews had decided midway through Ellis's first term to try to unseat the mayor. Compared with Dillard and Ensley, Andrews was a relative newcomer to both Macon and to local politics, and his vote totals suggest he drew most of the white anti-Ellis voters. Indeed, post-election analysis showed a large crossover vote of white Republicans in North Macon, almost all of whom supported Andrews. In those largely-Republican precincts hundreds more votes were cast than in the only Republican city council race, and Bibb County Republican chairperson Debra Lyons acknowledged that a crossover vote took place, although without official party encouragement.[43]

Predictably, a *Macon Telegraph* editorial suggesting that North Macon Republicans had voted for a candidate who "had little going for him beyond the color of his skin," struck a raw nerve and drew a flurry of protests from whites. They had voted, they insisted, on the basis of the content of Andrews's character rather than on the color of Ellis's skin. While denying the racial element in their votes, they also pointed out black Maconites' tendency to vote along racial lines. White denial has a long history in the South and the tradition continues in twenty-first century Macon. Ellis did have white support in his initial victory in 1999, but still a majority of white voters supported his white opponent Buck Melton. In the 2003 referendum on the Ellis administration, the mayor lost most of his white support. And while whites chalked this up to the mayor's ineptitude, the stark differences between the white and black precincts suggest that both groups engaged in racial bloc voting.[44]

Indeed, it is silly to deny that whites did at least unconsciously take race into account in their voting. The Republican crossover vote could have gone to a black candidate with much more experience in public office, Dillard or Ensley. Instead, it gravitated toward Andrews, a white newcomer to Macon with no experience in public office. If Ellis's shortcomings were his inexperience and ineptitude rather than his race, and if Andrews's race were not a major selling point, why did the North Macon Republicans not vote for more experienced Dillard or Ensley, particularly when Ensley was endorsed by the *Macon Telegraph*?[45]

Add to this the public statements of some whites that an Ellis re-election would induce them to leave the city. On election eve, a white voter put a sign in front of his Vineville Avenue home, "This house for sale if Ellis wins." After the election, he told reporters his family would look for a new home "anywhere but Bibb County," adding, "I've had enough of this town." Eight days later another white Maconite announced to *Telegraph* readers his intention to move to Jones county rather than to "endure another four years with C. Jack Ellis." Another voter confessed she would "leave in a heartbeat," complaining of the non-cooperation between the city's white and black populations. "It's like we're two foreign countries living in one city," she told a reporter.[46]

Moreover, white flight from the city accelerated since Ellis's initial election as mayor. Between 1999 and 2003 Macon lost some 10 percent of its registered voters. Most of these were white voters whose departure raised the black share of voters from 53 to 56 percent. Such realities prompted black Councilperson Brenda C. Youmas to attribute black control of the mayor's office and city council, to white flight. "It's not because people thought they should vote for them, it's because white flight went to unincorporated areas and the blacks stayed in. Politics is so racial, and has very little to do with qualifications in Macon. It's racially divided and it didn't become racially divided because of Jack Ellis. I think it showed its face more. It's always about race on both sides of the coin."[47]

Similar dynamics surfaced in the general election, in which Ellis had no Republican opposition. Instead two white candidates launched write-in campaigns. Bibb County Libertarian Party president David Corr argued against Ellis's fiscal irresponsibility, as did house painter Michael Kilpatrick. In November the two "white-in" candidates garnered 30 percent of the votes, only to lose to Ellis by more than 5,000 votes. State and local election officials, however, were shocked at the result, saying they could never recall so great a vote for a write-in campaign. Not so surprising was the fact that the nine precincts carried by David Corr were an average of 86 percent white. In those nine precincts Corr averaged 67 percent of the vote, while Ellis could manage only an average of 22 percent.[48]

Racially-polarized voting of this degree cannot reasonably be attributable merely to a general dissatisfaction with an incumbent. White protestations to the contrary, only the historically naive could leave racial animus out of the anti-Ellis equation. Of course, black Maconites also voted along racial lines, leading whites to judge them as equally guilty of racialized voting. They reasoned that if whites are racist for voting for white candidates, the same can be said of blacks who vote for black candidates. Such reasoning oversimplifies the difference between historically dominant and dominated groups of people. Members of a long-dominated group vote for a member of their own group mostly to assert their self-esteem and group pride and to protect themselves from possible future domination. Minority groups—like Catholics in the Kennedy election or Greeks voting for Michael Dukakis in 1988—vote for their own kind to celebrate their arrival at the table. To the contrary, when whites reject black candidates in favor of white ones, the vote has more to do with helping a dominant group maintain its ownership of the table. Both kinds of electoral decision-making may deviate from an ideal of "objective" voting, but their meanings are hardly the same. They should not be confused by the pretense that either race is color-blind when clearly they are not.

Despite white objections that anti-Ellis sentiment is not because of his race, most of Macon's African Americans defended him and believed whites held him to a higher standard than they did previous mayors. Albert Billingslea and Lonzy Edwards both note that trips to Japan by mayors George Israel and Tommy Olmstead hardly caused a ripple, in stark contrast to Ellis's trips to Ghana. (This discrepancy existed because expenses for these trips were paid by Macon's YKK company, which had a plant in Kurobe, Japan, while Ellis's expenses were borne by the city.[49]) "While he has an ego that gets him in trouble sometimes," Billingslea asserted, "he's not been any better or worse than any of the other mayors that we've had. Fact is, if you look at the Ronnie Thompsons, he's been much better." Wesleyan College sociologist Catherine Meeks faults the mayor as "being kind of silly" in actions that were obviously "going to be like a lightning rod." She added, "He's made choices that he should have known better than to make, and by doing that the good of the people has been lowered." Many other African Americans, she speculated, felt the same way without being willing to say so publicly. But she also acknowledged her view that whites had been unfairly critical of Ellis. Most black Maconites seemed to agree with Herbert Dennard, editor of the *Georgia Informer,* who told a white interviewer, "He's not as bad as y'all think he is and he's not as good as we think he is."[50]

Clearly, the presence of C. Jack Ellis in the mayor's office has exacerbated racial tensions in Macon that lay barely beneath the surface. He lost most of his white support, which was always quite soft, by his public relations miscues. By March 2004, Ellis was partly blamed for the defeat of a special option local sales tax referendum that would have partially relieved the city's fiscal crisis. This claim created what could be called a spiritual crisis in Macon, and in the aftermath, some Maconites felt a quiet ferment was precipitating modest efforts to address the city's growing racial tensions. One example was Mt. Moriah Baptist Church's sponsorship of "In Search of Community: A Conversation on Racial Reconciliation." Reverend Lonzy Edwards's periodic efforts to start such a conversation had fallen on deaf ears in recent years. This time, however, some seventy to eighty citizens, evenly divided by race, met consistently over four Tuesday night sessions to address such concerns. While this increased concern was a hopeful sign, progress would require honest reflection on both sides of the racial divide. Both races would need to face unflinchingly the racial realities of their community and nation.

CONTEMPORARY RACIAL REALITIES

Beyond Macon's resegregating public schools, racial realities remain central. Indeed, it is difficult to think any facet of life in Macon and Bibb County that is not hampered by the persistent and unutterable separation. The 2000 US Census indicates that the city itself is 35.5 percent white, 62.5 percent black, and 2 percent American Indian, Asian, or Hispanic. For greater Bibb County, the demographics run 50.1 percent white, 47.3 percent black, and 2.6 percent "Other."[51] This reality will continue to affect city and county politics in a number of ways. The long-standing issue of city-county consolidation, the makeup and quality of the public schools, the need to attract new business into the area are issues that all hinge on the problem of black-white relations. Those relations, problematic since Macon's founding in 1823, continue to create tension and suspicion.

This tension was clearly reflected in surveys of Macon conducted by the 2002 Community Indicators Project of the John S. and James L. Knight Foundation. In cooperation with the Princeton Survey Research Association, the Knight Foundation surveyed Macon[52] and twenty-five other American communities to document changes in their quality of life. Among its many findings, the survey of Macon revealed a high level of distrust, particularly among the city's African-American population. According to the survey, whites and blacks in Macon continue to be deeply divided on many issues. For example, 64 percent of white Maconites give their city positive overall marks, 73 percent African Americans did likewise. A similar Knight survey conducted in 1999 indicated that blacks had become more satisfied, while whites grew less content. Knight researchers found this trend to run counter to the norm among its other communities, where blacks tended to be less satisfied than whites. In the 2002 report, black Maconites (57 percent) were almost twice as likely to be favorable toward the local government than whites (29 percent). Conversely, 64 percent of whites gave the city government negative ratings, compared with 35 percent of black Maconites.[53] Given reactions to the city's first black mayor, Jack Ellis's election in 1999 appears to have made the difference.

On questions of social trust, blacks were less optimistic than whites. Only 19 percent of black Maconites believed "most people can be trusted," compared to 41 percent of whites. In addition Macon's overall level of social trust, 44 percent, was 5 points lower than the national figure.[54] Comments from both white and black Maconites supplement these percentages. The *Telegraph's* Charles Richardson believes blacks in Macon are "so used to seeing white people as the enemy that can't get out of it. Same way with some whites, they can't see it any other way." Betty Slater, who has found it difficult to fund and find acceptance for a positive "Ethnic Awareness Program" she devised for the public schools, fumed, "I've gone to programs that black people have given and everything you heard was negative about the white man." At Wesleyan College Catherine Meeks spoke poignantly about this knee-jerk lack of trust: "I just know how deep the mistrust is in black people towards white people. It's just really, really deep. I can't speak for every black person, but I know that I encounter that in almost every black person that I know and read about. There's that level of 'Well, you know, you gotta be careful. They may look like they're this way, but you never know when they're going to turn into being white on you.'" In response, city council member and moderate white Democrat Richard Hutto would appeal to African Americans in Macon: "I absolutely understand your distrust and it's completely justified. You have every reason not to believe anything I or somebody else says to you. But just for a minute, could you suspend disbelief?" But even young blacks born since the civil rights movement remain skeptical of the good intentions of whites. A black Central High School student noticed classmate Faira Holliday wearing a wearing a T-shirt that read, "Students for anti-racism." He shocked her when he pointedly asked, "What? Is that a joke?"[55]

The Ellis years have seen, if not caused, an increase in those who view racial and ethnic relations as a problem, with 66 percent saying so in 2002, compared with 57 percent in the 1999 Knight survey. In 2002 69 percent of whites saw this as a problem, compared to 61 percent of blacks. In general, 68 percent of Maconites believed race relations would remain the same or deteriorate over the next five years; 29 percent expected improvement in this area. Blacks, however, were more optimistic than whites, with 34 percent of blacks expecting improvement in race relations, compared to only 25 percent of whites. As to questions of treatment, 46 percent of African Americans believed whites were treated better than blacks; 44 percent said both races were treated equally; 1 percent believed blacks were treated better. Only 12 percent of whites believed whites were treated better; 63 percent said both were treated equally; 17 percent believed that blacks were better treated.[56]

Black Maconites (78 percent) were 11 percentage points more likely than whites to view unemployment as a problem facing Macon. In giving a report card to the Bibb County schools, white and black respondents canceled each other out. Among blacks some 55 percent rated the schools as excellent or good, compared with only 35 percent of whites. Thirty-six percent of blacks said the schools were only fair or poor, whereas 54 percent of whites put the schools in the fair or poor categories.[57]

When the results of the Knight Foundation survey were published in November 2002, reactions were unsurprising. Don Griggs, a black resident outside the city limits, credited Ellis's blunders as tarnishing the city government's reputation, not only among whites, but also to some degree among blacks. City council president Anita J. Ponder took the results to show that "we still have some work to do on race relations." Ellis himself lamented the persistent separation, noting, "There are exceptions, but we still have two separate societies here." Also, not surprisingly, some preferred not to deal with the subject. Shirley Miller told reporter Thomas Krause she did not like to talk about race, adding, "It causes trouble."[58]

A look beyond perceptions about race to hard demographic data points up even harder realities for black life chances in twenty-first century Macon. Between 1990 and 1999 almost three-quarters (74.86 percent) of all black births were to unwed mothers. This compares to just under one-fifth (19.57 percent) of all white births. Such a comparison figures prominently in continued negative white feelings toward African Americans, especially in a Bible Belt city like Macon. Even in these more secular times, many white Maconites, like others across America, often view unwed births as signs of sexual immorality and irresponsibility. Ultimately, the black community will have to make progress in reducing this statistic.[59]

Citing similar figures for out of wedlock births in Bibb and neighboring counties, Charles Richardson editorialized on the problem in early 2003. "What it says to me," he surmised, "is that many black women no longer believe that having a child by themselves is a bad thing. They don't realize that, most likely, their child will be raised in a situation where they will have access to just half of the time, energy and resources of a child in a two-parent family. That they are continuing the pattern of generational poverty that is a precursor to low educational attainment, crime and drug abuse." He noted that by 1998 only about a third of 1,222 out-of-wedlock births were to teenage mothers, suggesting to him that the African-American community now viewed raising children without fathers as acceptable. "Fathers are being let off the responsibility hook, and as a community we've seen it so many times that it's become OK," he complained. Then he wondered aloud whether African-American pastors had challenged their congregations on this problem or capitulated to it. Calling on pastors to take up a comforting but prophetic word, he concluded, "If we don't quickly figure a way to change our norms back to where having babies is a two-person affair, the wheel of generational poverty will continue to turn and crush the black community."[60]

A good deal of the division between whites and blacks in America today arises out of disagreement on the dominant white perception that the victories of the civil rights movement effectively leveled the playing field in America. White conservatives believe that America has more or less become a colorblind society, except for those all-too-frequent occasions when blacks get preferential treatment in affirmative action policies. Jim Lee, an Democratic member of city council who has not voted for a Democratic presidential nominee since Lyndon Johnson, commented that the Constitution "guarantees equal opportunity, but it does not guarantee everybody success whether they earn it or not." Liberals like Ted Kennedy and Jesse Jackson, he argued, may have excused personal irresponsibility and led many to lives of dependence, but "if they wanted to achieve and wanted to work for what they got, and didn't want to sit back and wait for somebody to give it to them whether they earned it or not, the opportunity was there for them to do that." Despite this hard-line approach, Lee has a reputation for color-blind work for his constituents and won his last election over two black candidates in a ward that is some 60 percent African American.[61]

Thirty-year-old F. Stebin Horne III, a recently-elected Republican member of city council, agrees. Acknowledging that "problems of race are real," he argues that the playing is level in a legal sense. "Blacks are understanding that now there is so much opportunity out there and so many opportunities are being opened up to them, and the only thing that gets in the way of that now are those who choose to abuse it and use it for their own personal agendas." He remains highly critical of reverse discrimination and "black leaders who abuse race for personal agendas." While generally blaming an earlier generation of white and black political leaders in Macon who too often engaged in racial politics, Horne also admitted that in his own time on the council some of his black colleagues bore a heavier burden of blame: "[E]xposing myself to race relations, I've seen it only abused by the black leaders who I've worked with." Horne's colleague on the council Cole Thomason and County Commissioner Charles W. Bishop share the view of an essentially level playing field. While admitting that blacks still experience roadblocks in "certain corporate arenas," Thomason cites college affirmative action policies as, in Bishop's words, "instances where it [the playing field] may be even tilted."[62]

In stark contrast to these views, common to whites all across the nation, a large majority of African Americans believe that racial inequality persists in Macon, as it does in the nation at large. Of twenty-five black Maconites interviewed for this book, none were willing to say the playing field of equal opportunity is level in America or Macon. In addition, recently 392 students enrolled in Social Science courses at Macon State College participated in an opinion poll on race relations in Macon. White students were four times more likely (24 percent) than African Americans (6 percent) to answer that the playing field was "just about level. Fifty-two percent of whites saw the field slightly or greatly tilted toward whites, compared with 85 percent of blacks. Conversely, whites were *twelve* times more likely (24 percent) to than blacks (2 percent) to answer that the playing field is either slightly or greatly tilted toward blacks. (See appendix for complete results of this poll.) Blacks thus believe that the nation remains color conscious, and still gives privilege to whites, and thus they generally call for the continuation of affirmative action. Statistical evidence of racial inequality from the US Census shows clearly that the playing field in Macon far from level and that the city is not yet colorblind. [63]

For example, in 1992 a *Macon Telegraph* article revealed that black infant mortality in Bibb County was nearly twice that of white infant mortality. Between 1990 and 1999 that comparison held steady, with 20.58 dying per every thousand black births and 10.82 deaths per every thousand white births. Thus a black baby born in Bibb County is twice as likely to die in its first year than a white baby. Although some might attribute this statistic to perceived weaknesses in black nurturing such as more physically abusive parenting styles, another statistic makes that assumption questionable. Blacks have more twice as many babies born with low birth weights than white Maconites. Sociologists generally consider this statistic as a sign of the overall health of a population. Between 1990 and 1999 low birth-weight babies composed 14.51 percent of all black births, while among white Maconites such babies constituted only 7.22 percent of all white births.[64]

Once black Maconites survive infancy, their chances of economic success are significantly below white chances. Thirty-four percent of all black households have annual earnings of $15,000 or less, compared with 12 percent of all white households. Thus a black Maconite is 22 percent more likely than a white Maconite to be at the bottom of the economic scale. At the other end of the economic ladder, white households earning $200,000 or more made up 1.8 percent of all white households, while blacks with such earnings constituted .49 percent of all black households. While figures naturally show that only a small sliver of white or black households earn this much, they show nonetheless that whites are more than three times more likely than blacks to find themselves in the uppermost income bracket.[65] In 2000, according to the US Census, median household income for whites in Bibb County was $44,736, compared to $23,110 for black households. Black per capita income was $12,414, compared to more than twice that ($25,499) for whites. By comparison, nationally black per capita income in 2002 was $14,953.[66]

Nationally, the poverty and unemployment rates for blacks are much more severe than for whites. In 2002, across the United States 23 percent of African Americans lived at or below the poverty line, compared with only 8 percent of whites. Figures for Bibb County in 2000 were even more dismal, with blacks (31.5 percent) more than four times more likely to live in poverty than whites (7.4 percent).[67] As for national comparisons in unemployment rates, in 2002 blacks (10.9 percent) were more than twice as likely to be unemployed as whites

(5.05 percent). In Bibb County the differential was even greater, with black unemployment at 8.92 percent, compared to 2.47 percent for whites. Thus, in 2000 blacks were more than three times more likely than white Maconites to be unemployed.[68]

Beyond these statistics are the anecdotes of discrimination that African Americans in Macon continue to experience despite marked improvements since the civil rights era. Attorney Brenda Youmas told of a client with a master's degree who sued a manufacturing company in Macon for paying her substantially less than a comparably educated and experienced white worker. Youmas, who also serves on the city council, found it impossible to find a position in any white law firm in Macon when she graduated from Mercer's Law School. She noted in 2004 that it is *still* difficult for black law students to find jobs in white firms in Macon, citing only one example to the contrary. Blacks with college degrees in general, she points out, have difficulty finding jobs in Macon and often have to move to Atlanta to find work.

In addition, observing many juvenile cases in her practice, she notes that young white offenders are often turned over to their parents with charges dropped, while black offenders more often find themselves in jail and in court. Along with Municipal Judge William C. Randall, Youmas notes that, Macon has no black superior or state court judges, unique for a Georgia city of its size. Randall argued that Governor Roy Barnes was poised to appoint him until a delegation from the city prevailed upon him to change his mind.[69]

African Americans continue to receive shabby treatment in stores and shops around the city. Charles Richardson tells the story of being followed around by a clerk at the Belk-Matthews department store for "shopping while black" and scruffily dressed. The clerk appeared shocked when Richardson presented a Gold MasterCard to pay for his items. Ella Carter, the principal of Northeast High School, had been trying on clothes in a downtown store for twenty minutes when the clerk offered coffee to two white patrons who had just entered. Offended, she asked the speechless young clerk why she had not made the same offer to her. Macon State College psychology professor Myra Jackson is often annoyed at grocery stores where long lines of black customers wait at the cash register. Only when a white customer gets in line, she notes, are additional registered opened up.[70]

Catherine Meeks finds the arts community very segregated: "I go to the symphony and I'm the only black person in Porter Auditorium, and I wonder, 'Are we ever going to get past this?' ... where I would be the only black there and nobody would make eye contact with me." Others complain that Macon Little Theater rarely cast blacks or put on productions that might be of specific interest to black Maconites. James Louis Bumpus, pastor of the Tremont Temple Baptist Church, cites as contemporary examples not being able to have a pizza delivered to homes in black neighborhoods or not being able to go to the bank that's on the edge of the neighborhood, and open a checking account."[71]

Former real estate agent Robert L. Scott, Jr., cited banks refusing to make housing loans to his African-American clients. He speculated also about limits on business loans to blacks.[72] Willie J. Shuler's experience in establishing his Compu-Print Company was a case in point. Arriving in Macon in 1990, Shuler built up his reputation in the computer field, despite wary looks from white clients who did not expect a young black man to have such expertise. But he found it difficult to secure a $300,000 loan to open his own business. He described the process: "They were asking me for stuff that I didn't have. I hadn't got to that point yet. And I've talked to other small businessmen who were white that didn't have to go through that, who didn't have to have the things they asked me to have.... the collaterals, the credit history—I had the credit history, but they wanted an elaborate credit history.... How could I have $300,000 for collateral when I don't even have a business yet.... Even with an A+ credit history, I was denied."[73] On his third attempt, this time with a smaller bank, his loan was finally approved.

Related to Shuler's experience is the issue of higher interest or "subprime" loans. In 2002 a study by the Washington, DC-based Center for Community Change found that Macon ranked twenty-ninth out of 331 American metropolitan areas in the percentage of high interest loans to African Americans. Of blacks who received loans in Macon, 57 percent were "subprime" loans with high interest. In addition, the study showed that blacks in Macon were slightly more than three times more likely to receive high interest loans than whites. Nationally, the study found consistent disparities "to borrowers of color at all income levels," raising questions as to whether "factors other than risk alone" account for such disparities.[74]

Most Maconites, black or white, remain oblivious to these statistical comparisons or anecdotes. Even if they were made aware of them, most of their eyes would glaze over or they would re-interpret them in accord with their own perceptions or even prejudices. How then do whites and blacks in Macon feel about race relations at the beginning of a new century?

CONTEMPORARY RACIAL FEELINGS

Since 1986, the Martin Luther King, Jr. holiday has afforded Macon and the nation a regular and ritualized opportunity to reflect on issues of racial justice. As in all rituals, civil as well as religious, King observances can be reduced to merely going through the motions. As surely one can entertain oneself by counting the number of times the word "dream" is used in a typical King service, we can also expect the local newspaper to run a story that gives some variation of the now clichéd theme—American has come a long way since King called America to dream his dream, but we have a long way to go before that dream comes true. Indeed we have. Indeed we do.

So in 2002 the *Macon Telegraph* ran its obligatory article, seeking out the opinion of prominent and not-so-prominent Maconites. How fares King's dream in Macon today? Seventy-eight-year-old Joe Frank Bell, now a resident of nearby Lizella, grew up in Macon. For him much of Macon's old-style prejudices, like the firm social etiquette that governed how blacks and white talked to or walked past each other, have disappeared. Bell thinks the major problem is that young blacks squander the opportunities that King won for them. "In this day," he observed, "don't nobody keep you down. You keep yourself down." Gail King said her friends could not tolerate the fact that she works for an African American. Nevertheless, she believed other parents should follow her example and teach racial acceptance to their children, noting, "If you find somebody prejudiced, you know they were taught that." Director of Macon's Tubman African American Museum Carey Pickard is regularly approached by reporters, whom he regularly tells that there is much left to do: "Blacks still struggle to fight drugs and crime, to gain equal educational and economic opportunities, and to be treated fairly in sentencing by the courts. Macon is not what it was. But neither is Macon what it could be."[75]

The following year brought forth another article, which quoted Mayor C. Jack Ellis as saying economic progress among blacks is as important to making the "Dream" come true as political representation. Affirmative action is still important, he argues, for providing blacks greater access to higher education. Republicans Don Layfield and Calder Clay thought otherwise. Layfield argued, "You don't want to be practicing discrimination to end discrimination. It emphasizes a division, rather than a cohesion. Having run unsuccessfully to represent Macon in the US House, with a critical eye focused on affirmative action, Clay opined, "I do believe that discrimination still exists in our society, and I mean both ways." Once again, the Reverend Lonzy Edwards blasted Macon's unwillingness or inability to talk about race matters: "It's hard to talk about, so we don't talk about it."[76]

Race matters in Macon and Maconites do talk about race—but usually not in the same room at the same time. And since the beginning of the new century Maconites have had a sense of deja vu of certain race-related blasts from the past. One of these was the volatile issue left over from Zell Miller's 1992–1993 effort to change the Georgia state flag. The matter was taken up again in 2001 by Miller's successor, Governor Roy Barnes, who worked the Democratic Georgia House to change the flag that greatly minimized the Confederate flag's visibility. Changing the flag galvanized large numbers of angry white voters, who lined up behind 2002 Republican gubernatorial candidate, Sonny Perdue. While Barnes campaigned for re-election by defending his flag decision and changing the subject, Perdue promised to hold a referendum on the state flag if elected. The promise was the most significant factor in Perdue's being elected Georgia's first Republican governor since Reconstruction. During the campaign bumper stickers around Macon carried a Confederate-Georgia flag atop the golden dome of the state capital and a caption that read, "I Have a Dream." On election day large numbers of white Maconites voted for Perdue, whose prize was a new Atlanta address. Barnes nursed his wounds with conscience intact and a "Profile in Courage" Award from Caroline Kennedy and the JFK Library. Forty-five miles away in Cochran, Georgia, a white storekeeper spoke for many whites in Macon and Georgia, saying, "I don't know of anybody that voted for Roy Barnes."[77]

The other issue that caused even conservative commentator Bill O'Reilly to "look away" from Dixie was the news that in the South Georgia city of Butler, the Taylor County Board of Education was still allowing high school seniors to have separate, privately-sponsored proms for its white students, along with a mixed prom for both groups of students. In a rare instance of agreement, the editors of the *Telegraph* agreed with O'Reilly's criticism of the practice, but many Maconites wrote in to defend Taylor County's honor. An editorial by Charles Richardson took on a number of the Taylor defenders. These were privately sponsored parties, rather than a county sponsored prom. As a private party, the party givers determine the guest list. "All races still enjoy freedom of association," argued another writer. Most disturbing were those who used biblical arguments to condone the practice. One Maconite wrote, "Even the creator of mankind segregated the different races and nationalities to individual countries and principalities." Another cited the example of Jesus, who chose all of his disciples from among his own race and had he "dated, danced and married, we can be sure it would have been with a lady of his own race."

In another letter, another defender cited the existence of the NAACP, the United Negro College Fund, Black Entertainment Television, and Miss Black America as acceptable expressions of black heritage. Whites, he argued, should have the same opportunity to embrace their heritage. For his part, Richardson simply wondered why, in the years since separate, private proms were devised as a way to keep black boys from dancing with white girls, or vice versa, no one had ever risen up to declare the segregated proms morally wrong. To those who continued to use the Bible to defend such racism, Richardson could only shake his head in disbelief.[78]

Beyond these two divisive issues, many Maconites addressed matters they viewed as troubling the racial waters. Bennie Stephens, one of the first three blacks to venture into the halls of Mercer University, saw at least one that made contemporary racial realities worse than the old days. He observed, "Whereas we used to say a whole generation of whites have got to live and die before we can get along, maybe now we're looking at a time when a whole generation of blacks and whites have to live and die before we can get along." Barbara Hawthorne, a black mother, launched a broadside against a black community she saw as its own worst enemy. Fed up with hearing "how blacks are treated by the 'white race,'" she denounced fellow black parents for foisting their problem children on the schools, while leaving them at home without moral supervision. "Some of these black men today," she complained, "feel as though they are not a man if they can't help produce more babies than there are men in the armed forces." A contemporary Mercer student is disturbed by both whites who continue to view blacks as inferior and blacks "who feel the white population owes them something," but neither of which make any effort to cross the great racial divide. He adds: "I am sorry for the oppression many minorities (not only blacks) have experienced in the past, but if true diversity and unification is to be attained, the finger pointing must stop."[79]

Others lean less on rhetoric than on retelling some of what they have seen and heard. Korey Johnson recalled that a large number of his white classmates at Westside High School played hooky to protest the beginning of Black History Month. A newcomer who arrived in Macon in the mid-1990s discovered a game some of her co-workers played to amuse themselves when business was slow. Looking at birth announcements in the *Telegraph*, they challenge a colleague to "Name that race" and call out names like Latonia or Kaneshia. Having come to Macon from central Virginia, she is surprised at such blatant bigotry in the workplace. Longer-term Maconites find other employment concerns. Charlene Goodwin has taught in the dental hygiene program at Macon State College since 1977. When her first black student completed all the requirements and received her license in the mid-1980s, she experienced great difficulty finding a position. Dentists who interviewed her indicated they could not hire her because they knew their patients would not accept a black hygienist.[80]

When Scott Peaster was interviewed for a job at a freight-shipping warehouse, he found an older black man in the waiting room. Striking up a conversation, both applicants waited for the white interviewer to show up. His interview lasted five minutes, after which he was told to wait outside the office, while he interviewed the other candidate. Three minutes later the interviewer came out and told Scott he had the job. As he and the other applicant left the office, Scott asked him why his interview had been so short. "He told me blacks always start trouble and slow down the production," came the answer. Scott then advised him to get a lawyer and sue the company. Eventually, both Scott and his new friend were hired, said Peaster, "and we take care of each other at work." The hiring agent, however, was fired.[81]

Another student had taken a job waiting tables at the local Red Lobster Restaurant. On one occasion a family of ten sat at her station, but when she approached the table, the father commented that he did not wish to be served by a "Negro." While he continued making racial remarks, his daughter apologized and tried to no avail to quiet her father down. Deciding to discuss the problem with her boss, she accompanied him back to the table. He informed the man that in his restaurant employees were subject to dismissal if they made any racial remarks. Deciding to apply that same policy to customers as well as employees, the manager asked the family to leave. Both the family and the manager were from Macon.[82]

Twenty-year-old Renata Mathews complained that in her experience prejudice has reversed. More African Americans her age have shown bigoted attitudes toward whites than vice versa. On one occasion a middle-aged black woman approached the counter where a group of whites were placing their orders. Sidling up to Mathews, the black woman muttered under her breath, "I hate white folks. I can't stand them. They think they better than everybody else." Frustrated with her own people, she makes a pointed contrast: "In my twenty years of life I have never experienced any type of racism from any other person towards me." A white student at Macon State College believes "we all bleed one color, red," but tires of hearing about civil rights history and "racism against the blacks." She adds, "We are now living in the twenty-first century and now whites are also experiencing the racism."[83]

Joyce Grubbs works in Jack Ellis's office as the mayor's receptionist. After growing up in Chicago and having lived in Hawaii and Warner Robins, she has lived in Macon for six years. Compared to the other places she has lived, she would give Macon a D on its race relations report card. She illustrates the reasons for this low grade by telling of a particular white woman who calls the mayor's office every week to complain about blacks—she calls them "those people"—who have recently moved into her neighborhood. Their children play on the sidewalks in front of her house and she demands that the mayor do something to keep them in their own yards. "They don't know how to control themselves appropriately," says the woman, which Grubbs takes to mean that they are louder than she thinks they should be.[84]

These stories sample the many new and unexpected turns that racial prejudice often takes in these latter days. The same stories can often reveal contradictory forms of racism. Hope for healing and racial reconciliation remain buried beneath new ways of reacting to old animosities. Two final anecdotes reveal that ancient forms of racism still lurk in the darkness, occasionally made visible by an unexpected light. At a church day care center in South Macon, Jessica Annis was tending the children when one of the few black boys in the group accidentally brushed against a white girl in her care. Annis found herself speechless when the three-year-old recoiled, whirled, and said, "I don't like black boys. Tell him not to touch me!"

Then one summer day in 2002, Chamoya Faulks, a student at Macon State College, saw a similar example at the other end of the life cycle. She had just arrived when a short, sprightly, elderly white man entered the store where she worked. A regular customer, he began to regale the employees with stories and light banter. This time, somehow, his demeanor was different. The only African American in the store, Faulks stood off to one side within earshot, but out of the man's line of vision. On this occasion the customer was unusually annoyed. He began a "friendly" rant about what's wrong with this country. "United States is goin' down," he asserted. "And you know who's takin' us down? It's the Jews, the Catholics, and the niggers!" Not quite believing his ears, the dumbfounded manager could only ask, "Really?" "Yep," the man continued, "Them niggers taken over just about everything. You reckon they'll learn their lesson if we hang enough of 'em?" Then the man paid his bill, said his goodbyes, and walked out of the Macon Christian Bookstore, where he always came to buy Sunday school material for his church.[85]

Epilogue:
Prescriptions for Racial Healing

At this point in such an investigation, historians usually spend a few pages looking back over their work with a view toward making some insightful generalizations or drawing some useful conclusions. Some general statements are indeed proffered, but in this case it is done more out of convention than conviction. This is based on the feeling that from a historian writing about the city in which he lives a look to the future may be more beneficial than setting forth some generalizations about the century past.

Nevertheless, a quick review of Macon's racial history going back to Booker T. Washington suggests a handful of minor observations. First, surveying an entire century of black-white relations in Macon reveals that there were some important heroic figures who pushed the city uphill toward a summit of racial equality. They were both black and white. They were both famed and unnamed. They did their unpopular work early in the century and they did it late. Second, the story also reveals, indeed requires, some villains—figures who made the journey toward racial justice longer and bumpier than necessary. Here, frankly, they become more one-sidedly white, as it is impossible to unearth blacks who did not in one way or another hope to see what King called the "Dream" come true. Third, none of the heroes were fully heroic and none of the villains were devoid of some heroism. Fourth, African Americans carried the heaviest burden and traveled farther, but there could have been no victory, pyrrhic or otherwise, without winning progressive whites to their cause. Finally, black-white relations in Macon were shaped at different times by different forces, sometimes local, sometimes statewide, sometimes national or even international, and sometimes two or more of these in combination.

More substantively, this survey of a century's impact on blacks and whites in Macon reinforces the importance of those shaping influences mentioned at the outset. The *Macon Telegraph* has dominated the public media in the city and on balance has been a progressive influence. This was especially true under the leadership of publisher W. T. Anderson, whose editorials combated the worst elements of Southern racist radicalism, particularly his criticisms of lynching and the Klan. At crucial times, however, the editorial voice of the *Telegraph* remained more silent than certain events warranted. During the integration era, under the leadership of Bert Struby, the paper took a more conservative turn and did not challenge white Macon's turn from the public school system and toward private education.

In fits and starts Macon's branch of the NAACP became a central voice for African Americans beginning early in the twentieth century, but more urgently and successfully since the 1940s. Building on the work of the national organization, the NAACP became a local force for change with the 1962 bus boycott. Along with the black First Baptist Church of Macon, it also gave rise to Macon's first black mayoral candidate, the Reverend Julius Hope in 1975. To be sure, it provided the training ground for Macon's black political class and was also a center of support for the city's first black mayor, C. Jack Ellis.

Overlapping at times with the NAACP were various interracial efforts led in 1930s and '40s by the Macon Interracial Committee, a local extension of the Atlanta-based Commission on Interracial Cooperation (CIC). Central to the success of the Macon Interracial Committee was the work of Louise Harrold and other members of the Association of Southern Women for the Prevention of Lynching. By the 1950s, after the CIC had melded into the Southern Regional Council, the Macon Interracial Council evolved into the Macon Council on Human Relations and remained the singular venue for interracial discussions in the city until its demise in the 1970s. Since the 1980s Macon's interracial efforts took a different turn with Father Richard Keil's founding of the Harriet Tubman African American Museum and occasional efforts by the churches.

From such a base of interracial activity, white progressives like Joseph Hendricks, Kelly Barnett, Ray Brewster of Mercer University, and Thomas Gossett and Carl Bennett of Wesleyan College, did courageous work to push Macon faster toward racial justice. Their work also points up the important contributing role of the city's institutions of higher learning. Mercer in particular has distinguished itself with exemplary leaders like professor G. McLeod Bryan and presidents Rufus C. Harris and R. Kirby Godsey. Since 1979 Godsey's leadership has developed stronger ties between the university and the city, has resisted the impulse toward white flight to remain in the central city, and contributes to the revitalization of downtown Macon through the Mercer Center for Community Development. While the university has never been the prophetic voice that McLeod Bryan hoped for, as the first black students at Mercer will readily attest, on balance it has nudged Macon to take larger strides toward racial harmony and justice.

Non-local factors also shaped the lives of blacks and whites and their interrelations in Macon. No locality develops in a vacuum, especially since the dawn of mass communications. Statewide, national, and even international events powerfully shaped racial matters in Macon at crucial times in the twentieth century. A turn-of-the-century cultural negrophobia engulfed Georgia and Macon, as it did the entire South and most of the North, and largely spawned the Southwide hysteria to disfranchise black voters. Events in Europe and the Allies' war against Hitler gradually helped white Maconites and other Americans clearly see the irony of fighting Nazi racism with a racism of our own. Even without a conflagration of violence of its own, like all of America, Macon was greatly influenced by the civil rights movement and the South's "massive resistance" to it. Racial riots in Watts and around the nation during the late 1960s helped create the "Reagan Revolution," which has lured many Maconites and many other Southern Democrats into the Republican Party, with important ramifications for black-white relations.

The overall theme of this study has been a certain continuity that has characterized relations between white and black Maconites as an "unutterable separation." As a century has come and gone this unutterability has changed its meaning from being unspeakably tragic during the early "nadir" years to being simply unspeakable, something too few citizens wish to discuss. Thus racial tensions are still the elephant in the room that African-American and white Maconites, when they are together, pretend not to notice.

Beyond this continuity, this history shows the undeniability of change. Whatever tensions still persist, no one can convincingly argue that nothing has changed. Most of that change has indeed been for the better. Change, however, is not always positive. The editorial voice of the *Macon Telegraph*, so potent in the anti-lynching and anti-Klan efforts, became more muted during the civil rights movement and virtually silent in the face of white flight from the city and the public schools. Happily, change can also mean growth toward wider human values. In 1949 a local lawyer named William Augustus Bootle represented Vineville residents seeking to stop the building of a swimming pool for blacks near their homes. In the arguments over that issue, one prominent black Maconite asserted he was not aware that Mr. Bootle "ever did [anything] for the advancement of Negroes." This assessment would be significantly revised when *Judge* Bootle ordered the desegregation of the University of Georgia (1961) and the Bibb County public schools (1970). Today, the Federal Courthouse where he presided in Macon is named after him and he is universally revered as a civil rights hero.

So much for concluding observations. But since change *is* possible, even undeniable, and since it can go in progressive or regressive directions, some practical suggestions may be in order. No reader who has made the journey from Emory Speer and Booker T. Washington to C. Jack Ellis with the story's theme in mind can easily emerge without giving voice to the title of one of Martin Luther King's last books, penned after the victories of the Civil Rights Act of 1964 and the 1965 Voting Rights Act—"Where do we go from here?" It seems unimaginable that one could traverse a hundred years of "unutterable separation" without issuing the logical challenge: You've described the disease, but can you suggest a cure? We know what is broken, but how do we fix it? To lead readers through ten decades of persistent and unutterable racial separation only to leave them without an action plan for racial reconciliation would be to surrender to despair and hopelessness.

One can, however, call the glass half full rather than half empty, choosing to build on the positive signs and move in hope toward the twin goals of both racial equality *and* reconciliation. To venture toward hope in these final pages, however, requires the author to exchange hats. Perhaps the historian's hat must be replaced by that of the preacher. In truth, these hats are very similar. Both the historian and the preacher study old documents, try to understand and explain them, and in the end draw from them some lessons for contemporary life. Further, both the preacher and the historian seek to help persons learn from the past and avoid its pitfalls. Both the preacher and the historian are in essence teachers, and both are shaped by powerful reformist impulses. They both hope, and at least one of them prays, that their work will make something better. Perhaps the major difference between them is that the historian has no "Thus says the Lord," no divine action, and no certainty that his or her "sermons" will convert the sinner. The historian cannot say what God has done or might do. Like the preacher, however, the historian must suggest what human beings can do or even ought to do to move his or her society from the actual toward to the ideal. The publication of this book finds that particular city struggling to find its footing lest it slip into an abyss of non-community. Peter C. Brown, director of the Mercer University Center for Community Development, put it bluntly:

> The communities that have developed the capacity to work across ethnic lines, across social class lines, across historical divisions, across different levels of education are going to move forward. They're going to be successful. The ones that can't do that, the ones that play the old special interest politics—"I've got mine or I've got my street paved in my neighborhood"—are gonna lose in this incredibly fluid global economy.... And in this community we haven't developed the capacities to do that.[1]

Macon's economic and social well-being depends upon overcoming black-white tensions. If Macon can bridge this chasm, perhaps there is hope for the rest of the nation. So having indirectly experienced twentieth century Macon's unutterable separation, we ask, "How then can the black-white chasm be bridged? How can the untterability of race relations be broken in Macon?

Before talking, however, a different way of thinking is very much in order. For half of the last century the Reverend Fred Shuttlesworth has toiled heroically as a civil rights leader and local pastor. His exploits as the central figure in the black freedom struggle in Birmingham, Alabama, made him perhaps the most unsung hero of the movement. Like his more famous colleague, Martin Luther King, Jr., in mass meetings or in his statements to the press, Shuttlesworth had a collective message for white Americans: It is time that you as a people, represented by your government, take action to "live out the true meaning of your creed" that all men and women are created equal. He and the entire civil rights movement called upon whites to take some corporate (meaning as a body and using political means) action to move American society toward racial equality. The message was more than merely individual, telling white Americans they should overcome racial bigotry and learn to accept black Americans as equals. Such individual action was useful, even indispensable, for getting to some semblance of equality, but political action was necessary to effect any lasting change.

In his black congregations, however, as with most evangelical preachers, Shuttlesworth's message focused more on individual responsibility. Addressing his African-American congregations, Shuttlesworth's prophetic fire burned just as fervently as in his mass meeting addresses, but his fiery spirituality was trained on stirring up the individuals in his pastoral care to bear up under their personal responsibilities. As a prophet of personal responsibility, Shuttlesworth addressed not only ethereal spiritual matters, but often spoke in earthy terms about very mundane responsibilities. His church sermons pointedly called on his congregants to live disciplined lives. Along with calling them to faith in Jesus, he regularly admonished them to take baths, discipline their children, educate themselves, develop a strong work ethic, and avoid out-of-wedlock pregnancies.[2]

By joining these two emphases, Shuttlesworth's message was holistic. In this it reflected one of the distinguishing marks of African American evangelicalism, which has more effectively balanced otherworldly and this-worldly concerns than its white counterparts. It avoided the "spirituality of the church," a notion by which white ministers in the antebellum South restricted themselves to dealing with spiritual, rather than social or political, matters. It also avoided the polarization of current dialogue on racial problems in America. Conservatives have typically called upon the "pathological" black community to exercise individual responsibility, while liberals have typically said that America must take corporate or political action. By contrast, Shuttlesworth's example suggests that the prescription for racial healing in Macon and the nation at large must be a holistic blend of both individual responsibility *and* corporate action. Any attempt to address black-white relations in Macon or throughout America would be wise to follow this example and make both emphases to both groups.

One key reason for doing so is that such a holistic approach is the only one that matches the holistic reality of human nature. Paradoxically, human beings are individuals who must live in community in order to be truly healthy. Human beings are not mere individuals, nor are they just "social creatures"; they are both. This paradox is what biblical scholar Frank Stagg called the "polarities of human existence."[3] This dichotomy is a given element in our humanity. Thus, to think rightly about the nature of humanity requires recognizing both our individual and corporate natures. To deny or ignore either human individuality or human sociality is to lose an essential element of human nature and to misconceive the kind of beings we humans are.

Beyond this theoretical or even theological reason for a holistic approach to black-white relations, there is also a practical one. Whites in America have often emphasized individualism, rugged or otherwise, as the central element of the "American mind." Whites have continually been taught to see persons as individuals whose personal effort could lead to success in life. Thus they have not often seen the societal nature of racism embedded in our culture and the institutions of society. They see racism as mere prejudice, as exclusively a matter of individual acts and attitudes. Blacks as well as whites, they argue, must as individuals be tolerant of other individuals. Whites also see individual responsibility as the answer to whatever inequality may still exist for African Americans. They argue that the playing field is now level, and all that is necessary is for African Americans to succeed is for them to develop their individual responsibility and their work ethic. These understandings are accurate as far as they go, but they do not address institutional or cultural racism.

At the same time, some civil rights leaders have so overemphasized the corporate responsibility of white America that, unlike Fred Shuttlesworth, they seemed to many whites to have forgotten individual responsibility altogether. As a result the "civil rights community" has run the danger of relegating African Americans to permanent victim status, always complaining that white America has done and continues to do them wrong.

Taking an either-or approach in effect lets either whites or blacks off the hook. An individualistic message suggests blacks are solely responsible for their own lot in life. If they would work hard, as have Asian Americans, they could progress economically and harmonious race relations could be restored. An exclusively corporate or political approach suggests that white America is solely responsible for racial inequality. If white Americans would eliminate their racism, reduce their self-interest, and share power with African Americans, all would be right with the world. Both approaches miss the practical reality that both sides are typically at fault when a relationship breaks down. Any successful effort to repair America's or Macon's racial relationships must holistically address both individual and corporate (political) responsibility for both white and black America.

Applying this model to black-white relations in America would require several realizations. First, there must be candid and regular dialogue. Despite reservations and evasions Maconites must overcome the unutterability of the problem. Despite "race fatigue," they must talk about race and do so in the same room. Whites must get over it—namely their reluctance to hear more discussions of race and history. Creede Hinshaw, pastor of the overwhelmingly-white Mulberry Street United Methodist Church, addressed this problem in an interview:

> Whites are really not interested in talking about race, period. As far as their concerned, there really *are* no problems, and if blacks would just quit talking about things, everything would be fine.... "Quit making everything a racial issue," is commonly stated. That's the traditional white view.... Anything that [seems] too confrontational would drive white folk away. I feel for African Americans because if you just play by the rules of the white game, you never get anything done, and if you jump up and down and say things are bad, then they leave.[4]

Indeed, many whites who believe America is now or ought to be color-blind seem to view African-American neighbors as the racists if they even mention racism as a continuing problem. This perspective perpetuates what Councilman Richard Hutto described as "two armed camps, people who don't trust the other side." Just after joining the council, he attended a Christmas party where he related the story of colleague reneging on a promise to vote a certain way. "Well, that's what you have to expect from blacks," came the reply from a party-goer who looked surprised when Hutto shot back, "Maybe so, but I'm talking about a white Republican." The exchange was naturally premised on the assumption that it is safe to talk about race in an all-white group.[5]

Like most family conflicts, this deep, painful rift in the American family cannot mended without a long, candid conversation in which both parties truly desire reconciliation. On this point, many African Americans not only wonder how long they will have to wait for equality, but also why, as Councilwoman Brenda Youmas asks, "the blacks have to initiate it and be the forgiving ones. It's never from the other side."[6] In Macon as throughout the nation, let the conciliatory conversation begin. But given the fact that whites historically initiated the relations between Africans and themselves, it is incumbent on whites, who still have most of the economic and social influence in Macon, to initiate it.

Macon's history provides plenty of precedent. At various times during the twentieth century, white and black Maconites formed interracial meetings or organizations to help black and white individuals get to know one another. Typically, however, those meetings were ad hoc, crisis-driven affairs. An exception to this rule was the Macon Council on Human Relations, which from the 1930s to the late 1970s met regularly to foster dialogue. But other, larger efforts of this sort have usually fizzled after public attention was diverted from the crises that sparked them by other events. Nowadays, every King Holiday observance includes some call for renewed dialogue. Even Mayor Jack Ellis's Community Diversity Committee, having begun with good intentions, has so far failed to carry through to become a regular, high profile factor in the life of the city. Maconites can and should find ways of building on these established structures to expand and deepen racial dialogue in their city.

There have been other suggestions. In May 2003, the Reverend Lonzy Edwards, a voice in the wilderness who has often tried to nudge a reluctant city toward more honest dialogue, issued another of his many appeals. On this particular occasion Edwards wrote a column for the *Macon Telegraph* entitled, "Race and Reconciliation: Can It Happen in the Here and Now?" calling upon the cities Christian churches to take the lead in such efforts. "As our churches go," he argued, "so will our communities." Edwards recommended, among other things, that churches establish "sister church" relationships whereby the congregations yoke themselves together for regular meetings for fellowship and joint mission projects. There is no real reason why such "sister congregation" relationships could not include synagogues and mosques. In a related idea, Michael Bell, pastor of the Greater St. Stephens Baptist Church in Fort Worth, Texas, suggests that white and black churches swap fifty to a hundred members for six months to a year. But such relationships, if taken seriously as a congregational priority, could foster dialogue and mutual understanding in many ways.[7]

Two other efforts could also be helpful. Given the threat of stagnation in the city, and the need for whites to initiate the process of reconciliation, it is well past time for Macon's white clergy to enter the fray. White ministerial timidity on the issue of race has long been documented by historians of the South and Southern religion. Macon's own history provides some crucial examples of courageous Protestant prophets like J. Rufus Moseley, W. Lowry Anderson, or George E. Clary in the 1930s or Walter Moore and Thomas Holmes in the civil rights era, whose ministries went beyond pious platitudes to push white Maconites toward racial brotherhood. The same must be said of Father Richard Keil and other priests at St. Peter Claver Catholic Church. As Paul Kivel has perceptively noted, racism is like a fire raging across our country. At times it flares up into a firestorm and at others it merely smolders, but all Americans are in varying degrees burned by it. Most importantly, Kivel argues, "Only justice can put out the fire."[8] Important as are individual relationships between blacks and whites, the smoldering racial tensions in Macon and in America will never be completely addressed without also dealing with the matter of racial or social justice. Social justice means more than "bringing criminals to justice" or punishments fitting crimes. In Judeo-Christian ethics social justice means fairness and a commitment to fix what human evil has broken. White ministers of the twenty-first century must address the questions of racial reconciliation *and* justice. They must also do so intentionally and regularly.

In addition, they should commit themselves to preaching a sermon on such matters on the Sunday nearest the Martin Luther King National Holiday, along with taking the initiative to participate in public events on the holiday itself. To do so may be controversial with their congregations, but the King Holiday has an unrivaled importance in the

African-American community. It has largely replaced blacks' earlier celebrations of Emancipation Day. Thus for the white clergy more fully to embrace the King Holiday will be a powerful sign of their interest in reconciliation. Likewise, African-American ministers and other leaders should take care not to view the King Holiday as the special preserve of the black community or church. As they plan their King Holiday activities, let them include whites on their programs and in the planning. Thus local efforts to celebrate King's birthday could become more than the African-American holiday it has become.

A second realization is that efforts toward reconciliation must go beyond dialogue between individuals to address unequal power relationships. Dialogue alone is insufficient. Dialogue is focused on helping white and black individuals learn to know, appreciate, and accept one another. This knowledge is crucial and requires an unswerving intentionality in order to happen—and happen it must. But human reality is collective and societal as well as individual. Dealing only with individual relationships leaves institutional or cultural racism untouched and intact. Dialogue alone does not deal with power and politics where inequality still stacks the deck against African Americans.

This fact reflects historical realities in the American South, where, even in the midst of Jim Crow, relationships between individual blacks and whites were often warm and loving. Whites have usually overestimated that warmth, because blacks, in unequal power relationships with whites, could not with impunity express their resentments. If whites only seek better individual relationships with blacks, without addressing their political and economic power advantage, black resentment cannot help but persist. They would almost inevitably be driven to the implication, "Sure, we can all get along…as long as we are willing to accept our disadvantaged place in American society."

Third, everything must be said and done within a context of repentance and forgiveness. This attitude need not be understood in any particularly Christian or even religious context. Mending a broken marital relationship requires one or both parties to say, "I'm sorry" and "I forgive you," no matter how secular they may be. Thus, during 350 years of shared history on this continent both whites and blacks have had ample opportunity to mistreat and distrust one another. Admittedly, because whites have had most of the power most of the time, whites have a greater burden and more for which to repent. That does not mean, however, that African Americans can avoid repentance of their own. They have, for example, at times over-generalized whites as "white devils." They have at times engaged in destructive and indiscriminate rioting (Watts, the King assassination, the Rodney King verdict). They are often overly sensitive to slights that may be more attributable to the growing coarseness or simple impoliteness of American society than to racial hatred. However understandable such reaction may have been, by acknowledging their wrongdoing in such episodes blacks can move the dialogue of repentance and forgiveness forward.

Fourth, real repentance requires sacrifices from both parties. There are many examples in all religions and in everyday life whereby penitents are called upon to fix that which their misdeeds have broken. If a philandering husband wishes to repent of his adultery, he must do more than simply say he is sorry; he must give up his mistress and all reminders of her. Since both parties are usually at fault when a marital relationship is broken, both parties must take responsibility, both must give and receive forgiveness, and both must take some sacrificial steps to mend the breach.

Fifth, white Americans must realize the continued existence and work toward eliminating "white privilege." This is a corporate reality that white Americans must come to understand in spite of their cultural predisposition toward individualism. Here is the weak link in current American race relations. Whites typically believe the Civil Rights Act of 1964 and the 1965 Voting Rights Act effectively leveled the playing field, and if it were not for the "reverse discrimination" of affirmative action, America would be a colorblind society. As a general rule, black Americans continue to feel the effects of inequality and discrimination and are frustrated and often enraged that whites cannot or will not acknowledge the privilege they still enjoy in American life.

In Macon, as across America, most whites allow anecdotes about occasional "reverse discrimination" to mask the steady, unrelenting reality that white skin still bestows advantages upon the individual Americans who have it. At the most basic level of life expectancy, a person randomly "thrown" into the world and landing in America with black skin is statistically likely to live 5.7 years less than a random white American—in Georgia the figure is 1.7 years.[9] On the basis of mere *quantity* of life, whites are advantaged in America, and much more so when it comes to quality of life. White Maconites are still privileged over blacks in every major economic index. This fact is also true in the United States as a whole.

As sociologist Thomas M. Shapiro and others have shown, when one looks beyond mere income differentials (which are startling enough) and compares racial differences in net worth (all accumulated financial assets minus all debt), the effects of generational opportunity are all the more dramatic. In 2000, the average net worth of white families was ten times that of black families ($81,000 to $8,000). Some 50 percent of white families have received head start assistance like college tuition payments or down payments on first homes from the accumulated wealth of their parents and grandparents. For black families this figure is 20 percent. In the 1990s, some 25 percent of white families inherited a financial legacy averaging $144,000 at the death of a parent or grandparent. Only 5 percent of black families received such inheritances, and those averaged only $42,000.[10]

When it comes to home ownership, the most important factor in attaining middle-class status, whites continue to benefit from past discrimination and current racism. According to a report by David Rusk, because of white flight and the habit of whites leaving neighborhoods that become more than 10 percent black, white families in America pay an average interest rate of 8.12 percent on home mortgages, compared to 8.44 percent for blacks. Over the life of a typical thirty-year loan, this higher interest would amount to paying an additional $11,750 in interest for the same house. Rusk also shows that in the largest 100 American cities the homes of white families are valued 18 percent higher than those of black families earning the same income. In Southern cities the differential was smaller at 11 percent, with white homes being appraised at $2.08 for every dollar of income. For black families earning the same income, the ratio is $1.85 for every dollar.[11]

In a recent column, Walter Williams dismissively attributed such advantages to hard work by whites' grandparents and great-grandparents.[12] While celebrating American individualism and a strong work ethic, this deliberately myopic perspective refuses to acknowledge the many local, state, and federal programs and policies that discriminated *for* white forebears and *against* black ancestors. Not even counting the head starts white families gained from generations of slavery and segregation, several federal programs specifically aided white families move into middle-class status. Among these was the 1862 Homestead Act, which granted 1.5 million families, almost all of them white, plots of up to 160 acres of land for a nominal fee and a promise to live on the land for five years and make improvements. Forty-six million Americans—nearly a quarter of the current adult population—are descended from Homestead Act recipients.[13]

The first generation of Social Security beneficiaries did not include those who worked in agricultural workers or domestic servants, the two vocations in which most blacks worked. Thus, unlike most whites, the grandparents of most of black families today had no retirement help from our government.[14] A number of programs after World War II helped white poverty rates decline from 66 percent in 1940 to 20 percent in 1960. Because blacks were rejected for military service during the war at a rate of 48 percent, compared to 28 percent for whites, fewer African Americans were eligible to benefit from the GI Bill. Among those black veterans who did gain from the Veterans Employment Service, most were placed in low-paying, unskilled jobs, 92 percent of which were filled by blacks. By contrast, 86 percent of the professional or managerial positions were filled by white veterans. As a result, median income for black veterans was 65 percent of white median income.[15]

Finally, federal programs provided access to new home ownership to returning veterans through Veterans Administration and Federal Housing Administration policies. In both agencies low-interest loan policies were color-coded. Blacks received only 2 percent of the $120 billion worth of new homes financed by the VA and FHA between 1934 and 1962. Those who did receive loans got them with higher interest rates and were restricted to poorer, predominantly black neighborhoods where their homes appreciated at much slower rates.[16]

Thus, before whites hail individual responsibility and their own bootstraps, while inveighing against government programs for blacks and other poor, it may be instructive to remember benefits *they* received from race-conscious government programs of the recent past. Paul Kivel's checklist of white benefits is long and includes the following:

—My ancestors were legal immigrants to this country when immigrants from Asia, South and Central America, or Africa were restricted.

—My ancestors came to the US of their own free will and never had to relocate unwillingly.

—I or my ancestors received federal farm subsidies, farm price supports, agricultural extension assistance, or other federal benefits.

—My parents or I went to racially segregated schools.

—I served in the military when it was still racially segregated, or achieved a rank where there were few people of color, or served in a combat situation where there were large numbers of people of color in dangerous combat positions.

—My ancestors took jobs in railroads, streetcars, construction, shipbuilding, wagon and coach driving, house painting, or any other occupation where blacks were excluded.

—I or my ancestors received job training in a program where there were few or no people of color.

—I or my ancestors worked or work in a job where people of color made less for doing comparable work or did more menial jobs.

—I have worked in a job where people of color were hired last or fired first.

—My parents were able to vote in any election they wanted without worrying about poll taxes, literacy requirements, or other forms of discrimination.[17]

For whites to recognize and acknowledge the past effects on both blacks *and on themselves* may very well be the most important step toward racial reconciliation Americans can take in the twenty-first century. By contrast, compared to benefits this extensive, whites who are "disadvantaged" by affirmative action or "reverse discrimination" have quite little to complain about. Frankly, to do so is comparable to someone with an ingrown toenail complaining to a person with a broken leg about how difficult it is to walk.

But beyond the statistical and economic advantages enjoyed by whites, they also enjoy unearned benefits of a cultural nature. Peggy McIntosh, professor of Women's Studies at Wellesley College, has explained both the meaning and specific examples of white privilege in an article called "Unpacking the Invisible Knapsack." Rather than viewing racism as merely individual acts of meanness against persons because of their race, she argues that racism must also be understood as "invisible systems conferring dominance on my group." If racism actively puts African Americans at a disadvantage, as a corollary it also puts whites at an advantage. That advantage is "white privilege." McIntosh also cites a long list of up to fifty cultural examples of white privilege. Among these are the following:

1. If I should need to move, and if I can be pretty sure of renting or purchasing housing in an area that I can afford and in which I would want to live, I benefit from white privilege.

2. If I can be pretty sure that my neighbors in such a location will be neutral or pleasant to me, I benefit from white privilege.

3. If, whether I use checks, credit cards or cash, I can count on my skin color not to work against the appearance of financial reliability, I benefit from white privilege.

4. If can swear, or dress in second hand clothes...without having people attribute these choices to the bad morals, the poverty, or the illiteracy of my race, I benefit from white privilege.

5. If I can do well in a challenging situation without being called a credit to my race, I benefit from white privilege.

6. If I am never asked to speak for all the people of my racial group, I benefit from white privilege.

7. If I ask to talk to the "person in charge," and be fairly certain that I will be facing a person of my race, I benefit from white privilege.

8. If a traffic cop pulls me over and I can be sure I haven't been singled out because of my race, I benefit from white privilege.

9. If I have low credibility as a leader and I can be sure that my race is not the problem, I benefit from white privilege.

10. If I am more likely to be taken seriously than a black person when I talk about racism or white privilege, I benefit from white privilege.[18]

Coupled with the economic advantages of whiteness, this sort of privilege clearly confers unearned dominance upon white Americans because of their race. Even if whites born since 1965 do not use the N-word, have black friends, have never owned a slave, or never supported segregation, they still enjoy white privilege. They still have more favorable life chances than a black American. Their comparative place in the economic and/or political pecking order is at least partly determined by where their parents stood in the pecking order. Likewise their parents before them and their parents before them and their parents before them. If somewhere in that family chain someone voted for a politician who supported the Jim Crow system or was a beneficiary of government programs that aided only whites, then persons at the contemporary end of that chain still enjoy accumulated benefits from the Jim Crow system that privileged whites and disadvantaged blacks.

Thus, interracial dialogue and acceptance are not enough. Even if by some magic spell all Americans could wake up tomorrow fully purged of all prejudice against persons of another race or culture and fully committed to loving acceptance of all others, white privilege would still exist. No amount of dialogue or good will can deeply affect black-white relations in America unless white Americans realize that white privilege is still a reality, to whatever degree whites may seek to deny it. When asked what whites could do to improve race relations in Macon, the Reverend Eddie B. Smith, Sr., pastor of the Macedonia Baptist Church, did not focus on any situation or problem specific to Macon. Rather, he expressed a more general wish that whites could come to comprehend the continuing effects of slavery and segregation on blacks. "Most whites," he observed, "have yet to understand the depth of those effects on blacks, how it affected the psyche of African Americans even today."[19]

What then to do about it? No one can go back and undo this tangled history. But whites can take action to reduce its effects. That action must be political, however. Most prominently, whites can and should embrace affirmative action as a moral course of action. Upwards of 60 percent of white Americans currently reject affirmative action. They typically look at it in an abstract, non-historical manner: Racial preference for whites was wrong; racial preference for blacks is wrong; two wrongs don't make a right. In the abstract, this deduction is logical and compelling. In the *real world*, however, where history has put and kept whites in an advantaged position, this approach conserves or at least prolongs a status quo that continues to advantage whites.

As Lincoln told Congress when he sought its support for the Emancipation Proclamation, black and white Americans "cannot escape history." Since twenty "negars" arrived at Jamestown on a Dutch man-o-war in 1619, during some 250 years of slavery and another 100 years of segregation, our colonial, national, state, and local governments deliberately built a system of affirmative action that gave unearned privilege to whites. Then came the civil rights laws of the mid-1960s, by which white America "gave" blacks equal access to public accommodations and equal access to the voting booth. In stark reality, such a "gift" should have at least been given in 1789 when the Constitution was ratified and never really cost white America anything but its racial prejudice.

After 1965, America rather half-heartedly and temporarily committed itself to Lyndon Johnson's Great Society program, which included affirmative action policies *for* blacks instead of against them. Within a mere thirteen years, as indicated by the 1978 *Bakke* ruling, white America determined it had paid enough to atone for its historic racial sins. Imagine believing that just thirteen years of half-hearted effort could fully correct problems of inequality that took over 350 years to create. Since then America's political swing to the right has made affirmative action a four-letter word to a majority of whites and the only place in America where many can recognize discrimination.

White Americans should embrace affirmation action as morally demanded, not by abstract logic, but by the hard realities of history. As Jimmie Samuel, executive director of the Macon-Bibb County Economic Opportunity Council and one of the first black students at Mercer University, has said:

> I'm afraid most white folks have not been willing to come to grips [with the idea] that to be white in America, you get privileges. You have historically got them. Now the laws—the Voting Rights Act, the Civil Rights Acts and all that—have tried to level the playing field. But you've got so much history and baggage that it really can't do that. It can help things go forward from here. But you still got all of this stuff that's rooted in there that's privileges. And unless you're willing to give up a *little bit* of that, nothing can change.[20]

Although it may be as likely as the proverbial snowball surviving the fires of Hell, a conversion of the American mind on this point would be a monumental symbol to black America that white Americans were finally willing to make some sacrifices for the sake of racial reconciliation. Particularly if coupled with government training and job programs, which contrary to contemporary political rhetoric were quite successful in reducing poverty in America, an culture-wide embrace of affirmative action could very likely have healthy effects on black-white relations. It would signal to African Americans that their white fellow Americans were prepared to go beyond mere platitudes about racial equality and actually begin to share their cultural, political, and economic power with them. It would be a giant step toward convincing them that white Americans had, to paraphrase John the Baptist, borne "fruit worthy of repentance." And how long should America continue such policies? How about for 350 years or until black life expectancy and income and poverty and unemployment are equal to those of whites, whichever comes first?

Finally, African Americans as individuals (and as a separate community) must assume responsibility for their own advancement. Does government have a responsibility? Absolutely. Therefore, whites should sacrifice their aversion to government programs and affirmative action. Since whites used government to create America's historic racial inequalities, morally they should be willing to use government to remedy those inequalities. But if government has a role to play and whites must sacrifice something for racial reconciliation, so do individuals in the black community. They must push individual initiative to address those aspects of black life that not only hinder black advancement, but also antagonize whites with whom African Americans must live in peace.

In particular, middle-class and professional blacks must re-invest their time and resources in helping the larger African American community. Macon business leader Alex C. Habersham admonishes other successful blacks like himself: "A lot of brothers and sisters got these jobs, moved to River North, and got a nice car, and gave little or no consideration to the fact that 'Now I'm up here. I've done well. Now let me reach back and help somebody else.' You got a lot of black folks that don't recognize that we have a responsibility to help because somebody helped us."[21] He calls on black professionals to lead the way back to the inner city schools to work with administrators, teachers, and students in aiming toward discipline and academic excellence.

If whites can no longer excuse themselves from responsibility by embracing affirmative action and other government programs for the poor, blacks must no longer excuse individual irresponsibility in their own community. (This negligent attitude occurs much less than most whites think, but the tendency should be countered wherever it exists.) Black parents and churches must redouble their efforts to curb teen pregnancies and out-of-wedlock births. Black leaders must increase efforts to inculcate values of education and the work ethic. Black America must acknowledge that while poverty and hopelessness and white racist institutions do contribute to black crime, the black community itself also contributes to higher levels of crime by often excusing it or blaming it on conditions created by "the White Man." If whites will sacrifice their privilege and power, blacks can be more willing to sacrifice their internalized rage and sullenness about white America. African Americans must gradually learn to sacrifice their suspicion of whites, and in those places, like Macon, where they have achieved a measure of political power, they will take care to administer that power fairly where whites are concerned. If, after 350 years of being the Americans most committed to calling the nation to "live out the true meaning of its creed," what a tragedy it would be if African Americans failed to live out that creed when and where they have come to power.

Finally, some may be tempted to dismiss these prescriptions as just another expression of "liberal guilt." In the political climate of early twenty-first century America, these suggestions may very well be classified by the four-letter word "liberal." If so, I embrace the designation gladly. But I do so not out of guilt, but because of what is really a very conservative value system. I am convinced that a truly biblical sense of justice demands such a course of action. How odd it is that conservatives who complain that America has drifted from its supposedly Judaeo-Christian moorings always focus on praying in schools or saying "under God" as part of the Pledge of Allegiance, but never on the biblical concept of making restitution for that which has been unjustly taken from others.

Nevertheless, whether or not Maconites and Americans more generally conceive of our race problem in religious, theological, or biblical terms, depends on the personal choices that they make. Those who *do* have Jewish or Christian commitments would do well to seek out what their religious traditions of justice (*mishpat* in Hebrew) require of a society that claims to be God's chosen nation. Yet even if we do not understand race and racism as situated within the biblical or theological category of "sin," even the most secular of Americans can agree that it *is* a moral issue. Dealing with the continuing racial inequality in Macon and America, especially through government policy, has not been very high on the American political agenda in the past quarter century. But for Americans, who see themselves as the most moral people on the planet, it is high time that it return to our *moral* agenda.

The American Century has come and gone, as have the three centuries that preceded it, but both the color line and the inequality on either side of it yet remain. "How long?" asked Martin Luther King, Jr., in a famous speech in Montgomery, Alabama. "Not long," he answered, "because the arc of the moral universe is long, but it bends toward justice."[22] Before we get much further into this new century, it is time that those who concern themselves with basic right and wrong inquire into the moral demands of justice. It is time for Americans and Maconites—black and white together—to meet those demands.

Thus endeth the lesson.

Notes

Introduction

[1]See Philip S. Foner and Robert James Branham, eds., *Lift Every Voice: African American Oratory, 1787–1900* (Tuscaloosa: University of Alabama Press, 1998) 802.

[2]*Macon Telegraph*, 19 September 1895, 2, 7.

[3]*Macon Telegraph*, 24 September 1895, 4; Foner and Branham, *Lift Every Voice*, 802.

[4]*Macon Telegraph*, 17 October 1901, 1.

[5]*Macon Telegraph*, 18 October 1901, 4.

[6]*Macon Telegraph*, 22 October 1901, 4.

[7]*Macon Telegraph*, 31 October 1901, 2; *Macon Telegraph*, 1 November 1901, 4.

[8]*Macon Telegraph*, 25 October 1902, 4; *Macon Telegraph*, 3 November 1901, 4; *Macon Telegraph*, 7 November 1901, 4.

[9]John Hammond Moore, "Jim Crow in Georgia," *South Atlantic Quarterly* 66 (Autumn 1967): 556–57; *Macon Telegraph*, 3 November 1901, 1; *Macon Telegraph*, 5 November 1901, 1; *Macon Telegraph*, 6 November 1901, 1.

[10]R. Kirby Godsey, "Opening Remarks," Founder's Day Convocation, Mercer University, 12 January 1994, Joseph M. Hendricks personal papers, Macon GA.

[11]J. Scott Key and Danny Palmer, "Reflections on Founders Day 1994," 13 January 1994, Joseph M. Hendricks papers.

[12]John Winthrop, "A Modell of Christian Charity," in David A. Hollinger and Charles Capper, eds., *The American Intellectual Tradition*, 2nd ed., vol. 1. (New York: Oxford University Press, 1993) 15.

[13]Readers familiar with the literature on American civil religion will recognize this interpretation of Winthrop as being heavily indebted to Robert N. Bellah's many works on the subject. Among these are "Civil Religion in America," *Daedalus* 96 (Winter 1967): 1–21; *The Broken Covenant: American Civil Religion in Time of Trial* (New York: Seabury Press, 1975). For discussions of civil religion in the South, see Charles Reagan Wilson, *Baptized in Blood: The Religion of the Lost Cause, 1865–1920* (Athens: University of Georgia Press, 1980) and Andrew M. Manis, *Southern Civil Religions in Conflict: Civil Rights and the Culture Wars* (Macon GA: Mercer University Press, 2002).

[14]Susan Myrick, "W. T. Anderson's Editorial Influence," *Publishers Service Magazine* (5 January 1933): 7–8. Copy of article in the W. T. Anderson biographical files, Washington Memorial Library, Macon GA.

[15]Stephen N. G. Tuck, *Beyond Atlanta: The Struggle for Racial Equality in Georgia, 1940–1980* (Athens: University of Georgia Press, 2001).

Chapter 1

[1]For a discussion of this theme, see Eric Foner, *Nothing But Freedom: Emancipation and Its Legacy* (Baton Rouge: Louisiana State University Press, 1983).

[2]Donald L. Grant, *The Way It Was in the South: The Black Experience in Georgia* (New York: Carol Publishing Group, 1993) 96–97.

[3]Ida Young, Julius Gholson, and Clara Nell Hargrove, *History of Macon, Georgia* (Macon GA: Lyon, Marshall & Brooks, 1950) 301, 304.

[4]Glenda E. Gilmore, *Gender and Jim Crow: Women and the Politics of White Supremacy in North Carolina, 1896–1920* (Chapel Hill: University of North Carolina Press, 1996) 3. On the general fear of blackness in the post-Emancipation South, see Joel Williamson, *A Rage for Order: Black-White Relations in the American South Since Emancipation* (New York: Oxford University Press, 1986) 238.

[5]Young et al., *History of Macon*, 304.

[6]On the Georgia Equal Rights Association meeting in Macon, see Grant, *The Way It Was*, 102. The *New Haven Courier and Journal*, 11 August 1867, carried the story of the attack on a black congregation in the Rutland community near Macon. On 6 September, the *Georgia Weekly Telegraph* issued an angry denial. See Kristina Simms, *Macon: Georgia's Central City* (Chatsworth CA: Windsor Publications, Inc., 1989) 39.

[7]Horace Calvin Wingo, "Race Relations in Georgia, 1872–1908" (Ph.D. diss., University of Georgia, 1969) 5–6.

[8]For the text of the speech, see Philip S. Foner and Robert James Branham, eds., *Lift Every Voice: African American Oratory, 1787–1900* (Tuscaloosa: University of Alabama Press, 1998) 476–83.

[9]Quoted in Stephen Ward Angell, *Bishop Henry McNeal Turner and African-American Religion in the South* (Knoxville: University of Tennessee Press, 1992) 90–91

[10]Grant, *The Way It Was*, 122.

[11]Wingo, "Race Relations in Georgia," 6, 15; *Augusta Daily Constitutionalist*, 4 October 1872; *Americus Sumter Republican*, 4 and 11 October 1872; on Maynard and the Klan, see Young et al., *History of Macon*, 314.

[12]Wingo, "Race Relations in Georgia," 269; J. Morgan Kousser, *The Shaping of Southern Politics: Suffrage Restriction and the Establishment of One-party Rule, 1880–1910* (New Haven: Yale University Press, 1974) 215–21. For percentages of Georgians voting in presidential elections between 1876 and 1906, see Kousser, *The Shaping of Southern Politics*, 212.

[13]John Michael Matthews, "Studies in Race Relations in Georgia, 1890–1930" (Ph.D. diss., Duke University, 1970) 86; John Dittmer, *Black Georgia in the Progressive Era, 1900–1920* (Urbana: University of Illinois Press, 1977) 94. This 6.25 percentage of black voters in Macon was significantly lower than the 28.3 percent statewide. See Kousser, *The Shaping of Southern Politics*, 61–62.

[14]*Atlanta Journal*, 7 October 1904.

[15]On the rise and fall of Populism, see John Hope Franklin, "Legal Disfranchisement of the Negro," *Journal of Negro Education* 26 (Spring 1957): 242–43; Alex M. Arnett,

The Populist Movement in Georgia: A View of the "Agrarian Crusade" in the Light of Solid South Politics (New York: Columbia University Press, 1922); Dewey W. Grantham, Jr., *Hoke Smith and the Politics of the New South* (Baton Rouge: Louisiana State University Press, 1958); C. Vann Woodward, *Origins of the New South, 1877–1913* (Baton Rouge: Louisiana State University Press, 1951); *Tom Watson, Agrarian Rebel,* 2nd ed. (New York: Macmillan Company, 1938; reprint, Savannah: Beehive Press, 1973); Russell Korobkin, "The Politics of Disfranchisement in Georgia," *Georgia Historical Quarterly* 74 (Spring 1990): 20–58. It should be noted that, in the early twentieth century, most white Southern newspapers, in line with their assumptions of black inferiority, did not capitalize the word "Negro," In such quotations I will leave the term in lower case.

[16]Korobkin, "The Politics of Disfranchisement," 39; Woodward, *Tom Watson*, 321; *Atlanta Constitution*, 2 September 1904. See also Mark Bauerlein, *Negrophobia: A Race Riot in Atlanta, 1906* (San Francisco: Encounter Books, 2001) xvi.

[17]Wingo, "Race Relations in Georgia," 103; Korobkin, "The Politics of Disfranchisement," 43–44.

[18]Thomas W. Hardwick to Tom Waston, 26 June 1905, in "Some Letters From Thomas W. Hardwick to Tom Watson Concerning the Georgia Gubernatorial Campaign of 1906," *Georgia Historical Quarterly* 34 (December 1950): 328–40.

[19]*Atlanta Independent*, 18 November 1905; "Speech of the Honorable Hoke Smith, Delivered at Madison, Georgia, 29 June 1905," pamphlet (Atlanta: Bennet Print House, 1905), Georgia Room, Hargrett Rare Book and Manuscript Library, University of Georgia, Athens; Grantham, *Hoke Smith*, 149, citing *Atlanta Journal,* 10 December 1905; Woodward, *Tom Watson*, 324–25. See also Bauerlein, *Negrophobia*, 21.

[20]*Macon Telegraph*, 11 January 1906, 6–7.

[21]*Macon Telegraph*, 10 January 1906, 4; *Macon Telegraph*, 11 January 1906, 1.

[22]*Macon Telegraph*, 2 January 1906, 6; *Macon Telegraph*, 21 January 1906, 4.

[23]*Macon Telegraph*, 4 January 1906, 4.

[24]Dittmer, *Black Georgia in the Progressive Era*, 173–74; The Macon News, *History of Macon: The First One Hundred Years, 1823–1923* (Macon GA: The J. W. Burke Company, 1929) 84.

[25]David Levering Lewis, *W. E. B. Du Bois: Biography of a Race, 1868–1919* (New York: Henry Holt and Company, 1993) 326–27.

[26]*Macon Telegraph*, 14 February 1907, 3.

[27]Grant, *The Way It Was*, 286; Dittmer, *Black Georgia in the Progressive Era*, 173–74; *Athens Georgian*, 27 October 1875; *Atlanta Journal*, 12 August 1893; *The Independent* 52 (June 7, 1900): 1398–99; *Macon Telegraph*, 15 February 1906, 3; *Macon Telegraph*, 19 February 1906, 1.

[28]Grant, *The Way It Was*, 112–15.

[29]*Macon Telegraph*, 22 February 1906, 4.

[30]*Macon Telegraph*, 15 February 1906, 4.

[31]*Macon Telegraph*, 7 July 1906, 2–3.

[32]Ibid.

[33]*Macon Telegraph*, 20 February 1906, 5.

[34]*Macon Telegraph*, 20 February 1906, 4.

[35]*Macon Telegraph*, 15 March 1906, 4.

[36]Wingo, "Race Relations in Georgia," 407; Letter to *Macon Telegraph*, 2 August 1906, quoted in the *Atlanta Journal*, 5 August 1906.

[37]*Macon Telegraph*, 10 August 1906, 2; *Macon Telegraph*, 11 August 1906, 4.

[38]*Macon Telegraph*, 12 August 1906, 3.

[39]*Macon Telegraph*, 14 August 1906, 4.

[40]See advertisement in *Macon Telegraph*, 21 August 1906, 2; Bacon's comments were carried on p. 4 of the same issue.

[41]Bauerlein, *Negrophobia*, 101.

[42]Wingo, "Race Relations in Georgia," 113; Korobkin, "The Politics of Disfranchisement," 49.

[43]Grantham, *Hoke Smith*, 154; *Macon Telegraph*, 22 August 1906, 1; *Macon Telegraph*, 23 August 1906, 1. Smith received 1,327 votes to Howell's 947. Other candidates were J. H. Estill, 74 votes; Richard B. Russell, 294 votes, and James M. Smith, 7 votes.

[44]*Macon Telegraph*, 2 September 1906, 1; *Macon Telegraph*, 5 September 1906, 1, 5; Grantham, *Hoke Smith*, 154.

[45]Quoted in Bauerlein, *Negrophobia*, 103.

[46]*Atlanta Constitution*, 1 August 1907, 9.

[47]*Atlanta Constitution*, 23 July 1907, 7; *Atlanta Journal*, 3 August 1907, 1.

[48]*Atlanta Constitution*, 3 August 1907, 7.

[49]*Atlanta Constitution*, 13 August 1907, 1, 3.

[50]*Atlanta Constitution*, 15 August 1907, 1.

[51]*Atlanta Journal*, 30 July 1907, 4; *Atlanta Constitution*, 31 July 1907, 6; *Macon Telegraph*, 19 August 1907, 1.

[52]*Atlanta Constitution*, 28 July 1907, 5; *Atlanta Journal*, 30 July 1907, 4.

[53]*Macon Telegraph*, 7 August 1907, 3.

[54]*Macon Telegraph*, 8 October 1908, 1.

[55]*Atlanta Journal*, 8 October 1908, 8.

[56]*Atlanta Journal*, 11 October 1908, 8.

[57]Korobkin, "The Politics of Disfranchisement," 56–57.

[58]See Rayford W. Logan, *The Negro in American Life and Thought: The Nadir, 1877–1901* (New York: Random House, 1954); On the ideas of "Negro retrogression," see Williamson, *Rage for Order*, 78–86.

[59]Charles Carroll, *The Negro a Beast* (St. Louis: American Book and Bible House, 1896); Frederick L. Hoffman, *Race Traits and Tendencies of the American Negro* (New York: Macmillan, 1900). These books are discussed in Bauerlein, *Negrophobia*, 58. Eighteen years later Madison Grant published another important example of "scientific racism" in *The Passing of the Great Race* (New York: Charles Scribners' Sons, 1918; reprint, New York: Arno Press, 1970), which argued that racial intermixing would destroy the racial purity of the Anglo-Saxon people.

[60]Penelope Bullock, "Atlanta Race Riot," in David C. Roller and Robert W. Twyman, eds., *Encyclopedia of Southern History* (Baton Rouge: Louisiana State University Press,

1979) 89; See also Wingo, "Race Relations in Georgia," 450. Williamson, *Rage for Order,* 106–16, provides an excellent discussion of Thomas Dixon and his writings. In addition to *The Clansman,* Dixon promulgated these views of Reconstruction and the "bestial" nature of blacks in *The Leopard's Spots* (1902), *The One Woman* (1907), *The Traitor* (1907), and *The Sins of the Father* (1910).

[61]*Macon Telegraph*, 9 January 1906, 3; *Macon Telegraph*, 31 January 1906, 1.

[62]*Macon Telegraph*, 12 September 1906, 4.

[63]*Macon Telegraph*, 9 November 1910, 8.

[64]*Macon Telegraph*, 12 November 1910, 7.

[65]One of the first persons to prove this was Memphis editor Ida B. Wells-Barnett, whose 1892 books *Southern Horrors: Lynch Law in All Its Phases* and *Red Record: Tabulated Statistics and Alleged Causes of Lynching in the United States* showed that only one-third of lynching victims were even accused (much less convicted) of rape. Most were terrorized for various forms of black assertiveness. See Jeffrey C. Stewart, *1001 Things Everyone Should Know about African American History* (New York: Doubleday, 1996) 125–26. In 1921, Georgia governor Hugh M. Dorsey's investigation of lynching in Georgia bore out Wells-Barnett's conclusions. Of 135 lynching incidents only two involved any crimes against white women. See "A Statement from Governor Hugh M. Dorsey as to the Negro in Georgia" (Atlanta: n.p., 1921), microform, Main Library, University of Georgia, Athens, and my relevant discussion in chapter 3 of this book.

[66]*Macon Telegraph*, 3 January 1906, 3.

[67]*Macon Telegraph*, 10 February 1906, 4; *Macon Telegraph*, 16 January 1907, 1.

[68]*Macon Telegraph*, 13 August 1906, 5

[69]*Macon Telegraph*, 31 January 1906, 5.

[70]*Macon Telegraph*, 4 August 1906, 4; *Macon Telegraph*, 29 August 1906, 2.

[71]Leon Prather, "Race Riots," in *Encyclopedia of Southern Culture*, ed. William Ferris and Charles Reagan Wilson (Chapel Hill: University of North Carolina Press, 1989) 1497; Bullock, "Atlanta Race Riot," 89. For the fullest description of the riot, see Bauerlein, *Negrophobia*, passim; Charles Crowe, "Racial Massacre in Atlanta, September 22, 1906," *Journal of Negro History* 54 (April 1969): 150–73.

[72]*Atlanta Evening News*, 21 and 22 September 1906, 1.

[73]*Atlanta Journal*, 22 September 1906, 1.

[74]Bauerlein, *Negrophobia*, 145–46.

[75]*Macon Telegraph*, 24 September 1906, 1.

[76]*Macon Telegraph*, 24 September 1906, 1; Young et al., *History of Macon*, 489; *Macon Telegraph*, 28 September 1906, 2.

[77]*Macon Telegraph*, 24 September 1906, 4. For a description of the dives and their pictures of "nude" (suggestively dressed) women, see Bauerlein, *Negrophobia*, 135–38.

[78]*Macon Telegraph*, 26 September 1905, 1; *Macon Telegraph*, 28 September 1906, 5. For Pendleton's editorial, "'The Clansman' Again," see page 4 of the 28 September issue.

[79]*Macon Telegraph*, 24 November 1915, 9. As a leader of the Georgia UDC, Blount was an articulate spokesperson for the traditional Southern view of Reconstruction and

Southern history. She is the namesake of Mercer University's annual Lamar Lectures on Southern history and culture.

[80]Bauerlein, *Negrophobia*, 189.

[81]Young et al., *History of Macon*, 489; *History of Macon: The First One Hundred Years*, 87.

[82]*Macon Telegraph*, 4 October 1906, 4.

[83]*Macon Telegraph*, 12 October 1906, 4.

[84]*Macon Telegraph*, 27 September 1906, 4.

[85]*Macon Telegraph*, 26 September 1906, 1.

[86]*Macon Telegraph*, 27 January 1907, 6.

[87]*Atlanta Constitution*, 13 August 1907, 1, 3.

Chapter 2

[1]Reinhold Niebuhr, *The Irony of American History* (New York: Charles Scribners' Sons, 1952) 2; C. Vann Woodward, "The Irony of Southern History," *Journal of Southern History* 19 (February 1953): 3–19. Woodward later took "A Second Look at the Theme of Irony," as one of his chapters in the *Burden of Southern History* (Baton Rouge: Louisiana State University Press, 1977) 213–33.

[2]*Macon Telegraph*, 10 November 1916, 1.

[3]*Macon Telegraph*, 6 April 1917, 4; *Macon Telegraph*, 7 April 1917, 4.

[4]Ida Young, Julius Gholson, and Clara Nell Hargrove, *History of Macon, Georgia* (Macon GA: Lyon, Marshall & Brooks, 1950) 498, 501–503; Billy Watson, "Military History of Macon," 14 April 1976, unpublished manuscript, Macon–Bibb County Historical Reference Files, Washington Memorial Library, Macon, Georgia. Watson was on the editorial staff of the *Macon Telegraph*.

[5]Watson, "Military History of Macon," 18.

[6]Du Bois's editorial was published in the July 1918 issue of the *Crisis*. Quoted in Jeffrey C. Stewart, *1001 Things Everyone Should Know about African American History* (New York: Doubleday, 1996) 211. For figures on black draft registration and military service, see Stewart, *1001 Things*, 208.

[7]*Macon Telegraph*, 6 April 1917, 4; *Macon Telegraph*, 11 April 1917, 6.

[8]*Macon Telegraph*, 19 April 1917, 3.

[9] *Macon Telegraph*, 17 May 1917, 12; *Macon Telegraph*, 25 May 1917, 7; *Macon Telegraph*, 25 May 1917, 11.

[10]*Macon Telegraph*, 26 May 1917, 10.

[11]*Macon Telegraph*, 26 June 1917, 9.

[12]*Macon Telegraph*, 3 April 1918, 5.

[13]*Macon Telegraph*, 24 June 1918, 1; *Macon Telegraph*, 25 June 1918, 14.

[14]*Macon Telegraph*, 26 June 1918, 6.

[15]Donald L. Grant, *The Way It Was in the South: The Black Experience in Georgia* (New York: Carol Publishing Group, 1993) 304.

[16]*Macon Telegraph*, 23 May 1918, 7; *Macon Telegraph*, 24 July 1918, 14.

[17]John Michael Matthews, "Studies in Race Relations in Georgia, 1890–1930" (Ph.D. diss., Duke University, 1970) 157. See also Grant, *The Way It Was*, 308.

[18]Grant, *The Way It Was*, 313.

[19]William P. Randall, interview by Clifford Kuhn and Duane Stewart, 4 February 1989, 5–6, Georgia Government Documentation Project, Special Collections Department, Pullen Library, Georgia State University, Atlanta, Georgia.

[20]*Macon Telegraph*, 3 December 1917, 10.

[21]*Macon Telegraph*, 21 October 1917, 1.

[22]*Macon Telegraph*, 22 October 1917, 1, 3; *Macon Telegraph*, 26 October 1917, 3.

[23]Grant, *The Way It Was*, 306; John Dittmer, *Black Georgia in the Progressive Era, 1900–1920* (Urbana: University of Illinois Press, 1977) 199.

[24]Dittmer, *Black Georgia in the Progressive Era*, 188.

[25]*Macon Telegraph*, 24 November 1917, 3.

[26]Leon Litwack, *Trouble in Mind: Black Southerners in the Age of Jim Crow* (New York: Alfred A. Knopf, 1998) 466.

[27]Ibid., 467.

[28]Grant, *The Way It Was*, 303.

[29]Stewart, *1001 Things*, 208–209.

[30]*Macon Telegraph*, 3 March 1918, 1; *Macon Telegraph*, 12 December 1918, 3.

[31]Fitzhugh Brundage, *Lynching in the New South: Georgia and Virginia, 1880–1930* (Urbana: University of Illinois Press, 1993) 8, 20. See also Orlando Patterson, *Rituals of Blood: Consequences of Slavery in Two American Centuries* (New York: Basic Civitas Books, 1998) 176–79, based on Daniel T. Williams, "The Lynching Records at Tuskegee Institute," in *Eight Negro Bibliographies*, comp. Daniel T. Williams (New York: Kraus Reprint, 1970).

[32]Litwack, *Trouble in Mind*, 284, 297; Ida B. Wells, *Crusade for Justice: The Autobiography of Ida B. Wells*, ed. Alfreda M. Duster (Chicago: University of Chicago Press, 1991) 154–55.

[33]Rebecca Felton to the *Atlanta Journal*, 15 November 1898; Litwack, *Trouble in Mind*, 301–302, citing D. P. Hale to Dr. J. B. Hawthorne, 27 December 1898, Rebecca Felton Papers, University of Georgia Library.

[34]Brundage, *Lynching in New South*, 270–80.

[35]*Macon Telegraph*, 4 February 1912, 1, 12; *Macon Telegraph*, 5 February 1912, 2.

[36]*Macon Telegraph*, 5 February 1912, 2.

[37]*Macon Telegraph*, 6 February 1912, 4.

[38]*Macon Telegraph*, 14 February 1916, 2.

[39]*Macon Telegraph*, 3 March 1916, 4.

[40]*Macon Telegraph*, 4 September 1918, 1; *Macon Telegraph*, 5 September 1918, 1.

[41]*Macon Telegraph*, 29 July 1919, 7.

[42]*Macon Telegraph*, 19 August 1919, 6.

[43]*Macon Telegraph*, 3 November 1919, 1, 10.

[44]*Macon Telegraph*, 4 November 1919, 9, 16.

[45]*Macon Telegraph*, 4 November 1919, 6.

[46]*Macon Telegraph*, 13 November 1919, 4.

[47]*Macon Telegraph*, 3 January 1920, 6.

[48]*Macon Telegraph*, 30 July 1922, 1, 10.

[49]*Macon Telegraph*, 30 July 1922, 1, 10; *Macon Telegraph*, 30 July 1922, 1, 2; *Macon Telegraph*, 31 July 1922, 1, 2; *Macon Telegraph*, 1 August 1922, 1; *Macon Telegraph*, 3 August 1922, 1.

[50]*Macon Telegraph*, 31 July 1922, 2; *Macon Telegraph*, 2 August 1922, 1, 9; *Macon Telegraph*, 3 August 1922, 4; Karl Evanzz, *The Messenger: The Rise and Fall of Elijah Muhammad* (New York: Pantheon Books, 1999) 47–50; *Atlanta Constitution*, 30 July 1922, 1A, 2A; *New York Times*, 30 July 1922, 28A; 2 August 1922, 19A.

[51]*Macon Telegraph*, 2 August 1922, 1, 9; *Macon Telegraph*, 3 August 1922, 1; *Macon Telegraph*, 3 August 1922, 1.

[52]*Macon Telegraph*, 3 August 1922, 5, 4.

[53]*Macon Telegraph*, 4 August 1922, 4; *Macon Telegraph*, 4 August 1922, 1.

[54]*Macon Telegraph*, 6 August 1922, 1, 6; *Macon Telegraph*, 9 August 1922, 1, 2.

[55]*Macon Telegraph*, 7 August 1922, 1, 9.

[56]*Macon Telegraph*, 6 August 1922, 4.

[57]*Macon Telegraph*, 29 August 1922, 1, 4; *Macon Telegraph*, 31 August 1922, 1, 9; *Macon Telegraph*, 11 September 1922, 1.

[58]*Macon Telegraph*, 12 September 1922, 1, 6.

[59]*Macon Telegraph*, 13 September 1922, 1, 2.

[60]*Macon Telegraph*, 12 August 1922, 1.

[61]*Macon Telegraph*, 24 September 1922, 1, 7.

[62]*Macon Telegraph*, 3 October 1922, 5.

[63]*Macon Telegraph*, 15 September 1922, 4

[64]*Macon Telegraph*, 26 September 1922, 4.

[65]*Macon Telegraph*, 3 August 1922, 12.

[66]*Macon Telegraph*, 6 August 1922, 9.

[67]*Macon Telegraph*, 13 August 1922, 4.

[68]*Macon Telegraph*, 29 August 1922, 4.

[69]*Macon Telegraph*, 14 April 1916, 12; *Macon Telegraph*, 21 October 1922, 4.

[70]*Macon Telegraph*, 1 February 1920, 1.

[71]*Macon Telegraph*, 10 October 1916, 4.

[72]*Macon Telegraph*, 21 October 1916, 4.

[73]*Macon Telegraph*, 31 October 1916, 8. During this period northern labor agents were unwelcome in Georgia, where business leaders insisted on checking migration of the black labor force. In 1917, when most Georgia cities charged "only" $1,000, Macon charged an exorbitant labor agent fee of $25,000. The state labor commission sought to suppress recruiting advertisements in Georgia newspapers, and the *Macon Telegraph* advocated jailing labor agents. Some 151,438 blacks left Georgia between 1920 and 1922. In 1923 the number of departures reached 1,500 per week. See Grant, *The Way It Was*, 291–95.

[74]*Macon Telegraph*, 7 November 1916, 4; *Macon Telegraph*, 10 November 1916, 4.

[75]*Macon Telegraph*, 26 May 1917, 7; *Macon Telegraph*, 25 May 1917, 4.

[76]*Macon Telegraph*, 5 September 1920, 7.

[77]Claude A. Clegg, *An Original Man: The Life and Times of Elijah Muhammad* (New York: St. Martin's Press, 1998) 11–13; Evanzz, *The Messenger*, 47–50.

Chapter 3

[1]George David Anderson, "A City Comes Of Age: An Urban Study of Macon Georgia During the 1920's" (MA thesis, Georgia College, 1975) 61, citing the 1920 census. The black population of Bibb County numbered an additional 10,000, with a total of 33,025. See http://fisher.lib.virginia.edu/census.

[2]The Macon News, *History of Macon: The First One Hundred Years, 1823–1923* (Macon GA: The J. W. Burke Company, 1929) 74.

[3]Anderson, "A City Comes of Age," 52–58, see also 14; A. B. Bernd, "Macon: Urba Futura," *Georgia Cracker*, November 1922, 16.

[4]Anderson, "A City Comes of Age," 89–91; *Macon Telegraph*, 15 November 1927, 2.

[5]*History of Macon: The First One Hundred Years*, 147; *Macon City Directory* (Richmond VA: Polk and Company, 1922) 820.

[6]In 1928, 1,527 were unemployed, 620 of whom were white and 907 black. See Anderson, "A City Comes of Age," 93.

[7]"Literacy Statistics, 1920, Georgia," in "Extract From Report of the Georgia Illiteracy Commission to the Governor of Georgia," n.d. [c. 1924], Rufus W. Weaver Papers, box 1, folder 156, Special Collections, Jack Tarver Library, Mercer University, Macon, Georgia; Rufus W. Weaver to Etta J. Wilson, 18 September 1925, copies in the Rufus W. Weaver Papers.

[8]*Macon Telegraph*, 18 January 1922, 16.

[9]Sesquicentennial Edition of the *Macon Telegraph*, 28 September 1973, section IV, 4; Catherine Meeks, *Macon's Black Heritage: The Untold Story* (Macon GA: The Tubman African American Museum, 1997) 58, 64; T. J. Woofter, Jr., *Progress In Race—Relations In Georgia* (Atlanta: Report of the Secretary of the Georgia Committee on Race Relations, 1922) 14; Works Progress Administration, *Georgia: The WPA Guide to Its Towns and Countryside* (Athens: University of Georgia Press, 1940; reprint, Columbia: University of South Carolina Press, 1990) 85.

[10]*Macon City Directory* (Richmond VA: Polk and Company, 1927) 14; Donald L. Grant, *The Way It Was in the South: The Black Experience in Georgia* (New York: Carol Publishing Group, 1993) 229–30.

[11]Letter to editor, H. Taylor, *Macon Telegraph*, 8 September 1923, 4.

[12]Both Ingram's letter and Anderson's editorial comments are found in the *Macon Telegraph*, 26 March 1923, 4.

[13]*Macon Telegraph*, 20 May 1921, 6.

[14]*Macon Telegraph*, 25 August 1923, 4.

[15]*Macon Telegraph*, 23 March 1921, 3.

[16]James F. Cook, *The Governors of Georgia, 1754–1995* (Macon GA: Mercer University Press, 1995) 210.

[17]*Macon Telegraph*, 17 August 1915, 1; Leonard Dinnerstein, *The Leo Frank Case* (Athens: University of Georgia Press, 1999); Cook, *The Governors of Georgia*, 208–209.

In one of the greatest miscarriages of justice in Southern history, Jim Conley, a janitor at the pencil factory who became the star witness against Frank, was later discovered to be the perpetrator of the crime. Irony remains a theme of this case, as in that moment, prejudice against a Northern Jew trumped anti-black prejudice.

[18]*Macon Telegraph*, 13 and 14 September 1916, 1; *Macon Telegraph*, 7 September 1916, 4; *Macon Telegraph*, 9 September 1916, 1.

[19]Grant, *The Way It Was*, 323–24.

[20]*Macon Telegraph*, 30 May 1921, 1. C. B. Wilmer was Episcopal bishop for Georgia and M. Ashby Jones was pastor of Ponce de Leon Avenue Baptist Church in Atlanta. *Atlanta Constitution*, 26 April 1921, 2.

[21]John Dittmer, *Black Georgia in the Progressive Era, 1900–1920* (Urbana: University of Illinois Press, 1977) 208–209.

[22]*Atlanta Constitution*, 23 April 1921, 1; Copy of the pamphlet in Commission on Interracial Cooperation Papers, reel 4, item 89, Archives Department, Robert W. Woodruff Library, Atlanta University Center, Atlanta, Georgia. (Hereinafter cited as CIC Papers.)

[23]*Atlanta Constitution*, 29 April 1921, 10; *Savannah Press* editorial reported in CIC Papers, reel 4, item 88; *Macon Telegraph*, 12 May 1921, 6.

[24]*Macon Telegraph*, 17 May 1921, 5.

[25]*Macon Telegraph*, 17 May 1921, 5; *Macon Telegraph*, 23 May 1921, 7.

[26]*Macon Telegraph*, 13 May 1921, 1, 6; *Macon Telegraph*, 15 May 1921, 1, 7; *Macon Telegraph*, 23 May 1921, 1.

[27]*Macon Telegraph*, 15 May 1921, 1, 7; *Macon Telegraph*, 17 May 1921, 6;*Macon Telegraph*, 20 May 1921, 6.

[28]My narrative of the entire mass meeting comes from the *Macon Telegraph*, 23 May 1921, 1, 7.

[29]*Macon Telegraph*, 26 May 1921, 6; *Macon Telegraph*, 27 May 1921, 4.

[30]*Macon Telegraph*, 21 May 1921, 6; *Macon Telegraph*, 30 May 1921, 8; *Macon Telegraph*, 30 May 1921, 1, 8; *Macon Telegraph*, 24 May 1921, 4.

[31]*Macon Telegraph*, 13 May 1921, 1, 4.

[32]*Macon Telegraph*, 19 May 1921, 9.

[33]*Macon Telegraph*, 24 May 1921, 1; *Macon Telegraph*, 26 June 1921, 2, 3.

[34]*Macon Telegraph*, 26 June 1921, 1, 2.

[35]*Macon Telegraph*, 8 November 1916, 4.

[36]Roger K. Hux, "The Ku Klux Klan in Macon, 1919–1925," *Georgia Historical Quarterly* 62 (Summer 1978): 155–56.

[37]*Macon Telegraph*, 16 August 1920, 6.

[38]*Macon Telegraph*, 5 July 1922, 1, 10; *Macon Telegraph*, 7 July 1922, 2.

[39]*Macon Telegraph*, 9 July 1922, 4.

[40]*Macon Telegraph*, 5 November 1922, 1; *Macon Telegraph*, 6 November 1922, 4.

[41]*Macon Telegraph*, 6 November 1922, 1, 13.

[42]*Macon Telegraph*, 7 November 1922, 1, 2; *Macon Telegraph*, 8 November 1922, 1, 13.

[43]*Macon Telegraph*, 7 November 1922, 1, 2; *Macon Telegraph*, 10 November 1922, 1.

[44]*Macon Telegraph*, 17 March 1923, 1; *Macon Telegraph*, 7 April 1924, 1, 5; *Macon Telegraph*, 1 May 1924, 6.

[45]*Macon Telegraph*, 30 May 1923, 1; *Macon Telegraph*, 4 June 1923, 1, 10; *Macon Telegraph*, 26 July 1923, 1.

[46]*Macon Telegraph*, 19 June 1923, 1; *Macon Telegraph*, 20 June 1923, 1, 9.

[47]*Macon Telegraph*, 19 August 1923, 1.

[48]*Macon Telegraph*, 19 August 1923, 4.

[49]*Macon Telegraph*, 20 August 1923, 1.

[50]Ibid.; *Macon Telegraph*, 24 August 1923, 1.

[51]*Macon Telegraph*, 28 August 1923, 1.

[52]*Macon Telegraph*, 1 September 1923, 1.

[53]*Macon Telegraph*, 2 September 1923, 1; *Macon Telegraph*, 6 September 1923, 1, 9.

[54]*Macon Telegraph*, 4 October 1923, 1; *Macon Telegraph*, 18 February 1924, 1; *Macon Telegraph*, 19 February 1924, 1.

[55]*Macon Telegraph*, 10 September 1923, 1, 2.

[56]*Macon Telegraph*, 12 September 1923, 1; *Macon Telegraph*, 13 September 1923, 1, 3.

[57]*Macon Telegraph*, 13 September 1923, 4; *Macon Telegraph*, 14 September 1923, 1, 4.

[58]*Macon Telegraph*, 15 September 1923, 1, 3; *Macon Telegraph*, 16 September 1923, 1, 4.

[59]*Macon Telegraph*, 25 September 1923, 1, 12; *Macon Telegraph*, 26 September 1923, 1, 8; *Macon Telegraph*, 30 September 1923, 1.

[60]*Macon Telegraph*, 23 October 1923, 1, 3; *Macon Telegraph*, 26 October 1923, 1, 8; *Macon Telegraph*, 6 December 1923, 1, 3.

[61]*Macon Telegraph*, 22 November 19214, 1, 5.

[62]*Macon Telegraph*, 20 November 1924, 1; *Macon Telegraph*, 25 November 1924, 8; *Macon Telegraph*, 8 December 1923, 1; Hux, "The Ku Klux Klan in Macon, 1919–1925," 160–61.

[63]*Macon Telegraph*, 13 June 1924, 4; *Macon Telegraph*, 22 June 1924, 3; *Macon Telegraph*, 25 June 1924, 1; *Macon Telegraph*, 29 June 1924, 1, 2; *Macon Telegraph*, 30 June 1924, 1, 7; *Macon Telegraph*, 1 July 1924, 6.

[64]*Macon Telegraph*, 2 October 1923, 1.

[65]*Macon Telegraph*, 3 October 1923, 1; Hux, "The Ku Klux Klan in Macon, 1919–1925," 162–63.

[66] Hux, "The Ku Klux Klan in Macon, 1919–1925," 162–63.

[67] *Macon Telegraph*, 2 February 1924, 1, 9.

[68]*Macon Telegraph*, 16 February 1924, 1, 4.

[69]*Macon Telegraph*, 5 September 1924, 4.

[70]*Macon Telegraph*, 5 September 1924, 1, 10; *Macon Telegraph*, 9 September 1924, 11.

[71]*Macon Telegraph*, 9 September 1924, 1, 8, 9.

[72]*Macon Telegraph*, 11 September 1924, 1; *Macon Telegraph*, 12 September 1924, 1, 12.

[73]Cook, *The Governors of Georgia*, 215; *Macon Telegraph*, 8 September 1924, 1; *Macon Telegraph*, 11 September 1924, 1; *Macon Telegraph*, 12 September 1924, 1.

[74]*Macon Telegraph*, 9 September 1920, 1; *Macon Telegraph*, 10 September 1920, 1; *Macon Telegraph*, 7 October 1920, 1; Cook, *The Governors of Georgia*, 217; Rufus W. Weaver to Clifford M. Walker, 30 November 1922, Rufus W. Weaver Papers, box 1, folder 10.

[75]*Macon Telegraph*, 14 September 1922, 1; *Macon Telegraph*, 10 November 1922, 2.

[76]*Macon Telegraph*, 15 November 1923, 1.

[77]Cook, *The Governor's of Georgia*, 216; *Macon Telegraph*, 14 October 1924, 1; *Macon Telegraph*, 15 October 1924, 4.

[78]*Macon Telegraph*, 15 October 1924, 4; *Macon Telegraph*, 19 October 1924, 4.

[79]*Macon Telegraph*, 17 October 1924, 4.

[80]*Macon Telegraph*, 18 October 1924, 1.

[81]*Macon Telegraph*, 15 March 1928, 1, 17.

[82]*Macon Telegraph*, 10 September 1924, 4.

Chapter 4

[1]Dan T. Carter, "From Segregation to Integration," in John B. Boles and Evelyn Thomas Nolen, eds., *Interpreting Southern History: Historiographical Essays in Honor of Sanford W. Higginbotham* (Baton Rouge: Louisiana State University Press, 1987) 414–15; John Shelton Reed and Dale Volberg Reed, *1001 Things Everyone Should Know About the South* (New York: Doubleday, 1996) 53.

[2]Stephen N. G. Tuck, *Beyond Atlanta: The Struggle for Racial Equality in Georgia, 1940–1980* (Athens: University of Georgia Press, 2001) 18.

[3]*Macon Telegraph*, 24 October 1979, 1A, 9A.

[4]US Census figures for 1930 and 1940 indicate total and partial unemployment in Bibb County in the following ratios: 1930 unemployment: whites 5.28 percent; blacks 8.35 percent. 1940 Unemployment: whites 7.29 percent; blacks, 12.85 percent. Over the decade white unemployment grew by 2.01 percent, compared to 4.5 percent for blacks. Over the same decade, white owned or operated farms in Bibb County fell from 642 to 596, a 7.2 percent decrease. By contrast, black owned or operated farms fell from 370 to 233, a 37.1 percent decrease. See US Census figures for 1930 and 1940, http://fisher.lib.virginia.edu/census.

[5]Paul Douglas Bolster, "Civil Rights Movements in Twentieth Century Georgia" (Ph.D. diss., University of Georgia, 1972) 44–45, 47.

[6]"Depression and the Race Problem: A Confidential Statement," n.d., Commission on Interracial Cooperation Papers, reel 4, item 72, Archives Department, Robert W. Woodruff Library, Atlanta University Center, Atlanta, Georgia.

[7]Bolster, "Civil Rights Movements,"39; John Hammond Moore, "Communism and Fascists in a Southern City: Atlanta, 1930," *South Atlantic Quarterly* 67 (Summer 1968):

445–46; Ann Wells Ellis, "'Uncle Sam Is My Shepherd': The Commission on Interracial Cooperation and the New Deal in Georgia," *Atlanta History* 30 (Spring 1986): 48.

[8]*Macon Telegraph*, 2 September 1930, 2A.

[9]Jesse O. Thomas, "The Negro Looks at the Alphabet," *Opportunity* 12 (January 1934): 12; *Macon Telegraph*, 2 August 1939, 1.

[10]*Macon Telegraph*, 20 September 1931, 1, 11; *Macon Telegraph*, 21 September 1931, 1.

[11]J. Morgan Kousser, *Colorblind Injustice: Minority Voting Rights and the Undoing of the Second Reconstruction* (Chapel Hill: University of North Carolina Press, 1999) 213. *Macon Telegraph*, 17 November 1933, 7; Donald L. Grant, *The Way It Was in the South: The Black Experience in Georgia* (New York: Carol Publishing Group, 1993) 352.

[12]Tuck, *Beyond Atlanta*, 16; Ralph Bunche, *The Political Status of the Negro in the Age of F. D. R.*, ed. Dewey E. Grantham. (Chicago: University of Chicago Press, 1973) 404; *Macon Telegraph*, 11 January 1939, 9A.

[13]*Mercer Cluster*, 1 December 1939, 3.

[14]*Macon Telegraph*, 4 May 1932, 8A.

[15]*Macon Telegraph*, 14 July 1938, 4.

[16]*Macon Telegraph*, 15 January 1933, 1, 9.

[17]*Macon Telegraph*, 19 January 1933, 1, 5; *Macon Telegraph*, 21 January 1933, 12; *Macon Telegraph*, 9 May 1938, 7.

[18]*Macon Telegraph*, 9 May 1938, 7.

[19]*Macon Telegraph*, 15 March 1939, 1.

[20]*Macon Telegraph*, 19 March 1939, 4.

[21]*Macon Telegraph*, 23 March 1939, 4.

[22]James F. Cook, *The Governors of Georgia, 1754–1995* (Macon GA: Mercer University Press, 1995) 228–31.

[23]William Anderson, *The Wild Man from Sugar Creek: The Political Career of Eugene Talmadge* (Baton Rouge: Louisiana State University Press, 1975) 111.

[24]*Macon Telegraph*, 28 August 1935, 1.

[25]Press release from Roosevelt's address, Lake Junaluska, North Carolina, 25 July 1944, Dorothy Tilly Papers, box 2, folder 1, Special Collections, Robert F. Woodruff Library, Emory University, Atlanta, Georgia.

[26]Anderson, *The Wild Man from Sugar Creek*, 136–37.

[27]*Macon Telegraph*, 26 January 1936, 1, 2; *Macon Telegraph*, 27 January 1936, 1, 7.

[28]*Macon Telegraph*, 28 January 1936, 1, 2.

[29]*Macon Telegraph*, 27 January 1936, 4.

[30]*Macon Telegraph*, 30 January 1936, 1, 10.

[31]Patricia Sullivan, *Days of Hope: Race and Democracy in the New Deal Era* (Chapel Hill: University of North Carolina Press, 1996) 159–60; as cited in Sullivan, "Blunt Criticism," reprint of *Georgia Women's World* article in *Columbia Observer*, n.d. [1936], FDR Papers, office files 93, box 2; Anderson, The *Wild Man from Sugar Creek*, 136–40.

[32]*Macon Telegraph*, 30 January 1936, 1, 2; *Macon Telegraph*, 30 January 1936, 4.

[33]*Macon Telegraph*, 13 September 1940, 19.

[34]*Macon Telegraph*, 2 February 1936, 4; *Macon Telegraph*, 3 February 1936, 4.

[35]Tuck, *Beyond Atlanta*, 19; Cook, *The Governors of Georgia*, 232.

[36]*Macon Telegraph*, 7 June 1942, 1, 2; *Macon Telegraph*, 9 June 1942, 1.

[37]*Macon Telegraph*, 10 September 1942, 3.

[38]Annual Report, Macon Chamber of Commerce, 1933, Spright Dowell Files, Special Collections, Jack Tarver Library, Mercer University, Macon, Georgia, box 7, folder 357; *Macon Telegraph*, 2 September 1933, 5A; David M. Kennedy, *Freedom From Fear: The American People in Depression and War, 1929–1945* (New York: Oxford University Press, 1999) 183.

[39]*Macon Telegraph*, 23 April 1933, 4; *Macon Telegraph*, 13 September 1933, 2.

[40]*Macon Telegraph*, 22 October 1938, 9A; *Macon Telegraph*, 18 January 1939, 7A; *Macon Telegraph*, 3 June 1938, 2; *Macon Telegraph*, 7 June 1938, 9.

[41]*Macon Telegraph*, 28 August 1935, 7; *Macon Telegraph*, 1 October 1933, 11; *Macon Telegraph*, 23 October 1933, 11; *Macon Telegraph*, 2 November 1937, 3; *Macon Telegraph*, 18 November 1933, 9.

[42]*Macon Telegraph*, 11 December 1933, 4; *Macon Courier*, 6 December 1978, 1, 7, 12.

[43]*Macon Telegraph*, 31 January 1933, 5; *Macon Telegraph*, 7 February 1933, cited in Titus Brown, *Faithful, Firm, and True: African American Education in the South* (Macon GA: Mercer University Press, 2000) 113; *Macon Telegraph*, 28 February 1933, 5; *Macon Telegraph*, 2 March 1933, 11.

[44]*Macon Telegraph*, 20 November 1936, 7.

[45]*Macon Telegraph*, 11 May 1937, 9; *Macon Telegraph*, 1 September 1937, 11.

[46]*Macon Telegraph*, 30 August 1938, 7.

[47]*Macon Telegraph*, 5 October 1938, 1, 2; *Macon Telegraph*, 28 October 1938, 1, 10; Catherine Meeks, *Macon's Black Heritage: The Untold Story* (Macon GA: The Tubman African American Museum, 1997) 48.

[48]*Macon Telegraph*, 17 September 1916, 5.

[49]*Macon Telegraph*, 15 February 1932, 5.

[50]*Macon Telegraph*, 23 March 1941, 5; Wayne McClain, *A Resurrection Encounter: The Rufus Moseley Story* (Minneapolis: Macalester Park Publishing Company, 1997) 112–13, 122, 164 (citing Moseley's book *Manifest Victory*, 185–87).

[51]Quoted in Will Campbell, *The Stem of Jesse: The Costs of Community at a 1960s Southern School* (Macon GA: Mercer University Press, 1994) 65.

[52]*Macon Telegraph*, 16 June 1933, 8; *Mercer Cluster*, 1 March 1935.

[53]Morton Sosna, "Commission on Interracial Cooperation," in the *Encyclopedia of Religion in the South* (Macon GA: Mercer University Press, 1984) 179–80; Ann Ellis, "The Commission on Interracial Cooperation, 1919–1944: Its Activities and Results" (Ph.D. diss., Iliff School of Theology, 1975).

[54]Benjamin E. Mays, "Realities in Race Relations," *Christian Century* 48 (1931): 404; E. Franklin Frazier, "Memorandum submitted by Dr. Guy B. Johnson," Myrdal-Carnegie Manuscripts, Commission on Interracial Cooperation (CIC) Papers, reel 4, 13–13C; Bolster, "Civil Rights Movements," 55–56; Ellis, "The Commission on Interracial Cooperation," preface.

[55]Morton Sosna, "Association of Southern Women for the Prevention of Lynching," in the *Encyclopedia of Religion in the South* (Macon GA: Mercer University Press, 1984) 77–78; Jacquelyn Dowd Hall, "The Legacy of Jessie Daniel Ames," *South Today*, n.d., 7, in Southern Regional Council Papers, reel 218, Robert W. Woodruff Library, Archives Department, Atlanta University Center, Atlanta, Georgia; Jacquelyn Dowd Hall, *Revolt Against Chivalry: Jessie Daniel Ames and the Women's Campaign Against Lynching* (New York: Columbia University Press, 1979).

[56]Reports, 1936; Jessie Daniel Ames to Mrs. E. B. Harrold, 15 May 1936; Mrs. Marshall J. Ellis to Mrs. Robert H. McDougald, 30 September 1936; Ames to Ellis, 1 April 1937, Association of Southern Women for the Prevention of Lynching (ASWPL) Papers, reel 5, Archives Department, Robert W. Woodruff Library, Atlanta University Center, Atlanta, Georgia.

[57]Mrs. Louise C. Harrold to Jessie Daniel Ames, 6 and 18 April 1936; Ames to Harrold, 21 April 21 and 15 May 1936, ASWPL Papers, reel 5.

[58]Editorial from *Macon News*, 2 June 1941; W. Lowry Anderson to Jessie Daniel Ames, 4 June 1941; Jessie Daniel Ames to W. Lowry Anderson, 30 June 1941, CIC Papers, reel 50, item 123.

[59]W. Lowry Anderson to Dr. R. L. Russell, 1 October 1938, CIC Papers, reel 51, section 144; W. Lowry Anderson, 21 August 1942 report, CIC Papers, reel 50, item 123.

[60]Aaron Brown, "Loopholes in the Educational Law," Macon Conference, Georgia Committee of the CIC, 3 November 1938, CIC Papers, reel 51, section 144.

[61]Report, Georgia Committee on Interracial Cooperation October 1938–July 1939, Interracial Conference, Macon, Georgia, 3 November 1938, CIC Papers, reel 45, item 46.

[62]Anderson to Clary, "Report on Work Done For Interracial Cooperation [July–September 1939]," 29 September 1939, CIC Papers, reel 51, section 144.

[63]Report on work done by W. Lowry Anderson, June 1940; George E. Clary to Ames, 11 November 1940, CIC Papers, reel 51, section 144.

[64]Biennial report, Department of Education, 1940, CIC Papers, reel 29, item 13; "History of the Booker T. Washington Community Center, [1939]"; Anderson to Clary, Report on Work Done For Interracial Cooperation [July–September 1939], 29 September 1939, CIC Papers, reel 51, section 144; Robert A. Burnham, "Interracial Cooperation in the Age of Jim Crow: The Booker T. Washington Community Center of Macon, Georgia," *Atlanta History* 42 (1999): 19, 22.

[65]Burnham, "Interracial Cooperation," 22–23; Macon Negro Demonstration Project, 4, Booker T. Washington Community Center office files, Macon GA; Booker T. Washington Community Center (BTWCC) board of directors, minutes, 29 May 1939; form letter to Mr. John Doe, 1 September 1939, BTWCC office files.

[66]Burnham, "Interracial Cooperation," 20–23; Macon Negro Demonstration Project, 4; BTWCC board of directors, minutes, 29 May 1939, BTWCC office files.

[67]Burnham, "Interracial Cooperation," 25; "Information Submitted to Community Chest," CIC Papers, reel 51.

[68]W. Lowry Anderson, 5 September 1941 report; 10 October 1941 report, CIC Papers, reel 50, item 123.

[69]W. Lowry Anderson, 5 September 1941 report; Anderson, report to Ames and Tilly, 14 December 1941, CIC Papers, reel 50, item 123.

[70]W. Lowry Anderson, 10 October 1941 report, CIC Papers, reel 50, item 123.

[71]*Macon Telegraph*, 21 October 1941, 2.

[72]Jessie Daniel Ames to Lowry Anderson, 14 October 1941; Anderson, Report to Ames and Dorothy Tilly, 14 December 1941, CIC Papers, reel 50, item 123.

Chapter 5

[1]Ida Young, Julius Gholson, and Clara Nell Hargrove, *History of Macon, Georgia* (Macon GA: Lyon, Marshall & Brooks, 1950) 558; US Census figures, 1940, 1950, http://fisher.lib.virginia.edu/census.

[2]Lee Finkle, "The Conservative Aims of Militant Rhetoric: Black Protest During World War II," *Journal of American History* 60 (December 1973): 692–713; Walter White, *A Rising Wind* (Garden City NY: Doubleday, 1945) 142, 144; Gunnar Myrdal, *The American Dilemma: The Negro Problem and Modern Democracy* (New York: Doubleday, 1944) xxv; Peter J. Kellogg, "Civil Rights Consciousness in the 1940s," *Historian* 42 (November 1979): 33–34; see also Neil Wynn, *The Afro-American and the Second World War* (London: P. Elek, 1976).

[3]Richard M. Dalfiume, "The Forgotten Years of the Negro Revolution," *Journal of American History* 55 (June 1968): 90–106; Patricia Sullivan, *Days of Hope: Race and Democracy in the New Deal Era* (Chapel Hill: University of North Carolina Press, 1996); Donald R. McCoy and Richard Ruetten, "The Civil Rights Movement: 1940–1954," *Midwest Quarterly* 11 (October 1969): 11–34.

[4]John W. Summerford to NAACP, 10 October 1941, NAACP Papers, part 26, series A, reel 10; John W. Summerford to Governor Eugene Talmadge, 12 September 1941, NAACP Papers, part 26, series A, reel 10, Emory University, Atlanta, Georgia.

[5]*Macon Telegraph*, 27 April 1942, 4; *Macon Telegraph*, 17 May 1942, 22.

[6]*Macon Telegraph*, 17 June 1942, 1, 2.

[7]*Macon Telegraph*, 20 June 1942, 1.

[8]*Macon Telegraph*, 21 February 1943, 7.

[9]*Macon Telegraph*, 2 March 1943, 4A.

[10]Tuck, *Beyond Atlanta*, 30–31; Sullivan, *Days of Hope*, 66.

[11]*Macon Telegraph*, 11 June 1942, 1; *Macon Telegraph*, 18 June 1942, 4; *Macon Telegraph*, 21 June 1942, 1, 2.

[12]Donald L. Grant, *The Way It Was in the South: The Black Experience in Georgia* (New York: Carol Publishing Group, 1993) 311; John W. Summerford to NAACP, 10 October 1941, NAACP Papers, part 26, series A, reel 10; application for charter to NAACP board of directors, 30 April 1942, NAACP Papers; *Macon Telegraph*, 25 May 1942, "Colored People's Page"; *Macon Telegraph*, 29 May 1942, 9; report of the election of officers of the Macon, Ga. branch, June 1, 1942, NAACP Papers, part 26, series A, reel 10. Other prominent black Maconites in the charter membership were John H. Jenkins, R. E. Hartley, Fischer M. Mosley, Frank J. Hutchings, and Minnie Singleton.

[13]Memorandum for the file in re Macon, Georgia Branch, 27 June 1942, NAACP Papers, part 26, series A, reel 10; *Macon Telegraph*, 7 June 1942, 24.

[14]Memorandum for the file in re Macon, Georgia Branch, 27 June 1942, NAACP Papers, part 26, series A, reel 10; *Macon Telegraph*, 9 June 1942, 1.

[15]Tuck, *Beyond Atlanta*, 53; *Macon Telegraph*, 7 and 10 June 1942.

[16]*Macon Telegraph*, 9 June 1942, 1.

[17]*Macon Telegraph*, 10 June 1942, 1, 4.

[18]*Macon Telegraph*, 24 June 1942, 6; *Macon Telegraph*, 28 June 1942, 6; *Macon Telegraph*, 6 June 1942, 4. Ethridge served as managing editor and associate editor of the *Telegraph* from 1919 to 1933. *Macon Telegraph*, 6 April 1981, 1.

[19]*Atlanta Daily World*, 21 June 1942, 1; John A. Jenkins to Thurgood Marshall, 17 July 1942, NAACP Papers, part 26, series A, reel 10; John A. Jenkins narrative, 20 July 1999; *Macon Telegraph*, 9 June 1942, clipping in Gus A. Kaufman personal papers, copies in author's possession. Jenkins' narrative has Dr. C. W. Dyer inviting the grand jury to the Washington Avenue church. As a member of the laity and a physician, Dyer would have had no authority to extend such an invitation. The *Macon Telegraph* article of 9 June 1942, however, noted Stennett, the pastor of the church in question, acting as spokesperson for the NAACP group. Unlike Dyer, Stennett would have the authority of inviting a group to the church. This fact, as well as the fact that Jenkins' memory has proven faulty on some details, my narrative identifies Stennett as the speaker.

[20]Memorandum, Walter White to the National Legal Committee, 30 June 1942, NAACP Papers, part 26, series A, reel 10. This committee was composed of William H. Hastie, Thurgood Marshall, and Prentice Thomas.

[21]Walter White to J. A. Jenkins, 30 July 1942; Prentice Thomas to J. A. Jenkins, 22 July 1942; Memorandum, Thurgood Marshall to Walter White, 31 July 1942, NAACP Papers, part 26, series A, reel 10.

[22]*Macon Telegraph*, 30 June 1942, 1.

[23]W. Lowry Anderson to Robert Redfield, 26 June 1942, CIC Papers, reel 50, item 123.

[24]*Macon Telegraph*, 21 August 1942, 1, 5; John A. Jenkins narrative, 20 July 1999, Gus A. Kaufman personal papers, Macon GA; Young et al., *History of Macon*, 601.

[25]*Macon Telegraph*, 23 September 1942, 1.

[26]*Macon Telegraph*, article, n.d., clipping in Gus A. Kaufman papers; Also signing the statement of black leaders were Dr. E. M. Calhoun, Rev. J. T. Saxon, Sol C. Clemens, J. S. Williams, M.D., Rev. R. Waite Stennett, and M. L. Fleming.

[27]*Macon Telegraph*, 8 September 1942, 1; *Macon Telegraph*, 23 September 1942, 1.

[28]W. Lowry Anderson to Jessie Daniel Ames, 26 August 1942, CIC Papers, reel 49, section 114. Frank J. Hutchings, Jr., interview with author, 13 February 2004, audio recording, Tubman African American Museum, Macon GA.

[29]*Macon Telegraph*, 6 August 1942, 1, 4.

[30]Cited by Adam Fairclough, "State of the Art: Historians and the Civil Rights Movement," *Journal of American Studies* 24 (1990): 387–98; *Macon Telegraph*, 28 May 1940, 3; *Macon Telegraph*, 14 January 1944, 9A.

[31]*Macon Telegraph*, 5 January 1945, 3.

[32]*Macon Telegraph*, 8 September 1944, 9.

[33]Georgia Council on Human Relations to Georgia State Democratic Committee, 29 June 1944, Southern Regional Council Papers, Robert W. Woodruff Library, Archives Department, Atlanta University Center, Atlanta, Georgia, reel 64, item 1989.

[34]Southern Regional Council, "The White Primary 1944 With Special Reference to Georgia," Clarence Bacote Papers, box 22, folder 27, Archives Department, Robert W. Woodruff Library, Atlanta University Center, Atlanta, Georgia.

[35]John Egerton, *Speak Now Against the Day: The Generation Before the Civil Rights Movement in the South* (New York: Alfred A. Knopf, Inc., 1994) 406–407; *Macon Telegraph*, 13 September 1945, 2; *Macon Telegraph*, 15 September 1945, 2; *Macon Telegraph*, 13 October 1945, 1, 5; Will Campbell, *The Stem of Jesse: The Costs of Community at a 1960s Southern School* (Macon GA: Mercer University Press, 1994) 15.

[36]McCoy and Ruetten, "The Civil Rights Movement: 1940–1954," 15–16; John Hammond Moore, "Jim Crow in Georgia," *South Atlantic Quarterly* 66 (Autumn 1967): 559.

[37]*Macon Telegraph*, 10 September 1942, 1; Memo to Governor Ellis Arnall, "Racial Adjustment After the War," [c. 1945], Southern Regional Council Papers, reel 4, 1–3.

[38]Mark Newman, "The Georgia Baptist Convention and Desegregation, 1945–1980," *Georgia Historical Quarterly* 83 (Winter 1999): 685; Grant, *The Way It Was*, 358, 363–64; Howard Sitkoff, *The Struggle for Black Equality, 1954–1992*, rev. ed. (New York, 1993) 11, 13–14, 18–19.

[39]Newsletter, Georgia Committee on Interracial Cooperation, May 1945, Southern Regional Council Papers, reel 64, item 1989.

[40]Clarence A. Bacote, "The Negro Voter in Georgia Politics Today," *Journal of Negro Education* 26 (Summer 1957): 307.

[41]Grant, *The Way It Was*, 62–66.

[42]*Hapeville Statesman,* 11 April 1946, 1, cited in J. Morgan Kousser, *Colorblind Injustice: Minority Voting and the Undoing of the Second Reconstruction* (Chapel Hill: University of North Carolina Press, 1999) 200.

[43]*Mercer Cluster*, 1 May 1946; *Macon Telegraph*, 5 May 1946, 7.

[44]Joseph L. Bernd, "White Supremacy and the Disfranchisement of Blacks in Georgia, 1946," *Georgia Historical Quarterly* 66 (Winter 1982): 492–500.

[45]*Macon Telegraph*, 16 June 1946, 1, 4.

[46]William P. Randall, interview by Clifford Kuhn and Duane Stewart, 4 February 1989, 15, Georgia Government Documentation Project, Special Collections Department, Pullen Library, Georgia State University, Atlanta, Georgia.

[47]*Macon Telegraph*, 19 July 1946, 7; *Macon Telegraph*, 17 July 1946, 14.

[48]*Macon Telegraph*, 20 April 1947, 1, 3.

[49]*Macon Telegraph*, 1 June 1947, 1; *Macon Telegraph*, 12 June 1947, 1; *Macon Telegraph*, 13 June 1947, 1.

[50]*Macon Telegraph*, 21 July 1947, 1.

[51]*Macon Telegraph*, 14 June 1947, 1; *Macon News*, 14 June 1947, 1, 8. During the gubernatorial campaign of the previous year, Marshall and Calhoun, both stockholders of the *Macon Voice*, engaged in a bitter battle over control of the paper, and over which

candidate to endorse. Calhoun and other majority stockholders filed suit against Marshall and another minority stockholder, A. L. Thomas. When Judge Mallory Atkinson placed the paper into receivership, Marshall began his own paper, the *Macon World.* See *Macon Telegraph*, 23 August 1946, 1, 4; *Macon Telegraph*, 30 August 1946, 16. Black Maconites were divided over the role of Larkin Marshall and the two black newspapers. Letters to the *Macon Telegraph*, suggested that many, including the black Evangelical Ministers' Union, objected to Marshall as a political boss. On 17 June 1947, the Union voted to "condemn this self-styled leader and urge our people to vote their own individual conviction and allow no man to block them," *Macon Telegraph*, 19 June 1947, 6.

[52] *Macon Telegraph*, 21 June 1947, 1; *Macon News*, 21 June 1947, 1. On the aldermanic races, see *Macon Telegraph*, 22 June 1947, 12.

[53] *Macon Telegraph*, 6 January 1948, 1; *Macon Telegraph*, 8 January 1948, 1.

[54] *Macon Telegraph*, 3 September 1948, 10; *Macon Telegraph*, 5 September 1948, 8; *Macon Telegraph*, 1 September 1948, 6.

[55] *Macon Telegraph*, 5 September 1948, 19.

[56] *Macon Telegraph*, 3 September 1948, 6; *Macon Telegraph*, 6 September 1948, 4.

[57] *Macon Telegraph*, 9 September 1948, 1, 2.

[58] Quoted in David McCullough, *Truman* (New York: Simon and Schuster 1992) 570.

[59] *Macon Telegraph*, 2 November 1947, 29.

[60] McCoy and Ruetten, "The Civil Rights Movement: 1940–1954," 20–21; *Macon Telegraph*, 3 February 1948, 1.

[61] *Macon Telegraph*, 4 February 1948, 1; *Macon Telegraph*, 5 February 1948, 6.

[62] *Macon Telegraph*, 20 February 1948, 6.

[63] *Macon Telegraph*, 18 March 1948, 1.

[64] Clive Webb, "Charles Bloch, Jewish White Supremacist," *Georgia Historical Quarterly* 83 (Summer 1999): 271–73; 281.

[65] Webb, "Charles Bloch," 268–69; *Macon Telegraph*, 19 July 1948, 4.

[66] *Macon Telegraph*, 8 August 1948, 1; *Macon Telegraph*, 9 August 1948, 2.

[67] *Macon Telegraph*, 3 November 1948, 1.

[68] *Macon Telegraph*, 30 March 1948, 4; *Macon Telegraph*, 26 April 1948, 4.

[69] *Macon Telegraph*, 7 January 1948, 32; *Macon Telegraph*, 14 January 1948, 6.

[70] *Macon Telegraph*, 20 January 1948, 1; *Macon Telegraph*, 21 January 1948, 5; *Macon Telegraph*, 5 June 1948, 1.

[71] *Macon Telegraph*, 14 May 1949, 1; *Macon Telegraph*, 1 June 1949, 1.

[72] *Macon Telegraph*, 26 July 1949, 1; *Macon Telegraph*, 27 July 1949, 1.

[73] *Macon Telegraph*, 14 July 1946, 1.

[74] *Macon Telegraph*, 2 October 1946, 1; *Macon Telegraph*, 11 October 1946, 1, 3; *Macon Telegraph*, 8 December 1946, 16.

[75] *Macon Telegraph*, 11 and 12 December 1948, 1.

[76] *Macon Telegraph*, 5 February 1948, 1; *Macon Telegraph*, 8 February 1948, 8; *Macon Telegraph*, 1 May 1948, 4.

[77] *Macon Telegraph*, 17 June 1948, 1; *Macon Telegraph*, 28 June 1948, 4.

[78] *Macon Telegraph*, 20 July 1948, 1.

[79]*Macon Telegraph*, 7 January 1949, 1; *Macon Telegraph*, 8 March 1949, 1; Carl D. Bennett, telephone interview by the author, 14 March 2003, notes in author's possession.
[80]*Macon Telegraph*, 13 May 1949, 1; *Macon Telegraph*, 15 June 1949, 1; Walton Smith to *Macon Telegraph*, 26 January 1949, 4.
[81]*Macon Telegraph*, 21 March 1948, 8; Grant, *The Way It Was*, 362.

Chapter 6

[1]Mills Lane, ed., *Georgia: History Written by Those Who Lived It* (Savannah: Beehive Press, 1995) 323–25.
[2]Numan V. Bartley, *The Rise of Massive Resistance: Race and Politics in the South During the 1950's* (Baton Rouge: Louisiana State University Press, 1969); Earl Black, *Southern Governors and Civil Rights: Racial Segregation as a Campaign Issue in the Second Reconstruction* (Cambridge: Harvard University Press, 1976); Robbins L. Gates, *The Making of Massive Resistance: Virginia's Politics of Public School Desegregation, 1954–1956* (Chapel Hill: University of North Carolina Press, 1964); Alexander Leiholdt, *Standing before the Shouting Mob: Lenoir Chambers and Virginia's Massive Resistance to Public-School Integration* (Tuscaloosa: University of Alabama Press, 1997); Charles P. Roland, *The Improbable Era: The South Since World War II* (Lexington: University Press of Kentucky, 1975); Francis M. Wilhoit, *The Politics of Massive Resistance* (New York: G. Braziller, 1973). See also John Bartlow Martin, *The Deep South Says "Never"* (New York: Ballantine Books, 1957).
[3]Herman Talmadge, quoted in Mark Newman, "The Georgia Baptist Convention and Desegregation, 1945–1980," *Georgia Historical Quarterly* 83 (Winter 1999): 691; *Macon Telegraph*, 18 May 1954, 1, 3; *Macon Telegraph*, May 20 1954, 1; *Macon Telegraph*, 24 May 1954, 1. Herman Talmadge, *You and Segregation* (Birmingham AL: Vulcan Press, 1955).
[4]*Macon Telegraph*, 18 May 1954, 1, 3, 8.
[5]*Southern School News* 1 (1 October 1954): 6; *School Southern News* 1 (8 June 1955): 3.
[6]*Macon Telegraph*, 9 September 1954, 1; *School Southern News* (4 November 1954): 10.
[7]*Macon Telegraph*, 8 October 1954, 1; *Macon Telegraph*, 22 October 1954, 1; *Macon Telegraph*, 23 October 1954, 4.
[8]*Macon Telegraph*, 8 October 1954, 8; *Macon Telegraph*, 2 November 1954, 4.
[9]Walter F. Murphy, "The South Counterattacks: The Anti-NAACP Laws," *Western, Political Quarterly* 12 (June 1959): 385; *Macon Telegraph*, 3 November 1954, 1; "Georgia," *School Southern News* 1 (1 December 1954): 6.
[10]*Macon Telegraph*, 14 July 1955, 4; *Macon Telegraph*, 5 August 1955, 18; *Macon Telegraph*, 8 August 1955, 4; *Macon Telegraph*, 16 August 1955, 4; *Macon Telegraph*, 16 August 1955, 1; *Macon Telegraph*, 22 August 1955, 4; *Macon Telegraph*, 15 November 1955, 4; *Macon Telegraph*, 9 September 1955, 8. Inasmuch as the Georgia Constitution required racially segregated schools, to require teachers to support the

constitution was tantamount to requiring that they support segregated education. The board's action did drop specific concerns with NAACP affiliation among teachers.

[11]*Macon Telegraph*, 7 August 1956, 1.

[12]Address by attorney General Eugene Cook, "The Ugly Truth About the NAACP," 1955, Southern Regional Council Papers, Robert W. Woodruff Library, Archives Department, Atlanta University Center, Atlanta, Georgia, reel 19.

[13]*Macon Telegraph*, "Mr. Cook Weakens His Argument by Adopting McCarthy's Tactics," Southern Regional Council Papers, reel 64; "Response to Eugene Cook," October 1955, Southern Regional Council Papers, reel 134; *Macon Telegraph*, 11 September 1955, 1.

[14]*Macon Telegraph*, 31 August 1955, 1; *Macon Telegraph*, 29 September 1955, 3.

[15]"Report on 1956 Legislation," Department of Racial And Cultural Relations, National Council of the Churches of Christ in the United States of America, Southern Regional Council Papers, reel 218; *Macon Telegraph*, 6 February 1956, 4.

[16]*Macon Telegraph*, 10 February 1956, 1; *Macon Telegraph*, 11 February 1956, 6.

[17]*Macon Telegraph*, 6 February 1956, 4; *Macon Telegraph*, 7 February 1956, 4; *Macon Telegraph*, 10 February 1956, 6; *Macon Telegraph*, 16 March 1957, 8.

[18]*Macon Telegraph*, 17 December 1958, 1; *Macon Telegraph*, 1 October 1958, 5; *Macon Telegraph*, 3 December 1958, 4.

[19]Reid H. Cox to Spright Dowell, 3 January 1947, Spright Dowell Files, Special Collections, Jack Tarver Library, Mercer University, Macon, Georgia, box 23, folder 1290.

[20]Horace Calvin Wingo, "Race Relations in Georgia, 1872–1908" (Ph.D. diss., University of Georgia, 1969) 156; John Roach Straton, "Will Education Solve the Race Problem?" *North American Review* 170 (June 1900): 785–801.

[21] Honorary degree committee minutes, 1958–1959, George B. Connell Papers, Special Collections, Jack Tarver Library, Mercer University, Macon, Georgia.

[22]Thomas Gossett to Gus Kaufman, 5 July 1999, Gus A. Kaufman personal papers, Macon GA, copies in author's possession.

[23] Rufus W. Weaver to Guy M. Wells, 29 April 1921; Guy M. Wells to Weaver, 14 May 1921; Guy M. Wells to Rufus W. Weaver, 30 July 1922, Rufus W. Weaver Papers, box 3, folder 101, Special Collections, Jack Tarver Library, Mercer University, Macon, Georgia.

[24]Will Campbell, *The Stem of Jesse: The Costs of Community at a 1960s Southern School* (Macon GA: Mercer University Press, 1994) 15.

[25]Spright Dowell, Address to memorial service for Robert Russa Moton, 4 December 1949, Tuskegee Institute, Spright Dowell Files, box 24, folder 1352, Special Collections, Jack Tarver Library, Mercer University, Macon, Georgia.

[26]Spright Dowell, A History of Mercer University, 1833–1953 (Macon: Mercer University Press, 1958) 327–28; *Macon Telegraph*, 4 February 1940, 2; report by Buford Boone, Spright Dowell Files, box 12A, folder 585; Louie D. Newton, letter to potential donors, 10 April 1941, Spright Dowell Files, box 16, folder 814; Spright Dowell to Joseph P. Duffy, 31 May 1941, Spright Dowell Files, box 16, folder 814.

[27]Joseph M. Hendricks, interview by Andrew Silver, 3 August 2001, 1–2, , Special Collections, Jack Tarver Library, Mercer University, Macon, Georgia.

[28]Howard G. McClain to Guy B. Johnson, 16 October 1946; Guy B. Johnson to Howard G. McClain, 21 November 1946, Southern Regional Council Papers, reel 23; Howard McClain to Mrs. M. E Tilly, 13 November 1947, Southern Regional Council Papers, reel 67.

[29]G. McLeod Bryan, interview by Andrew Silver, 21–22 May 2001, , Special Collections, Jack Tarver Library, Mercer University, Macon, Georgia; Das Kelly Barnett, "Lecture on Old Testament Sources of Christian Ethics," class notes, "History of Christian Ethics," 2 January 1947; "Biblical Ethics," summer 1948, Robert G. Gardner Papers, Special Collections, Jack Tarver Library, Mercer University, Macon, Georgia.

[30]R. L. Russell to Spright Dowell, 10 April 1947; Hansford D. Johnson to R. L. Russell, 12 April 1947, Spright Dowell Files, box 24, folder 1359; *Macon Telegraph*, 31 January 1948, 1; *Macon Telegraph*, 1 February 1948, 6. "Mercer Students Protest the Klan," *Light* 2 (March 1949): 3.

[31]*Mercer Cluster*, 17 January 1958, 3. Joseph Hendricks estimated that "racial radicalism" among Mercer students in the mid-1950s amounted to only some 5 percent. Hendricks interview, 3.

[32]Hendricks interview, 5.

[33]Andrew Silver, *Combustible/Burn: A Play* (Macon GA: Mercer University Press, 2002) x. While this source is a dramatic presentation of the integration of Mercer University, it is based exclusively on more than a hundred interviews with participants. The lines of the play come directly from the words of those interviewees, and thus quality as primary source material.

[34]G. McLeod Bryan, interview by Andrew Silver, 21–22 May 2001, 1, 7, Special Collections, Jack Tarver Library, Mercer University, Macon, Georgia.

[35]Bryan, interview, 21–22 May 2001, 18–19; Joseph M. Hendricks, interview by the author, 2 June 2000, audio recording, Harriet Tubman African American Museum, Macon GA; Charles W. Walker to Rufus C. Harris, 3 August 1962, Rufus C. Harris Papers, box 2, folder 44, Special Collections, Jack Tarver Library, Mercer University, Macon, Georgia.

[36]*Macon Telegraph*, 29 May 1954, 6.

[37]*Macon Telegraph*, 24 June 1954 1; *Macon Telegraph*, 29 June 1954, 1; Silver, *Combustible/Burn*, 57–63.

[38]*Macon Telegraph*, 4 December 1955, 1.

[39]G. McLeod Bryan, *Voices in the Wilderness: Twentieth Century Prophets Speak to the New Millennium* (Macon GA: Mercer University Press, 1999) 7–8; G. McLeod Bryan, interview by the author, 29 March 2003; Bryan, interview, 21–22 May 2001, 2.

[40]*Mercer Cluster*, 15 November 1957, 1.

[41]Thomas Gossett to Gus Kaufman, 5 July 1999, Gus A. Kaufman papers.

[42]Carl D. Bennett to Gus Kaufman, 25 June 1999, Gus A. Kaufman papers; Newman, "The Georgia Baptist Convention," 690, citing Bennett's letter to the *Christian Index*, 17 December 1953.

[43]Carl Bennett. interview by Andrew Silver, Special Collections, Jack Tarver Library, Mercer University, Macon, Georgia, copy in author's possession.

[44]"'Immoral, Illegal, Undemocratic!', Bennett Attacks White Primary," *The Watchtower*, 11 February 1947, copy in Gus A. Kaufman papers.

[45]Carl D. Bennett to Gus Kaufman, 25 June 1999, Gus A. Kaufman papers.

[46]*Macon Telegraph*, 21 July 1946, 8.

[47]"Race in the News," report by the Southern Regional Council, September 1949; clippings from *Time* and *Newsweek,* copies in Gus A. Kaufman papers; Thomas F. Gossett, *Race: The History of an Idea in America* (New York: Oxford University Press, 1963). An updated revision of this classic text was reissued in 1997.

[48]*Macon Telegraph*, 18 May 1954, 1, 8.

[49]*Macon Telegraph*, 14 October 1955, 1.

[50]"Colored People's Page," *Macon Telegraph*, 16 October 1955.

[51]*Macon Telegraph*, 2 February 1956, 1; *School Southern News* 2 (March 1956): 10–11.

[52]*Macon Telegraph*, 11 February 1956, 6.

[53]"Proposals for Program and Organization 1957–58: The Situation in the State," Southern Regional Council Papers, reel 154.

[54]*Macon Telegraph*, 21 January 1958, 2; minutes, Georgia Council on Human Relations, Atlanta, Georgia, 14 October 1959, Georgia Council on Human Relations newsletter, November 1959, Joseph M. Hendricks personal papers, Macon GA, copies in author's possession.

[55]*Macon Telegraph*, 18 May 1954, 1, 8.

[56]*Macon Telegraph*, 24 May 1954, 1; *Macon Telegraph*, 25 May 1954, 1; *Macon Telegraph*, 6 November 1954, 1. The golfers' request was ignored. In November, Mayor B. F. Merritt and city attorney Cloud Morgan declined comment on the matter pending further study. See *Macon Telegraph*, 8 November 1955, 1.

[57]*Macon Telegraph*, 12 November 1954, 1; *School Southern News* 2 (6 January 1955): 7; "Report on Georgia, Current Segregation-Desegregation 1962," 21, Southern Regional Council Papers, reel 123, item 508.

[58]*Macon Telegraph*, 14 July 1955, 1; *Macon Telegraph*, 15 July 1955, 3.

[59]*School Southern News* (8 June 1955): 3; *Macon Telegraph*, 3 August 1955, 1; *Macon Telegraph*, 14 August 1955, 1.

[60]*Macon Telegraph*, 26 August 1955, 1; *Macon Telegraph*, 27 August 1955, 7; *Macon Telegraph*, 8 September 1955, 1; *Macon Telegraph*, 9 September 1955, 1. Board president J. D. Crump appointed former Superior Court Judge Mallory Atkinson to head the committee, which also included McKibben Lane, Wallace Miller, Jr., Charles Hertwig, and George P. Rankin. Blacks who signed the petition were Dr. E. M. Calhoun, Arthur J. Wrice, Jr., Walter E. Davis, Allen Habersham, Harold B. Ingram, Mrs. Rose Walden, Solomon Mims, Guy Johnson, Evelyn Byron, Alice M. Brown, Henry G. Mixon, J. S. Williams, and Atlanta attorney Donald Hollowell.

[61]*Macon Telegraph*, 11 September 1955, 1; *Macon Telegraph*, 13 September 1955, 4; *Macon Telegraph*, 14 October 1955, 1.

[62]*Macon Telegraph*, 23 May 1954, 39; report, Amos O. Holmes to Gloster B. Current, 21 July 1958; report, Amos O. Holmes to Gloster B. Current, 21 August 1958, NAACP Papers, part 25, series D, reel 17, Emory University, Atlanta, Georgia; report on membership statistics, 1962, NAACP Papers, part 25, series B, reel 3.

[63]Amos O. Holmes, "Annual Report, 1959," NAACP Papers, part 25, series B, reel 3; *Pittsburgh Courier*, 16 September 1959, 3; draft article, *Pittsburgh Courier*, 26 September 1959, Trezzvant W. Anderson Papers, box 15, folder 83, Department of Archives, Robert W. Woodruff Library, Atlanta University Center, Atlanta, Georgia; draft article, *Pittsburgh Courier*, 1959, Trezzvant W. Anderson Papers, box 15, folder 82.

[64]*Macon Telegraph*, 30 May 1956, 7.

[65]*Macon Telegraph*, 12 June 1956, 4; *Macon Telegraph*, 19 June 1956, 4.

[66]*Macon Telegraph*, 5 December 1952, 1.

[67]*Macon Telegraph*, 15 October 1955, 1.

[68]*Macon Telegraph*, 20 February 1957, 1; *Macon Telegraph*, 22 February 1957, 2; *Macon Telegraph*, 23 February 1957, 1; *Macon Telegraph*, 21 April 1957, 1; *Macon Telegraph*, 29 April 1957, 1; *Macon Telegraph*, 26 May 1957, 1.

[69]*Macon Telegraph*, 10 January 1957, 1; *Macon Telegraph*, 21 January 1957, 4.

Chapter 7

[1]John Dittmer, *Local People: The Struggle for Civil Rights in Mississippi* (Urbana: University of Illinois Press, 1995); Glenn T. Eskew, *But for Birmingham: The Local and the National Movements in the Civil Rights Struggle* (Chapel Hill: University of North Carolina Press, 1997); Andrew M. Manis, *A Fire You Can't Put Out: The Civil Rights Life of Birmingham's Reverend Fred Shuttlesworth* (Tuscaloosa: University of Alabama Press, 1999); Stephen N. G. Tuck, *Beyond Atlanta: The Struggle for Racial Equality in Georgia, 1940–1980* (Athens: University of Georgia Press, 2001) 245. All of these important studies emphasize the local elements in the civil rights movement. For a short article on the indigenous character of Macon's civil rights movement, see George A. Doss, Jr., "Homegrown Movement in Macon," *New South* 18 (April 1963): 3–10.

[2]Rev. Van Joseph Malone, Sr., interview by WMAZ, 25 August 1992, videocassette, Genealogy Department, Washington Memorial Library, Macon, Georgia. Interviews by WMAZ and the Macon Arts Alliance provided raw footage that was later edited for inclusion in a four-part television series entitled Black Cultural History in Macon, Georgia, which was aired on WMAZ-TV in 1993. Hereinafter cited under the interviewee's name and interviewed by WMAZ.

[3]Williams had left Macon in 1956 to begin a new medical practice in Detroit, in response to increased pressure from the white community for his NAACP activities. Malone, interview, 25 August 1992; *Macon Telegraph*, 6 June 1966, 14.

[4]*Macon Telegraph*, 25 June 1959, 1; Buckner Melton, Sr., interview by the author, 10 April 2003, audio recording, Harriet Tubman African American Museum, Macon GA. In Ed Wilson's first run for political office, the Mercer law professor foiled Denmark Groover's re-election campaign as a member of the Georgia House. Groover contributed to his own defeat in alienating the county's black voters by having served as Governor

Marvin Griffin's floor leader. In that capacity he supported the governor's "massive resistance" agenda, including leading the fight in the Georgia House to incorporate the Confederate emblem into the 1956 Georgia flag.

[5]J. Morgan Kousser, *Colorblind Injustice: Minority Voting and the Undoing of the Second Reconstruction* (Chapel Hill: University of North Carolina Press, 1999) 213.

[6]Draft article, *Pittsburgh Courier*, 21 February 1962, Trezzvant W. Anderson Papers, box 9, folder 65, Department of Archives, Robert W. Woodruff Library, Atlanta University Center, Atlanta, Georgia; *Macon Telegraph*, 22 February 1962, 1.

[7]*Macon Telegraph*, 7 June 1960, 1; *Macon Telegraph*, 7 June 1960, 2; *Macon Telegraph*, 9 June 1960, 1.

[8]*Macon Telegraph*, 8 June 1960, 1, 6.

[9]*Macon Telegraph*, 8 June 1960, 4; *Macon Telegraph*, 9 June 1960, 1; *Macon Telegraph*, 10 June 1960, 1.

[10]*Macon Telegraph*, 9 June 1960, 1; Gus B. Kaufman, interview by the author, 8 June 2000, audio recording, Harriet Tubman African American Museum, Macon GA.

[11]*Macon Telegraph*, 14 June 1960, 2; *Macon Telegraph*, 28 June 1960, 14; *Macon Telegraph*, 2 July 1960, 1.

[12]Doss, "Homegrown Movement," 3–4; *Macon Telegraph*, 2 July 1960, 2.

[13]*Macon Telegraph*, 4 July 1960, 4; *Macon Telegraph*, 6 July 1960, 2.

[14]William P. Randall to Wiley Branton, 29 September 1964, Southern Regional Council Papers, Robert W. Woodruff Library, Archives Department, Atlanta University Center, Atlanta, Georgia, reel 184; William P. Randall, interview by Clifford Kuhn and Duane Stewart, 4 February 1989, 5–6, Georgia Government Documentation Project, Special Collections Department, Pullen Library, Georgia State University, Atlanta, Georgia; William P. Randall, interview by WMAZ, 12 August 1992, videocassette, Genealogy Department, Washington Memorial Library, Macon, Georgia.

[15]Report, Amos O. Holmes to Gloster B. Current, 1 July 1960; Amos O. Homes, "Special Report: Investigation of the Grand Jury Investigation on Negro Bloc Voting in Macon and Bibb County," 26 July 1960, NAACP Papers, part 25, series D, reel 18, Emory University, Atlanta, Georgia; William P. Randall to Wiley Branton, n.d., NAACP Papers.

[16]Georgia House of Representatives *Journal*, 1963, 301, 352, 549, 645–48 and the deposition by Denmark Groover, 23 April 1984 in *US v. Lowndes County*, 19–20, 22–23, 26–28, 48–49, cited in Kousser, *Colorblind Injustice*, 198, 213–15, 228–29.

[17]Clarence A. Bacote, "The Negro in Atlanta Politics," *Phylon* 16 (Winter 1956): 343, in Southern Regional Council Papers, reel 208.

[18]*Macon News*, 21 February 1961; "Cross Burned Here At Home Of Minister," newspaper clipping, n.d., Joseph M. Hendricks personal papers, Macon GA, copy in author's possession; Hendricks, interview with author, 2 June 2000, audio recording, Harriet Tubman African American Museum, Macon GA.

[19]Malone, interview, 25 August 1992; *Macon Telegraph*, 9 June 1960, 1; *Macon Telegraph*, 5 April 1961, 1; Robert L. Anderson, "Leadership Politics and Popular Empowerment: Divisions in the Black Movement in Macon, Georgia," unpublished

manuscript, Yale University, copy in author's possession, 29 September 1986, 4–5; *Macon Telegraph*, 31 May 1961, 5; *Macon Telegraph*, 1 November 1961, 1.

[20]*Macon Telegraph*, 17 May 1960, 6; *Mercer Cluster*, 20 May 1960, 2; statement by the Macon Council of Human Relations, 15 March 1960; Willis B. Glover to Frank J. Hutchings, Sr., 25 April 1960, Joseph M. Hendricks papers.

[21]Doss, "Homegrown Movement," 7; *Macon Telegraph*, 3 June 1961, 1; F. Robert Otto, "Mercer and the Admission of Black Students—A Memoir of Robert Otto," n.d., 4, Joseph M. Hendricks papers.

[22]*Macon Telegraph*, 7 July 1961, 1; *Macon Telegraph*, 1 November 1961, 1.

[23]*Wall Street Journal*, 16 January 1962, 16, in Southern Regional Council Papers, reel 174.

[24]*Macon Telegraph*, 26 February 1961, 1; *Macon Telegraph*, 29 July 1961, 1; Doss, "Homegrown Movement," 6; William P. Randall, interview, 12 August 1992.

[25]*Macon News*, 9 March 1961, 4; *Macon News*, 11 March 1961, 4.

[26]*Macon Telegraph*, 8 August 1961, 8; clipping, *Atlanta Journal*, 9 October 1961, Trezzvant W. Anderson Papers, box 17, folder 1; *Macon Telegraph*, 28 December 1961, 1; *Macon Telegraph*, 5 January 1962, 1; *Macon Telegraph*, 9 February 1962, 1.

[27]*Macon Telegraph*, 10 February 1962, 1.

[28]William P. Randall. interview, 12 August 1992; Hendricks, interview by Andrew Silver, 3 August 2001, 5, Special Collections, Jack Tarver Library, Mercer University, Macon, Georgia.

[29]*Macon Telegraph*, 10 February 1962, 1; Malone, interview, 25 August 1992.

[30]Newsreel footage in *Black Cultural History in Macon, Georgia, Part III: 1930–1970*, Macon Arts Alliance and WMAZ-TV, 1993, videocassette, Geneology Department, Washington Memorial Library, Macon, Georgia.

[31]*Macon Telegraph*, 10 February 1962, 1; *Macon Telegraph*, 11 February 1962, 1, 7; *Macon Telegraph*, 12 February 1962, 1.

[32]Malone, interview, 25 August 1992; *Macon Telegraph*, 13 February 1962, 1, 5; *Macon Telegraph*, 15 February 1962, 1.

[33]Draft article, *Pittsburgh Courier*, 13 February 1962, Trezzvant W. Anderson Papers, box 15, folder 78.

[34]*Macon Telegraph*, 14 February 1962, 1; *Macon Telegraph*, 15 February 1962, 1, 4.

[35]*Macon Telegraph*, 16 February 1962, 1; *Macon Telegraph*, 17 February 1962, 1.

[36]*Macon Telegraph*, 18 February 1962, 4; Melton, interview, 10 April 2003.

[37]Draft article, *Pittsburgh Courier*, 21 February 1962, Trezzvant W. Anderson Papers, box 9, folder 65; *Macon Telegraph*, 22 February 1962, 1.

[38]*Macon Telegraph*, 24 February 1962, 4; *Macon Telegraph*, 27 February 1962, 4; *Macon Telegraph*, 26 February 1962, 1.

[39]*Macon Telegraph*, 27 February 1962, 1.

[40]Melton, interview, 10 April 2003; draft article, *Pittsburgh Courier*, 1 March 1962, Trezzvant W. Anderson Papers, box 7, folder 85; draft article, *Pittsburgh Courier*, 7 March 1962, Trezzvant W. Anderson Papers, box 14, folder 45; Tuck, *Beyond Atlanta*, 140–43; "Synopsis of Recent Civil Rights Developments: Macon, June 25–December 31 1963," Southern Regional Council Papers, series 16, reel 219.

[41]William C. Randall, interview with author, 26 January 2004.

[42]*Macon Telegraph*, 3 October 1962, 8; Rufus C. Harris, "Growing Up To What?" formal university convocation address, 2 October 1962, Thomas J. Homes Papers, box 1, folder 46, Special Collections, Jack Tarver Library, Mercer University, Macon, Georgia; H. L. Young to Rufus C. Harris, 6 October 1962, Rufus C. Harris Papers, box 2, folder 44, Special Collections, Jack Tarver Library, Mercer University, Macon, Georgia.

[43]Will Campbell, *The Stem of Jesse: The Costs of Community at a 1960s Southern School* (Macon GA: Mercer University Press 1994) 41; *Mercer Cluster*, 17 January 1958, 3; *Mercer Cluster*, 8 December 1961, 2; *Christian Index*, 22 November 1962, 8; The 1961 student poll, reported in *Macon News*, 3 February 1961, 3, indicated 309 students (63 percent) saying they would be willing to attend college with blacks; 180 (37 percent) indicated they would not. The poll was cited by Harris in a public statement in which he indicated favoring the integration of Mercer. See *Christian Index*, 2 August 1962, 3.

[44]*Christian Index*, 2 August 1962, 3; W. G. Moffat [Maconite] to Rufus C. Harris, 24 July 1962; Crockett Odom to Rufus C. Harris, 26 July 1962, Rufus C. Harris Papers, box 2, folder 44.

[45]Rev. John C. Forsman and Mrs. Arnold Davis to Rufus C. Harris, 23 October 1962; Rufus C. Harris to Rev. John C. Forsman, 26 October 1962, Thomas J. Holmes Papers, box 1, folder 46; Andrew Silver, *Combustible/Burn: A Play* (Macon GA: Mercer University Press, 2002) 86.

[46]Rufus C. Harris, "Report to the Trustees, October 18, 1962," Rufus C. Harris Papers, box 4, folder 53.

[47]*Mercer Cluster*, November 30, 1962, 2.

[48]*Mercer Cluster*, 26 October 1962, 1; Ben F. Bloodworth, Citizens' Council circulars, in Rufus C. Harris Papers, box 2, folder 44; *Mercer Cluster*, 9 November 1962, 1; *Mercer Cluster*, 9 November 1962, 3, 6; anonymous letter to Rufus C. Harris, 17 November 1962; John M. Martin to Rufus C. Harris, 10 December 1962, Rufus C. Harris Papers, box 2, folder 44; *Christian Index*, 22 November 1962, 3; Alan Scot Willis, "A Baptist Dilemma: Christianity, Discrimination, and the Desegregation of Mercer University," *Georgia Historical Quarterly* 80 (Fall 1996): 599–600.

[49]G. McLeod Bryan to Joe Hendricks, 4 February 1994, Joseph M. Hendricks papers; John T. Mitchell to Rufus C. Harris, Rufus C. Harris Papers, 20 December 1962, box 3, folder 52.

[50]Kent Anglin to Rufus C. Harris, 5 February 1963, Rufus C. Harris Papers, box 4, folder 50; *Macon Telegraph*, 19 April 1963, 1; *New York Times*, 19 April 1963, 12; Campbell, *Stem of Jesse*, 73–76, citing official minutes of the meeting; G. McLeod Bryan to Rufus C. Harris, 29 April 1963, Rufus C. Harris Papers, box 4, folder 53.

[51]*Mercer Cluster*, 20 September 1963, 2; *Houston Post*, 27 January 1991, E4.

[52]Campbell, *Stem of Jesse*, 107–150. Campbell tells the story in detail, along with that of the Black Studies Program at Mercer.

[53]Quoted in Silver, *Combustible/Burn*, 92–96; *Christian Index*, 3 October 1963, 1; Mark Newman, "The Georgia Baptist Convention and Desegregation, 1945–1980," *Georgia Historical Quarterly* 83 (Winter 1999): 702; Grace Bryan Holmes, *Time to*

Reconcile: The Odyssey of a Southern Baptist (Athens: University of Georgia Press, 2000) 226.

[54]F. Robert Otto, interview by Andrew Silver, 3 June 2001, 13–14, Special Collections, Jack Tarver Library, Mercer University, Macon, Georgia; Otto, "Mercer and the Admission of Black Students," 1; Holmes, *Time to Reconcile*, 226–27.

[55]Thomas J. Holmes, *Ashes for Breakfast* (Valley Forge PA: Judson Press, 1969) 18, 20, 21.

[56]Holmes, *Time to Reconcile*, 227; Thomas J. Holmes to congregation, July 27, 1966, Joseph M. Hendricks papers; *Macon Telegraph*, December 15, 1985, 1E.

[57]Holmes, *Time to Reconcile*, 235–36; Holmes letter, ibid.

[58]Thomas J. Holmes to Congregation, 27 July 1966, Joseph M. Hendricks papers; Holmes, *Time to Reconcile*, 238–39; *Macon Telegraph*, 26 September 1966, 3; *Atlanta Constitution*, 26 September 1966, 1, 10.

[59]*Atlanta Constitution*, 2 September 1966; *Christian Index*, 27 October 1966, 3; *Macon Telegraph*, 28 September 1966, 11A; *Macon Telegraph*, 29 October 1973, 3A; Holmes, *Time to Reconcile*; *Baptist Man's Journal* (April/ May/June 1967): 1–7; *Mercer Cluster*, 30 September 1966, 4; Tuck, *Beyond Atlanta*, 140–43; *Mercer Cluster*, 6 November 1973, 3; Fred and Elizabeth Hinesley, *History of Tattnall Square Baptist Church, 1891–1991* (Macon: Tattnall Square Baptist Church, 1991) 10–11, 14–15. The church's seventy-fifth anniversary history, which is reprinted in the 1991 volume, includes two paragraphs noting the July 1966 decision to refuse black worshippers, but nothing on the dismissal of the ministers.

[60]*Macon Telegraph*, 7 November 1966, 4.

[61]*Atlanta Journal Constitution*, 16 October 1962, 16.

Chapter 8

[1]Rayford W. Logan, *The Negro in American Life and Thought: The Nadir, 1877–1901* (New York: Random House, 1954).

[2]Mary Ann Berg Richardson, "The City of Macon, Georgia's Sacrifice to Jim Crow: A. O. Bacon's Gift of Baconsfield Park, 1911–1972" (MA thesis, Georgia College, 1988).

[3]*Macon Telegraph*, 11 April 1963, 2; Buckner Melton, Sr., telephone interview by the author, 22 April 2003, notes in author's possession.

[4]Bacon's 1868 journal, 124–26, and Bacon's manuscript will, 17, 20–21, cited in Richardson, "Georgia's Sacrifice to Jim Crow," 13, 16–17, 20.

[5]Richardson, "Georgia's Sacrifice to Jim Crow," 60–63.

[6] William P. Randall, interview by Clifford Kuhn and Duane Stewart, 4 February 1989, Georgia Government Documentation Project, Special Collections Department, Pullen Library, Georgia State University, Atlanta, Georgia, cited in Richardson, "Georgia's Sacrifice to Jim Crow," 65–66, 68.

[7]Richardson, "Georgia's Sacrifice to Jim Crow," 68, 70–71; *Evans, et al. v. Newton, et al.*, 220 Georgia 280 (1964). On the *cy pres* doctrine, see *Evans et al. v. Abney*, 396 US 435 (1970) www.law.umkc.edu/faculty/projects/ftrials/conlaw/abney.html.

[8]Richardson, "Georgia's Sacrifice to Jim Crow," 71–72; *E. S. Evans, et al. v. Charles E. Newton, et al.*, 382 US 296, 86 US 186, 15 L. Ed. 2d 373 (1966).

[9]Richardson, "Georgia's Sacrifice to Jim Crow," 73–76; *Evans v. Newton et al.*, 221 Georgia 870 (1966); Long's Order and Decree, 14 May 1968; *Evans, et al. v. Abney, Trustee, et al.*, 244 Georgia 286 (1968).

[10]*Evans et al. v. Abney*, 396 US 435 (1970).

[11]*Macon Telegraph*, 10 December 1989, 1C, 2C; Richardson, "Georgia's Sacrifice to Jim Crow," 85.

[12]*Macon Telegraph*, 26 June 1963, 1.

[13]*Macon Telegraph*, 27 June 1963, 1.

[14]*Macon Telegraph*, 4 November 1964, 1. Herbert Dennard, interview with author, 10 January 2004, audio recording, Harriet Tubman African American Museum, Macon GA.

[15]James F. Cook, *The Governors of Georgia, 1754–1995* (Macon GA: Mercer University Press, 1995) 282–85; *Macon Telegraph*, 15 September 1966, 1; *Macon Telegraph*, 29 September 1966, 1.

[16]*Macon Telegraph*, 10 November 1966, 21; Cook, *Governors of Georgia*, 285.

[17]*Macon Telegraph*, 2 November 1967, 1.

[18]*Macon Telegraph*, 6 November 1967, 2; *Macon Telegraph*, 9 November 1967, 1; *Macon Telegraph*, 12 November 1967, 8. Vote totals: Thompson, 14,604 (53.3 percent); Merritt 12,787 (46.7 percent).

[19]*Macon Telegraph*, 5 April 1968, 16; *Macon Telegraph*, 6 April 1968, 3.

[20]William C. Randall, interview with author, 26 January 2004, audio recording, Tubman African American Museum, Macon GA.

[21]*Macon Telegraph*, 5 April 1968, 16; *Macon Telegraph*, 6 April 1968, 3; *Macon Telegraph*, 7 April 1968, 1, 2.

[22]*Macon Telegraph*, 7 April 1968, 1; Joseph M. Hendricks, interview by author, 28 April 2003, notes in author's possession.

[23] Hendricks, interview, 28 April 2003.

[24]*Macon Telegraph*, 7 November 1968, 1. Vote totals: Wallace, 17,296 (42.9 percent); Nixon, 13,413 (32.5 percent); Humphrey, 10,559 (25.6 percent).

[25]Manley F. Brown and Edward Lukemire, "An Oral Interview by Judge W. A. Bootle, Part I," *Journal of Southern Legal History* 7 (1999): 96, 198; Robert A. Pratt. *We Shall Not Be Moved: The Desegregation of the University of Georgia* (Athens: University of Georgia Press, 2002) 89.

[26]Manley F. Brown and Edward Lukemire, "An Oral Interview by Judge W. A. Bootle, Part II," *Journal of Southern Legal History* 8 (2000): 96.

[27]*Macon Telegraph*, 7 January 1961, 1; Brown and Lukemire, "Bootle, Part II," 102–103; *Macon Telegraph*, 11 January 1961, 1; *Mercer Cluster*, 13 January 1961, 2.

[28]*Macon Telegraph*, 11 January 1961, 1; *Macon Telegraph*, 17 January 1961, 2.

[29]Brown and Lukemire, "Bootle, Part II," 107.

[30]Brown and Lukemire, "Bootle, Part II," 107–108; *Macon Telegraph*, 16 January 1961, 4.

[31]*Macon Telegraph*, 17 May 1979, 1, 2; Macon Council on Human Relations, "From Compliance to Cooperation," 30 July 1964, Southern Regional Council Papers, Robert

W. Woodruff Library, Archives Department, Atlanta University Center, Atlanta, Georgia, reel 142.

[32]*Macon Telegraph*, 11 August 1985, 3D; "Not So Civil," 1998 retrospective article, *Macon Telegraph*, n.p., clipping in Gus A. Kaufman papers.

[33]*Macon Telegraph*, 9 December 1969, 9B; *Macon Telegraph*, 15 January 1970, 1, 2A.

[34]Brown and Lukemire, "Bootle, Part II," 109–10; *Macon Telegraph*, 15 January 1970, 1.

[35]*Macon Telegraph*, 19 January 1970, 1, 2, 4A.

[36]*Macon Telegraph*, 22 January 1970, 1, 3A.

[37]*Macon Telegraph*, 23 January 1970, 1, 2A; *Macon Telegraph*, 27 January 1970, 4A.

[38]*Macon Telegraph*, 3 February 1970, 4; *Macon Telegraph*, 2 February 1970, 4.

[39]*Macon Telegraph*, 3 February 1970, 3A; *Macon Telegraph*, 5 February1970, 1, 2.

[40]*Macon Telegraph*, 8 February 1970, 1; *Macon Telegraph*, 8 February 1970, 1, 2; *Macon Telegraph*, 11 February 1970, 1; *Macon Telegraph*, 13 February 1970, 1, 2A; *Macon Telegraph*, 14 February 1970, 1, 4.

[41]*Macon Telegraph*, 14 February 1970, 1, 2, 4A; *Macon Telegraph*, 15 February 1970, 1, 4.

[42]*Macon Telegraph*, 16 February 1970, 1, 2, 4A.

[43]*Macon Telegraph*, 17 February 1970, 1, 2, 3A.

[44]*Macon Telegraph*, 20 February 1970, 1; *Macon Telegraph*, 25 February 1970, 1, 2A.

[45]*Mercer Cluster*, 17 February 1970, 2, 3.

[46]*Macon Telegraph*, 21 February 1970, 4; *Macon Telegraph*, 1 March 1970, 5A; *Macon Telegraph*, 24 February 1970, 4; Palmyra Braswell, interview with author, 24 January 2004, audio recording, Tubman African American Museum, Macon GA.

[47]*Macon Telegraph*, 25 February 1970, 1, 2A.

[48]*Macon Telegraph*, 26 February 1970, 1; *Macon Telegraph*, 27 February 1970, 1.

[49]*Macon Telegraph*, 4 March 1970, 1; *Macon Telegraph*, 14 March 1970, 3A.

[50]*Macon Telegraph*, 16 July 1970, 5; *Macon Telegraph*, 16 February 2002, 1A, 12A.

[51]*Macon Telegraph*, 25 March 1970, 1, 2A.

[52]*Macon Telegraph*, 9 May 1968, 1A; *Macon Telegraph*, 11 May 1968, 1A; Robert L. Anderson, "The Role of Leadership in the Civil Rights Movement in Macon, Bibb County, Georgia: 1959–1971," unpublished research paper, Yale University, copy in author's possession, 1985, 25, based on interviews with Ronnie Thompson and Burton Lee.

[53]*Macon Telegraph*, 2 April 1970, 4A; *Macon Telegraph*, 26 March 1970, 1, 2A.

[54]*Macon Telegraph*, 18 February 1979, 18. Percentages have been rounded off.

[55]*Macon Telegraph*, 26 March 1970, 1, 2A.

[56]William P. Randall, interview, 4 February 1989, 58–60; Anderson, "Role of Leadership," 3–4, citing an interview by Robert Brown; Robert L. Anderson, "Leadership Politics and Popular Empowerment: Divisions in the Black Movement in Macon, Georgia," unpublished research paper, Yale University, copy in author's possession, 29 September 1986, 12.

[57]Anderson, "Leadership Politics," 13–14.

[58]*Macon Telegraph*, 10 June 1970, 3A.

[59]*Macon Telegraph*, 17 June 1970, 1.

[60]Anderson, "Leadership Politics," 15; *Macon Telegraph*, 24 June 1970, 1, 2A.

[61]*Macon Telegraph*, 20 June 1970, 1, 2.

[62]Ibid; *Macon Telegraph*, 21 June 1970, 1, 2.

[63]*Macon Telegraph*, 1 July 1970, 1, 2A; Anderson, "Leadership Politics," 20–22.

[64]*Macon Telegraph*, 5 July 1970, 8A.

[65]*Macon Telegraph*, 6 July 1970, 4A.

[66]*Macon Telegraph*, 16 July 1970, 1A; *Macon Telegraph*, 17 July 1970, 5A; Thompson was convinced that BLF rhetoric made it likely that the young militants intended to burn down the city. Asked by an interviewer what he expected to happen in Macon if he had not issued that order, Thompson replied, "The city would have burned…. The fact is [that] a building *was* burned. We stopped it all. We didn't have a building burned in that particular period. But I think that downtown Macon would have been devastated." Later in the interview, he indicated that he took the "you won't have a town threats" very seriously. See Ronnie Thompson, interview by Andrew Silver, 28 May 2002, 6, 16, Special Collections, Jack Tarver Library, Mercer University, Macon, Georgia.

[67]*Macon Telegraph*, 27 June 1971, 11A; *Macon Telegraph*, 28 June 1971, 1A.

[68]*Macon Telegraph*, 3 July 1971, 1, 2A; *Macon Telegraph*, 6 July 1971, 1A; Anderson, "Leadership Politics," 26–29, citing his interviews with Robert Brown and William P. Randall.

[69]*Macon Telegraph*, 16 July 1971, 1A; *Macon Telegraph*, 17 July 1971, 1A.

[70]*Macon Telegraph*, 16 July 1971, 1, 2A.

[71]*Macon Telegraph*, 17 July 1971, 1, 10A; *Macon Telegraph*, 18 July 1971, 1, 3A.

[72]*Macon Telegraph*, 18 July 1971, 3A; Thompson, interview, 28 May 2002, 20; *Macon Telegraph*, 4 November 1971, 6.

[73]*New York Times*, 8 July 1971, 39; 11 May 1974, 17; Henry Ficklin, interview with author, 30 January 2004, audio recording, Tubman African American Museum, Macon GA; Robert L. Scott, Jr., interview with author, 22 January 2004, audio recording, Tubman African American Museum, Macon GA.

[74]*Mercer Cluster*, 11 October 1974, 2.

[75]*Macon Telegraph*, 9 August 1972, 1A; *Macon Telegraph*, 18 February 1979, 10A.

[76]*Macon Telegraph*, 18 February 1979, 10A; Anderson, "Leadership Politics," 30–31.

[77]*Macon Telegraph*, 18 April 1975, 1, 2A; *Macon Telegraph*, 5 September 1975, 1; *Macon Telegraph*, 9 September 1975, 1, 2A; *Macon Telegraph*, 6 September 1975, 4A.

[78]*Macon Telegraph*, 11 September 1975, 1, 2A; *Macon Telegraph*, 20 September 1975, 1, 2A; *Macon Telegraph*, 25 September 1975, 1, 2A; *Macon Telegraph*, 5 February 1995, 2B; *Macon Telegraph*, 10 April 1978, 1B.

[79]*Macon Telegraph*, 30 March 1976, 3A; *Macon Telegraph*, 1 December 1979, 1B.

Chapter 9

[1]Dinesh D'Souza, *The End of Racism: Principles for a Multiracial Society* (New York: Simon and Schuster, 1996).

[2]Reagan's words come from his 28 October 1980 debate with President Jimmy Carter. Transcript from the Public Broadcasting Service, http://www.pbs.org/newshour/debatingourdestiny/newshour/80_carter–reagan.html.

[3]The term comes from James Davison Hunter, *Culture Wars: The Struggle to Define America* (New York: Basic Books, 1990). Two years later the appearance of Hunter's work, the term became part of common journalistic parlance after Patrick Buchanan told the Republican National Convention that the nation was embroiled in "a religious and cultural war...for the soul of America." By discussing race in only fifteen, nonconsecutive pages in a 400–page study, Hunter greatly downplays the role of race in America's culture war. For a different perspective, see Andrew M. Manis, *Southern Civil Religions in Conflict: Civil Rights and the Culture Wars* (Macon GA: Mercer University Press, 2002).

[4]This image of America has existed at least as long as the melting pot metaphor, first put forward by Horace Kallen, "Democracy Versus the Melting–Pot," *The Nation,* 18 February 1915, 13; 25 February 1915, 14, cited in Arthur M. Schlesinger Jr., *The Disuniting of America* (New York: Whittle Direct Books, 1991) 13, 86.

[5]*Macon Telegraph*, 25 October 1978, 4A.

[6]Cashin survey cited in Stephen N. G. Tuck, *Beyond Atlanta: The Struggle for Racial Equality in Georgia, 1940–1980* (Athens: University of Georgia Press, 2001) 245.

[7]Jay Vitalian, "Letter to the Editor," *Mercer Cluster*, 1 April 1983, 1.

[8]Karen Jacob, "Living In Oz," *Mercer Cluster*, 22 April 1988, 6; "Discrimination Exist on Campus," *Mercer Cluster*, 12 October 1992, 4.

[9]*Macon Telegraph*, 5 April 1988, 1D; *Mercer Cluster*, 8 April 1983, 3; *Mercer Cluster*, 20 April 1990, 2.

[10]*Macon Telegraph*, 14 January 1980, 1; Mercer *Cluster*, 16 January 1981, 3.

[11]Taylor Branch, "Uneasy Holiday Redux," *New Republic*, 18 January 2002. See http://www.tnr.com/express/branch011802.html.

[12]*Macon Telegraph*, 18 January 1988, 1, 5A; Jonathan Miller, "Opinion: King Holiday Is More Than One Day," *Mercer Cluster*, 23 January 1989, 5.

[13]Richard Keil, interview with the author, 3 February 2004, audio recording, Tubman African American Museum, Macon GA.

[14]*Macon Telegraph*, 23 May 1986; 3D; *Macon Telegraph*,13 June 1987; 2B; *Macon Telegraph*, 11 November 1988; 3D.

[15]*Macon Telegraph*, 17 September 1997, B1; *Macon Telegraph*, 20 February 1998, B2; *Macon Telegraph*, 29 July 1998, B1; *Macon Telegraph*, 2 September 1998, B1.

[16]*Macon Telegraph,* 30 April 2001, A1; *Macon Telegraph*, 19 December 2001, A1; *Macon Telegraph*, 26 April 2002, B1; *Macon Telegraph*, 25 August 2002, A1; *Macon Telegraph*, 22 November 2002, A1; *Macon Telegraph*, 17 August 17, 2003. Special Section, 8. See also the Tubman website (http://www.tubmanmuseum.com/geninfo/history.htm).

[17]*Macon Telegraph*, 4 October 1980, 3B; *Macon Telegraph*, 12 June 1984, 1D, 2D.

[18]*Macon Telegraph*, 18 February 1986, 1B, 2B.

[19]*Macon Telegraph*, 20 March 1987, 1B, 2B; *Macon Telegraph*, 21 April 1987, 1B.

[20]*Macon Telegraph*, 29 June 1996, 1C; *Macon Telegraph*, 21 September 1996, 1C; Rev. Eddie B. Smith, Sr., telephone interview by author, 23 May 2003, notes in author's possession.

[21]*Macon Telegraph*, 20 January 1998, 1A; *Macon Telegraph*, 3 February 1998. 1B.

[22]*Macon Telegraph*, 5 April 1998. 1A.

[23]*Macon Telegraph*, 10 April 1981, 1B; *Macon Telegraph*, 13 July 1981, 1B. See also http://www.mindspring.com/~teeth/caution/macontg100years.htm.

[24]*Macon Telegraph*, 2 November 1980, 1C; *Macon Telegraph*, 11 January 1981, 1A.

[25]*Macon Telegraph*, 14 March 1981, 1B; *Macon Telegraph*, 15 April 1981, 1B; *Macon Telegraph*, 13 July 1981, 1B; *Macon Telegraph*, 12 September 1981, 1B.

[26]*Macon Telegraph*, 22 October 1981, 1B; *Macon Telegraph*, 25 October 1981, 1C; *Macon Telegraph*, 9 November 1981, 1B.

[27]*Macon Telegraph*, 6 November 1980, 1C.

[28]*Macon Telegraph*, 8 July 1983, 1A, 7A.

[29]*Macon Telegraph*, 1 February 1981, 1C; *Macon Telegraph*, 31 August 1983, 1B. *Macon Telegraph*, 1 September 1983, 1B.

[30]*Macon Telegraph*, 20 June 1983, 1B.

[31]*Macon Telegraph*, 20 June 1983, 1B; *Macon Telegraph*, 11 March 1984, 1C, 2C.

[32]*Macon Telegraph*, 14 March 1984, 1A, 4A, 11A, 1B; *Macon Telegraph*, 18 March 1984, 1B; *Macon Telegraph*, 3 June 1984, 2C.

[33]*Macon Telegraph*, 16 October 1984, 1A, 10A, 11A.

[34]*Macon Telegraph*, 24 October 1984, 7A.

[35]*Mercer Cluster*, 2 November 1984, 1; *Macon Telegraph*, 7 November 1984, 1B, 6B; *Macon Telegraph*, 8 November 1984, 1C; *Macon Telegraph*, 11 November 1984, 1A; *Macon Telegraph*, 9 November 1988, 1A, 9A. Bibb County votes totals for 1984: Mondale, 26,427 (52.6 percent); Reagan, 24,170 (47.4 percent). 1988 totals: Bush, 22,179 (50.1 percent); Dukakis, 22,084 (49.9 percent).

[36]*Macon Telegraph*, 4 November 1992, 1A, 4A; *Macon Telegraph*, 6 November 1996, 1A; *Macon Telegraph*, 8 November 2000, 3B. Republicans Bob Dole and George W. Bush carried Georgia in 1996 and 2000, despite losing Bibb County. Between 1980 and 2000 white Bibb County voters trended clearly toward the Republican Party, as seen in the percentages of voters who voted against the Democratic candidates: 1980, 33.5 percent; 1984, 47.4 percent; 1988, 50.1 percent; 1992, 48 percent; 1996, 49 percent; 2000, 49.1 percent. Since upwards of 90 percent of Bibb's county's black voters have supported Democrats, voting patterns over the last fifth of the twentieth century show significantly racial polarization.

[37]This narrative of the related Rodney King incidents, as well as the quotation, comes from David K. Shipler, *A Country of Strangers: Blacks and Whites in America* (New York: Alfred A. Knopf, 1997) 387–89.

[38]*Macon Telegraph*, 5 June 1992, 11A; *Macon Telegraph*, 6 June 1992, 1A, 13A.

[39]*Macon Telegraph*, 1 May 1992, 4A; *Macon Telegraph*, 3 May 1992, 4B.

[40]*Macon Telegraph*, 2 May 1992, 13A; *Macon Telegraph*, 3 May 1992, 1B.

[41]*Macon Telegraph*, 13 May 1992, 9A; *Macon Telegraph*, 17 May 1992, 5B.

[42]*Macon Telegraph*, 17 May 1992, 5B; *Macon Telegraph*, 24 May 1992, 5B; *Macon Telegraph*, 25 May 1992, 12A.

[43]*Mercer Cluster*, 12 October 1992, 4, 5.

[44]*Macon Telegraph*, 13 May 1992, 9A.

[45]*Macon Telegraph*, 23 May 1992, 16A.

[46]*Macon Telegraph*, 6 May 1992, 1A.

[47]*Macon Telegraph*, 14 May 1992, 9A; *Macon Telegraph*, 13 May 1992, 13A; *Macon Telegraph*, 5 June 1992, 11A.

[48]*Macon Telegraph*, 4 June 1992, 11A.

[49]*Macon Telegraph*, 14 May 1992, 9A.

[50]*Macon Telegraph*, 3 June 1992 1B, 2B.

[51]*Macon Telegraph*, 31 May 1992, 4B; *Macon Telegraph*, 1 June 1992, 3A, 4A.

[52]*Macon Telegraph*, 28 May 1992, 2B.

[53]*Macon Telegraph*, 7 June 1992, 5B.

[54]*Macon Telegraph*, 16 June 1992, 7A.

[55]*Macon Telegraph*, 29 May 1992, 1, 8A; *Macon Telegraph*, 2 June 1992, 1B.

[56]*Macon Telegraph*, 4 June 1992, 11A.

[57]*Macon Telegraph*, 29 May 1992, 1, 8A.

[58]*Macon Telegraph*, 31 May 1992, 12A; *Macon Telegraph*, 5 June 1992, 11A.

[59]*Macon Telegraph*, 8 March 1995, 1B.

[60]Vote totals: Marshall, 7,458 (50.4 percent); Ellis, 7,338 (49.6 percent). See *Macon Telegraph*, 13 September 1995, 1A.

[61]*Macon Telegraph*, 13 May 1997, 1A.

[62]*Macon Telegraph*, 11 June 1997, 3A.

[63]*Macon Telegraph*, 13 June 1997, 18A.

Chapter 10

[1]W. E. B. Du Bois, *The Souls of Black Folk* (New York: Vintage Books, 1990) 16.

[2]*Macon Telegraph*, 20 July 1999, 1A; *Atlanta Journal and Constitution*, 21 July 1999, 3C; *Macon Telegraph*, 22 July 1999, 1A.

[3]*Macon Telegraph*, 22 July 1999, 1A.

[4]*Macon Telegraph*, 14 December 1999, 14A.

[5]*Macon Telegraph,* 24 December 1999, 1A; *Macon Telegraph,* 23 December 1999, 1C; *Macon Telegraph,* 7 January 1999, 1A; *Macon Telegraph,* 2 January 2000, 10B.

[6]*Macon Telegraph,* 26 December 2000, 6D; *Macon Telegraph***,** 2 January 2000, 11D; *Macon Telegraph,* 2 January 2000, 10B; *Macon Telegraph***,** 13 January 2000, 1A.

[7]*Macon Telegraph,* 26 December 2000, 6D; *Macon Telegraph***,** 2 January 2000, 11D; *Macon Telegraph,* 29 December 2000, 13A.

[8]*Macon Telegraph***,** 5 January 2000, 1B; *Macon Telegraph,* 8 January 2000, 1A, 12A; *Macon Telegraph,* 26 December 1999, 6D.

[9]*Macon Telegraph*, 7 January 2000, 1C; *Macon Telegraph*, 13 January 2000, 1A; *Macon Telegraph,* 2 March 2000, 1A.

[10]*Macon Telegraph,* 2 January 2000, 10B; *Macon Telegraph,* 4 January 2000, 8A; *Macon Telegraph,* 18 January 2000, 6A; Charles Richardson, interview with author, 2 June 2003, audio recording, Tubman African American Museum, Macon GA.

[11]"New 'Segregation Academies' Are Flourishing in the South," *South Today,* October 1969, in Southern Regional Council Papers, reel 218, Robert W. Woodruff Library, Archives Department, Atlanta University Center, Atlanta, Georgia.

[12]Ibid.

[13]Leonard Levine and Kitty Griffith, "The Busing Myth: Segregation Academies Bus More Children, and Further," *South Today,* 7, in Southern Regional Council Papers, reel 218.

[14]*Macon Telegraph,* 11 March 1960, 1A; *Macon Telegraph,* 27 April 1960, 12A.

[15]*Macon Telegraph,* 24 April 1969, 1A.

[16]*Macon Telegraph,* 25 April 1969, 1A, 2A; *Macon Telegraph,* 1 February 1970, 9A.

[17]*Macon Telegraph,* 13 September 1969, 3A; *Macon Telegraph,* 8 November 1998, 1E.

[18]All figures come from the US Census, 1960, 1970, 1990, and 2000 (www.census.gov.) and the Georgia Department of Education (http://www.doe.k12.ga.us/_dbs/schools/private.asp?u_SystemID=611); *Macon Telegraph,* 3 February 2002, 1A, 4A; Richardson, interview, 2 June 2003; Peter C. Brown, interview with author, 30 January 2004, audio recording, Tubman African American Museum, Macon GA. Brown, director of the Mercer University Center for Community Development, cited percentages from a presentation by Linda Barrs, chairperson of the Georgia Board of Education.

[19]*Macon Telegraph,* 1 September 1975, 1, 2A; *Macon Telegraph,* 3 September 1975, 1, 2A.

[20]The story of "Susie" and "Vanessa" comes from a narrative on black-white relations solicited from my students during the course of my research for this study. I have, of course, changed the names to protect their privacy.

[21]F. Stebin Horne III, interview with author, 4 February 2004, audio recording, Tubman African American Museum, Macon GA, and Cole Thomason, interview with author, 21 February 2004, audio recording, Tubman African American Museum, Macon GA.

[22]*Macon Telegraph,* 3 February 2002, 1A, 4A.

[23]Alex C. Habersham, interview with author, 20 February 2004, audio recording, Tubman African American Museum, Macon GA.

[24]Richardson, interview, 2 June 2003; conversation with Jessica Annis, a student at Macon's Central High School, December 2003.

[25]*Macon Telegraph,* 18 July 2001, 1, 10A.

[26]Reverend James Louis Bumpus, interview with author, 28 February 2004, audio recording, Tubman African American Museum, Macon GA.

[27]Ibid.

[28]*Macon Telegraph,* 3 February 2002, 1A, 4A; Brown, interview, 30 January 2004.

[29]*Macon Telegraph*, 20 February 2002, 1B; *Macon Telegraph,* 7 March 2002, 1A; *Macon Telegraph,* 17 December 2002, 1A. For final redistricting plan, see http://www.bibb.k12.ga.us/final.htm.

[30]*Macon Telegraph*, 22 March 2001, 2B.

[31]*Macon Telegraph*, 14 April 2001, 2B; *Macon Telegraph,* 5 September 2002, 1B; *Macon Telegraph*, 8 September 2002, 1B.

[32]*Macon Telegraph*, 10 September 2002, 1B; *Macon Telegraph*, 5 April 2002, 1B; *Macon Telegraph,* 3 May 2002, 12C.

[33]*Macon Telegraph,* 19 November 2000, 1A.

[34]*Macon Telegraph*, 15 June 2001, 1B; *Macon Telegraph,* 19 July 2001, 1, 8A.

[35]*Macon Telegraph,* July 2001, 1B; *Macon Telegraph,* 19 May 2001, 1B.

[36]Neal Boortz, See http://www.boortz.com/july12.htm.

[37]See http://www.fortunecity.com/meltingpot/harrow/505/KennyBglossary.html; See also *Macon Telegraph, 2* February 2001, 1B.

[38]See http://www.fortunecity.com/meltingpot/harrow/505/SCLNphotos.htm.

[39]Palmyra Braswell, interview with author, 24 January 2004, audio recording, Tubman African American Museum, Macon GA; Elaine Lucas, interview with author, 31 January 2004, audio recording, Tubman African American Museum, Macon GA.

[40]*Macon Telegraph*, 20 August 2001, 8A.

[41]C. Jack Ellis, 2003 State of the City Address, 14 March 2003. See http://www.city ofmacon.net/ CityDept/mayor/speeches/State%20of%20City%20Release.doc.

[42]*Macon Telegraph,* 28 November 2000, 1A; Chester Fontenot to members of the Mayor's Community Diversity Committee, 4 November 2002, Joseph M. Hendricks personal papers, Macon GA; Joseph M. Hendricks, interview with author, 27 May 2003, audio recording, Tubman African American Museum, Macon GA; *Macon Telegraph,* 21 November 2002, 1B; *Macon Telegraph*, 22 November 2002, A8.

[43]*Macon Telegraph*, 16 July 2003, A1; *Macon Telegraph*, 16 July 2003, A4.

[44]*Macon Telegraph,* 17 July 2003, A7; *Macon Telegraph,* 20 July 2003, A8; *Macon Telegraph*, 21 July 2003, B5; *Macon Telegraph,* 22–25 July 2003, see Letters to the Editor pages.

[45]*Macon Telegraph*, 13 July 2003, A8.

[46]*Macon Telegraph*, 16 July 2003, A4, A5; *Macon Telegraph,* 16 July 2003, A8; *Macon Telegraph*, 24 July 2003, A8.

[47]*Macon Telegraph*, 16 July 16, 2003, A4; Brenda C. Youmas, interview with author, 26 February 2004, audio recording, Tubman African American Museum, Macon GA.

[48]*Macon Telegraph*, 3 September 2003, B1; *Macon Telegraph*, 5 November 2003, A1; *Macon Telegraph*, 9 November 2003, A10; *Macon Telegraph*, 10 November 2003, B5. Voter registration percentages and vote totals in these nine precincts are derived from a report on "Active Voters by Race/Gender," 1 March 2004, and a printout of the 2003 general election returns, both courtesy of the Bibb County Board of Elections.

[49]*Macon Telegraph*, 31 July 2003, B5.

[50] Albert Billingslea, interview with author, 17 January 2004, audio recording, Tubman African American Museum, Macon GA; Lonzy Edwards, interview with author, audio recording, Tubman African American Museum, Macon GA; Catherine Meeks,

interview with author, 29 January 2004, audio recording, Tubman African American Museum, Macon GA; Herbert Dennard, interview with author, 10 January 2004, audio recording, Tubman African American Museum, Macon GA.

[51]*Macon Telegraph,* 21 November 2002, 1B.

[52]The survey was based on telephone interviews with a representative sample of 800 adults over eighteen years of age, conducted 16–30 July 2002.

[53]"An Update of Public Opinion on Local Issues in Macon, Georgia," October 2002, 5, John S. and James L. Knight Foundation Community Indicators Project, see http://www.knightfdn.org/indicators/2002/mac/macon_reports_2002.pdf. Hereinafter cited as *Knight Report.*

[54]*Knight Report*, 8.

[55]Charles Richardson, interview author, 31 May 2003, audio recording, Tubman African American Museum, Macon GA; Betty Jean Slater, interview author, 20 February 2004, audio recording, Tubman African American Museum, Macon GA; Meeks, interview, 29 January 2004; interview with Richard Hutto, 6 February 2004; conversation with Faira Holliday, 16 March 2004.

[56]*Knight Report*, 9.

[57]*Knight Report*, 13, 15.

[58]*Macon Telegraph*, 17 November 2002, 1A, 10A.

[59]"Georgia County Guide," Center for Agribusiness and Economic Development, http//:wwwgeorgiastats.uga.edu.

[60]*Macon Telegraph,* 11 March 2003, 6A.

[61]Jim Lee, interview with author, 10 January 2004, audio recording, Tubman African American Museum, Macon GA.

[62]Horne, interview, 4 February 2004; Thomason, interview, 21 February 2004; Charles W. Bishop, interview with author, 23 January 2004, audio recording, Tubman African American Museum, Macon GA.

[63]This poll was constructed by the author and administered in twenty-three different classes in the Social Science Division (education, history, political science, psychology, and sociology) at Macon State College during the spring 2004 semester. The total number of respondents (392) represents 7 percent of the college's total enrollment. Racial composition of the respondents was 60.2 percent white, 34.4 percent African American, and 5.4 percent Hispanic, Asian, or Other. In addition, the average age of students at Macon State College is twenty-seven years, older than the traditional age college student. Thus, although admittedly unscientific, the poll is nonetheless fairly representative of opinion among this group of college students.

[64]"Georgia 2000 Information System," http://www.georgia2000.org.

[65]Ibid.

[66]US Census, 2000; *Annual Demographic Supplement to the March 2002 Current Popular Survey.* See http://factfinder.census.gov.

[67]Jesse McKinnon, "The Black Population in the United States: March 2002," 7; US Census, 2000. See http://factfinder.census.gov.

[68]Ibid.

[69]Youmas, interview, 26 February 2004; William C. Randall, interview with author, 26 January 2004, audio recording, Tubman African American Museum, Macon GA.

[70]Richardson, interview; Ella Carter, interview with author, 17 February 2004, audio recording, Tubman African American Museum, Macon GA; Myra Jackson, interview with author, 4 May 2003, audio recording, Tubman African American Museum, Macon GA.

[71]Meeks, interview, 29 January 2004; Bumpus, interview, 28 February 2004.

[72]Robert L. Scott, Jr., interview with author, 23 January 2004, audio recording, Tubman African American Museum, Macon GA.

[73]Willie J. Shuler, Jr., interview with author, 6 February 2004, audio recording, Tubman African American Museum, Macon GA.

[74]*Macon Telegraph*, 2 May 2002, A1, 10A; See Allen Fishbein, "CCC Study Finds Subprime Lenders Target Minorities," *Housing and Neighborhood* 1 (Spring 2002): 10–12. This is the official newsletter of the Center for Community Change.

[75]*Macon Telegraph*, 21 January 2002, 1A.

[76]*Macon Telegraph*, 20 January 2003, 1A, 6A.

[77]*Macon Telegraph*, 10 November 2002, 1A, 10A; *Macon Telegraph*, 13 November 2002, 1A, 10A.

[78]*Macon Telegraph*, 25 May 2003, 8A; *Macon Telegraph*, 29 May 2003, 10A.

[79]Bennie Stephens, interview with Andrew Silver, 26 July 2001, 17–18, Special Collections, Jack Tarver Library, Mercer University, Macon, Georgia; *Macon Telegraph*, 26 January 1992, 7B; Adam Land, "Letters to the Editor: Race a Problem at Mercer," *Mercer Cluster*, 7 February 2002, 16.

[80]Korey L. Johnson, personal narrative on black-white relations in Macon, Macon State College, 12 December 2002, in author's possession; the Virginia transplant to Macon is the author's wife; Charlene Goodwin, interview with author, 21 August 2002, in author's possession.

[81]Scott Peaster, personal narrative on black-white relations in Macon, Macon State College, 29 October 2002, in author's possession.

[82]Shynobia Williams, personal narrative on black-white relations in Macon, Macon State College, , 28 April 2003, in author's possession.

[83]Renata Mathews, personal narrative of black-white relations in Macon, Macon State College, , 1 April 2003, in author's possession; Brittany M. Shepherd, "Culture Credit Reaction Paper," 18 January 2002, in author's possession.

[84]Joyce Grubbs, interview with author, 13 May 2003, in author's possession.

[85]Email from Jessica Annis to author, 1 February 2004; Chamoya Faulks, personal narrative of black-white relations in Macon, Macon State College, , 23 July 2002, in author's possession.

Epilogue

[1]Peter C. Brown, interview with author, 30 January 2004, audio recording, Tubman African American Museum, Macon GA.

[2]Andrew M. Manis, *A Fire You Can't Put Out: The Civil Rights Life of Birmingham's Reverend Fred Shuttlesworth* (Tuscaloosa: University of Alabama Press, 1999).

[3]Frank Stagg, *Polarities of Human Existence in Biblical Perspective*, rev. ed. (Macon GA: Smyth and Helwys Publishing, 1994).

[4]Creede Hinshaw, interview with author, 2 March 2004, audio recording, Tubman African American Museum, Macon GA.

[5]Richard Hutto , interview with author, 6 February 2004, audio recording, Tubman African American Museum, Macon GA.

[6]Brenda C. Youmas, interview with author, 26 February 2004, audio recording, Tubman African American Museum, Macon GA.

[7]*Macon Telegraph*, 10 May 2003, 6A; "After 30 Years, King's Legacy Still Bleeds," *Baptist Standard*, 8 April 1998.

[8]Paul Kivel, *Uprooting Racism: How White People Can Work for Racial Justice* (Gabriola Island, BC, Canada: New Society Publishers, 2002) 1–4.

[9]In 2002, white life expectancy in the United States was 76.9 years, compared to a black life expectancy of 71.2 years. See *National Vital Statistics Report* 50 (16 September 2002): 2. In Georgia, white life expectancy was 82.5 years in 2001. Black life expectancy was 80.8 years. Printed report, Office of Health Information and Policy, Georgia Division of Public Health, 2001.

[10]Thomas M. Shapiro, *The Hidden Cost of Being African American* (New York: Oxford University Press, 2004) 47, 64–67.

[11]David Rusk, *The "Segregation Tax": The Cost of Racial Segregation to Black Homeowners*. Brookings Institution, 2001. Available at www.brookings.edu/es/urban/publications/ruskexsum.htm.

[12]Walter Williams, "Shameful College Practices," *Macon Telegraph*, 15 April 2004, 8A. Williams complained about a "White Privilege Forum" held in spring 204 semester at the University of Louisville.

[13]Trina Williams, "The Homestead Act: A Major Asset-building Policy in American History," presented at the Inclusion in Asset Building: Research and Policy Symposium organized by the Center for Social Development, September 2000. Available at gwbweb.wustl.edu/csd/Publications/2000/wp00-9.pdf.

[14]Eric Foner, "Hiring Quotas for White Males Only," *The Nation,* 26 June 1995, 24.

[15]Shapiro, *The Hidden Cost,* 75–77.

[16]Stephen Grant Meyer, *As Long As They Don't Move Next Door: Segregation and Racial Conflict in American Neighborhoods* (Lanham MD: Rowman & Littlefield Publishers, Inc., 2000) 7–8; Andrew Wiese, *Places of Their Own African American Suburbanization in the Twentieth Century* (Chicago: University of Chicago Press, 2004); George Lipsitz, *The Possessive Investment in Whiteness: How White People Profit From Identity Politics* (Philadelphia: Temple University Press, 1998) 6; Shapiro, *The Hidden Cost,* 77–79.

[17]Kivel, *Uprooting Racism,* 32–34. Kivel's checklist includes a total of thirty-five such benefits.

[18]Peggy McIntosh, "White Privilege and Male Privilege: A Personal Account of Coming to See Correspondences through Work in Women's Studies," working paper

189, 1988, Wellesley College Center for Research on Women. See http://seamonkey.ed.asu.edu/~mcisaac/emc598ge/"\l"daily.

[19]Eddie B. Smith, Sr., interview with author, 23 May 2003, in author's possession.

[20]Jimmie Samuel, interview with author, 5 February 2004, audio recording, Tubman African American Museum, Macon GA.

[21]Alex C. Habersham, interview with author, audio recording, Tubman African American Museum, Macon GA.

[22]Martin Luther King Jr., "Our God is Marching On," 25 March 1965, Montgomery, Alabama. The speech was delivered in front of the Alabama state Capitol, at the end of the historic Selma-to-Montgomery March. The full text of the speech is available at the Martin Luther King, Jr. Papers Project at Stanford University. See http://www.stanford .edu/group/King/publications/speechesFrame.htm.

Appendix

Comparative Results on Race Relations Poll

Poll was conducted by Andrew M. Manis among students enrolled in Social Science courses at Macon State College during the Spring 2004 semester.

Total Respondents (392)

White:	60.2% (236)
African American:	34.4% (135)
Hispanic, Asian, or Other:	5.4% (21)

1. In Macon whites talk about race...

	Whites	African Americans	Other
Too much	55%	28%	43%
Too little	8%	24%	10%
About the right amount	32%	41%	43%
No Answer	5%	7%	5%

2. In Macon, African Americans talk about race...

	Whites	African Americans	Other
Too much	73%	50%	71%
Too little	4%	10%	5%
About the right amount	20%	36%	24%
No Answer	3%	4%	0%

3. Which is the bigger problem in keeping the US from being a colorblind society?

	Whites	African Americans	Other
Whites discriminating against blacks	8%	22%	19%
Blacks blaming whites	35%	13%	24%

for their problems

	Whites	African Americans	Other
Both of these equally	43%	49%	28%
Other (Specify)	14%	13%	28%
No Answer	0%	3%	0%

4. When do you think the US will achieve racial equality?

	Whites	African Americans	Other
Never	27%	43%	24%
Not in my lifetime	48%	38%	38%
In my lifetime	11%	13%	19%
We're pretty close to it now	8%	6%	10%
We have it now	3%	0%	5%
No Answer	0%	1%	5%

5. How would you rate black-white relations in contemporary Macon?

	Whites	African Americans	Other
Excellent	0.4%	0%	0%
Good	28%	23%	19%
Fair	49%	64%	38%
Poor	20%	10%	29%
Terrible	0.8%	2%	14%
No Answer	1.8%	1%	0%

6. In America today the "playing field" of equal opportunity is…

	Whites	African Americans	Other
Just about level	24%	6%	24%
Tilted slightly toward whites	41%	44%	28%
Tilted greatly toward whites	11%	41%	28%
Tilted slightly toward blacks	21%	2%	10%
Tilted greatly toward blacks	3%	0%	10%
No Answer	0%	7%	0%

Bibliography

I. PRIMARY SOURCES
A. Manuscript Collections
Atlanta University Center
Association of Southern Women for the Prevention of Lynching Papers.
Clarence Bacote Papers, Robert W. Woodruff Library.
Commission on Interracial Cooperation Papers.
Countee Cullen /Harold Jackman Collection.
Georgia Council on Human Relations Papers.
Southern Conference on Human Welfare Papers.
Southern Regional Council Papers.

Jack Tarver Library at Mercer University
George B. Connell Papers.
Robert G. Gardner Papers.
Rufus C. Harris Files.
Rufus W. Weaver Files.
Spright Dowell Files.
Thomas J. Holmes Papers.
Walter L. Moore Papers.
William Heard Kilpatrick Papers.

Archives and Geneology Department, Washington Memorial Library
Ballard Normal School Historical Collection.
Charles J. Bloch Papers.

Booker T. Washington Community Center office files.
Jessie Daniel Ames Collection, University of North Carolina, Southern History
        Collection, Chapel Hill, North Carolina.
Julian Harris Papers, Emory University, Atlanta, Georgia.
Joseph M. Hendricks papers.
Gus B. Kaufman papers.
NAACP Papers. Robert Woodruff Library, Emory University, Atlanta, Georgia.

B. Interviews

Unless otherwise indicated, all interviews with were conducted by the author.
Abrams, Albert J. 11 February 2004.
Adams, Virgil. Interview with Richard Hyatt, 2 August 2001.

Bennett, Carl. 14 March 2003.

Bennett, Carl. Interview with Andrew Silver, 25 August 2001.

Bennett, Margaret. 14 March 2003.

Billingslea, Albert. 17 January 2004.

Bishop, Charles W. 23 January 2004.

Bootle, William Augustus. Brown, Manley F. and Edward Lukemire. "An Oral Interview with Judge W. A. Bootle, Part I" *Journal of Southern Legal History* 7 (1999): 115–99.

———. "An Oral Interview with Judge W. A. Bootle, Part II" *Journal of Southern Legal History* 8 (2000): 95–171.

———. Interview with Robert A. Pratt, 1 March 2001.

Braswell, Palmira. 24 January 2004.

Brown, Peter C. 30 January 2004.

Bryan, G. McLeod. Interview with Andrew Silver, 21–22 March 2002.

Bryan, G. McLeod. 29 March 2003.

Bumpus, Reverend J. Louis. 28 January 2004.

Carter, Ella. 17 February 2004.

Dennard, Herbert. 10 January 2004.

Edwards, Lonzy. 17 September 2002.

Ficklin, Henry. 30 January 2004.

Goodwin, Charlene. 21 August 2002.

Gossett, Thomas. 14 March 2003.

Grubbs, Joyce. 13 May 2003.

Habersham, Alex C. 20 February 2004.

Hart, Samuel F., Sr. 23 January 2004.

Hendricks, Joseph M. 27 May 2003, 2 June 2000.

———. Interview with Andrew Silver, 3 August 2001.

Hinshaw, Creed. 2 March 2004.

Horne, Stebin III. 4 February 2004.

Hutchings, Frank, Jr. 13 February 2004.

Hutto, Richard. 6 February 2004.

Jackson, Myra. 4 May 2003.

Kaufman, Gus B. 6 June 2000.

Keil, Richard. 3 February 2004.

Lee, Jim. 16 January 2004.

Lucas, Elaine. 31 January 2004

Malone, Reverend Van J., Sr. Interview with WMAZ-Macon Arts Alliance, 25 August 1992. Videotape in Genealogy Department, Washington Memorial Library, Macon, Georgia.

Meeks, Catherine. 29 January 2004.

Melton, Buckner, Sr. 10 April 2003

———. 22 April 2003.

Middleton, Susan Y. 11 February 2004.

Otto, F. Robert. Interview with Andrew Silver, 3 June 2001.

Olmstead, Tommy. 13 February 2004.

Ponder, Anita. 16 January 2004.

Randall, William P., Sr. Georgia Government Documentation Project, 4 February 1989, Special Collections Department, Pullen Library, Georgia State University, Atlanta.

_____. WMAZ-Macon Arts Alliance Interview, 12 August 1992.

Randall, William C. 26 January 2004.

Richardson, Charles. 2 June 2003

Samuel, Jimmie. 5 February 2004.

Scott, Robert L., Jr. 22 January 2004.

Shuler, Willie J., Jr. 6 February 2004.

Slater, Betty Jean. 20 February 2004.

Smith, Reverend Eddie B., Sr. 23 May 2003.

Stephens, Bennie. Interview with Andrew Silver, 26 July 2001.

Terry, Ronald E. 15 February 2004.

Thomason, Cole. 21 February 2004.

Thompson, Ronnie. Interview with Andrew Silver, 28 May 2002.

Youmas, Brenda C. 19 February 2004.

C. Books

Ames, Jessie Daniel. *Repairers of the Breach* (Georgia Problems: Excepts...Race Relations (1937*)*.

Arnett, Alex Mathews. *The Populist Movement in Georgia: A View of the "Agrarian Crusade" in the Light of Solid South Politics.* New York: Columbia University Press, 1922.

Brooks, Robert Preston. *The Agrarian Revolution in Georgia, 1865-1912.* No. 639 of the University of Wisconsin *Bulletin.* Madison, 1914.

Bryan, G. McLeod. *Voices in the Wilderness: Twentieth Century Prophets Speak to the New Millennium.* Macon: Mercer University Press, 1999.

Cable, George Washington. *The Negro Question.* New York: Charles Scribner's Sons, 1903.

Douglass, H. Paul. *Christian Reconstruction in the South.* Boston: Pilgrim Press, 1909.

Dowell, Spright. *A History of Mercer University, 1833-1953.* Macon: Mercer University, 1958.

Holmes, Grace Bryan. *Time to Reconcile: The Odyssey of a Southern Baptist.* Athens: University of Georgia Press, 2000.

Holmes, Thomas J. *Ashes for Breakfast.* Valley Forge: Judson Press, 1969.

LeConte, Joseph. *Man and the State, Studies in Applied Sociology.* New York: D. Appleton and Company, 1892.

Park, Orville, editor. *Macon Methodism from 11826 to 1903.* Macon: Macon Methodist Churches, 1903.

Parks, Willis B., editor. *The Possibilities of the Negro in Syumposium.* Atlanta: Franklin Printing and Publishing Company, 1904.

Ragsdale, B. D., editor. *Memoirs of Pinckney Daniel Pollock.* Macon: self-published, 1942.

Silver, Andrew. *Combustible/Burn: A Play.* Macon: Mercer University Press, 2002.

Stephenson, Gilbert Thomas. *Race Distinctions in American Law.* New York: Doubleday, Page, and Company, 1908.

Talmadge, Herman E. *You and Segregation.* Birmingham AL: Vulcan Press, 1955.

Wells, Ida B. *Crusade for Justice: The Autobiography of Ida B. Wells.* Edited by Alfreda M. Duster. Chicago: University of Chicago Press, 1991.

Woofter, Thomas J. *Progress in Race Relations in Georgia: Report of the Secretary of the Georgia Committee on Race Relations for 1922.* Atlanta: Georgia Committee on Race Relations, 1922.

Works Progress Administration. *Georgia: The WPA Guide to Its Towns and Countryside.* New Introduction by Phinizy Spalding. Columbia: University of South Carolina Press, 1990. Originally published in 1940.

D. Articles

Avery, W. A. "Inter-Racial Cooperation in Georgia," *Southern Workman* 51 (April 1922): 185f.

Crowe, Charles. "Racial Massacre in Atlanta, September 22, 1906" *Journal of Negro History* 54 (April 1969): 150–73.

Doss, George A., Jr. "Homegrown Movement in Macon" *New South* 18 (April 1963): 3–10.

DuBois, W. E. B. "The Relation of the Negroes to the Whites in the South" *Annals of the American Academy of Political and Social Science* 18 (1901): 121–40.

"Lynching in Georgia" *Time* (28 July 1941): 37

Straton, John Roach. "Will Education Solve the Race Problem?" *North American Review* 170 (June 1900): 785–801.

E. Government Documents

Report of the Special Inspector of Misdemeanor Convict Camps of Georgia, n.p., 1897.

F. Newspapers

Atlanta Journal and Constitution
Mercer Cluster
Macon Courier
Macon News
Macon Telegraph
Southern School News, 1958–1970

II. SECONDARY SOURCES

A. Books

Anderson, Nancy Briska, *Macon: A Pictorial History.* Virginia Beach VA: Donning Company/Publishers, 1979.

Anderson, William. *The Wild Man from Sugar Creek: The Political Career of Eugene Talmadge.* Baton Rouge: Louisiana State University Press, 1975.

Angell, Stephen Ward. *Bishop Henry McNeal Turner and African-American Religion in the South.* Knoxville: University of Tennessee Press, 1992.

Aptheker, Herbert. *A Documentary History of the Negro People in the United States.* New York: The Citadel Press, 1951.

Bartley, Numan V. *The Creation of Modern Georgia.* Athens: University of Georgia Press, 1983.

————. *The Rise of Massive Resistance: Race And Politics in the South During the 1950's.* Baton Rouge, Louisiana State University Press, 1969.

Bauerlein, Mark. *Negrophobia: A Race Riot In Atlanta, 1906.* San Francisco: Encounter Books, 2001.

Batts, H. Lewis, and Rollin S. Armour, *History of the First Baptist Church of Christ at Macon.* Macon: First Baptist Church, 1991.

Bayor, Ronald H. *Race and the Shaping of Twentieth-Century Atlanta.* Chapel Hill: University of North Carolina Press, 1996.

Black, Earl. *Southern Governors and Civil Rights: Racial Segregation as a Campaign Issue in the Second Reconstruction.* Cambridge: Harvard University Press, 1976.

Brown, Michael K., Martin Carnoy, et al. *Whitewashing Race: The Myth of a Color-Blind Society.* Berkeley: University of California Press, 2003.

Brown, Titus. *Faithful, Firm, and True: African-American Education in the South.* Macon: Mercer University Press, 2000.

Brundage, W. Fitzhugh. *Lynching in the New South: Georgia and Virginia, 1880–1930.* Urbana: University of Illinois Press, 1993.

Chalmers, David M. *Hooded Americanism: The History of the Ku Klux Klan.* New York: Franklin Watts, 1981.

Clegg, Claude A. *An Original Man: The Life and Times of Elijah Muhammad.* New York: St. Martin's Press, 1998.

Coleman, Kenneth, editor. *History ofGeorgia.* Athens: University of Georgia Press, 1977.

Conway, Alan. *The Reconstruction of Georgia.* Minneapolis: University of Minnesota Press, 1966.

Cook, James F. *The Governors of Georgia, 1754-1995.* Revised and expanded edition. Macon: Mercer University Press, 1995.

Dittmer, John. *Black Georgia in the Progressive Era, 1900-1920.* Urbana: University of Illinois Press, 1977.

————. *Local People: The Struggle for Civil Rights in Mississippi.* Urbana: University of Illinois Press, 1995.

Egerton, John. *Speak Now Against the Day: The Generation Before the Civil Rights Movement in the South.* New York: Alfred A. Knopf, Inc., 1994.

Evanzz, Karl, *The Messenger: The Rise and Fall of Elijah Muhammad.* New York: Pantheon Books, 1999.

Foner, Eric. *Nothing But Freedom: Emancipation and Its Legacy.* Baton Rouge: Louisiana State University Press, 1983.

Foner, Philip S. and Robert James Branham, editors. *Lift Every Voice: African American Oratory, 1787-1900.* Tuscaloosa: University of Alabama Press, 1998.

Gates, Robbins L. *The Making of Massive Resistance: Virginia's Politics of Public School Desegregation, 1954–1956.* Chapel Hill: University of North Carolina Press, 1964.

Gilmore, Glenda E. *Gender and Jim Crow: Women and the Politics of White Supremacy in North Carolina, 1896–1920.* Chapel Hill: University of North Carolina Press, 1996.

Goldfield, David R. *Black, White, and Southern: Race Relations and Southern Culture, 1940 to the Present.* Baton Rouge: Louisiana State University Press, 1990.

Grantham, Dewey W. Jr. *Hoke Smith and the Politics of the New South.* Baton Rouge: Louisiana State University Press, 1958.

Hacker, Andrew. *Two Nations: Black & White, Separate, Hostile, Unequal.* New York: Scribner, 2003.

Hall, Jacquelyne Dowd. *Revolt Against Chivalry: Jessie Daniel Ames and the Women's Campaign Against Lynching.* New York: Columbia University Press, 1979.

Hill, Samuel S. *Encyclopedia of Religion in the South.* Macon: Mercer University Press, 1984.

Inscoe, John C., editor. *Georgia in Black and White: Explorations in the Race Relations of a Southern State, 1865–1950.* Athens: University of Georgia Press, 1994..

Iobst, Richard W. *Civil War Macon: The History of a Confederate City.* Macon: Mercer University Press, 1999.

Gossett, Thomas F. *Race: The History of an Idea in America.* New York: Oxford University Press, 1963.

———. *Uncle Tom's Cabin and American Culture.* Dallas: Southern Methodist University Press, 1985.

Grant, Donald L. *The Way It Was in the South: The Black Experience in Georgia.* New York: Carol Publishing Group, 1993.

Kennedy, David M. *Freedom From Fear: The American People in Depression and War, 1929-1945.* New York: Oxford University Press, 1999.

Kitwana, Bakari. *The Hip Hop Generation: Young Blacks and the Crisis in African-American Culture.* New York: Basic Civitas Books, 2002.

Kivel, Paul. *Uprooting Racism: How White People Can Work for Racial Justice.* Gabriola Island, BC, Canada: New Society Publishers, 2002.

Klinkner, Philip A. and Rogers M. Smith. *The Unsteady March: The Rise and Decline of Racial Equality in America.* Chicago: University of Chicago Press, 1999.

Kousser, J. Morgan. *Colorblind Injustice: Minority Voting Rights and the Undoing of the Second Reconstruction.* Chapel Hill: University of North Carolina Press, 1999.

_____. *The Shaping of Southern Politics: Suffrage Restriction and the Establishment of One-Party Rule, 1880–1910.* New Haven: Yale University Press, 1974.

Lane, Mills, editor. *Georgia: History Written by Those Who Lived It.* Savannah: Beehive Press, 1995.

Leidholdt, Alexander. *Standing Before the Shouting Mob: Lenoir Chambers and Virginia's Massive Resistance to Public-School Integration.* Tuscaloosa: University of Alabama Press, 1997.

Lewis, David Levering. *W. E. B. DuBois: Biography of a Race, 1868–1919.* New York: Henry Holt and Company, 1993.

Lipsitz, George, *The Possessive Investment in Whiteness: How White People Profit From Identity Politics*. Philadelphia: Temple University Press, 1998.

Litwack, Leon F. *Trouble in Mind: Black Southerners in the Age of Jim Crow*. New York: Alfred A. Knopf, 1998.

Macon News. *History of Macon: The First One Hundred Years, 1823–1923*. Macon: The J. W. Burke Company, 1929.

McCullough, David. *Truman*. New York: Simon and Schuster, 1992.

McElreath, Walter. *A Treatise on the Constitution of Georgia*. Atlanta: The Harrison Company, 1912.

Meeks, Catherine. *Macon's Black Heritage: The Untold Story*. Macon: The Tubman African American Museum, 1997.

Meyer, Stephen Grant. *As Long As They Don't Move Next Door: Segregation and Racial Conflict in American Neighborhoods*. Lanham MD: Rowman & Littlefield Publishers, Inc., 2000.

McClain, Wayne. *A Resurrection Encounter: The Rufus Moseley Story*. Minneapolis: Macalester Park Publishing Company, 1997.

Patterson, Orlando. *Rituals of Blood: Consequences of Slavery in Two American Centuries*. New York: Basic Civitas Books, 1998.

Pratt, Robert A. Pratt. *We Shall Not Be Moved: The Desegregation of the University of Georgia*. Athens: University of Georgia Press, 2002.

Roland, Charles P. *The Improbable Era: The South Since World War II*. Lexington: University Press of Kentucky, 1975

Shapiro, Thomas M. *The Hidden Cost of Being African American*. New York: Oxford University Press, 2004.

Simms, Kristina. *Macon: Georgia's Central City*. Chatsworth CA: Windsor Publications, Inc., 1989.

Sitkoff, Harvard. *A New Deal for Blacks: The Emergence of Civil Rights as a National Issue*. New York: Oxford University Press, 1978.

Sosna, Morton L. *In Search of the Silent South: Southern Liberals and the Race Issue*. New York: Columbia University Press, 1977.

Sullivan, Patricia. *Days of Hope: Race and Democracy in the New Deal Era*. Chapel Hill: University of North Carolina Press, 1996.

Tuck, Stephen N. G. *Beyond Atlanta: The Struggle for Racial Equality in Georgia, 1940–1980*. Athens: University of Georgia Press, 2001.

Wiese, Andrew . *Places of Their Own African American Suburbanization in the Twentieth Century.*Chicago: University of Chicago Press, 2004.

Wilhoit, Francis M. *The Politics of Massive Resistance*. New York: G. Braziller, 1973.

Williamson, Joel, *A Rage for Order: Black-White Relations in the American South Since Emancipation*. New York: Oxford University Press, 1986.

Woodward, C. Vann. *Origins of the New South, 1877–1913*. Baton Rouge: Louisiana State University Press, 1951.

———. *The Strange Career of Jim Crow*. 2nd edition. New York: Oxford University Press, 1966.

———. *Tom Watson, Agrarian Rebel*. 2nd edition. Savannah: Beehive Press, 1973 [originally Published 1938].

Young, Ida, Julius Gholson, and Clara Nell Hargrove. *History of Macon, Georgia.* Macon: Lyon, Marshall & Brooks, 1950.

B. Articles

Bacote, Clarence A. "The Negro Voter in Georgia Politics Today" *Journal of Negro Education* 26 (Summer 1957): 307–18.

Bernd, Joseph L. "White Supremacy and the Disfranchisement of Blacks in Georgia, 1946" *Georgia Historical Quarterly* 66 (Winter 1982): 492–513.

Burnham, Robert A. "Interracial Cooperation in the Age of Jim Crow: The Booker T. Washington Community Center of Macon, Georgia" *Atlanta History* 42 (Summer 1999): 19–35.

Carter, Dan T. "From Segregation to Integration" In *Interpreting Southern History: Historiographical Essays in Honor of Sanford W. Higginbotham.* Edited by John B. Boles and Evelyn Thomas Nolen. Baton Rouge: Louisiana State University Press, 1987.

Dalfiume, Richard M. "The Forgotten Years of the Negro Revolution" *Journal of American History* 55 (June 1968): 90–106.

DuBois, W. E. B. "Race Relations in the United States" *Phylon* 9 (1948): 234–47.

Ellis, Ann Wells. "'Uncle Sam Is My Shepherd': The Commission on Interracial Cooperation and the New Deal in Georgia" *Atlanta History Journal* 30 (Spring 1986): 47–64.

Fairclough, Adam. "Historians and the Civil Rights Movement" *Journal of American Studies* 24 (1990): 387–98.

Finkle, Lee. "The Conservative Aims of Militant Rhetoric: Black Protest During World War II" *Journal of American History* 60 (December 1973): 692–713.

Franklin, John Hope. "Legal Disfranchisement of the Negro" *Journal of Negro Education* 26 (Spring 1957): 241–48.

Foner, Eric. "Hiring Quotas for White Males Only" *The Nation* (26 June 1995): 24.

Grantham, Dewey W., editor. "Some Letters to Tom Watson Concerning the Georgia Gubernatorial Campaign of 1906" *Georgia Historical Quarterly* 34 (December 1950): 328–40.

Holmes, Michael S. "Blue Eagle as 'Jim Crow Bird': The NRA and Georgia's Black Workers" *Journal of Negro History* 57 (1972): 276–83.

_____ . "The New Deal and Georgia's Black Youth" *Journal of Southern History* 38 (August 1972): 443–60.

Hux, Roger K. "The Ku Klux Klan in Macon, 1919–1925" *Georgia Historical Quarterly* 62 (Summer 1978): 155–68.

Kellogg, Peter J. "Civil Rights Consciousness in the 1940s" *Historian* 42 (November 1979): 18–41.

Korobkin, Russell. "The Politics of Disfranchisement in Georgia" *Georgia Historical Quarterly* 74 (Spring 1990): 20–58.

McCoy, Donald R. and Richard Ruetten. "The Civil Rights Movement: 1940–1954" *Midwest Quarterly* 11 (October 1969): 11–34.

Meier, August, and Elliott Rudwick. "The Boycott Movement Against Jim Crow Streetcars in the South" *Journal of American History* 55 (March 1969): 756–75.

Moore, John Hammond. "Jim Crow in Georgia" *South Atlantic Quarterly* 66 (Autumn 1967): 554–65.

Murphy, Walter F. "The South Counterattacks: The Anti-NAACP Laws" *Western Political Quarterly* 12 (June 1959): 371–90.

Newman, Mark. "The Georgia Baptist Convention and Desegregation, 1945–1980" *Georgia Historical Quarterly* 83 (Winter 1999): 685–705.

Rable, George C. "The South and the Politics of Antilynching Legislation, 1920–1940" *Journal of Southern History* 51 (May 1985): 201–20.

Rusk, David. *The "Segregation Tax": The Cost of Racial Segregation to Black Homeowners.* Brookings Institution, 2001.

Seligman, Herbert. "Slavery in Georgia, A.D. 1921" *Nation* (20 April 1921): 591.

Sitkoff, Harvard. "Racial Militancy and Interracial Violence in the Second World War" *Journal of American History* 58 (December 1971): 661–81.

Stephenson, Gilbert T. "The Segregation of the White and Negro Races in Cities" *South Atlantic Quarterly* 13 (January 1914): 1–18.

Webb, Clive. "Charles Bloch, Jewish White Supremacist" *Gerogia Historical Quarterly* 83 (Summer 1999): 267–92.

Willis, Alan Scot. "A Baptist Dilemma: Christianity, Discrimination, and the Desegregation of Mercer University" *Georgia Historical Quarterly* 80 (Fall 1996): 595–615.

C. Dissertations and Theses

Allred, William Clifton, Jr. "The Southern Regional Council, 1943-1961." MA thesis, Emory University, 1966.

Anderson, George. "A City Comes Of Age: An Urban Study of Macon Georgia during the 1920's" MA thesis, Georgia College, 1975.

Bacote, Clarence Albert. "The Negro in Georgia Politics, 1880–1908." Ph.D. dissertation, University of Chicago, 1955.

Bolster, Paul Douglas. "Civil Rights Movements in Twentieth Century Georgia," Ph.D. dissertation, University of Georgia, 1972.

Ellis, Ann. "The Commission on Interracial Cooperation, 1919–1944: Its Activities and Results" Ph.D. dissertation, Georgia State University, 1975.

Matthews, John Michael. "Studies in Race Relations in Georgia, 1890–1930." Ph.D. dissertation, Duke University, 1970.

Richardson, Mary Ann Berg. "The City of Macon, Georgia's Sacrifice to Jim Crow: A. O. Bacon's Gift of Baconsfield Park, 1911–1972." MA thesis, Georgia College, 1988.

Wingo, Horace Calvin. "Race Relations in Georgia, 1872–1908." Ph.D. dissertation, University of Georgia, 1969.

D. Other Unpublished Sources

Anderson, Robert L. "The Role of Leadership in the Civil Rights Movement in Macon, Bibb County, Georgia: 1959-1971" Unpublished research paper, Yale University, 1985.

————. "Leadership Politics and Popular Empowerment: Divisions in the Black Movement in Macon, Georgia." Unpublished Research Paper, Yale University, 29 September 1986.

Brown, Titus. " 'Faithful, Firm, and True': Ballard Normal School, Macon, Georgia, 1865–1949." Unpublished manuscript, 1999.

Horton, Lelia J. "Macon—Unknown Frontier to Modern City: Turn of the Century 1901–1945" Address to the Macon History Club, 7 April 1983.

Williams, Trina. "The Homestead Act: A Major Asset-building Policy in American History." Presented at the Inclusion in Asset Building: Research and Policy Symposium, September 2000. Available at gwbweb.wustl.edu/csd/Publications/2000/wp00-9.pdf.

Index

Abernathy, Ralph David, 258
Abney, Guyton G., 238
Adams, Charles, 42
affirmative action, 10, 235, 275, 277, 278, 287, 289, 331, 337 353, 359, 360, 361
Africa, 2, 9, 24, 27, 225
African Americans: and African emigration, 24-25; accommodationist leadership style among, 1; activism among, 10; advancement of, 17, 54; as beasts, 26, 35-7, 41; as brutes, 38; business development among, 78, 287; criminality, 37-38; death rate among, 23; deportation of, 27; education of, 2, 23, 25, 27, 37, 38, 50, 72-3, 79-81, 123, 131-2; employment statistics for, 259; home ownership among, 354; illiteracy among, 78-9; as inferior race, 36, 182; intimidation of, 17, 19; as lazy, 41; majority status of, 8; medical care of, 112-3, 124-5; migration of, 50, 54, 73-5, 77; ministers, 18, 17-9, 24-5, 29, 49, 51, 52, 70, 71, 127, 128, 138, 145, 147, 192, 200, 215, 216, 219, 237, 253, 265, 346, 352; and personal responsibility, 361; politics, 3, 8, 15, 17, 29; 112, 258-71, 285, 289, 290, 332; population in Macon, 16, 77, 316; responsibilities of the middle class, 360;as sexually obsessed, 36; violence against, 17, 19, 39-45, 82, 89, 95, 132, 144 (*See also* Atlanta race riot (1906); voting of, 15, 17, 19-20, 31, 34, 112, 151, 154-5, 157, 164-5, 198, 205-211; voting tests for, 26; voter registration among, 19-20, 22, 27-8, 34, 111, 153, 155, 205; unemployment among, 78, 109; and World War I, 48-53, 120; and World War II, 139-151
African Methodist Episcopal Church (AME), 24, 49, 52, 62, 126, 127, 134, 217, 290

agitators, 145, 234
Agrarianism, Agrarian movement. *See* Populism.
Agricultural Adjustment Act, 109
Ainsworth, Bishop W. N., 97
Akins, Coleman, 49
Alexander, J. F., 96, 98, 99, 101
Alexander, Rev. Cameron, 219
Alexander, Will W., 7, 108, 128, 129
Allen Chapel AME Church, 217
amalgamation, 175
"American century," 6, 362
"American Creed," 6
(The) American Dilemma, 140
American exceptionalism, 9, 362
American flag, 24, 297, 298
American Loyalty League, 122
American Missionary Association, 79, 123
American Order of Fascisti, 109
Americus Sumter Republican, 19
Ames, Jessie Daniel, 7, 108, 129, 130, 137, 150
Anderson, A.M., 206
Anderson, Clifford, 40
Anderson, Dock, 54
Anderson, Nancy, 284
Anderson, Rev. W. Lowry, 130, 131, 132, 135, 136, 137, 138, 148, 150-1, 351
Anderson, Robert L., 212, 263, 269
Anderson, Trezzvant, 198, 218, 221
Anderson, Wilfred, 249
Anderson, W. T. (William Thomas), 11, 14, 47, 48, 52, 53, 59, 62, 65, 66, 69, 70, 72, 73, 75, 80, 81, 86, 87, 91, 92, 93, 100, 102, 105, 110, 113, 114, 124, 145, 151, 203, 343; comment on the Great War, 47-48; comment on the, 91; comment on lynching, 59, 65-66; comment on NAACP, 81
Andrews, Dominick, 324, 325
Anglo-Saxons, Anglo-Saxonism, 2, 3, 53, 89
Annis, Jessica, 341